RON SCHARA'S
MINNESOTA
FISHING
GUIDE

WITH "RAVEN," STAR OF "MINNESOTA BOUND"

TRISTAN OUTDOORS

Tristan Outdoors is an imprint of Tristan Publishing, Inc.

Tristan Publishing, Inc.
2300 Louisiana Avenue North
Suite B
Golden Valley, MN 55427

Photographs from Bill Lindner Photography and the North American Fishing Club

Remarkable design support from Bolger Concept to Print

Printed in China by Pettit Network, Inc. Afton, MN

Edited by Gail Plewacki

ISBN 0-9726504-4-X

First Printing

Please visit **www.tristanoutdoors.com**

To daughters, Simone and Laura,
Whose fishing days lie ahead
(with their significant others).
And to Denise, wonderful wife, mother and friend,
who long has tolerated my angling passions.

Prologue

Why Do I Fish?

Why do I fish?

It's a fair question with no easy answer.

For one thing, we anglers are seldom asked to explain what keeps us casting, keeps us hoping to catch a fish.

To those of us who fish, it is no mystery. Perhaps the only folks who are puzzled by fishing are those who haven't done it.

It's been said the essence of fishing is much more than casting or retrieving or playing the catch. It's the wind in your face, the sound of awakening birds as the sun peeks over the eastern horizon.

In every fishy place there is magic and mystery. And it's just waiting to be discovered by the next angler who comes along. What's more, the quest to unlock those fishy secrets takes you to nifty places, including some of the world's garden spots.

But let's not forget the pure joy of catching, the moment when a fishing dream is dancing on the end of the line. Memories are made of this.

Fishing is also a teacher. The lessons learned in a fishing boat are not forgotten when you return to shore. For example, patience. Patience is absolutely required to be an angler. But you learn that patience also pays in other of life's endeavors.

To go fishing is a lesson in humility. Put another way, to fish is to be humbled. Not once, but time and time again.

An angler accepts these lessons taught by a fish. Life itself is kept in perspective by the things a fish teaches.

Some of us who fish are known to exaggerate a fish or two. Nobody ever said the exact truth was necessary to tell a good story.

Just remember, for every exaggerated tale of giant whoppers caught and stuffed for the wall, there are many true stories about the big one that got away.

Beyond the fish stories, there is something more, something spiritual and eternal in this pursuit we call angling. Clearly, those of us who fish tend to do so for a lifetime.

You're never too old to start fishing. And you're never too old to quit. I like that about fishing. As my own fishing seasons wind down to a precious few, it's nice to know I'll still be there.

There as long as I can be.

As long as I can bait a hook and make a cast.

As long as I am living, I intend to go fishing.

Good fishing,

Ron Schara

Contents

Acknowledgements

The fishing expert who wrote this book is not me.

The skills shared in these pages were garnered from my many angling companions who through the seasons offered their expertise. I was like a sponge in a leaky boat, soaking up the knowledge and friendship they shared.

First, thanks to my wife, Denise, who for years tolerated my shortcomings in husbandry skills while I logged time in search of angling skills. My daughters, Simone and Laura who, as little girls, willingly tagged along with Dad. They now have their own angling dreams to fulfill.

My first fishing companions, my parents, Harlan and Evelyn Schara, are gone now. Until I make my last cast, I'll be forever grateful I had parents who loved fishing. Gone, too, are Uncles Edward Dickens, Lawrence Dickens and Harvey Dickens, who shared their fishing days with me.

I've been blessed by countless moments with good fishing company. My uncles who shared their knowledge and time with me: Uncles Bob Dickens, Ray Schara, Kenny Schara and Charles Schara. Gary Roach, a.k.a. Mr. Walleye, who 25 years ago first brainstormed the idea of a Minnesota fishing guide written by me.

So many others, in no particular order, are:

The Griz, a guide extraordinaire; Dick Sternberg, thinking man's angler; Al and Ron Lindner, friends and In-Fisherman entrepreneurs; Ron Weber and Ray Ostrom, great anglers, businessmen and stars of the Rapala story; Dave Perkins, sport show guru; Bill Plantan and Dave Frink, inventive canoe makers; Larry Bollig, fishing bear; Gary Lake, tournament partner; Mark Fisher, fishing talk star; "Woody," a fairly reliable guide.

Frank Schneider and Gil Hamm, gifts to muskies; John Larson, pilot and fishing buddy; Mark Bundgaard, my daddy; Billy Dougherty, great Rainy guide; Doc

fishin' family   Ron, Laura, Denise and Simone Schara

Acknowledgements

Norb Epping, ovary bait specialist; Jay Anderson and Jim Cook, memorable lake trout; Bill Dedrick, Mr. Electronics; Ron Payer, fish manager with class; Duane Shodeen, gift to metro fishing; Mel Haugstad, fighter for trout habitat; Jim McDonnell, the fishin' is always good, the catchin' not always; Babe Winkelman, paid his fishing dues; Marv Koep, baitman entrepreneur; Fred Priewert, like a father; Wayne Bartz, trout bug pro; Tom Helgeson, love that fly; Dan Gapen, loves rivers; Scott Sparlin, save the Minnesota River; Bobby Brouillet, Don Koenig and Joe Ball, high school fishin' buddies; Bob Nybo, my favorite river rat; Dick Knapp, first muskie guide; Lynn Schultz, founded first B.A.S.S. chapter; Bud and Ted Burger, store front anglers; Leroy Ras, teacher of angling; Bob Taintor, memorable fly tyer; Tony Herbert, loved Mille Lacs; Ivan Burandt, uncanny fish finder; Duane Betker, let's make a deal; Frankie Dusenka, build a bait shop and they will come; Ron and Sharon Hunter, fans of Winni; Joe Fellegy, speaks his angling mind; John and Duane Peterson, a pair of fireballs; Ted Takasaki, fished his way to the top; Nick Adams, anglers will buy it.

Dozens of others have shared a boat or fishing bank with me. I can say I've never had a fishing partner I didn't enjoy, although over time a few of their names drifted away. If your name is missing, please forgive my fading memory.

A special thanks to all of DNR's dedicated fisheries managers for helping shorten the time between bites. Thanks also to Noel Vick, a fellow fishing writer, who so ably assisted in gathering research to update a new Minnesota Fishing Guide.

Finally, a nod of appreciation to my brothers and sisters who share my genetics as well as my love of fishing: Mary Jane Orth, Robert Schara, Richard Schara, Roger Schara and DeAnn Curnow, who'll always be younger than me—darn. Over the years, we've captured many fishing exploits on videotape for *Minnesota Bound* audiences on KARE 11 and for fans of ESPN2's *Backroads With Ron and Raven*. For every good catch, there's an even better cameraman working behind the pictures. My thanks to Joe Harewicz, Steve Plummer and Mike Cashman for their great "catches." Thanks also to Kelly Jo Weiner and Simone Schara-Gonse, who keep our Minnesota Bound operations running while I'm casting away.

Ron Schara

P.S. Please accept this apology to fisherpersons. My use of masculine nouns such as fisherman inadequately represent the interest, passion and contributions of women to the angling sport. While I've tried to use "angler" as the catch-all word, there are times when "fisherman" is more painless to the reader's eye. Blame the language. And please don't be offended. My Grandmother, Blanch Dickens, always said she was a better "fisherman" than Grandpa Clate.

And she was.

Introduction

Let Us Wet a Line...

When you start a fishing book, the most difficult words to write are the first ones.

How do you capture and put down on paper the excitement and joy of angling and what it means to the soul?

Capturing the glory of angling is a task even more overwhelming when it's *fishing in Minnesota*. You're talking major league. Fishin' is big time in the Land of 10,000 Lakes; lordy, we tell the world on our license plates.

So—how do you describe the essence of Minnesota fishing? And do it in the first words of a book?

Frankly, I faced this same dilemma back in 1978 when I wrote my first Minnesota Fishing Guide. The first words? What would they be? I pondered the question and struggled for the answer for what seemed like hours. Suddenly, I thought of an old fishing companion by the name of J.D. Fletcher.

J.D. was a self-styled hillbilly who lived in the country and didn't think much of city life. He drove a rusty pickup truck that rattled and rocked on the road, which meant J.D. had to yell when his passenger asked him a question.

"What do people do around here?" I asked J.D. as we bounced along a back road.

J.D. thought for a second and then uttered the words I'd use to start my first Minnesota Fishing Guide.

"Those folks around here that don't fish, dig worms for those that do," said J.D.

Indeed, fishing is what we're about. This is the land the Dakota Indians so appropriately called "Minnesota"— meaning sky-tinted waters.

We still don't win Super Bowls and our political leaders still only reach vice-presidencies. We might not be first in pork production or dairy cows, but if your idea of heaven is a land laced with the world's finest natural fishing waters, that's Minnesota.

Our major holidays are Thanksgiving, Christmas and the Fishing Opener. Our common bond consists of fathead minnows, bug dope and a nice walleye chop. A statewide poll found that nearly 6 of every 10 Minnesota residents go fishing at least once a year.

According to the Department of Natural Resources (DNR), the number of adults and children who wet a line every year is estimated to be 2.3 million folks. Fishing license sales exceed $18 million. Golly, we spend collectively $50 million for live bait, minnows, worms, and night crawlers. Sport fishing is close to a $2 billion industry in the state, consisting of money spent on fishing tackle, fishing boats, lodges and so forth.

The DNR's fisheries budget is about $22.4 million a year, consisting of funds generated almost totally from the angling and boating public. On that point, in the future Minnesotans need to expand their support to sustain and manage the state's fishing resources.

Historically, fishing programs were based on the user-pay model. But times

have changed. There are human pressures on lakes and rivers and management programs that anglers alone cannot afford to finance. Angling fees cannot keep going up. In truth, state businesses and taxpayers contribute very little in dollars to DNR fish programs. In a perfect world, all of us who benefit from clean water and good fishing would help pay the price. This is includes key segments of the business community, such as tourism. And, of course, all tax-paying Minnesotans eventually enjoy a higher

quality of life if we all contribute to maintain a healthy fishing environment.

Wonderfully, Minnesota has so many angling opportunities to enjoy but also so much to care for.

I'm not sure who did the counting, but the DNR says there's about 3.8 million acres (that's 3,800,000) of fishing water in Minnesota. If my math is right that's almost 6,000 square miles.

While our license plate boasts of 10,000 lakes, the number is actually much higher than that (closer to 12,000

Introduction

lakes more than 10 acres), although only about 6,000 are managed for fishing. Just to finish this numbers game, the DNR says we have about 15,000 miles of fishable rivers.

So—there you have it. We got fishin' water. Now what about the fish?

Let's not pretend that Minnesota is some newly discovered hotspot. We've been pulling fish out of our waters now for 150 years or so and there's bound to be change.

Less than 35 years ago, commercial netting of walleyes and other species was still allowed on lakes, such as Rainy or Lake of the Woods. It slowly became obvious that gillnetting and sport fishing could not co-exist. Why sell a netted walleye for $2 when anglers would spend ten times that amount to *catch* the same fish? The Legislature eventually saw the wisdom of such hook and line economics and the netting of valuable game fish was halted statewide by law.

Nevertheless, remember, we are no longer casting into pristine waters, except perhaps for a few lakes in the Boundary Waters Canoe Wilderness Area. By virtue of increasing fishing pressure, a Minnesota fishing experience seldom can match that of a Canadian lake that is far removed from the angling masses.

Yet, nature has been kind to Minnesota. We have natural fishing water that is capable of yielding high fish populations. If we manage our fishing resources wisely, if we recycle our fish where necessary (catch and release), we can almost ensure that the "good ol' days" of fishing in Minnesota will never end.

Need proof?

Consider the walleye-catching history on Lake Mille Lacs. When did anglers set a record for catching pounds of walleyes? The late 1800s? 1930? 1951? A long time ago? No, Mille Lacs anglers set the record in the 90s. Making the right decisions in fish management is the key to Minnesota's angling future.

Today, Rainy and Lake of the Woods—two walleye lakes once fished by commercial netters and two lakes once noted for their small walleyes or lack thereof—have rebounded and offer exceptional sport angling. Why? Because the right decisions were made about managing the lakes, controlling fish harvest, water levels and so forth.

Most of us who fish are optimists. That's the essence of fishing. Hoping for a bite. I'm also an optimist about Minnesota's fishing future.

Over the last three decades in Minnesota, I've been witness to remarkable success stories.

Included is the comeback of muskie fishing, the stability of our large walleye lakes, the restoration of trout streams, the addition of new fishing water via aeration, the decline of lake winter-kills, the effectiveness of slot limits, the return of sport fishing on Lake Superior, the protection of wild rivers, and the cleanup of the Mississippi River in the Twin Cities. Minnesotans should be proud; we all want happiness on the angling faces of tomorrow.

This may explain why on a perfectly good fishing day I'm am pounding out the words to this newly revised Minnesota Fishing Guide.

In the coming pages, together let's seek the spirit of angling and appreciate the eternal quest to fool a fish. It's nothing new. We've been trying to fool fish for a million years now.

My goal, dear reader, is to increase for you the number of bended rods. Yes, we all love the cry of loons, the beauty of a sunset, the calm that comes with being on the water. If that's why you fish, why tie on a hook?

No, let's be honest.

I enjoy all those things, like loons and sunsets, but I like 'em even more if I've just caught a fish or if I'm just about to catch one.

Thus, these pages are written with the hope of shortening your time between bites. Does this mean if we keep reading we'll never again get skunked fishing in Minnesota?

Oh, lordy, no.

Fooling a fish ain't that easy. And that's a good thing, I say. Getting skunked is a rite of passage in an angler's life. It won't happen just once. Catching nothing keeps us humble and tries to keep us honest.

Fishing is not something to do in life. It's an adventure in life. Along the way an angler learns things about fish, about places where fish live, about those who fish with you and you discover things about yourself. This happens whether you catch fish or not.

So—together let's continue the adventure. Maybe we'll catch something. Maybe it'll be a trophy for the wall. Or maybe we won't catch a thing.

Just remember, the best fishing memories to bring home usually are those that need no dusting.

However, if you feel your fishless days are endless, if you feel there's nothing left to catch in Minnesota, please grab the nearest shovel.

And dig me some worms.

Basics Briefly

Tools of the Game

Minnesota's fishing tools aren't much different from other places where water is fresh and not salty.

While it's true an angler never can have enough fishing rods, the rod models and reel types that will serve your angling needs are not extensive or expensive. The only odd stuff you'll have to gather is for ice fishing, a sport that most of the country finds puzzling if not repulsive. What do they know? In Minnesota, if there's ice, folks will drill a hole and fish.

When buying workable fishing tackle, keep in mind the fish do not know the difference between a $25 reel and a $250 model. The best stuff will not necessarily turn you into a fishing professional. Sometimes your hunch is as important as the price tag on your depth finder or graphite rod.

To catch fish in Minnesota, we tend to use rods, reels and weather predictions courtesy of Grandma's lumbago. Our fish know both how to open their jaws like a starved wolf or clamp them tighter than a shoemaker's vice.

Every lake is different and every day of fishing is different, too. Catching fish is a new challenge every time you try. Even casting to the same spot.

We haven't even mentioned weather yet. Oh, lordy, does Minnesota have weather, all varied and seldom predictable when it's your turn to head for the water.

We also have evil weather, known as cold fronts. When a cold front passes through, the fish sulk and seal their lips in silence. True.

While it may help to hold your mouth right or spit on your hook to catch fish, expensive preparations are usually unnecessary.

However, it is possible to justify buying and using a different fishing rod for each game fish species in the state. Fishing rods are just like shoes. One rod cannot do it all.

Suffice it to say, you'll need several different rods, because they are designed to accomplish different tasks. That said, whatever you own now in the way of basic fishing gear is good enough to catch something.

After all, there are about 156 different fish species living within the state's borders. Some of them, of course, are not considered game fish and are never caught by conventional angling methods.

Basically, most of us fish for only a few of those 156 species, of which a goodly number can be caught with one style of fishing rod and one style of reel. Other fish species simply require techniques so specialized that a variety of rods or reels becomes a piscatorial necessity.

So—let's take a look:

Rods and Reels

First decide what you most like to fish for and in which way. In Minnesota, that usually means you'll fish for walleyes, northern pike and panfish. You'll use live bait most of the time, occasionally pitch-

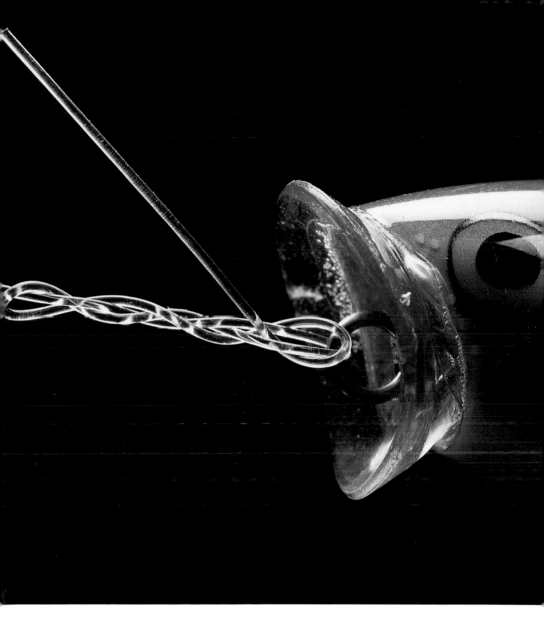

ing an artificial lure or two. That also means you can get by with one rod, maybe two.

If you're the type who's looking for a good walleye rod that you can also use during the winter months, while you're vacationing in the Florida Keys, I'd suggest you buy one of everything. You can afford it.

But if I had but one rod to choose for

Minnesota, it would include these credentials: It would be made with a blank of graphite with a cork handle. A product of space technology, graphite has revolutionized rod making for its combination of important properties, strength, light weight and sensitivity.

A rod's length is important, but the choice is mostly personal. What do you like? A longer, say 7-foot rod has advan-

tages in hook setting and casting. But a shorter, say 5-1/2-foot rod, may cast easier in tight situations, may be lighter to hold and easier to pack.

Of greater importance when selecting a rod is the rod's action. How do you know? Check the fine print located above the handle of every rod. Each manufacturer provides the rod's vital data, including length, range of lure weights in ounces and the type of "action," such as light or medium or heavy and so forth.

(The action of a rod is based largely on its spine and flex. A stout rod, one with a stiff tip end, is classed as a "heavy" action rod; the opposite extreme is an ultra light or light action, one with flexibility of a bullwhip.)

For your first fishing rod, I'd suggest a medium action. Medium action rods normally are designed to handle lures or weights ranging roughly from 1/8th to 1/2 ounce, which almost covers every weight you'd cast for walleyes, bass or northern pike.

Keep in mind, a medium rod won't be the best for casting panfish lures, although most use a bobber for such fish. And since we often use bobbers 10-times bigger than we need, you'll have no prob-

lem casting tiny lures with a medium action rod.

I'm betting you soon won't be satisfied long with just one fishing rod. Sooner or later, you'll discover that different rods are like different tools that enhance the angling experience.

You looking for fun?

Fun is fishing for scrappy panfish with an ultra light or light weight fishing rod with 2- or 4-pound test line. Bluegills, crappies, perch, white bass tend to have fighting hearts but light weights. On a medium rod, they're overpowered. With a whippy ultra light rod, the same fish is nothing but fishing fun.

If you thrill to the sight of a fully arched fishing rod, the ultra light will bend double on a 1-pound crappie. Don't use such a rod for muskies, however, unless you've never seen a rod tied into an overhand knot.

Speaking of muskies or, for instance, 10-pound northern pike, a do-it-all medium action rod won't be worth a hoot on these monsters, either. Oh, you can land big fish but you'll have trouble casting or trolling the kind of lures that normally catch big pike or muskie. That's why pool cues are preferred.

Raven's tidbit

You need a heavy or extra-heavy action rod to toss most of the conventional muskie-fooling plugs. If you don't use big plugs, you'll still need a stout rod to set the hooks in a muskie's jaws. 'Course, you can always take your chances. But muskies are elusive enough without knowingly hurting your odds. You don't climb mountains with a stepladder.

For a few other game fish in Minnesota you could argue a special rod is important. Fishing for Minnesota's steelhead trout on North Shore streams comes to mind. Again, if you want to give yourself a chance, steelhead catching requires investing in a long, stout fly rod. Not to fish with artificial flies, but to use much like a cane pole. Come to think about it, a cane pole would work. Until a steelhead hit and turned it into toothpicks.

A special rod might also be necessary if you choose to stalk the brook trout streams that wind through the jungles of Minnesota's Northeast. For fishing in the boondocks, you might want an extremely short rod with a reel on one end and a mosquito swatter on the other to defend yourself in the bush.

Otherwise, the best-equipped angler on Minnesota's lakes and streams need not own a sporting goods store. Speaking of fishing tackle, my preferred retail store is one that hires knowledgeable clerks in the fishing department. Anybody can ring up my charges. What most anglers want and need is product information.

If I'm going to Alaska to fish king salmon, I'm hoping the clerk will know what I need in the way of rods, reels, line and tackle or be smart enough to pass me onto a clerk who does. Many times I've shared fishing camps with traveling anglers who were misguided and were sold gear that was largely worthless for the task at hand.

However, fish are not humbled by rod or reel alone.

A couple of Minnesota fishing characters, Larry Bollig and Mark Fisher, the stars of Bear Facts and Fish Tales on KSTP 1500, once said, "If you don't know the fish, it won't matter what kind of rod you use."

We anglers are always looking for a shortcut to success. We mistakenly think you can buy fishing success along with

Raven's birthday is September 15th.

the best gear. Wrong. Study the fish first, then read your reel's operating directions.

Speaking of reels, there are three basic types—open-faced or spinning, closed-face or spin-cast and bait-cast or casting.

(Actually there's a fourth type, the fly reel, but it's for fly rods and functions mostly as a place to store fly line.)

Each reel type has advantages and shortcomings. What is important is to choose the reel type that you can handle best.

Stick with brand names and buy top models. Expect to pay $30 to $60 for a reel and slightly more for a rod. There are higher prices, of course. Generally, you get what you pay for.

Some of my earliest memories of fish-

ing frustration are the result of a casting reel, which was the cheapest model sold by a cheap reel company. It wouldn't cast with 10 sinkers unless I swung the rod sidearm like a double-bit axe.

Higher price reels, for instance, tend to have more ball bearings, more workmanship and more features. Higher rods usually feature more line guides, top quality graphite and some kind of replacement guarantee against breaking.

While expensive gear alone won't make you a better fisherman, it also won't stop you from being one, either. As you advance in your angling passions, you'll want to fish with the best gear possible. If you're a beginner, you'll be happy with cheaper gear because you won't know the difference yet.

improved clinch knot

The improved clinch knot has a double loop around the hook eye and is one of the strongest hook-attachment knots.

1) Pass the end of the line through the hook eye or swivel. Double back and make five or more twists of the line end around the standing line.

2) Holding the coils, bring the end back through the first loop formed between the coils and the hook eye and then back through the big loop as shown.

3) Hold onto the end and standing line and pull up tight. Clip off excess.

The good news is today's rods and reels are the best the industry has ever produced. You probably can't go wrong, rod or reel, if you purchase the medium-priced selections on the fishing tackle shelves.

Lines and Knots

To paraphrase W.C. Fields, there never was a man so bad at tying knots he couldn't serve as a good example.

Allow me to volunteer.

I once was stricken with inept knot-tying disease and still suffer occasional relapses. I know what it's like to tie on a new lure, heave it towards fishy-looking waters and watch it sail out of sight. We all could blame the line if it wasn't for the pigtail on the end, indisputable evidence of knot disease.

For Minnesota's fishing demands there's no excuse. The knots any angler needs to know to keep lures and fish on the end of the line are simple to learn and easy to tie. If you are knot-challenged, check out the website: www.netknots.com/fishing.

In the meantime, here are tying instructions for five knots that ought to serve your every knot tying wish:

Improved Clinch Knot - The basic knot for tying on lures, hooks, flies or snaps.
1) Pass the end of the line through the hook eye or swivel. Double back and make five or more twists of the line end around the standing line.

palomar knot

The Palomar knot, like the improved clinch knot, has a double loop around the hook eye, but some anglers find it easier to tie.

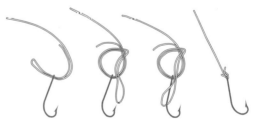

1) Pass line through eye of hook and return through eye making a 3" or 4" loop as shown.
2) Hold line and hook eye with one hand and use other hand to tie a loose overhand knot in doubled line. Do not tighten.
3) Hold loose overhand knot and pull loop over hook, swivel or lure.
4) Pull on doubled line to draw knot up making sure loop does not hang up in hook eye or swivel. Pull both line ends to tighten. Clip off end about 1/8" from knot.

2) Holding the coils, bring the end back through the first loop formed between the coils and the hook eye and then back through the big loop as shown.

3) Hold onto the end and standing line and pull up tight. Clip off excess.

Palomar Knot - Another basic knot for tying on hooks, lures, swivels. You may find it easier to tie than the Improved Clinch knot. Properly tied it's just as strong.

1) Pass line through eye of hook and return through eye making a 3" or 4" loop as shown.

2) Hold line and hook eye with one hand and use other hand to tie a loose over-hand knot in doubled line. Do not tighten.

3) Hold loose overhand knot and pull loop over hook, swivel or lure.

4) Pull on doubled line to draw knot up making sure loop does not hang up in hook eye or swivel. Pull both line ends to tighten. Clip off end about 1/8" from knot.

Surgeon's Knot - For tying a leader to a line end, where the diameters are unequal.

1) Overlap ends of lines for several inches. Tie a simple overhand knot treating both strands as one.

2) Pass the two strands through the loop again. Pull up tight. Trim ends.

surgeon's knot

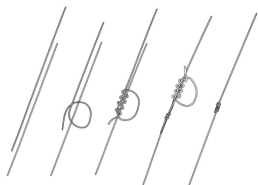

The surgeon's knot is the best way to splice mono to superline. It works well for any lines of different material or diameter.

1) Overlap ends of lines for several inches. Tie a simple overhand knot treating both strands as one.

2) Pass the two strands through the loop again. Pull up tight. Trim ends.

Blood Knot - The best knot for tying one to line when the diameters of the two are the same or nearly so. Makes a strong, small joint that slips through most rod guides easily.

1) Overlap the ends of the two lines for several inches. Hold at the middle of the overlap and twist one end around the other line five or more turns. Bring end back and through strands as shown.

2) Still holding the lines, turn other end around line the same number of turns in the opposite direction. Bring end back and pass between lines from opposite direction of first end.

3) Tighten by pulling up slowly on both lines. Clip off short ends.

Double Surgeon's Loop - Quick, easy and strong. Tie it at the end of line leaders or snells.

1) Double up line end for a few inches. Form loop in doubled line holding it in place, between thumb and forefinger.

2) Pass end of doubled line through loop twice. (For greater strength pass doubled line through loop four times.) Pull doubled end up tight to form final loop.

Solving Line Mysteries

Monofilament line—the most popular and practical fishing line in use today—sometimes acts like a necessary evil. It tangles, twists, breaks or flies off our reels in professional overruns, otherwise known as a backlash.

In truth, one's troubles with mono-

blood knot

A blood knot looks complex, but is quite simple to tie. Don't try it with lines of greatly different diameters or different materials.

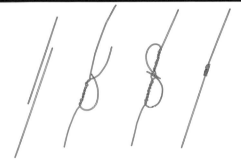

1) Overlap the ends of the two lines for several inches. Hold at the middle of the overlap and twist one end around the other line five or more turns. Bring end back and through strands as shown.

2) Still holding the lines, turn other end around line the same number of turns in the opposite direction. Bring end back and pass between lines from opposite direction of first end.

3) Tighten by pulling up slowly on both lines. Clip off short ends.

filament are usually more deeply rooted with the user than the line. Keep in mind, line twist can be avoided with swivels. Allowing the twisted line to drag a few minutes behind a moving boat also can cure line twist.

A backlash is caused by not having enough brains in your thumb. Overloading a reel also can cause it.

Line troubles on closed-face or open-faced reels also tend to be caused by overloading or under loading. Keep the line spool filled to within 1/8th inch and your troubles may disappear.

Also, add new line to the reel without twisting. Every line maker I know offers twist free directions that may be found inside every new box of mono. Follow the directions.

The Hi-tech Fishing Lines

In the last 20 years, line manufacturers have invented a number of new line concoctions featuring braided this, spun that. Some of them were poor substitutes for mono and they've disappeared. Still others, such as Berkley's Fireline or Spiderwire, have survived angling scrutiny and have found a home on fishing reels. Once again, the new lines are best in specific fishing situations, such as trolling crankbaits or flipping lures into heavy cover.

There's no such thing as one line to serve all. It's also true that monofilament is still the line of choice for most uses.

double surgeon's loop

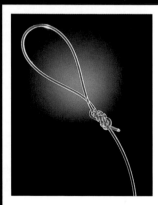

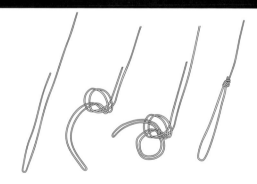

The double surgeon's loop is very easy to tie and makes a secure loop in the end of your line or leader.

1) Double up line end for a few inches. Form loop in doubled line holding it in place, between thumb and forefinger.

2) Pass end of doubled line through loop twice. (For greater strength pass doubled line through loop four times.) Pull doubled end up tight to form final loop.

Yes, but what strength line?

Again, no one size or weight line fits all fishing needs. However, most of your fishing requirements in Minnesota will be easily met with an assortment of line ranging from 6 to 12 pound test. Walleyes, pike and bass tend not to be line shy.

However, trout is another story. Having sharp vision and a suspicious nature, trout require more fooling, meaning thinner, more invisible lines of 1- to 4-pound test are usually necessary.

On the contrary, muskie fishing demands heavy weight lines, say 30 to 50 pound test plus wire or steel leaders of 50 to 100 pounds test.

Some fishermen insist on arming themselves with the heaviest line possible, say 20-pound test, for all kinds of fishing just in case that trophy fish hits.

The problem is the trophy usually doesn't. Why? Because the heavy line disrupted the action of the lure or bait and the trophy kept its mouth shut.

Excessively heavy line causes more problems than it's worth. Most spinning and spin-cast reels won't function properly; finely balanced lures won't swim right; casting distance is severely limited.

If you're uncertain about selecting the proper test line, make your mistake on the lighter side. Your reel and casting performance won't suffer. And it's already been proven that you can land any fish, no matter what size, on light line if you know the art of fighting a fish and have a reel with a smooth, working drag.

Troubleshooting Line

Monofilament fishing line can seem to go haywire. It'll curl or twist. It'll age and turn brittle and weak. It'll test your nerves, monofilament will.

Curls develop when the line has been coiled on a reel for a length of time. It's very common and doesn't mean your line needs changing. To remove the curls, simply stretch that part of the mono line that you'll use in a long cast. The stretching seems to realign the nylon molecules and its like creating new line.

Line twist is the result of several possible errors in your fishing savvy. You'll know when it happens; your slack line will twist on itself like its alive.

A common cause is when a lure twists or revolves and there's a cheap swivel or none at all to keep the line from twisting as the lure does.

Free-turning swivels placed ahead of lures, such as spoons and spinners, will help reduce some of the twisting. But sooner or later, you'll get the twists and your line will curl up on itself and eventually make a nest any robin would be proud to own.

Another cause of line twist is to reel without retrieving line. Let's say you have a large fish on the line and a reel drag that's set on the light side. If you reel and the pickup reel revolves without gaining line on the spool, you are creating twist faster than a fish blinks.

Sometimes line twist simply happens for no good reason at all.

Fortunately, line twist is easily avoided and easily eliminated.

If you've got twists only in the front few feet of line, hold your rod tip high, letting your lure dangle free. It will slowly unwind. When it quits turning, the twists will be gone.

If you've got a severe case of the twists, cut everything off the end of your line—snaps, swivels, lures. Hop in a boat or stand in a stream and let the line peel out behind the moving boat or current. Let out enough line to cover the twisted portion. The friction of the water against the monofilament works as a magical untwister. In minutes, your line will be like new again.

What else should you know about fishing line?

While it's not necessary to replace monofilament line on the reel every year, I would recommend adding new line, say 50 to 100 yards to the business end each season.

Keep in mind, monofilament will tend to fray or develop weak spots near the terminal end or that line nearest the hook. Check for line nicks by occasionally running the line between your fingers. Or simply snip off 3 or 4 feet of the old line.

Keep line stored out of sunlight and excessive heat to make it last longer. And please don't throw waste monofilament line overboard. Dispose of it properly. Old line tossed away inevitably ends up breaking seals on outboard motors or ends up wrapped around unsuspecting birds, often causing their death.

Our lake bottoms are fishing grounds, not dumping grounds.

Magic of Polarized Sunglasses

Every angler should wear them. They're kinder to your eyes in bright sunlight. For anglers, Polarized lenses are important tools, cutting surface glare and allowing improved vision for several feet underwater.

Dr. Jerry Poland, a Crosby eye surgeon, is a staunch advocate of wearing Polarized lenses at all times when fishing and for a variety of reasons. First, the eye is protected from ultra-violet rays and from flying hooks.

In some boating situations, the reduction in water glare and the Polarized view showing shallow water may help you avoid rocks and stumps.

Seeing edges of weed beds or tops of rock piles with the help of Polarized lenses is also a tool for making more accurate casts to catch more fish.

(By the way, my fishing buddy, Dr. Poland, has a trick if you're unsure your sunglasses are Polarized. Place your eyeglass lens against a known Polarized lens and turn your lens. If both are Polarized, the view through both lenses will turn dark as turned. If there is no change in light through both lenses when turned, your glasses are *not* Polarized.)

Cold Fronts, Wind and Other Excuses

If you hang around Minnesota's bait shops, boat docks or lakeside taverns, sooner or later you'll hear some piscatorial moaning about cold fronts.

When a cold front hits a fishing lake the conversation usually goes like this:

"Catch anything?"

"Naw."

"Weren't biting, huh?"

"Naw. Think it was that danged cold front."

Cold fronts have one benefit; they're the perfect excuse for an empty stringer. You can say the front just arrived or just left and be, technically correct. Listeners will gush with sympathy. They may not know what a cold front is, but it sounds official.

However, cold fronts do happen and fish don't like 'em.

Cold fronts arrive in various forms, weak to strong, but there's little doubt that your fishing will suffer. A strong cold front might shut down the bite for 72 hours or more.

You might be asking: What's a cold front?

Good question, since a cold front can show up without any drastic change in air temperature. But let's leave the science of cold fronts to the meteorologists.

What fishermen need to know is this:

Cold fronts are generally recognized by and associated with a day that breaks with bright, cloudless, high blue skies along with a brisk (and often cool or downright chilly) northwest wind. Cold fronts can appear in winter or summer, of course.

When a cold front arrives, anglers generally will find little to cheer about. Belinda Jensen, a popular TV meteorologist and an angler herself, says there is no scientific explanation that she knows

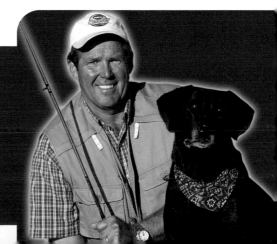

Fishing has played a large part in my life since boyhood. My grandparents, my uncles and aunts on both sides of the family were avid anglers or at least tolerated lots of Sunday afternoons spent fishing.

about that explains why fish act as they do in the presence of a cold front.

Yet from the moment a cold front arrives, fishing action will falter until reaching rock bottom on the day after the front passes. Depending on the strength of the weather pattern, the action often begins to pick up by the second or third day.

Are these cold front rules absolute? Of course not. We're talking fish and fishing. Yes, I've seen reasonably good catches under cold front conditions, but normally the action will be "slow" all over the lake.

Also know this: Not all fish are created equal when it comes to cold fronts. Although I don't have any scientific evidence to back my hunches, I'd say largemouth bass and muskies are the most sensitive fish to cold fronts, followed by walleyes and panfish. It's been my experience the fish least affected by cold fronts are northern pike and stream trout.

So—what to do?

A cold front is apt to affect everything from schools of baitfish to muskies longer than oars. A persistent fisherman can improve his luck during a cold front by changing his objective. That is, switching from bass to bluegills, for example. Perch seem to bite all the time, although they may be less aggressive, too. Ron and Al Lindner, a pair of fish-thinking brothers and founders of In-Fisherman, often confronted the bad odds of cold fronts. In their guiding

days, their worst luck was under the influence of cold fronts. But they also discovered a few last resorts. "Generally we fished deeper water or the heaviest cover during cold fronts," Ron explains. "Our luck wasn't always phenomenal, but we did catch something while other fishermen didn't."

Says Al, "And we went to live bait for everything. The guy who throws artificials during the effects of a cold front can usually forget it. I do think that walleyes are less affected by cold fronts than say bass. But still, you should fish deeper and SLOWER. That's the key."

When The Wind Blows

Minnesota has its share of fishy wind. Former Gov. Jesse Ventura was always good for a gust or two. (Just kiddin' ol Jesse, the Body. Was I your favorite jackal?) We anglers also face our share of pesky wind.

Although angling poems are written about wind direction—"wind from the east, fish bite the least"… and so forth— the wind's intensity, rather than direction may do more to make or break your fishing luck. After all, the wind's direction depends on the location of pressure systems and frontal movements. Fish, indeed, may bite the least with an east wind, but the culprit is the weather phenomenon, not the wind's direction. The wind's velocity is something else again.

Winds that whip up dangerous boating conditions need no explanation. Fishermen shouldn't be out on big waters on those stormy occasions. I was once or

twice and my fingerprints are still imbedded on the gunwales of the boat.

No, I'm referring to winds that are safe, but affect your fishing success. For example, largemouth bass, roaming in bulrush shadows, are almost impossible to catch when the bulrushes are buffeted by wind and waves. I don't know if this is true, but a fella once told me bass don't like bobbing in windy shallows. The answer, of course, is to find those bassy-looking weed beds that on any given day are out of the wind. Or pursue deepwater bassin' spots.

Walleye fishermen are always hoping for a "walleye chop," a brisk breeze that ripples the waters or forms small whitecaps. Wind and walleyes go together.

Wind does two things: reduces sunlight penetration for the light-sensitive walleyes and often triggers a feeding binge. In addition, wind is like a boat control tool for drifting while you drag a line in search of walleyes.

There is a point, however, when the winds become a detriment to a drifting walleye fisherman. In those times, I've found a great aid to angling is a drift sock, which slows the speed of your drift. Pro-anglers Sam Anderson and Gary Roach, who fish walleyes under all conditions, learned to expand the uses for a drift sock. Eventually, they fine-tuned their own version, the Drift Control Sea Anchor.

At first glance, having a drift sock (or drift bag) trailing alongside the boat looks like a line or fish tangle just waiting to happen. Don't worry. You'll adjust and, as a result, the sock is seldom in the way. Most models also are designed to collapse quickly when you're ready to bring the sock onboard.

Sometimes there is no defense against an overpowering wind. Hey, you're uncomfortable and getting wet. You're drifting too fast to stay on the bottom. What to do? Move out of the wind or call it a day. Don't risk your boat safety for a bite.

The important thing to remember is that wind does affect most game fish in Minnesota. It can be an advantage or disadvantage. A wind impacts your fishing techniques, the way your bait is presented and your ability to detect strikes.

To get along with wind, stay versatile. Use wind to your advantage whenever possible. There may be times when you'll intentionally want to fish in wind-rumpled waters. Then again, your best success may be waiting in quieter places...lakeshores, islands, and points on the leeward side. If your luck is still lousy, go ahead; blame it on a cold front. No one will be the wiser.

Using Your Eyes

A Minnesota lake map is an indispensable angling aid when you venture onto strange water. There are now hundreds of Minnesota's fishing lakes that have been charted into hydrographic maps, showing depth contours, physical features, vegetation and so forth.

Keep in mind, many lakes were mapped decades ago and the accuracy is

Basics Briefly

often unreliable. Still, a lake map is useless unless you know how to read one (see illustration on page 17).

You can also "read" a lake with your eyes. All fish like to be near something. Boat docks, weed beds, brush, rock piles, tree stumps, boulders—these features may be visible.

Of course, there are "objects" underwater we cannot see that also attract and hold fish. That's where a lake map is invaluable, even one with inaccuracies. A typical lake map will show the approximate location of sunken islands, drop-offs, underwater points, rock bars and the like. More importantly, the maps also show where the bottom is rather uninteresting and flat and most likely fishless. But don't pass up places that, on the map, don't look fishy. Maps don't show submerged weed beds, a major fish attractant.

Thus, you must use both you eyes and a hydrographic map.

New Age Fish Maps

GPS, the global positioning system developed by the U.S. to navigate the world, has made many Minnesota lake maps more reliable. A Minnesota Company, SonarMap, took GPS mapping technology to another level, creating lake bottom contours with extreme accuracy taken from literally thousands of GPS waypoints. They're called ReelBottom Fishing Maps and are now available at retail fishing outlets. Other GPS-made maps are also more accurate and offer the necessary navigational coordinates to known fishing hotspots.

GPS receivers are now common on fishing boats, which means an angler merely plugs in the coordinates of a known fishing location and the GPS unit—communicating with satellites more than 11,000 miles up above the Earth—directs you to the spot. Some GPS units have built-in lake maps showing, not only fish haunts, but marinas, restaurants, public accesses, bridges, rivers, roads and more.

GPS technology has clearly found a home in Minnesota fishing boats, meaning the age of old guide fishing secrets is going the way of the dinosaur. While we may regret the changing times, you can't stand in the way of progress. As we march along, anglers should ask themselves: how much farther do we go in the name of fishing success and still retain angling mysteries and skunked days?

Fortunately, so far, the fish bite when they want to, in spite of all our fancy gadgetry.

Using Electronic Fishing Eyes

The electronic angling age arrived in Minnesota in the late 1960s when Carl Lowrance, an Oklahoma engineer, brought his magical green box to show Marv Koep's Nisswa Guides how to read the newfangled devices. Carl had invented a portable sonar fishing device, utilizing technology first developed for U.S. Navy submarines.

One by one, Carl took the guides for a ride on the lake demonstrating how a

Basics Briefly

lake maps

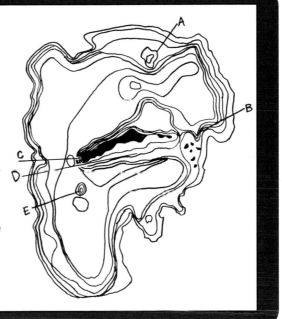

A typical lake map: note contour lines, which show depths, islands, points, bays. (A) Indicates underwater hump. (B) Shows how point extends underwater with fast drop-off outside of point; note small islands are in rather dull water. (C) Shows very sharp drop-off. The closer the contour lines the sharper the drop-off. As compared to (D) which shows contour lines farther apart, indicating a gradual increase in water depth. (E) Shows typical sunken island with 10 feet of water over top of the island.

flashing gizmo in the green (or red) box would indicate what was below the boat—mud bottoms, rock bottoms, sand bottoms and EVEN fish.

I was one of the lucky anglers to receive a personal lesson from Carl that day. Now, 30 years later, my eye-opening experience with Carl remains a fond memory of time spent with a real fishing pioneer.

Today, we know these things as fish finders, depth finders, wide screen, multi-pixel, liquid crystal, full color, high speed, blah, blah, blah wonders. While the new models offer many nifty features, the basic sonar technology remains unchanged.

Let's also put an end to a couple of myths about sonar units.

Can you really tell the size of a fish? What part of "no" don't you understand?

A sonar unit emits a sound wave and measures the distance it travels before the sound hits a target and bounces back to the transducer. In an instant, the sonar unit measures the distance and converts the reading into feet for you to read on the screen.

But some fish marks on the sonar screen are larger than others. That's because the fish is closer to the middle of the cone-shaped sonar signal.

Can I tell a walleye from a carp on my sonar screen? Not really.

Should you look for fish before you start fishing?

Many anglers do. My walleye tournament teammate, Gary Roach, rarely stopped to fish a sandbar or rock pile or other deepwater spot unless he saw fish marks on his Lowrance. (Obviously, you wouldn't run your boat over shallow water walleyes—less than 10 feet—to see if any are there because you'd spook them in the process.)

On the other hand, if you don't see fish on the sonar it doesn't mean there's nothing below to catch. Often fish will hunker between rocks or in thick weeds and will not be detected by sonar.

Your electronic eyes are most valuable if used to find—not fish—but bottom contours where fish might live. If you drive the lake until you see the screen fill with fish you might never wet a line.

Generally, a lake map will give you a good idea of where to start fishing and the depth finder will show where you might want to drop bait.

When I leave the dock, my eyes, my depth finder, is already looking. I may not trust the maps but I'll trust the sonar signal. You never know when—on the way to a spot marked on the map—you'll cross an underwater hump or some other fishy-looking structure that's not on the map.

You may want to make a cast there.

It could be the pot-of-piscatorial-gold that every angler dreams of finding.

Floating Right

There is no doubt; today's modern fishing boats are the safest in the history of boat making. Still, too many anglers capsize and drown every year. In Minnesota, a large percentage of boating accidents, sometimes nearly half, are associated with fishing.

And drinking.

Minnesota has some mighty big water. Big enough to challenge the seaworthiness of many boats, not to mention the fisherman at the helm.

One unfortunate day on Mille Lacs, a storm hit without warning and tossed 23-foot boats around like corks. I know. Frank Hans and I were out there watching the sky turn mean as a powerful wind slowly turned Mille Lacs into a field of angry whitecaps.

Later, we learned, two men in a smaller craft capsized and drowned. Both were wearing lifejackets.

That particular storm hit with very little warning. That's not usually the case. Most storms in Minnesota approach from the northwest, west, or southwest. Whenever you're fishing, keep an eye peeled in those directions. Marine radios are a handy source of weather, but most fishing boats aren't equipped.

The key is don't take chances, especially on big water. Give yourself enough time to reach the safety of shore. One sign of pending trouble is a sudden change of wind direction. That usually means a weather change and it could be for the worse.

If you suspect bad weather later in your fishing day, try one of Minnesota's many smaller lakes instead of chancing ocean-size waves on big waters.

If you're a visitor and unfamiliar with local lakes, seek advice from local bait shops and fishermen. Chances are if a local angler is skeptical about a lake's boating condition ("I wouldn't go out there if I were you") or the weather ("She looks nasty to the west") you'd be wise to heed the advice.

In addition, some lakes react differently to storms or strong winds, depending on their direction. For example, a gusty south wind on Lake X may not be dangerous to fishermen. However, the same wind from the west on Lake X could turn the water surface into white froth.

Many of today's boats could handle such a white froth if today's anglers all knew how to handle the boat. Whenever two or more fishermen head out, somebody invariably wants to ride in the bow seat.

In rough water, passengers should stay low and arrange weight to keep the bow light enough to respond to the waves. The key is to keep weight off the bow so that the boat can respond to the wave action.

Seats were placed in a boat for comfort under normal boating conditions. Rough waters are not normal. Don't hesitate to place your passengers on the deck or floor of the boat to ride out the bad water. Have them sit near the centerline of the boat to increase the craft's stability. Wise canoeists know the value of that lesson. For those who stand or ride high in a canoe will soon ride under.

So what's the perfect Minnesota fishing boat?

That's a loaded question, which I shall refrain from triggering.

Raven, the quiet dog folks see on television, is not such a quiet dog in a fishing boat. Will she ever quit hunting for fish or digging her paw into the minnow bucket? No way. If she catches a minnow, will she eat it? Like...right now.

Aluminum or fiberglass? Another personal decision.

I do have my opinions, of course. But it's important that each boat buyer determine where and how he intends to use the boat much of the time. Those fishermen who are in love with the state's giant lakes, such as Leech and Mille Lacs, should consider boats in the 18-foot or larger category and certainly no smaller than 16-feet.

If you fish some big waters, but mostly smaller lakes, then a 17- to 15-footer may be the best compromise.

As every angler knows, there's a place for 12-foot johnboats, canoes, and other small car toppers. They're portable and ideal for fishing on that hidden out-of-the-way lake or floating a river.

But rarely do small craft belong on big water unless you're looking for trouble.

How Much Outboard?

The amount of outboard engine power is a personal thing and dependent on the boat being powered. However, the choice is critical for fishermen who like to troll for northern and muskies or back troll (run the boat in reverse, stern-first) for walleyes.

Years ago, an angler who took fishing seriously settled for outboards in the 25 to 50 horsepower class.

Today, most anglers rely on large horsepower (115 to 225) to reach their fishing grounds and then switch to kickers (smaller outboards) or high-thrust electric trolling motors on the bow or stern for boat control.

Where the outboard power climb is going to end, who knows? We anglers always want to go further and faster and, as we all know, the fishing is always better on the other side of the lake.

Magic of Boat Control

When the subject of boat control comes up so does a question: Which style of fishing boat is best? Tiller or console?

A tiller model (where the angler operates the boat from a seat in the stern and controls the outboard with a tiller handle) is often considered the ultimate in boat control but tiller boating lacks in other ways.

A console model typically means somewhat less boat control but more comfort. In console models, most of the actual boat control is performed by an angler sitting or standing in the bow and controlling the boat with a bow mount electric trolling motor.

I must admit that for years, having honed my fishing skills with the likes of Gary Roach and Al Lindner, I was strictly a tiller man. No need to switch, I figured.

One day, Jim Antolik, of Crestliner Boats, suggested trying a console model, adding he expected me to be surprised at how the boat handled. At first, my bow fishing skills were quite rusty. On windy days, I struggled with the trolling motor. Sitting in the bow seat, my sense of movement or trolling speed was crude. I yearned for the return of my tiller seat.

However, as the fishing days went by, something changed. I gradually felt

more comfortable operating from the bow. Using bow-mount electric trolling motors with adequate power is the key. On some windy days I learned to utilize the help of drift socks (also known as drift bags) to slow the drift and maintain boat control.

Lastly, I learned to adjust to any situation and be contented with either tiller or console boat models.

Keep in mind, boat control for angling isn't about getting someplace first or fastest. It's about turning your boat into a fishing tool that will help you properly cover fishing spots and allow you to present baits in the right manner to unseen quarry below.

If your boat control is right, you'll catch fish. If not, it won't matter if you're the fastest boat on the lake.

Hiring a Guide

When in doubt, hire a fishing guide.

It's the cheapest fishing lesson around. A fishing guide will show you where to fish, how to fish and possibly even clean your catch.

If you're a fishing novice, a guide doubles as an excellent coach and most are anxious to help you increase your appreciation and enjoyment of fishing. A happy angler is probably a return customer.

Minnesota is blessed with a number of skilled anglers who go fishing for hire. Since it's your money, choose a

guide based on the recommendation of anglers who've used the guide's services. Ask for referrals. Talk to bait shop or resort owners. They'll know if the guide delivers. Resorts and lodges are particularly concerned about the guides they recommend or have on staff. If you have a lousy time with a guide (regardless of what is caught), you're apt to blame the resort or lodge.

Keep in mind, fishing has its slow days and so do guides. What you should expect, however, is a guide's best effort at having an enjoyable time, fish or no fish. Make sure you understand what the guide will or will not furnish so there are no surprises when it's time to pay.

Check the guide's equipment. If he's professional, his boat will be in good shape and safely adequate for the waters you will be fishing.

Ask about his fishing style before you make a reservation.

If you like casting for northern pike and the guide is a trolling specialist, you're not going to have a fun day.

It's also unfair to ask a guide to fish your way. You're paying him for his experience and expertise, so get the most out of it.

So—if you like to flip for bass in slop, choose a guide who likes to do the same thing. In that way, the guide will be at his best and you'll have a good time. And you might even catch something.

Guide fees vary. Make sure you know what the charges are for half-day or full-days and how many rods (anglers) are included. Don't hire one guide and expect to include Uncle Kenny, Aunt Eva and two kids in the same boat.

Launch Fishing

Launch fishing is for the angler who wants a bargain and company.

Launch services are offered on a number of Minnesota lakes, including Mille Lacs, Lake Minnetonka, Leech Lake, Winnibigoshish, Lake of the Woods and Rainy.

Most launches can handle 15 to 20 or more passengers at a time. In most cases, you can buy a seat on the next scheduled trip. Or, you and friends can rent the whole launch and the captain or pay a certain amount per angler. Fish cleaning service is usually extra.

Again, inquire about how much time you're buying on a launch and what is

Raven's tidbit

provided (baits, rods, refreshments, life jackets, etc.?).

If you feel safer in big boats on big water, launch fishing is ideal. Most captains are excellent guides and they work hard to put you on fish. The more fish, the better the tip.

Lake Superior Charter Fishing

The greatest fishing comeback story in Minnesota is also about the state's largest lake. Fact is, Lake Superior is the largest freshwater lake in the world.

It's a long story but Superior is back as a sport fishing lake. Thanks to state and federal fish managers, lake trout stocks have been restored and various salmon species, such as Coho (silver) and Chinook (king) salmon have been introduced.

Hiring a Lake Superior charter boat is the ideal way to discover this grandiose body of clear and cold water. In a nutshell, lake trout action on Superior—from the Duluth Harbor to Grand Marais— seems to be getting better every year.

My last outing with Capt. Bill Judnick onboard his charter, Summer Heat, was a real eye opener as we caught lakers ranging from 4 pounds to 15 pounds. This was on an August day when the air temps were in the 90s. On Superior, however, the only thing hot was the fishing action.

Charter boats are available at half-day and full-day rates and provide all fishing tackle. All you need is a jacket, snacks and personal items.

To contact charter boats on Lake Superior, call the Duluth Visitor's Bureau at 800-4-DULUTH. Or visit website: www.visitduluth.com.

Other charters on the North Shore may be found by searching the Web using key words Superior and fishing.

Keeping Minnows Happy

As Izaac Walton once wrote, "A dead worm is but a dead bait, and like to catch nothing, compared to a lively, stirring worm."

While Walton's wisdom speaks for itself, I might add that a dead minnow or a mushy night crawler represents the most expensive rotten meat you've ever bought.

I once figured that night crawlers, selling for $2 a dozen comes out to $64 per pound. The point being, if you don't take care of your live bait, you'd be better off going to the fish market where

**Her full name is
Rum River's Black Raven**

minnow buckets

Popular minnow buckets include: 1) Styrofoam, which "breathes"; 2) plastic and 3) metal buckets perforated inserts; 4) flow-through; and 5) aerated bucket, which runs off a boat's 12 volt electrical system.

walleyes sell for considerably less than $64 per pound.

Before you can keep bait healthy, it first must be purchased in that condition.

Look before you buy.

When buying night crawlers, reputable bait dealers will encourage you to open the carton of how lively the 'crawlers are. Touch a few. They should react. If not, they're probably ready to die.

Healthy 'crawlers also are plump like a short, fat cigar. Pick one up. If it looks like a shoestring, chances are you couldn't feed it to a robin much less a walleye.

Never buy a carton of night crawlers that contains one dead member. The others likely will be dead, shortly.

Of all live bait, leeches are the easiest to judge. Again, check the carton. Dead leeches turn white or gray. So make sure you're buying a lively dozen.

Once the bait is out of the store, it's up to you to keep it alive and active.

Your greatest challenge will be lake shiners. Shiners are magical walleye attractants, especially in early season. The problem is a perfectly happy shiner will likely turn belly up roughly three minutes after you leave the bait shop.

How do they know?

This is not the fault of the bait dealer. Shiners must be kept in cold, aerated water or they'll die before they try.

It might be needless to say, but good bait is important for good fishing. Sure, you can grind up a night crawler and still feed it to bluegills or perch. And sun-ripened minnows will attract catfish for

15 miles. But for walleyes, crappies, northern pike, muskies and other fish, you'll want active bait.

The best way to learn to care for bait is to follow the advice of the experts. The late John Vados spent most of his life as a keeper of live bait. Another bait specialist is Frankie Dusenka, who started selling worms as a boy in his father's hardware store in Chisago City.

John always told me he'd seen most of the mistakes anglers made and made a few himself. Same with Frankie.

They know how to make minnows happy.

Minnows

1. The best way to transport minnows successfully is to use an ordinary Styrofoam bucket with a good lid. Styrofoam buckets keep water fresh much longer than metal. Don't buy too many minnows each time and over-crowd your bucket. The more oxygen, the better the fishing.

2. Put 8-10 ice cubes in your bucket when transporting minnows long distances. If the ice cubes are made with ordinary tap water and contains chlorine, put them in a plastic bag first. Remember, keep the lid on!

3. Don't buy more minnows than you plan to use. Minnows quickly grow stale in an unnatural environment and aren't nearly as effective as when fresh.

4. When it's necessary to change minnow water (usually when all the minnows come topside for oxygen) refill only half the bucket each time. A whole

new bucket of lake water of a different temperature could likely cause shock and shorten minnow life. Any new water added to minnows should not change the temperature more than 10 degrees higher or lower than the water being replaced. Fresh water from a lake or well should be used. Do not use tap water from a municipal supply.

5. When you take fish home in your minnow bucket, be sure to wash it well before it's used for minnows again. Slime remaining in the bucket after fish are removed contains bacteria that use up valuable oxygen. Wash your bucket with regular baking soda for best results.

Night Crawlers and Worms

1. Night crawlers and worms are usually packaged in special bedding material, which includes food as well as habitat. There is enough food in each box to last 3-4 weeks and keep night crawlers and worms as fresh as if in their natural environment. Do not add moisture; packages contain just the right amount.

2. Night crawlers and worms should be kept within a temperature range of 40-60 degrees. A Styrofoam bucket is ideal for traveling. Just put a few ice cubes in a plastic bag, place in the bucket and you've got a great refrigerator for one or several boxes. Between fishing trips you can keep them in your refrigerator at home.

3. Boxes of night crawlers or worms should never be left in areas exposed to direct sunlight. While fishing be sure to keep them shaded beneath a boat seat. Boxes exposed for less than 10 minutes to direct sunlight can results in dead night crawlers and worms.

Leeches

1. Keep leeches cool. To store, change water daily and refrigerate. No feeding is necessary.

Miscellaneous Baits

1. Grubs, wax worms, mousies should be kept refrigerated (about 60 degrees) between fishing trips.

Filleting: No Bones About It

One of the best fish cleaners I ever met was Danny Stott. At the time, Danny was 11. He was earning money to buy a bike. Danny's a married man now, but he'll still fillet a walleye if his father, Buster, ever catches one.

Danny's boyhood skill with a fillet knife proves that practice makes perfect.

If your fillet looks like they've been through a meat grinder, it probably means you seldom catch much.

Besides practice, you need a decent fillet knife. Decent mean two things: sharp with a flexible blade and comfy handle.

There are more ways than one to skin a cat. Same goes for a fish.

The method illustrated here works as good as any, but I'm amazed at the variations in filleting in vogue around the country.

By the way, almost any Minnesota fish can be filleted, except catfish and bull-

how to filet a fish

(1) Make first cut just behind the gills. Slice down to the bone, then, without removing blade, turn it and slice straight along backbone...

(2) ...to the tail. Note that the fillet has been cut away from the rest of the fish. After slicing fillet off at tail, turn fish over and repeat procedure on the other side.

(3) With both sides removed, you have cut away both fillets without disturbing the fish's entrails. This is the neatest and fastest way to prepare fish. Now to finish the fillets...

(4) Next step Is to remove the rib section. Again, a sharp, flexible knife is important to avoid wasting meat. Insert blade close to rib bones and slice entire section away. This should be done before skin is removed to keep waste to a minimum.

(5) Removing the skin from each fillet is simply a matter of inserting knife at tail and "cutting" meat from the skin. With the proper knife, it's easily done.

(6) Here is each fillet, ready for the pan, or freezer. Note there is no waste. Remember not to overwash fillets. This will preserve tasty juices and keep meat in its firm natural state.

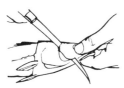

(7) Cutting out the "cheeks" is the next important step. Few fishermen know that cheeks are the filet mignon of the fish. Though small, they're tasty and well worth saving.

(8) Slice into cheek where indicated then "scoop out" meat with blade peeling away skin. Repeat on the other side. Many fishermen save cheeks until they have accumulated enough for a real gourmet's delight.

(9) Here are all the parts of the fish after you've finished. Note fish head, entrails, spine, tail and fins stay intact. This is the neatest way to prepare most game fish, and once you've mastered these few steps, the easiest.

heads. These two bewhiskered fishes are best skinned and gutted, preferably by somebody other than you. The late DNR Commissioner Joe Alexander was an expert at filleting panfish, especially crappies. Joe took great delight in demonstrating his advanced filleting skills in front of folks at the Minnesota State Fair. He also loved to challenge outdoor writers. Yes, I lost to Joe but I beat the guy from the St. Paul Pioneer Press.

Fish you intend to eat are best keep in a live-well or on ice until ready to be filleted. And one more thing. Fillet with respect. This means giving the fish a solid bonk on the head for a quick and humane death. Then, fillet.

Y-Bone Blues

Anglers anxious to dine on northern pike must face the problem of troublesome Y-bones, which are hidden and not removed by the usual filleting methods.

So extra steps are necessary. Again, there are several ways to achieve bone-free pike.

This is a simple version (see illustration on page 27).

Fillet as usual, except do not remove the skin. With the fillet flesh-side up, make an angular cut along the "lateral" line, which runs length-wise in the middle of the fillet. Fold over the flap of flesh containing the Y-bones (you can feel them with a finger) and make another cut, removing the flap. That should eliminate every bone in the fillet. Then, remove the skin. Again practice makes perfect.

Legal Lines

If the sport of fishing is worth doing, then it is worth preserving and protecting.

That's what Minnesota's fishing laws are about.

Basically, a Minnesota angler needs to know three things: if the fishing license is valid, if the fishing season is open and the fish limits.

There also is one stamp required, an $8.50 trout and salmon stamp.

Today, the subject of fish limits is becoming more complicated as the DNR begins to manage each lake individually. If you think about it, individual lake management only makes sense, because no two lakes are alike.

What this means is the book of Minnesota fishing rules is getting thicker.

In addition to daily fish limits, many lakes now have "slot" limits that dictate what size fish can be kept or must be released. Still other lakes have "minimum" size limits on certain fish species, meaning the fish must be of a certain length before it can be possessed. These special regulations are often posted at public accesses. Remember, it's your responsibility to know the law.

If you plan to fish for trout, be aware that at certain times some portions of trout streams are off-limits. In some cases, multiple hooks are prohibited.

Minnesota is bounded by four states and Canada. On the border lakes or rivers, the fishing seasons and limits often are different from Minnesota's inland waterways.

Non-residents share all of the fishing privileges enjoyed by residents with one exception: nonresidents are not allowed to spear.

A synopsis of Minnesota's fishing laws is available annually at license outlets, such as county license centers, sporting goods stores, hardware stores, bait shops and many resorts.

The Business End of Fishing

Fishing is big business in Minnesota.

And nature isn't the only worker.

The business end of fishing ranges from the state's huge tourism industry to outdoor products to the task of managing the fishing resources.

There are about 2.3 million of us who wet a line each year in Minnesota.

We anglers spend an estimated $1.8 billion (yes, *billion*) a year on fishing-related pursuits, according to DNR estimates.

Beyond buying fishing boats, we fork over $50 million on live bait, $34 million on lures and stuff and $8 million on ice to keep our fish, bait and beer cold.

Don't tell your spouse, but a typical state angler spends about $1,086 on fishing. Sounds cheap to me.

To maintain fishing, the DNR Fisheries Division employs about 320 workers, operates 18 fish hatcheries and operates on a budget that ranges between $22 to $30 million a year.

Minnesota's fish hatcheries raise and stock 235 million fish a year. Most are walleyes, followed (in order of numbers stocked) by rainbow trout, northern pike, brown trout, lake trout, Chinook salmon, channel catfish, brook trout, splake, smallmouth bass, muskies, largemouth bass and tiger muskies.

Minnesota has 12 hatcheries that raise walleyes and other warm water fish; five coldwater hatcheries for trout and salmon; 10 walleye spawning stations (where eggs are collected); 239 walleye rearing ponds; 4 northern pike spawning areas and 30 muskie-rearing ponds.

A Minnesota resident angler receives the aforementioned fish management program plus the privilege of fishing for the whole year for an individual license fee of $17. That's 365 days of fishing for less than... a nickel a day. Think about it? That's $.05 cents for a day of fishing.

It's a price not even Wal-Mart can beat.

Catch and Release

Is catch and release the answer?

Yes, but what was the question?

Allow me to confess, I am a proponent, practitioner and believer in the benefits of catch and release. The reasons are very simple. The greatest thrill in angling is catching a big fish. Big fish tend to be old fish. A 30-pound muskie needs about 15 years to reach that size. If we don't give fish time to grow, there'll be no big ones to catch.

The importance of releasing part of one's catch, hit home one day when I joined Al Lindner to fish for largemouth bass on one of Al's favorite lakes. In fact, Al was conducting a bass-catching research project with the blessings of DNR. His research consisted of catching and tagging as many bass as he could.

Basics Briefly

When I joined Al that day we fished hard and caught many bass. And guess what? Most of them had been caught and released previously. It dawned on me that if Al had chosen to legally keep every bass he'd caught that summer, the bass population in that lake would have been down to a precious few. Does that mean we no longer can keep anything? No, let's not make it a sin to eat a fish.

I'm a moderate on the subject of catch and release. I don't release everything I catch. Deep-fried walleye is too delicious to quit eating.

In other words, what I really practice is SELECTIVE catch and release.

Simply put, we should release the larger game fish because they are so rare. And, if we want a meal of fish fillets, keep the smaller fish, because they are the most abundant.

Of course, it's foolish to release a fish that has no chance of surviving. But don't make a hasty decision.

In early season, under cold-water conditions, a walleye hooked on live bait or artificial lures has an excellent chance of survival. In fact, a DNR study indicated an almost 100 percent survival rate for walleyes in water temperatures below 70 degrees. In warmer water, fish mortality increases, but still, the majority of fish, 80 percent or more, survived if released immediately.

A fish that is bleeding after being hooked only in the lips and handled carefully (preferably released with little or no handling), will almost certainly survive to bite again.

A fish taken to the frying pan has no chance.

Today, our fishing regulations are filled with special regulations, including slot limits, requiring the release of fish of certain sizes EVEN if the fish is fatally injured and about to die.

This hurts. I remember the disgust I felt one day for a Mille Lacs fishing rule that required me to release a 23-inch walleye that, despite my efforts to revive, was dying. When I last saw the fish, it was floating lifeless, its white belly shining in the sun and waiting for the next hungry sea gull.

Obviously, we don't want laws that require wanton waste. On the other hand, if we keep all the big walleyes, they will soon be gone, too.

We must also face Minnesota's piscatorial reality. Every year there are more of us catching more fish. For this to continue and grow, we have no choice but to recycle our fish by practicing catch and release. We also know it works.

We know by limiting ourselves, we are making fishing better in Minnesota. For everybody, including you and me.

How Fast They Grow

If Minnesota traded climates with Florida, the list of state record fish would be shattered. Our fish would grow to be giants; muskies would be capable of smashing small boats. Fishing might even become a dangerous pastime. Kids couldn't swim in northern pike waters.

It's probably a good thing that Minnesota has long winters with cold water. Our fish can get big, but they do it slower.

The growth rate of fishes is determined by a number of factors: water fertility, food supply, competition, species differences and individual differences. All rainbow trout, for instance, may look alike but each is an individual.

The number one factor controlling the growth rate of Minnesota's fishes is the cold water.

Fish that live in warmer climates with warmer water grow the year around. The biggest largemouth bass I've ever caught weighed slightly more than 13 pounds. A remarkable fish, yes. But that fish also reached this hefty weight in less than 14 years in the warm waters of Mexico's El Salto Lake.

In Minnesota, the water is warm for only a few months every year. When the water cools, the fish's metabolism is greatly reduced. It eats less and grows less. Slow growth doesn't mean Minnesota doesn't produce big fish, however. They just take more years to become lunkers.

The age of most scaled fish is determined by counting the annular rings on the scales, much like counting the growth rings on a tree. In fish without scales, the age can be determined by counting the rings present in a cross-section of the backbone.

Minnesota fisheries biologists often collect scale samples from fish caught by anglers to monitor the growth rates of fishes from various lakes. If the rates aren't normal, biologists may be alerted to problems with the lake.

Rough estimates of a fish's age may be determined by measuring the length. The chart on page 32, compiled by Minnesota's Department of Natural Resources, can be used as a guide.

You may be surprised at how many years are required to produce a heavy weight fish.

Keeping Memories

There are only four things you can do with a fish: eat it, mount it, photograph it, and release it.

Kinda makes you wonder why we try so hard to catch one, doesn't it? Still, we often botch the choices.

While it takes a terrible cook to ruin a frying pan of walleye or bluegill fillets, most of us easily take terrible photographs. Let's see if we can improve.

The key to interesting fish pictures is to keep it simple. Choose an uncluttered background, such as the sky. Get close to your subject, the fisherman and his catch.

Don't add three limits and the neighbor's dog. An angler holding one or two fish makes a much better picture. The more fish in a picture, the less fish actually noticed by the viewer.

Your angler model may want to look like a Tom Cruise or Cindy Crawford and insist on wearing sunglasses. That's a no-no. Remove the dark shades and take a picture so we can see those joyful eyes. In addition, watch for harsh shadows across

Basics Briefly

YEAR	1	2	3	4	5	6	7	8	9	10
Black crappie	2	5	7	8	10	11	12	12	13	14
Bluegill	2	3	5	6	7	8	8	9	9	10
Lake trout	5	9	12	16	18	20	23	26	28	28
Largemouth bass	4	7	9	12	13	15	16	18	18	—
Muskellunge	7	13	17	22	26	29	33	39	42	44
Northern Pike	8	13	18	21	24	27	29	31	33	35
Pumpkinseed	2	3	4	6	6	7	8	8	9	—
Rainbow trout	5	9	13	16	21	—	—	—	—	—
Rock bass	2	3	5	6	7	8	9	10	10	11
Sauger	4	8	10	12	13	14	14	—	—	—
Smallmouth bass	4	7	10	12	18	21	—	—	—	—
Yellow perch	3	5	6	7	8	9	10	11	11	—
Walleye	5	9	12	15	17	19	21	22	23	25

the face, created by hats and bright sun. Take the hat off or tilt it back or use a filler flash.

Check the background so that tree branches, light poles or street signs aren't growing out of the happy angler's head.

Action shots are fun to try, although you must keep your camera handy. But invariably, in the excitement of landing a fish, the camera will not be held evenly—and the horizon in the picture will look like a mountain slope. And who's ever seen a lake tilted on its side? Concentrate on keeping the horizon level and hope that the action captured is what you wanted.

Remember, it's the fisherman and his catch that are important. The rule is get close to what's important. Why have George standing on the dock and holding his walleye with half the lake and forty

acres of trees also in the picture. We want to see George and his fish.

And take several pictures. Chances are, if you only snap one photo of George, his eyes will be closed and his tongue out. Film is a cheap price to pay for fond memories.

Mounting A Trophy

Once in awhile, we each get lucky enough to catch a fish worth putting on the wall, to treasure for a lifetime. Fine, but you've got some important decisions to make right now.

Do you kill the fish and take it to a conventional taxidermy shop? Or do you choose to order a graphite replica, which means you photograph and measure the fish (length and girth) and quickly release the fish to bite again another day?

It's not a sin to go the conventional

route. Some trophy fish simply won't survive, even if released, so there's nothing wrong with going to the taxidermy shop.

But do it right: first, take several color photographs of the fish to give to the taxidermist. They'll be used to paint the fish and recapture its basic shape.

If you're close to a reputable taxidermist, deliver the fish as soon as possible. If not, freeze the whole fish in a plastic bag. Make sure the fins are folded back against the carcass. To protect the tail from breaking or splintering after it's frozen solid, place the tail between two pieces of cardboard and wrap securely before freezing.

When you first catch such a trophy, everybody and his brother will want to hold it, handle and show it to Uncle Louey. Avoid over-handling the fish, since some fish lose their scales easily. And missing scales will show up later, despite the best efforts of a taxidermist.

Make sure you discuss with the taxidermist how much you want to pay and what wall you expect to hang the trophy on. That may determine which way the fish is facing. You may also want lifelike settings added, all of which raise the price, of course.

The Wonder Of Graphite Mounts

Choosing a graphite mount has one great advantage. The lunker lives.

In my den room, I have two special replica mounts, a 22-inch smallmouth bass and a 46-inch northern pike. The smallmouth, the largest of its kind I've ever caught, is special for several rea-sons. The smallie was kind enough to hit while our Minnesota Bound television cameras were rolling.

When I caught the northern pike, it was, at the time, the largest pike of my angling career. Since then, I've caught and released a 49-incher.

In both cases, my fishing memories are on the wall while the trophies, hopefully, are still swimming.

The point is: there really is no reason today to kill a big fish in order to have it preserved as a trophy memory. You really can have your cake and eat it, too.

How To Release

A few suggestions:

1. Do not use the eye sockets of a fish as a grip. Tough to handle fish, such as northern pike or muskie, should be held by gripping the fish behind the head and gill plates. Better yet, slide the fish into a "cradle net" or large landing net to remove hooks.

2. Use long-nosed pliers to remove hooks. Keep your hands away.

3. Wanna take a picture? Fine, but be quick about it, holding the fish to support its weight and quickly returning the fish to water.

4. Before releasing, place the fish upright in water, grip by the tail, and slowly move the fish back and forth. You'll sense the fish regaining strength. Release when it's ready to swim and stay upright. The entire recovery may take several minutes so don't be in a hurry. The life you save may be your next catch.

How To Catch A State Record

Please read carefully. This is important. You will note that there's no promise here to help you break a Minnesota record fish.

Hey, there's 61 fish listed in the official record book. Surely, there's one that's breakable? I mean, what's wrong with having your name behind the Minnesota State Record… ahh… Redhorse? Why, there's even five different Redhorses from which to choose.

To report a possible record fish, the DNR says you must follow certain steps.

1. Weigh the fish on a state certified scale in front of two witnesses.
2. Take the fish to a DNR fisheries office for positive identification and to obtain a state record fish application.
3. Complete the application and submit to DNR along with a clear, full-length photo of the potential record fish.

If you insist on breaking an existing record, here's a tip. The next state record muskie is swimming in Mille Lacs or Leech Lake. All you have to beat is 54 pounds. Good luck.

Something To Shoot For

Minnesota's fishing waters have yielded but one world record. It was a dandy fish, weighing 55 pounds, 5 ounces, caught by Frank Ledwein on Clearwater Lake near Annandale on July 10, 1952.

It was a carp.

It's buried someplace.

The big fish was put on display at the 1952 World's Fair in New York. When the fair ended, Ledwein said he didn't want the fish back. Nobody's seen it since.

Can't blame Ledwein. Some say he never did catch that carp. No matter, with his name next to the carp record, Ledwein took enough ribbons for three lifetimes.

On a positive note, the record carp suggests that big fish can grow in Minnesota. These are important bragging rights.

Minnesota once claimed a former world's record muskellunge as its own state record, a 56-pound 8-ounce giant caught by J.W. Collins on Lake of the Woods. That was a feather in everybody's hat until Jimmy Robinson, that sage historian of outdoor events in *Sports Afield* magazine, proved that Collins was fishing on Ontario's side of Lake of the Woods when the big fish struck.

Yet, it happens.

Almost every year some lucky angler lands a new state record fish. And, yes, it could happen to you.

Consider "Red" Stuberud's tale of angling glory.

Minnesota's record rainbow trout, 17 pounds, 6 ounces, was caught by Ottway "Red" Stuberud of Knife River back in 1974. At the time, Red was living along the banks of the Knife. Fact is, he caught that state record while he was doing a little ice fishing almost in his backyard.

Proves you don't always have to travel far to get your name in the fish record books.

Some Minnesota record fish are caught as if fate itself had a hand.

For example, an Iowan, Bill Meyer, holds the state's record for brown bullhead. Now that probably doesn't surprise anybody. Iowans are known as infamous bullhead catchers, a reputa-tion they may or may not deserve. The last time I looked around the bullhead lakes at Waterville, the town that claims to be Minnesota's Bullhead Capitol, the Iowa license plates were only outnumbered by the Minnesota plates.

Now Meyer's fishing story only confuses the issue of bullhead claims. The trouble is, when Meyer tangled with that record 7-pound, 1-ounce bullhead, he wasn't fishing the famed bullhead water around Waterville.

No sir. Meyer had ventured to the land of pines and sky-blue water around Grand Rapids, which prides itself as a fishing paradise for about everything, 'cept bullheads.

In other words, when Waterville claimed the bullhead capitol title, not one tourism promoter in northern Minnesota argued. The late Claude Titus once served as the head honcho of tourism in Grand Rapids. Claude always sought the big spenders of the angling fraternity, the folks who fished for walleyes and smallmouth bass or trout and muskies.

(Bullhead fishing tourists are said to wear white shirts and carry $2 bills and not change either in a week.)

But Meyer threw a wrench in all that when he caught that record bullhead smack-dad amid the pines on Shallow Lake near Grand Rapids. Meyer said he was going to have his whiskered trophy mounted for display. Titus, it's rumored, was willing to bury it.

Now Grand Rapids has bullhead

braggin' rights and they still don't claim 'em.

I'll be honest. I'd love to see my name in the fish record book. Who wouldn't? There'd be no need to brag anymore. Just say, "Look it up in the records."

How To Enjoy Mosquitoes and Bugs

If you can play mind over mosquito, you'll be a happy Minnesota angler. Frankly, it's not that difficult to live peacefully with any bug that seeks to sip a little blood while you're fishing.

Just get used to it.

If you don't react (swell, bloat, bleed and so forth) to a bite from a black fly, you probably escaped from the University of Minnesota's medical research lab as a cadaver.

There also are no-see-ums to fear, but I always say out-of-sight, out-of-mind.

The good news for anglers about Minnesota bugs is that the most abundant, creepy, crawly thing you're apt to meet around the water is something called the tent caterpillar. They show up in the spring. Sometimes there are just two caterpillars in all of Minnesota; some years there's 2 gazillion trillion caterpillars. And that's just at your campsite.

Fortunately, the good news is those tent monsters have no teeth.

Bug Bite Defenses

In worst-case scenarios, my favorite defense is an offense. I swat. If I feel like being a pacifist, I wear a head net and

watch 'em act baffled because they can smell me but I ain't there. Ha.

The bug experts say that each of us has a peculiar odor, which breaks down into two categories: the smell that mosquitoes love; the smell that mosquitoes can't stand.

So—if you smell bad you won't have to worry about losing blood to mosquitoes. But for you sweet-smellers, mosquitoes are capable of making you wish you stunk.

Fortunately, there are excellent insect repellents available in Minnesota for those people who think we have mosquitoes. The most effect repellents are those containing high percentages of DEET. Use sparingly, however. Some folks have bad skin reactions to DEET.

Plus, you should know this: FISH HATE DEET.

When fish scientists at Pure Fishing (Berkley Co. in Spirit Lake, Iowa) were conducting taste tests on lab fish to research bait flavors, they discovered a surprising fact. The one flavor that fish disliked the most was—not gasoline or sun lotion or tobacco or peanut butter or beer or dozens of other flavors. No, fish despised the major ingredient in bug sprays, DEET.

Occasionally, native Minnesotans will talk about no-see-ums. You really can't see them easily but the same bug sprays will help reduce the attack. How do you know?

If you feel like somebody is jabbing

needles into your hide, then you're being attacked by no-see-ums.

Black flies look like miniature house-flies. They bite and then land. They like dark places, such as under your hair, behind your ear, around your belly button. When a black fly bites, you tend to bleed from about May to July. After that, they're gone.

In the battle against black flies, again, spray yourself. That'll put fear in a black fly's heart and it'll keep a respectable distance away from your face.

About an inch.

Planning a Minnesota Fishing Trip

Fishing in Minnesota never ends.

No matter what time of year, there is always some kind of fishing sport available. Some times are better than others, of course.

I've done my share of fishing in other states. I know how the fishing always seems greener across the state lines... until you get there. Then some wise ol' local angler will tell you that you picked the wrong time. What's the old saying? "You shoulda been here yesterday."

Visitors to Minnesota make the same mistakes. They show up on opening day for muskies or come in August and expect to slay walleyes. It doesn't work out that way very often.

Resident anglers also should adjust their fishing goals according to nature's timetable.

Yes, I know, the best time to go fishing is when you can. But do your homework

if you expect to catch something. Consider walleyes again. Yes, August can be a tough month for walleye action. But that's a dangerous generalization. I've experienced may great walleye fishing days on Lake of the Woods and Rainy Lake in, surprise, surprise, August.

Yet, following some rough guidelines offers the best odds and often the best fishing:

Walleyes - Season opens mid-May. Opening week is often good, but sometimes sketchy. Bring long underwear. Walleye action usually improves and holds steady from late May to late July.

June may be the prime walleye month, followed by July, a month when your odds for large walleyes goes up. In some waters, August walleye fishing is comparable to watching trees grow. The bite improves starting in mid-September and may get downright hot into mid-October. Bring long underwear again.

Best walleye ice fishing starts in mid-December (if there's ice) and runs into mid-January. Winter walleye action tends to slow considerably in late January and into February until the season closes.

However, the border waters of Minnesota-Canada, such as Lake of the Woods, remain open for walleye fishing and the action is usually good until the season ends in mid-April. Walleye fishing on the Rainy River and the Mississippi River can be excellent starting in early April.

Northern Pike - Northern fishing

tends to be sporadic from opening day (mid-May) until the warmer days of July. Top fishing begins in August and picks up after the fall turnover of water temperatures. Let's be honest. Big northern pike are rare. If you really want to catch one in Minnesota, start casting in September and October.

Largemouth Bass - The season usually opens in late May, often with excellent results in the warm shallows. Bass action improves in mid-June as bass move to summer haunts and continues through the summer into September. Bass feeding moods and occasional cold fronts can shut down the bite temporarily. A big bass month might be October, depending on timing of Old Man Winter.

Smallmouth Bass - Smallmouth action tends to improve in late May and only gets better with time. In some lakes, August tends to be slow but improves again in September and October.

Rivers are good most any time, especially if water levels are near normal or low. The largest smallmouth seem to show up in September and October in rivers and lakes.

Panfish - (Bluegills, crappies, perch)

Bluegills are always catchable but the fastest action begins when the bluegills spawn in early June. August is the top for platter-sized 'gills, although you'll have to fish deep.

Fastest crappie action follows the departure of ice in April and continues into May or early June.

Perch bite 365 days a year.

Muskellunge - Best times are when they happen. Muskie season usually opens in the first week of June. Top months are July through October. Early season can be fair, although the fish tend to run smaller.

Trout - In stocked streams, trout are not planted until threat of spring floods is over. Usually May.

Lake trout fishing in inland waters is best early, soon after ice-out when season opens in mid-May. As the water warms, lake trout go deep, which makes them more difficult to find.

Lake Superior trout and salmon are good in July through September. Starting in August, the size of Lake Superior lake trout tends to increase, according to Duluth charter boat captains.

For Duluth charter boat information,

that's why it's called fishing, not catching

call 1-800-4-DULUTH. Or visit web-site: www.visitduluth.com.

Steelhead fishing on North Shore streams is best from mid-April to mid-May. An $8.50 trout and salmon stamp is required when fishing in designated trout water, including Lake Superior.

A Note To Angling Visitors

Bring your own fishing tackle, by all means. But don't worry about running low. Minnesota has more tackle shops that beer parlors (I think) and more min-nows are never far away. Most bait stores also handle tackle in addition to such nat-ural baits as: minnows, night crawlers, leeches (of various sizes), earthworms. If you want crickets, you might have to bring your own.

Most resorts have boats to rent or a boat is included in the rental price of a cabin. Most also rent outboard motors and provide Coast Guard approved life jackets. Many resorts and bait shops also will provide fishing guides for hire (see section: Hiring a Guide).

Finding A Lodge or Resort:

For lodge and resort information, con-tact the local chamber office of your choice or contact: Minnesota Office of

Tourism, 100 Metro Square, 121 7th Place E., St. Paul, MN 55101 or call 800-657-3700.

Email address is: www.explore@state.mn.us

Wanna Camp N' Fish?

If you plan a combination fishing-camp-ing trip in Minnesota, information on public campgrounds in Minnesota State Parks or State Forests is available by con-tacting: DNR Information Center, 500 LaFayette Road, St. Paul, MN 55155. Call toll-free 888-MINN-DNR or local 651-296-6157.

Email address is: Info@dnr.state.mn.us

Private campgrounds also are avail-able. For a listing of private camping sites, contact the Minnesota Alliance of Campground Operators at 651-778-2400 on the Web at www.hospitalitymn.com.

Limited campsites also are listed on the DNR's maps of popular canoe routes from DNR's Trails and Water-ways Section.

Houseboat Fishin'

It just doesn't get much better. Oh, I

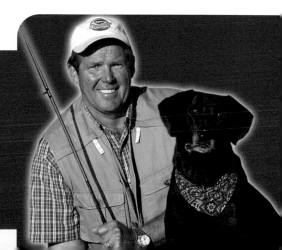

Of all the big muskies I've ever hooked, I've never landed one of them. Something bad always happens. To me, not the fish.

know, everybody makes that claim, but this time it's true.

Imagine these scenes: Cruising in a houseboat amid the island paradise of Rainy Lake or Lake Kabetogama or Lake of the Woods or Lake Vermilion and the list goes on.

Park the houseboat on a pristine sandy beach, tucked out of the wind. Aaaah, home for a few days. Hop into your fishing boat for a few hours in neighborhood hotspots. Return home. Cocktail time; steaks on the grill. Watch a sunset. Drift off to sleep to the sound of loon songs. Rise early and do it all again the next day.

Minnesota offers wonderful opportunities to rent a houseboat for fishing. For rental information, contact Minnesota Office of Tourism, 100 Metro Square, 121 7th Place E., St. Paul, MN 55101 or call 800-657-3700.

Email address is: www.explore@state. mn.us

Choosing The Right Lake

Troll the Internet. Minnesota's Department of Natural Resources has a unique "Lake Finder" feature on its Web page that is easy to follow and full of nifty information about what's catchable in every lake in the state.

To reach the "Lake Finder," log on to: www.dnr.state.mn.us.

Simply click your mouse on the lake finder banner. The DNR's "fish" page, as well as its "fishing" page is full of practical information any angler will find interesting. Of special note, check the latest fish population surveys on the lake.

The fish data will provide a hint of what to expect when you reach the lake.

Yes, you can learn a lot with the click of a computer mouse. But remember, surfing the Web is a far cry from trolling the bar.

Fishin' The BWCAW

Pack up all your cares and woes... and leave 'em at the first portage.

A canoe fishing adventure into Minnesota's Boundary Waters Canoe Area Wilderness (BWCAW) should be on everybody's must-do list.

Yes, the fishing can be great. Yes, the scenery is awesome. Yes, the solitude and quiet is refreshing. A paddle trip into the BWCAW can be all of those thing and more.

But the best reason for going is about you. You're apt to meet yourself out there in the boondocks. You'll learn to connect with nature and adjust to her schedule. You'll learn to cope with fewer material things and enjoy it. You'll learn you can do what you didn't think you could do.

Oh, sure, it might rain. Nobody can guarantee perfect weather.

Sure, the mosquitoes might come out at dusk. But they go away, too.

Sure, a black bear *might* wander into camp, but it's very unlikely and there are precautions to take.

Sure, this might happen and that might happen. But there's never a legitimate reason for not going. You have too much to gain by casting in wilderness waters.

No, you don't have to be Daniel Boone.

Canoe outfitters from Ely to Grand Marais are more than willing to make sure you have a good time. An outfitter's business depends on giving good advice and providing the right equipment from canoes and backpacks to cooking gear and food to sleeping bags and tents. Even fishing gear if you need it.

Gary Gotchnik, of Wilderness Outfitters in Ely, Minnesota, suggests that first time visitors or inexperienced wilderness travelers should utilize the advice and guidance of BWCAW outfitting businesses. "An outfitter also will help ease any confusion over planning your wilderness route and obtaining the necessary permits from the U.S. Forest Service," Gotchnik notes.

For more information about BWCAW canoe trips, contact the Ely Chamber of Commerce at 800-777-7281 or on the Web at www.ely.org.

BWCAW outfitters also are available in Crane Lake (800-362-7405; www.visitcranelake.com) and Grand Marais (888-922-5000; www.grand-marais.com).

Most outfitters also have guide packages where an experienced guide leads your group in and out of the boondocks. When my daughter Laura took her first BWCAW trip, veteran guide, Roger Skraba, famed for his "ya-ta-hay" greeting, joined us. The weather wasn't kind; we had lots of rain. But Roger's happy can-do attitude kept Laura and her friend, Brooke, smiling the whole trip.

"We call it liquid sunshine," Roger said of the rain.

It worked.

Fishing out of a wilderness canoe requires a few adjustments. First, remember not to lean over to land a fish or stand up to make a hard cast. If the wind is blowing hard, you may find control of the canoe and fishing don't go together.

I enjoyed the perfect solution a few years ago when Gary Gotchnik agreed to provide the paddle power while I did the casting. He said he didn't mind. He said he loved to paddle. When I started catching hefty smallmouth and 6-pound walleyes, I think Gary wanted to change his mind.

A wilderness angler is limited by weight, of course. If you bring a tackle box loaded with heavy jigs, remember you must carry everything over portages and paddle everything across the lakes.

Nevertheless, if fishing is your passion, don't skimp on the important things. Gary and I carried a lightweight digital Lowrance depth finder designed for canoe use. We had one spare rod and spare reel. We carried a light cooler bag to keep night crawlers. While the BWCAW walleyes, smallmouth bass and northern pike are willing biters most of the time; there are moments when only live bait will work.

My BWCAW tackle box is boiled down to basics. First, an assortment of lead head jigs of various sizes—1/16th to 1/2-ounce—prepared me to fish any depth if necessary. Berkley power baits featuring walleye colors, chartreuse, yellow and orange—would substitute for live bait.

Floating Rapalas of several colors served two purposes. The lure could be made to dive like a crankbait or allowed to flip on the surface like top water. The Rapala also would take walleyes one minute or smallmouth bass the next, depending on where it was cast.

A couple of fishing tools also are important in wilderness settings. A long-nosed pliers works to remove hooks or repair reels. A nail clipper will remove hangnails or cut fishing line.

The key to enjoying a BWCAW fishing trip is to avoid trouble. What could be worse, when you're miles from anywhere, than to bury a fishhook in your hand? For that reason, the best advice is to go barbless. Crimp down the hook barbs on every lure you use. If you accidentally hook yourself, you'll be glad you did.

Floating Rivers

So much water; so little time. I can't remember who said that but it's a dilemma faced by every Minnesota angler. And with so many lakes to fish, we tend to forget about rivers—all 15,000 miles of rivers.

This is a huge faux pas. It's wrong, too.

Over the years I've had the privilege with drifting with unabashed river folk who never wanted to be anywhere else. Rivers seem to capture those who follow its bends and turns. Most river addicts come to the current to catch smallmouth bass or walleyes.

At the moment, there are 24 rivers available with canoe route maps from the DNR's Trails and Waterways Section. The maps show accesses, campsites, historical attractions and so forth.

Be warned, however. Rivers in high water can be more dangerous than lakes.

Rivers also can be contagious. Among the river folk I've know, most became infected with the magic of rivers.

Years ago, Dan Gapen, of Big Lake, loved floating a stretch of the Mississippi above the Twin Cities and sharing it with others. But Gapen quickly realized the river was vulnerable to an ever-encroaching civilization as the Twin Cities' suburbs spread north. Today, stretches of the Upper Mississippi have special protection against excessive development on its banks, thanks to Gape's efforts.

Scott Sparlin of New Ulm had the same affliction for rivers, although his love was the Minnesota River, as ugly as it was.

One day Scott's son asked a simple question: Why was the Minnesota River the color of chocolate milk?

Scott didn't have a good answer. But the question inspired Scott to begin a tireless campaign to clean up the Minnesota from its headwaters on the state's western border to its mouth between Minneapolis and St. Paul.

And it's happening.

Bob Nybo, of Red Wing, is hooked on rivers, too, especially the Mississippi as it churns through bluff country between Minnesota and Wisconsin. Waterfowl

and walleyes keep Bob coming back to the enchanting Mississippi where he's active in community efforts to maintain the river's wildness.

A pair of canoe-making entrepreneurs, Bill Plantan and Dave Frink, of Rochester, also opened my river fishing eyes wider.

When we first met, Bill and Dave were sitting in one of their inventions, a canoe expressly designed for river fishing and angling comfort. It's called the River Ridge Custom Canoe (www.riverridge-customcanoes.com) and it's the result of their passion for fishing rivers. This special canoe is powered with an electric trolling motor for holding in current to cast or land a fish. The seats have backrests. An optional item is a solar panel to help maintain 12-volt battery power.

Most of all, the River Ridge is a stable craft and capable of carrying expensive Minnesota Bound television cameras without tipping.

Not yet, anyway.

Out of the Frying Pan

Minnesota's historic contributions to America include ore from the Iron Range, the beginning of the Father of Waters and beer batter.

The most perfect of these—given that iron rusts and the Mississippi floods—is the beer batter that coats a Minnesota fillet of walleye.

It's an intoxicating combination of the brewer's art from the land of sky blue waters and the fish that swim in it. We can only guess the historic birth of beer

batter. But, I'm guessing it was inspired on the shores of a Minnesota lake or river by anglers who had fresh fish, a little flour and, of course, beer.

And it was called: Shore lunch.

Bugs or mosquitoes, rain or snow, a shore lunch was always the tastiest meal this side of Chicago. Driftwood did the cooking. Your table was a log, your seat a slab of granite.

And, as every Minnesotan knows, if it's deep-fried walleye, it's got to be good.

I've had the pleasure of meeting a couple of exceptional chefs in my Minnesota travels.

My longtime friend, Gary Roach, didn't just work at catching walleyes. He worked at cooking them, too. After years of secretly concocting his own batter mix, one day Gary walked into the Pillsbury offices in Minneapolis. He talked his way into the kitchen and prepared walleye using his homemade batter. The folks at Pillsbury said it belonged on the market and they'd help him. That was the most unusual beginning of Gary Roach's Favorite, a dry or wet batter mix that is an exceptional addition to a walleye fillet. (I like the cajun style.)

Look for Gary Roach's Favorite in supermarkets or find it on the Web at www.mrwalleye.com.

Another friend, Tom Collins, didn't invent beer or beer batter, but he served plenty of it with walleyes at the old Collins Cafe in downtown Walker. The cafe is long gone now, but not the memory of Tom's great beer batter.

Collins' beer batter

HERE'S HOW

1. Combine eggs and beer.

2. Add dry ingredients all at once. Mix smooth, adjust consistency as required. If the batter is thick, adjust with small amounts of milk. If batter is too thin, adjust with cornstarch.

3. To fry, dredge fish lightly in cornstarch. Shake off excess, dip coated fillet in batter and immerse directly into deep cooking oil. Fry at about 375 degrees. Serve with appropriate sauce.

INGREDIENTS

2 eggs whole beaten
12 oz. beer
12 oz. flour
1/4 tsp. salt
1/4 tsp. pepper
1/4 tsp. nutmeg
1/2 tsp. baking powder
boneless fish fillets
cornstarch (for dredging)

Chef John, the Game Gourmet

One of my favorite fishing companions is also gifted chef, John Schumacher, of the famed New Prague Hotel. He's known as the "Game Gourmet" on the Minnesota Bound television shows and his talent is making tasty creations with simple recipes.

If you'd like a wider selection of Chef John's favorites, order the Minnesota Bound Game Cookbook ($12.95) or the Minnesota Bound Fish Cookbook ($12.95) by calling toll free 888-755-3155 or 952-546-3746 or on the Web at www.outdoorcalendars.com.

Here are some of Chef John's favorite fish recipes along with his comments about preparing game fish.

fish stir fry
serves 4

HERE'S HOW

Peel and cut vegetables. In a wok or heavy sauté pan heat oil until smoke hot. Add vegetables and cook for 3 minutes turning gently to keep from burning. Combine cornstarch, soy sauce, fresh ginger and chicken stock. Add to vegetables and bring to a simmer. Add fish tossing gently and cook until fish is tender and sauce is clear. Remove and serve over white rice.

CHEF JOHN'S NOTES:

- This is my favorite recipe for bluefish or bass.
- Firmer fish fillets work best for this dish.
- Leaving the skin on the fillets helps keep the fish pieces in tact.
- The vegetables look and cook best if sliced Chinese-style or on the bias.
- This is an easy campfire dish when made in an iron pan. The hotter the fire the better.

INGREDIENTS

3 c. fish fillets, sliced into finger sized pieces, skin on
1 c. onions, sliced 1/4"
1 c. carrots, sliced 1/4" thick on thebias
1 c. celery, sliced 1/4" thick on the bias
1 c. red pepper, sliced 1/4" thick, 3" long
1 c. fresh mushrooms, sliced 1/4"
1 1/2 Tbsp. vegetable oil or saffron oil
1 Tbsp. cornstarch
1 Tbsp. soy sauce
1 tsp. fresh ginger root minced fine
2 c. chicken stock, fish stock or clam broth
4 c. cooked white rice

Chef John's Tips For Cooking Fish

1. If you like to fish AND you like to cook, you're doubly blessed. Because every time you land a big one, cook it up, and draw appreciative raves from family or friends, you've had two successes in one day! Ordinary people are usually thrilled to have one success in one day.

2. I'm sure you know the ancient Greek saying, "moderation in all things." But what you may not know is that the origi-nal saying read, "moderation in all things—especially cooking fish." As a great seafaring people, the ancient Greeks knew that the most common mistake people make when cooking fish is to overcook it. So follow the wisdom of the ancient Greek philosophers. Protect the delicate flavor of your fish no matter what meal—breakfast, lunch or dinner. Don't cook it too long. Don't cook it too hot.

3. Like many people, you may assume that fish tastes bland at best. But in truth,

many fish have wonderfully interesting tastes. Your aim should be to bring out the taste of the fish you are cooking, not to bury it. Because no matter how many other ingredients and tastes you add, the true test of your cooking success will be the taste of the fish!

4. Never underestimate a fish. Most people think fish is just fish. Nothing could be further from the truth. Fish is a complete meat substitute that responds well to an enormous variety of sauces, spices and cooking methods. So please throw away any preconceptions you may still be carrying around about fish. I never cease to be amazed at all the interesting and exceptionally tasty dishes you can prepare with this amazingly versatile and often misunderstood food. A lot of wonderful side dishes go exceptionally well with fish.

yellow cornmeal and parmesan catfish
serves 4

HERE'S HOW

Place seasoned flour in a pie pan. Mix Parmesan cheese, corn meal and parsley flakes in another pie pan. Combine eggs and milk in a shallow bowl. Whisk mixture to a froth. Heat oil in an electric fry pan to 375°. When oil is hot, add butter. Dredge fish in flour mixture. Shake off excess flour. Dip fish in egg wash then roll in corn meal mixture. Shake off excess corn meal and place fish fillets in hot oil. Brown on one side for about 2 minutes being careful not to overcook. Turn and cook until done. Remove from oil and place on paper towel lined dish. Lightly splash with lemon juice and dust with your favorite seasoning.

INGREDIENTS

1 c. seasoned flour

1 c. freshly grated Parmesan cheese

1 c. cornmeal (yellow or white)

1 Tbsp. parsley flakes

2 eggs

3/4 c. milk

2 c. vegetable oil

1/4 c. butter

4 catfish fillets, skinned and cut into 5 inch slabs

1 Tbsp. fresh lemon juice

1 tsp. seasoning of choice (Cajun, taco or lemon pepper)

CHEF JOHN'S NOTES:

• This is an excellent breading for deep-frying all varieties of fish fillets.
• The oil needs to be at 375°. If it is too hot, the fish will burn. If it is too cold, the fish will absorb too much oil.
• To add some spiciness, fry chili peppers after removing stems and seeds.

grilled fish kabobs
(that work!) serves 4 – 6

HERE'S HOW

Cut fish into cubes and roll in seasoned flour in a pie plate. Remove to a rack and let dry for 10 minutes. Lay bacon out to temper. In a saucepan heat water and salt to boiling. Add red potatoes. Let boil for 10 minutes. Add whole shallots and boil for 5 minutes. Drain potatoes and shallots in a colander and let steam off. In a skillet heat olive oil hot. Add pepper cubes, zucchini slices, mushroom caps and sauté for 2 minutes. Add sherry. Turn and simmer for 2 minutes more. Remove vegetables to a rack to cool. Wrap each fish cube with 1/2 piece bacon. Place on platter seam side down.

To make kabob

Place a mushroom cap on one end of skewer, rounded side out. Next put on a zucchini slice, fish cube, pepper slice, fish cube, shallot, whole potato, shallot, fish cube, red pepper slice, fish cube, zucchini. Finish with mushroom, rounded side out.

INGREDIENTS

16 fish cubes cut into 1-inch squares

1 c. seasoned flour

8 strips bacon

1 qt. water for boiling vegetables

1 tsp. salt

8 small red potatoes

4 shallots, peeled

1 Tbsp. olive oil

2 large red peppers cut into 8 cubes

2 zucchini cut in 8 half-inch rounds

8 mushrooms, stems trimmed even
  to cap bottom

2 c. herbed dressing

1/2 c. sherry

2 lemons

4 long wooden or metal skewers

8 green onions, broomed

Place the 4 kabobs in a long baking pan. Top with 2 c. herb dressing. Cover with plastic wrap. Refrigerate for 1 hour or until needed.

To grill

Heat grill medium hot. Remove kabobs from pan. Let excess dressing run off. Place kabobs on grill until golden brown. Turn a quarter turn at a time until all sides are golden brown. Check fish for doneness. Put on a platter. Place broomed green onion on end of each skewer.

CHEF JOHN'S NOTES:

- This recipe is easier than it looks and is a great way to serve a large gathering in short time.
- Firm textured fish will stay on the skewer better than softer textured fish.
- This recipe works because the vegetables are pre-cooked.
- The bacon keeps the fish cubes moist.
- To broom green onions, remove root end. Cut in 2-inch lengths. Cut lengthwise strips halfway down the green onion pieces. Place in ice water to curl strips.
- Chicken breasts can be boiled with the potatoes and shallots. Chill breasts after cooking. Cut into pieces and add to the skewers.

Basics Briefly

crispy coconut fish
serves 4

HERE'S HOW

Sift chili powder, black pepper, garlic powder, mustard and seasoned flour into a pie plate. Combine fresh breadcrumbs with shredded coconut. In an electric fry pan or deep fryer, heat oil to 375°. Dredge fish fillets in flour mixture. Shake off excess flour. Dip in egg wash. Shake off excess. Cover with coconut/bread crumb mixture. Deep fry until golden brown. Remove to a paper towel lined plate. Serve with pineapple mayonnaise.

CHEF JOHN'S NOTES:

INGREDIENTS

1 1/2 tsp. chili powder
1/4 tsp. black pepper
1/4 tsp. garlic powder
1/4 tsp. dry mustard
1 c. seasoned flour
1 c. fresh white bread crumbs
1 c. shredded coconut
2 c. vegetable oil
12 boneless pan fish fillets (skins on)
1 c. egg wash
1 c. pineapple mayonnaise

• Fish fillets should not be thicker than 1/2 inch or longer than 3 inches. Larger fillets will absorb too much oil.
• I enjoy combining 1 tablespoon of sugar and 1/2 teaspoon of cinnamon and sprinkle it lightly over the cooked fillets as soon as they are removed from the fryer. Then I splash each fillet with fresh lemon juice.

heartland fish hash
serves 4

HERE'S HOW

In a large skillet, heat oil until hot. Add onions, celery and red peppers. Sauté until onions are tender. Add potatoes, corn, pickles, thyme, salt and pepper. Toss to combine and cook on medium heat until the potatoes and corn are hot. Place fish pieces evenly over the base and cover. Cook on low heat for 3 minutes. Remove pan from heat and let sit covered for 5 minutes. Remove cover and serve with poached or boiled eggs.

INGREDIENTS

1/4 c. olive oil
1/2 c. red onions diced 1/4 inch thick
1/2 c. celery diced 1/4 inch thick
1 c. red peppers diced 1/4 inch thick
2 c. red potatoes boiled with skins
　 on, diced 1/4 inch thick and cooled
1 c. frozen whole kernel corn
1/2 c. dill pickles diced 1/4 inch thick
1 tsp. thyme (dry leaves)
1 tsp. salt
fresh black pepper to taste
2 c. fish fillets diced 1 inch thick

fish and roasted vegetable napoleons
serves 4

HERE'S HOW

Preheat oven to 350°. Wash all vegetables thoroughly. Slice eggplant and brush lightly with olive oil. Heat a large skillet. Add eggplant slices 4 at a time and sauté until golden brown on one side. Remove to a paper towel lined sheet pan placing brown side down. Brush sweet potato slices with olive oil and sauté golden brown on both sides. Remove to sheet pan. Repeat with onions slices, zucchini slices and pineapple ring.

Slice tomatoes and season with salt, black pepper and thyme. Dredge fish in flour and sauté in 1 Tbsp. olive oil until golden brown on both sides. Remove to paper towel lined platter.

To build Napoleons, cover a baking sheet pan with aluminum foil. Brush with olive oil. Build all four Napoleons one at a time. First, place a slice of eggplant brown side up. Top with a slice of Cheddar cheese. Top with fish fillet. Sprinkle lemon pepper evenly over fish. Add zucchini slice, sweet potato, seasoned tomato slice, Mozzarella cheese, fish fillet, pineapple ring and second eggplant slice brown side down. Remove stem end and seeds from Anaheim pepper and stuff a sweet pickle inside pepper. Stick a sharp skewer through the stuffed Anaheim pepper and through the center of vegetable/fish stack. Place in a 350° oven for 25 minutes. Remove leaves from the bottom 3/4 of the rosemary sprigs and sharpen the ends. Remove from oven to warm plates. Replace skewers with rosemary sprigs. Serve with a lemon wedge.

INGREDIENTS

1 large eggplant, cut into 8 slices

1/4 c. olive oil

4 sweet potato slices, 1/4 inch thick

4 red onion slices, 1/2 inch thick

4 zucchini slices, 1/4 inch thick, 3 inches long

4 pineapple rings

4 jumbo-sized tomato slices, 1/2 inch thick

1/4 tsp. salt

1/2 tsp. fresh ground pepper

1 tsp. dry thyme

8 2 to 3 oz. boneless fish fillets

1 Tbsp. flour

4 slices Cheddar cheese

1 tsp. lemon pepper

4 slices mozzarella cheese

4 Anaheim or large jalapeno peppers

4 large sweet pickles

4 sprigs rosemary

1 extra-large lemon, cut in quarters

CHEF JOHN'S NOTES

• This recipe is fun to prepare.
• Use any vegetable or fruit of the season. Remember to precook them as the time in the oven only heats the Napoleons through.
• Any mild or hot chili pepper can be substituted for Anaheim peppers.
• If sweet potatoes are not available, use any large potato slices.

Twin Cities' Kids' Fishing Ponds

Every spring, Minnesota DNR fisheries crews take the first step in giving some lucky youngsters in the Twin Cities a few fond memories. The kids' fishing ponds are stocked with fish to catch.

In most cases, the ponds would not provide fishing if not for the DNR's help. Most ponds are stocked with crappies and bluegills. For annual updates on the kids' pond program, go online at www.dnr.state.mn.us/fishing/downtown/kids.

fishin' holes

Pond Name	Location
Lockness	Blaine (Lockness Park – Lexington & 111th Ave.)
Marthaler	West St. Paul (Wentworth Ave. & Humboldt Ave.)
Thompson	West St. Paul (Butler Ave.)
Wood Park	Burnsville (Portland Ave. & 145th St.)
Centennial	Edina (Centennial Lake Park – France Ave. S. & W. 76th St.)
Champlin Mill Pond	Champlin (Hwy. 169 & Hwy. 52)
Cornelia	Edina (66th St. & Valley View Rd.)
Loring	Loring Park (Hennepin Ave. S. & 15th St. E.)
Mallard (Boundary Creek)	Maple Grove (104th Ave. & Nathan Lane)
Powderhorn	Minneapolis (Powderhorn Park – 35th St. E. & 15th Ave. S.)
Smith	Bloomington (Smith Lake Park – Park Ave. S. & E. 80th St.)
Webber	Minneapolis (Camden Park – Webber Pky. & Aldrich Ave. N.)
Hanlos	White Bear Lake (White Bear Ave. & Orchard Ln.)
Langton	Roseville (Cleveland Ave. & Cty. Rd. C2)
Loeb	St. Paul (Marydale Park – Dale St. N. & Maryland Ave.)
Jordan Mill Pond	Jordan (Park Dr. & Sunset Dr.)
Lost	Mahtomedi (Wildwood Park – Hwy. 244 & Old Wildwood Rd.)

Basics Briefly

Twin Cities' Shore Fishing Sites

You don't need a boat to catch fish. Check the DNR's "Downtown Fishing Guide" for lakeshores where public fishing is permitted or go online at www.dnr.state.mn.us/fishing/downtown/waters.

In some cases, the DNR has installed fish attractors to make sure there's good fishing from the public docks or shores.

Metro Shore Fishing Lakes

Battle Lake; Woodbury; Bennett Lake, Roseville; Bryant Lake, Eden Prairie; Calhoun, Minneapolis; Cedar, Minneapolis; Como, St. Paul; Harriet, Minneapolis; Hiawatha, Minneapolis; Hidden Falls, Mississippi River, St. Paul; Island Lake, Shoreview; Islands of Peace Park, Mississippi River, Fridley; Lake of the Isles, Minneapolis; Keller Lake, Maplewood; Medicine Lake, Plymouth; Nokomis Lake, Minneapolis; Owasso and Wabasso, Shoreview; Lake Phalen, St. Paul; Pike Island, Mississippi River, St. Paul; Powderhorn Park, Minneapolis; Shady Oak, Hopkins; Snelling State Park, St. Paul; Tanners Lake, Oakdale and Wirth Lake, Minneapolis.

Wheelchair Accessible Shore Fishing Sites

These are on-shore fishing platforms or floating platforms designed for wheelchair access. Some platforms are built on-shore; others may be built over the water.

Freeborn County—Albert Lea Lake in Albert Lea, Minn.; Lake Fountain at North Edgewater Park.

Filmore County—Lanesboro Dam, S. Branch Root River in Preston; Camp Creek (three locations) along Harmony-Preston State Trail; Duschee Creek (five locations) near Lanesboro State Fish Hatchery; Sylvan Park Pond in Lanesboro, Minn.

Goodhue County—Lake Byllesby; Red Wing Pottery Pond in Red Wing, Minn.

Mower County—Austin Mill Pond in Austin, Minn.; Eastside Lake in Austin;

Olmsted County—Lake Zumbro; Chester Woods in Chester Woods Park; Foster Arends in Rochester's Foster Arend Park; Willow Creek Reservoir in Rochester.

Rice County—Two River Park in Faribault, Minn.; Wells Lake; Cannon River in Morristown, Minn.; Cody Lake near Lonsdale; Fox Lake, adjacent to public boat access; King's Mill Dam in King's Mille Park in Faribault.

Steele County—Beaver Lake, Beaver Lake County Park; Lake Kohlmeier in Owatonna.

Wabasha County—Lake Pepin in Lake City, Minn.; Mississippi River's Robinson Lake at Wilcox Landing.

Winona County—Middle Branch, Whitewater River in Whitewater State Park; Lake Winona on Lake Street in Winona, Minn.

Where Anglers Gather

Nothing beats hanging out with other folks who fish. Besides friendly saloons, here are a few spots you're apt to find

like-minded anglers to swap yarns and share the angling spirit.

MINNESOTA FISHING MUSEUM
304 West Broadway
Little Falls, Minn. 56345
320-616-2011
www.mnfishingmuseum.com

MINNESOTA FISHING
HALL OF FAME
P.O. Box 790
Walker, Minn. 56484
218-547-2000
www.minnesotafishinghalloffame.com

Fishing Schools
We could use more fishing schools in Minnesota. Drive around on a summer night anywhere in the state and you'll find adults teaching kids to play ball games, soccer and the like. But you'll never find someone teaching a group of kids how to cast or tie a knot.

Yes, I know, teaching kids how to fish was always the duty of parents or grandparents or Uncle Nicely. But times have changed and families have, too. Today, there's a greater need for adult anglers to "pass on" the tradition to youngsters willing to learn.

Frankly, I've never met a kid who wasn't fascinated with the mysteries of fishing.

Wisely, the Minnesota DNR launched the MinnAqua Program a decade ago to provide youngsters, especially those in urban areas, a chance to discover fishing.

Staff and volunteers from MinnAqua also assist with kid's fishing seminars at sport shows, including Ron Schara's Kid's Fishing School during the Minneapolis Aquatennial.

Youngsters might also discover the magic of angling from the following organizations or locations:

Underwater Adventures
Lower Level, Mall of America
The freshwater and saltwater fish exhibits offer nifty examples about fish behavior to further your fishing savvy.

For tour and school information, call 1-888-DIVE-TIME or the Web: *www.underwateradventures.cc*.

Becoming An Outdoors Woman in Minnesota
402 S.E. 11th St.
Grand Rapids, Minn. 55744
218-327-4564
www.dnr.state.mn.us/information_and_education/bow

Camp Lincoln For Boys
Camp Lake Hubert For Girls
10179 Crosstown Circle
Eden Prairie, Minn. 55344
1-800-242-1909 or 218-963-2339
www.lincoln-lakehubert.com

Minnesota 4-H Fishing Sports and Aquatic Ecology
University of Minnesota
Extension Service
1-800-444-4238
www.extension.umn.edu/distribution/youthdevelopment/da3560.html

Basics Briefly

Fly Fishing Minnesota
P.O. Box 6866
Lincoln, Neb. 68506
1-800-306-4111
www.schoolofflyfishing.com

Ma & Pa Gettel's Wilderness Camp For Kids
2987 State Highway 200
Mahnomen, Minn. 56557
1-866-744-CAMP (2267)
www.gettel.mahnomen.mn.us

Fishing Organizations
The fellowship of the angling fraternity is no more evident than in Minnesota.

A number of organizations—anglers all—have been formed to promote, protect, and enhance the future of a particular fish. These anglers believe that fishing means more today than just buying a license. It means that if there's going to be fishing tomorrow, fishermen must work together to fight pollution, fish habitat destruction and other threats. And they must contribute more time and money to boosting the fish and the sport so cherished. Anglers have to stay alert for new issues that could jeopardize their passion, including the use of lead sinkers. Lead shot was banned to protect waterfowl from lead poisoning. Lead sinkers could be next to protect Minnesota's loons. One split shot can poison a loon.

What the future of fishing needs more than anything else is informed and organized anglers. And all of the organizations will welcome new members.

Minnesota's Muskies, Incorporated
P.O. Box 120870
New Brighton, Minn. 55112
www.muskiesinc.org
Members work to sustain and expand muskie fishing water in the state. Emphasis on catch and release. Sponsors annual tournament in Leech Lake region. Associated with International organization.

Lake Superior Steelhead Association
Box 16034
Duluth, Minnesota 55816
Members are avid Lake Superior stream anglers concerned about future of steelhead populations in North Shore tributaries.

Minnesota B.A.S.S. Federation
P.O. Box 551
Howard Lake, Minn. 55349
www.mnbf.org
Members are avid largemouth bass anglers with emphasis on weekend tournaments. Sponsor state bass championships. Active in youth programs.

Minnesota Darkhouse and Angling Association
P.O. Box 1875
Burnsville, Minn. 55337
www.mndarkhouse.org
Members are avid darkhouse spearing enthusiasts who are concerned about northern pike populations and increased restrictions on spearing.

Women Anglers of Minnesota
P.O. Box 580653
Minneapolis, Minn. 55468
womenanglers@aol.com
Members are women who are avid anglers or are interested in learning to fish. Sponsor women-only tournaments and angling trips. Active in youth programs.

Wading Women of Minnesota
P.O. Box 11383
St. Paul, Minn. 55111
wadingwomen@hotmail.com
Members are fly fishing enthusiasts who are eager to share experience.

Trout Unlimited
Box 11465
St. Paul, Minn. 55111
www.mntu.org
Members are avid trout anglers who work to preserve streams and trout populations through scientific management. Sponsor banquets and fund trout stream improvement projects.

Federation of Fly Fishers
www.fedflyfishers.org
Members are avid fly anglers for game fish, mainly trout. Sponsor banquets and work to support fisheries management.

Minnesota Trout Association
Box 18
Preston, Minn. 55965
Members are active trout anglers in southeast Minnesota who are concerned about stream improvement, trout popu-

lations and DNR trout management programs.

Smallmouth Bass Alliance
www.smallmouth.org
Members work to protect and enhance smallmouth rivers and bass populations via size restrictions and habitat improvements. Sponsor annual banquet.

Minnesota Sportfishing Congress
2865 Matilda St.
Roseville, Minn. 55113
Members are active in legislative issues that impact fishing in the state. Sponsor banquet and appear before legislative hearings.

International Bowfishing Association
1049 Crystal Ct.
Lino Lakes, Minn. 55014
651-653-3279
www.iba-bowfishing.com
Members are active bow hunters of rough fish.

Minnesota Ice Team
P.O. Box 1172
Grand Rapids, Minn. 55745
www.iceteam.com
Members are avid ice anglers who share enthusiasm and winter fishing tips.

Minnesota Walleye Alliance
1159 Galtier St.
St. Paul, Minn. 55117
www.mnwalleyealliance.com
Members are avid walleye anglers who work to protect state walleye populations.

Basics Briefly

Fishing Has No Boundaries
215 Paul Bunyan Drive
Bemidji, Minn. 56601
218-751-8207
www.fhnbinc.org
Members work to help disadvantaged people overcome handicaps to go fishing. Sponsor events.

Capable Partners
P.O. Box 27664
Golden Valley, Minn. 55427
763-542-8156
www.capablepartners.org
Members team with disadvantaged outdoor enthusiasts to go fishing and hunting. Sponsor banquet and events.

Minnesota Lakes Association
P.O. Box 321
Brainerd, Minn. 56401
800-515-LAKE
www.mnlakes.org
Members are mostly lakeshore owners who are concerned about water quality and surface use issues.

Basics Briefly

1. **Minnesota has how many fishable lakes over 10 acres in size?**
   a) 15,233   b) 10,000
   c) 6,000   d) 2,303

2. **How many licensed and unlicensed anglers fish in Minnesota every year?**
   a) 1.5 million   b) 900,970
   c) 545,000   d) 2.1 million

3. **How many fish species swim in Minnesota waters?**
   a) 47   b) 76
   c) 156   d) 201

4. **What is the most caught fish in Minnesota?**
   a) Walleye   b) Panfish
   c) Northern Pike   d) Carp

5. **How much do anglers spend a year in Minnesota to buy fishing bait?**
   a) $42 million   b) $3.5 million
   c) $99 million   d) $800,000

6. **The Minnesota State Record Walleye weighs?**
   a) 17 lbs, 8 oz.   b) 17 lbs, 10 oz.
   c) 16 lbs, 7 oz.   d) 17 lbs, 17 oz.

7. **In 1979, the current Minnesota record walleye was caught where?**
   a) Rainy River   b) Seagull River
   c) St. Croix River   d) Straight River

8. **The most common contaminant found in Minnesota fish is?**
   a) Toxaphene   b) WD40
   c) Mercury   d) DDT

9. **What's the heaviest state record fish?**
   a) Lake Sturgeon   b) Muskellunge
   c) Bigmouth Buffalo   d) Carp

10. **What's the lightest state record fish?**
    a) Rock Bass   b) Hogsucker
    c) Green Sunfish   d) Pumpkinseed

11. **The Minnesota Fishing Hall of Fame is located where?**
    a) St. Paul   b) Walker
    c) Eveleth   d) Ely

12. **Which well-known Minnesota angler once worked as a nightclub singer?**
    a) Babe Winkelman   b) Jesse Ventura
    c) Ron Schara   d) Al Lindner

Basics Briefly

13. **How many years does it take for a muskie to grow from fingerling size to 50 pounds?**
    a) 50 years   b) 10 years
    c) 15 years   d) 25 years

14. **In a typical spring, how many walleye fry hatch naturally in Mille Lacs?**
    a) 3 million   b) 500 million
    c) 1 billion   d) 2 billion

15. **The most widespread game fish in Minnesota is?**
    a) Northern Pike   b) Bluegill
    c) Walleye   d) Largemouth Bass

16. **Minnesota's new perch limit is?**
    a) 100   b) 20
    c) 40   d) Unlimited

17. **On average, how many hours of fishing is required to catch a Minnesota muskie?**
    a) 24 hours   b) 48 hours
    c) 100 hours   d) 10,000 hours

18. **Which trout is native to Minnesota?**
    a) Brown   b) Brook
    c) Steelhead   d) Rainbow

19. **A walleye fry stocked in a Minnesota lake will grow to weigh one pound in how much time?**
    a) 2 years   b) 9 months
    c) 5 years   d) 1 year

20. **An adult female walleye will typically produce how many eggs?**
    a) 100,000   b) 250,000
    c) 8,000   d) 500

21. **The walleye is a member of which family of fishes?**
    a) Walleye   b) Pike
    c) Perch   d) Goldfish

22. **The whiskers on a bullhead or catfish are called?**
    a) Stingers   b) Horns
    c) Barbels   d) Feelers

23. **Which salmon has not been introduced into Lake Superior?**
    a) King   b) Sockeye
    c) Pink   d) Silver

Basics Briefly

24. Roughly, how much does the DNR spend a year on state fishing programs?
a) $55 million
b) $7 million
c) $22 million
d) $17 million

25. The hybrid fish known as Splake is a cross between a lake trout and what fish?
a) Brown Trout
b) Brook Trout
c) Sea Trout
d) Smelt

26. A northern pike has?
a) light markings on a dark body
b) dark markings on a light body
c) vertical bars on a light body
d) dark bars on a light body

27. What is a slot limit?
a) A special fish regulation
b) A casino rule
c) Dock restrictions on Lake Minnetonka
d) Catch and release

28. When was the brown trout introduced to Minnesota waters?
a) 1950
b) 1922
c) Early 1900s
d) Late 1800s

29. The reflective pigment in the eye of a walleye is called?
a) epidemial coating
b) tapetum lucidum
c) corneal micadum
d) lenscoat

30. The largemouth bass is the member of what family of fishes?
a) Striper
b) Sunfish
c) Perch
d) Bass

31. How many species of catfish swim in Minnesota?
a) Five
b) Three
c) Two
d) Six

32. Minnesota's tiger muskies are?
a) extinct
b) sterile
c) from Asia
d) a joke

Answers: 1-c; 2-d; 3-c; 4-b; 5-a; 6-a; 7-b; 8-c; 9-a; 10-c; 11-b; 12-c; 13-c; 14-d; 15-a; 16-b; 17-c; 18-b; 19-c; 20-a; 21-c; 22-c; 23-b; 24-c; 25-b; 26-a; 27-a; 28-d; 29-b; 30-b; 31-b; 32-b.

For Kids of Any Age

Panfish make the angling world go-round.

Bluegills, crappies, perch—without them the sport of fishing would be about much less catching.

Without them, some of the glamorous fishes of freshwater would be hard-pressed to survive. How would a large-mouth bass get such a big belly if it didn't have little bluegills to devour?

Of course, the real value of panfish is for kids. All of us kids. Who among us has ever tired of watching a bobber go under?

It's easy to be a fan of panfishing. More panfish are caught than any other fish in Minnesota. And why not? They provide action, yet they are not taken without some angling skill. They are small but, for their size, have huge fighting hearts. They also rank pretty high out of the frying pan.

Minnesota is blessed with an abundance of panfish water, featuring crappies or bluegills or perch or all three in lakes or rivers from one corner of the state to another. Only in the state's north and northeast, including the BWCA, is the bluegill absent.

What's the difference between sunfish and bluegills? Well, for the purpose of our discussion, it's the same fish. Technically, sunfish and bluegills are two separate species, although they crossbreed and, well, who knows what hybrids are swimming out there. But since they catch the same, taste the same and look the same (sorta), we'll treat 'em the same.

If panfish mean something stunted to you, then you've also come to the wrong place. Minnesota is noted for its lunker-sized panfish, including one-pound bluegills, crappies and "jumbo" perch. That's not to say stunted panfish lakes aren't a problem. It is. And DNR fish managers continue to experiment with ways to eliminate bluegill stunting and yield bigger bluegills of 8 inches or more.

In truth, we are part of the problem and maybe a big part, as we tend to cream off the larger bluegills as soon as they're caught. Look for more size restrictions or reduced limits in the future; otherwise, the stunted bluegill isn't going to go away.

Perch in recent years have faced the same problem of over-harvest, especially the larger specimens. Once upon a time, we had a 100 perch limit. If you think about it, who really needed to haul home 100 perch? Now the limit has been cut drastically to help maintain the state's jumbos.

The crappie story is the same. As more of us catch more, the state's limit on crappies has been reduced to maintain quality.

Catching Sunnies

That barefoot boy with his pant cuffs rolled, sitting on the bank, while holding a cane pole, next to a Folgers's coffee can of worms had the right idea.

You don't need much more than

Panfish

that—a cane pole, line, bobber, sinker and plain hook. Most of us have been weaned away from cane poles, which may or may not be fortunate. Whatever, no matter what you use, it must be used in the right waters.

Early summer—late May to mid-June—is the premium time for catching sunnies. The fish are spawning in the shallows and are easily located.

Minnesota has five kinds of sunnies, the popular bluegills, the pumpkinseed, the green sunfish, the warmouth and the orange-spotted sunfish. Most have similar habits and live in similar waters.

Panfish adore worms.

Let's start with the earthworm. The earthworm (not a night crawler) curled on a small hook undoubtedly catches more sunfish than any other bait.

I'd like to suggest a light line, maybe 6-pound test at the most, a small split-shot, a size 6 to 10 hook and a bobber about the size of a quarter.

sunnies and schara

If the abundance of bluegills was a problem, then one would not want to disrupt the spawning process. But, remember, most Minnesota waters suffer from an overdose of baby panfish.

Panfish

Not that tackle matters much. I've seen bluegills caught on chalk line with bobbers the size of basketballs. That's the beauty of it all.

There is a little trick in baiting the hook, however. Sunnies are famed bait stealers. Who can afford to feed thieves considering the price of worms or the work in digging 'em?

(By the way, night crawlers also work on bluegills. But use only a small 1-inch piece of night crawler at a time.)

The baiting trick is to weave the worm on the hook as if you were darning a sock (see photo). In that manner, the bluegill is almost forced to inhale the hook if it wants the worm.

There is no correct depth to fish bluegills with a bobber. That depth must be discovered by trial and error. When the sunnies are spawning, they usually are in less than 6 feet of water. Sometimes less than 2 feet. So the bobber has to be set accordingly. Some people are content to sit and watch a motionless bobber, waiting for it to move.

You can increase your sunfish action by occasionally jiggling the bobber, which causes the worm to twitch, thereby catching the bluegill's eye.

When bluegills are spawning in the shallows, they are spooky but very catchable. Where do they spawn? Use your eyes to find them. Look for moon-like craters on lake bottoms with sand or loam, but not mud. Often the spawning sites are located on the north shores of lakes or bays.

For panfish and other small fish that tend to nibble at bait, hook a small worm several times, letting only about 1/2 inch of the tail dangle. A long shank hook makes unhooking the fish easier because you can grab the hook more easily.

The moon-like craters are the spawning beds, which are created by the bluegill. The bed maker won't be far away.

It's a fair question whether we should catch spawning sunfish? If the abundance of bluegills was a problem, then one would not want to disrupt the spawning process. But, remember, most Minnesota waters suffer from an overdose of baby panfish.

When the bluegills have completed spawning, they move into deeper water and disappear amid the weed beds or along the deepwater edges. They are still highly catchable; it just takes more hunting.

Like most other fish, sunnies like to be near something—usually weed beds, where there's a good supply of insects,

WORM

SPONGE SPIDER   DRY FLY

POPPER

PORK RIND

NYMPHET OR
¹⁄₆₄ OZ JIG

snails and tiny minnows—the bluegill's favorite foods.

Other favored haunts include boat docks, bridge pilings, sunken treetops, and stump fields. Most people stand on a boat dock and cast out from it. Too bad. They'd have better luck if they quietly dropped a worm underneath the dock.

If you're looking for lunker bluegills (and who isn't?), the underwater weed beds adjacent to 20 or 30 feet of water are prime spots.

There are weed beds and then there are weed beds, however. The most productive aquatic vegetation consists of the various pondweeds, leafy plants that grow to just under the surface with small "seedy spikes" that peek above the water. But if you don't find pondweed, don't panic. There may not be any in the lake.

So find whatever aquatic vegetation you can find that is closest to deep water. Panfish also lurk in milfoil, the alien plant slowly invading state lakes.

Finding bluegills is no different than locating any other fish. It's done with trial and error.

Going Deep For Bluegills

Larger bluegills are likely found near deepwater structure on the outside of weed lines at depths in excess of 20 feet. Often big 'gills reside with the big boys, walleyes and the like. At other times, you'll likely find nice-sized bluegills suspended off the bottom but near weed lines.

To reach deeper bluegills, it's best to switch to a slip-type bobber rig or a regular live bait rig with no bobber.

canine catch

Anchor next to the outside weed edges and fan cast the bobber rig until you contact fish. Or, you may want to drift with a live bait rig as if you were fishing walleyes.

Still one more method is to go with a plain hook and a small splitshot pinched two or three feet up the line. Add bait. Cast the splitshot rig it along the edge of the weeds. Allow time for the bait to sink and then retrieve slowly. You'll apt to get a strike. I'd almost promise.

Best Bluegill Baits

You can be a very happy panfish seeker with a dozen worms. You know, earthworms. The kind that live in your garden or behind the barn. Thread one on your hook and you're ready to catch bluegills.

But bluegill fishing can be much more versatile than that.

Small leeches are excellent baits. Bluebills love 'em and the leech is tough on the hook, thwarting the bait stealers.

If you like fly-fishing, there's a bluegill always willing to inhale a wet fly, dry fly or fly rod popper. Floating spiders sponge with rubber legs are yummy to a bluegill. And one of the all-time great panfish

baits is a small 1-inch strip of white pork rind and a size 10 Aberdeen hook.

Plus you don't need a fly rod to catch sunnies on flies and poppers. You can cast a light fly or rubber spider with a conventional spinning or spin-casting rod and reel by using a small, clear-plastic "bubble" or "bobber" about 3 to 4 feet ahead of the fly.

The bubble provides enough weight to make the cast. Then merely twitch or slowly retrieve the bobber while the fly follows on 6-pound leader about three to six feet behind. Poppers may be fished in the same manner.

Bluegills Like Slow

As a general rule, bluegills don't like to chase their food. No matter if you're using live bait or artificials, fish slowly. Twitch enticingly. Bluegills are browsers. They feel no urgent need to chase any fast-moving morsel. That's why minnows seldom are the most effective bluegill bait. They'll work, of course, but tidbits of worm meat or imitation insects that hang and jiggle like an easy meal will catch more bluegills.

Early morning or late evening is prime

Raven loves to go fishing. For hours, she'll pace in the boat, staring blankly into the water in search of swimming fish. When I catch a fish, Raven gets very excited. Why? She wants to retrieve it!

times for bluegills, especially top water. Use your ears to find 'em. Listen for the "slurping" noise of bluegills feeding on the surface.

Like the sound of loons, bluegill sucking is music.

Catching Perch

Once upon a time, a Minnesota perch was just like Rodney Dangerfield. It got no respect. It was considered a pest, a bait stealer, a rather dull catch. Ice anglers toss 'em on the ice for the birds.

But no more. A perch may not be the brightest thing with fins, but it has a of admirers. Jumbo perch (10 inchers or more) roam in places like Lake Winnibigoshish or Leech or Mille Lacs. They are fun to catch and, being closely related to walleyes, even more fun to eat.

Now the only time a perch is a disappointment is when you were trying to catch something else.

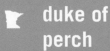

duke of perch

Catching small perch isn't much of a challenge, but it takes some refined techniques to consistently bag "jumbo."

When my daughters, Simone and Laura, were pretty little girls (now they're pretty big girls), the perch was their indoctrination to the joys of catching. Perch of any size. They bite. They fight. They make pretty girls scream with delight. If you need to teach a kid to fish, start with the perch under the dock.

Perch fishing techniques are similar to those for sunfish, except that big perch are more apt to take small minnows and leeches (although big bluegills will inhale leeches nicely).

In addition, perch are apt to be found more widely spread than sunfish. While the sunfish hangs around weed beds and sunken islands, perch will also frequent sand flats, sandbars, weeds, rocks, you name it. I've seen perch in 4 feet of water and caught them in 35 feet of water on the same lake on the same day.

Come to think about it, if you drag a worm around long enough I can't think of why you wouldn't catch a perch. It may not be a jumbo but it'll be a perch. Finding the jumbos just takes more searching.

The only time perch are difficult to catch is after sundown. Perch (and bluegills) feed almost entirely by sight. When the daylight fades, a perch quits feeding because it can't see.

One of my favorite jumbo perch-catching ploys is with a jigging spoon, tipped with only the head of a fathead minnow. Dave Genz, Minnesota's Mr. Ice Fishing, showed me his technique on day on Lake Winni. Jiggle the spoon and let

is slowly twist to a halt. Don't expect a strike. Perch just nibble.

Some perch days are better than others but I'm not sure if a perch angler ever gets skunked. You might get tired of catching. But that's a nice feeling to have.

At this point, I suppose you should be warned about eating "wormy" perch. Some perch have 'em; most don't. The little white worms are encased in a perch fillet; you can see em. But they won't hurt you. Once the perch fillet is dropped into the hot fish fry oil, the worm is just extra protein.

Catching Crappies

To a Minnesota fisherman, crappies are the first sign of spring.

In April, with the ice freshly melted, the snowdrifts gone and replaced by waves of water, the crappie is the first fish to greet the new season.

In fact, crappies are not only the first fish; they are the only fish. In the days immediately after ice-out, most other fish are still inactive. Not so with crappies.

Days after ice-out, if the day and night temperatures hang in the 50s, you can start expecting crappies to appear in the warmest shallows of the lake.

The warmest shores typically are those on the northerly shores of lakes and bays. It has to do with the angle of the sun's rays and the southerly winds. While south winds push the warmest surface water to the north end, the sun's rays also hit a north shore longer in the day to add a few degrees more of warmth.

The nice thing about crappies in

⚑ crappie baits

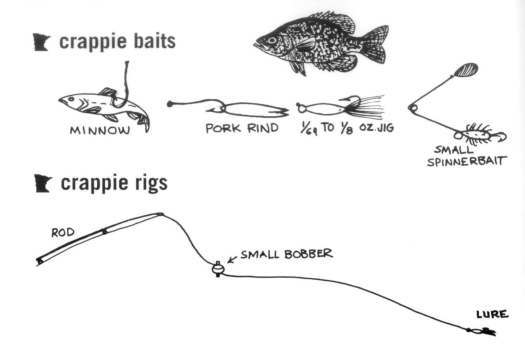

MINNOW

PORK RIND

1/64 TO 1/8 OZ. JIG

SMALL SPINNERBAIT

⚑ crappie rigs

ROD

SMALL BOBBER

LURE

springtime is two-fold: They gather in great numbers and they're all hungry. Check out lagoons, boat basins, channels, bays—any area of shallow water and you'll likely find concentrations of crappies.

Bring the spouse, the neighbors, the kids. Armed with light tackle, a bobber, splitshot, hook and small "crappie" minnows, anybody can catch crappies in the spring.

How To Say Crappie

By the way, the name crappie does not rhyme with crappy. To correctly pronounce crappie, the name rhymes with sloppy. Please refrain from saying crappie as crappy. It bothers Raven, my Black Lab.

Crappie Capers

Minnesota has two crappie species, the common "black" crappie and the not-so-common "white" crappie. Some lakes, such as Minnetonka, have both species. But generally the white crappie is found in more southerly waters in the state; the black in northern lakes.

The black crappie, as its name implies, is richly speckled with deep, dark marking. The white crappie is pale in comparison with faint markings.

Crappies spawn later in the spring, when the water temperature hits 60 degrees or so. Again, they are vulnerable to the fisherman who stalks their spawning grounds, usually on shallow, bulrush flats or other sandy bays. Small minnows and jig-minnow combinations are effective, used with or without a bobber.

If using jigs alone, light colors often work best, such as white, pink or yellow.

Since you're fishing shallow waters, depth is seldom a mystery. Later, when crappies move to 10-foot depths or more, you'll have better luck if your bait floats higher than the fish. Crappies love to move up to bite, but seldom will swim down. What depth is right? The answer comes with trial and error.

Casting and retrieving a crappie lure is also effective, although the speed of retrieve can be critical. Generally, the slower the better. If there's a slight ripple on the water, let the small waves bounce the bobber and in turn bounce the minnow or jig.

Mid and late-summer crappie fishing is a whole new ball game. By then, the crappies have re-gathered into schools and have moved to deeper water, sometimes 30 feet or more, and often suspended.

Suspended schools of crappies can be very difficult to find without the aid of electronic sonar depth finders. And once located, the school may move off, meaning your search must start all over again.

Keep in mind that crappies are structure fish. They will be adjacent or near drop-offs, humps, sunken islands, and so forth. Deep water next to bulrush clumps, points or flats are typical crappie hotspots. Concentrate your fishing in water 15 to 25 feet deep. Drop a lively minnow to the bottom and then slowly raise it a few feet at a time. If you don't make contact, repeat the process, working the edge of the drop-off until you find the crappies. Then, mark the spot. Anchor or drift over the area.

If you lose the school, keep drifting or troll slowly to cover as much water as possible.

Crappies love dusk. As the sun goes down, crappies think about their stom-

By the way, the name crappie does not rhyme with crappy. To correctly pronounce crappie, the name rhymes with sloppy. Please refrain from saying crappie as crappy, it upsets Raven.

ꙮ locating crappies and sunnies

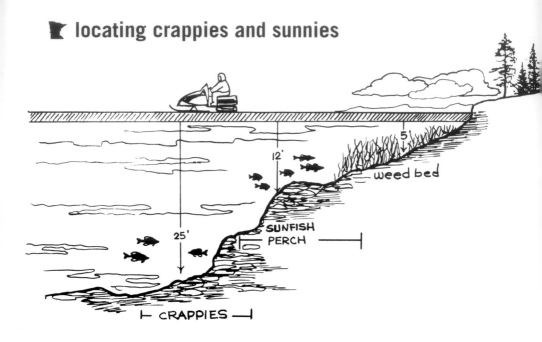

achs. Often the last sunlight of the day is the best crappie fishing of the day.

But don't count your crappies yet.

Both white and black crappies are known as "paper mouths," that is, their jaws appear to be held together with tissue paper.

If you set the hook on a crappie like it was a Mack truck, you'll lose every fish. The idea is to set the hook firmly but gently. Don't horse the crappie to shore or the boat. If you do, the hook may easily tear out, leaving the crappie somewhat shook but not seriously injured.

Ice Fishing for Panfish

If it weren't for panfish, ice fishing in Minnesota for pure excitement would be rated below watching haircuts.

Sure there are walleyes, northern pike and lake trout to keep the ice angler gushing with anticipation, but those species can be elusive when you're limited to a hole in the ice.

Fortunately, the abundant panfish take up the slack. By sheer numbers, they will be present just about anywhere you drill a hole.

You'll rarely find bluegills cruising in water deeper than 20 feet. Perch tend to range from 15 to 25 feet, much like crappies.

An early ice fishing ploy is to concentrate in the vicinity of weed beds and drop-offs where you fished last summer.

Crappies tend to be more elusive in the winter because the schools often suspend over deeper water. Nevertheless, stick near structure... drop-offs on underwater points, sunken islands and so forth. Plan to pursue crappies starting late afternoon and staying until an hour past dark. If crappies are near

the structure, they'll typically move in and feed as the daylight fades.

Gary Roach and I had that experience one afternoon on Birch Lake at Hackensack. We were fishing a sharp slope that ranged from 10 to more than 15 feet. When we first arrived, bluegills and perch kept us busy. There wasn't a crappie to be seen. Until sunset. Suddenly, crappies were everywhere.

When a lake is covered by 18 inches of ice and equal amounts of snow, it can be a little difficult finding fishy spots. Some anglers use their electronic depth finders, the portable models. The sonar signal will go through ice, although the transducer must be in some kind of liquid to work.

It also helps to eyeball the shoreline, looking for hints that indicate the existence of points. Then, it's guesswork. Drill a hole in the ice. Clip a heavy sinker on the end of your fishing line and drop it to the bottom to find the depth. By drilling several test holes you can find the drop-off or changes in depth. Such a trial and error method is hard work, or used to be with thick ice, an ice spud or hand auger. Today, there are gas or electric powered augers with laser-sharpened blades.

Ice fishing expert, Dave Genz, is a firm believer in drilling many holes before you start to fish even if you may never use them all. The reason? Noise. "Make your noise first, now you can quietly fish and change depths if necessary without making new noise," says Genz.

Clearly the key to winter success is found in the hole you make. Your bait choice is seldom critical. It's placement of the hole.

Fortunately, ice fishermen are a congenial bunch and rather gregarious. An ice fisherman with a hotspot seldom objects if other anglers stop to fish in the same vicinity. Panfish are abundant and prolific. You'll not fish them into extinction.

Winter sunfish and perch often may be caught with the same baits and lures used in the summer. Instead of earthworms, however, most ice fishermen use various grubs for live bait—wax worms, euro worms, goldenrod grubs, mousics, meal worms, red worms, and so forth. Most are available at bait shops. Or some anglers collect or raise their own.

White Crappie

Black Crappie

Compared to black crappies, white crappies have a more silver appearance, explaining why they're sometimes called silver bass. Like black crappies, they're also called specks, speckled perch, calico bass and many other regional names.

Panfish

Golden rod grubs are found in the galls (round bulges of the golden rod plant). Carefully cut open the gall and you'll find a small white grub.

Live grubs or worms may be fished on small, plain hooks (size 8 or 10) or with special hooks called ice flies. These are hooks with a dab of lead molded around the hook shank and painted. The painted lead acts as an attractor. Some ice flies have a small spinner blade for an attractor. Ice flies with glow paint also can be extremely effective.

One of the best bluegill lures—winter or summer—is a weighted rubber or sponge spider, tipped with a grub. Remember the bluegills and perch prefer hors d'oeuvres and not full course helpings.

The typical pan-fishing rig consists of an ultra light graphite rod or jiggle stick, light monofilament line (2- to 4-pound test), a splitshot or two, the hook or ice fly and a small bobber or float. Very small. About the size of a dime. Larger bobbers not only are unnecessary, they're a sure way of reducing your luck on panfish.

Give the grub or ice fly a little "action" once in awhile. Jiggle lightly, and then pause. Repeat several times a minute. The jigging action will attract attention and more bites. Plus, it'll give you something to do.

Winter crappie fishing gear is similar to that used for bluegills, except small fatheads (commonly called "crappie" minnows) are a bread and butter bait. Use a bare hook for the minnow or use a small 1/64- or 1/32-ounce mariboui jig.

When the crappies are in a feeding frenzy, it's fun to forget the live bait and base your luck strictly on artificial lures. With artificials, there's no fussing with grubs or minnows. Catch a fish, land it and sink the lure again.

An artificial lure is severely limited in winter, of course. All you can really do is fish vertically, up and down. A minnow in comparison is much deadlier. Yet, crappie caught on a fake bait under the ice is much more gratifying. And every angler should experience the feeling.

The great crappie explosion on Upper Red Lake was an interesting lesson in crappie feeding movements. Most days the crappie bite was a typical pattern, starting as the sun hit the horizon and lasting for an hour or two. Strangely, however, the sunset formula didn't work every day. Some anglers would arrive at noon and discover, much to their joy, that the Red Lake crappies were biting like mad. Go figure.

My strangest winter crappie fishing story begins on Rainy Lake, home to giant slabs, and made famous by such wily entrepreneurs as Barry "Woody" Woods, who operates a "fairly reliable" fish guiding service at Ranier, Minn.

By claiming to be "fairly reliable," Woody says that in a typical guiding season more than 95 percent of his customers are returned to the dock. (Hey, it's a joke, okay?)

One day Woody agreed to take us on a

winter crappie fishing trip and guaranteed us success. Wow, great, I thought. When you're shooting a Minnesota Bound fishing story, it helps to catch at least one or two fish. "No problem," Woody said.

We started fishing, each hunkered in a portable canvas shelter somewhere on frozen Rainy Lake.

Woody caught the first crappie. It was flopping when he showed it to me. A few minutes later, Woody caught the second crappie, bringing over for me to see.

I hadn't had a bite.

"Maybe you should fish in my hole," Woody said, trying to be generous. I said I would. Woody moved to where I had been fishing and immediately caught a third crappie.

I was bummed. How could I be so unlucky? What was I doing wrong? What was wrong with me?

Woody was laughing hard. The joke was on me. Woody had promised he'd catch fish and he wasn't taking any chances.

To make sure, he brought the crappies with him.

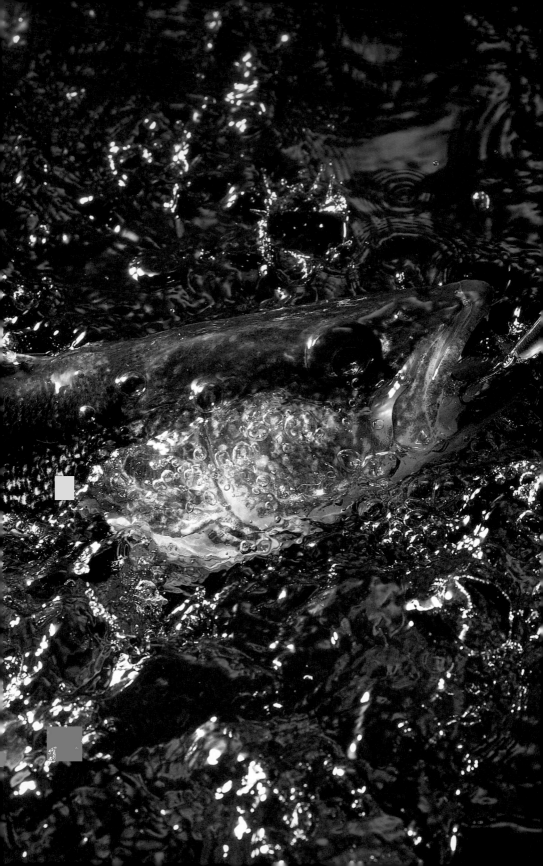

Minnesota's Filet Mignon

Without walleyes, Minnesota would be a cold Iowa.

Walleyes are us.

Outside of Canada, no other spot on earth has as many walleyes swimming around as Minnesota does. Nobody stocks more walleyes (230 million fry) from more hatcheries (12) in more lakes (900).

Minnesotans also lead the nation in walleye surveys, walleye meetings and walleye controversies.

Panfish may attract more state anglers if you're counting numbers. But no fish in Minnesota is more intensively sought or more highly prized than a walleye.

Its reputation as an epicurean delight is unmatched among freshwater fish. Browned in butter or coated with beer batter, the white, firm, walleye fillet has an exquisite taste of its own, not fishy, not mushy, not tough. It's absolutely… well, wait a minute.

The best tasting walleyes are the ones you've caught.

Pardon the pun, but that's the catch.

Wishing for walleyes is not enough to fill your plate unless you visit a restaurant that specializes in the aquatic fillet mignon. Two of my favorites are Tavern On Grand in St. Paul and Shelly's Restaurant in St. Louis Park.

The walleye may be the state's "official" fish, but I've never known a walleye to swim voluntarily into a frying pan.

Not even in Minnesota.

Yet, no matter where you roam in the state, you're not far from water with walleyes swimming in it. Walleyes have been introduced in dozens of lakes, including those surrounded by cows and farms in the state's southwest.

To the north, some of the state's largest water bodies, such as Mille Lacs, Leech, Winnibigoshish, Lake of the Woods, Red Lake, Vermilion, are among the best natural walleye lakes in the world.

These big waters rarely if ever require stocking because the lakes have an abundance of natural spawning ground with gravel shoals and rocky reefs. Nature supplies the walleye fishing. By itself, Mille Lacs raises more walleyes naturally, than all the state's hatcheries combined.

Many lakes will support walleyes but are incapable of maintaining their numbers naturally. These lakes then are stocked regularly or as needed based on fish surveys.

About The Walleye

Who, then, is this handsome fish with its golden sides, cream-white belly and glassy, pale blue eyes?

The walleye is a member of the perch family, closely related to both the perch and the similar-looking sauger.

In fact, many anglers confuse the walleye and sauger, since both fishes often occupy the same waters, the same habitat and may be caught in the same ways.

By the way, walleye and sauger are equally delicious. However, they are not the same fish. The walleye has a white marking on the lower tip of its tail; the sauger does not. Saugers usually have splotchy dark markings on their sides,

know the difference

Walleyes (top) have golden sides and a white belly. The spiny dorsal fin is not spotted, but has a black blotch at the rear base. The lower lobe of the tail has a large white tip. Saugers (bottom) are grayish to brownish with dark blotches. The dorsal fin has rows of distinct black spots and the pectoral fins have a dark spot at the base. The lower lobe of the tail may have a thin white streak.

which are much more defined than on a walleye. The spiny dorsal din in the sauger's back also is quite speckled whereas the walleye's dorsal fin is rather opaque with a single black spot at the rear base of the fin.

Sauger are not as abundant as walleye and tend to be found more in rivers than lakes, such as the Mississippi and St. Croix Rivers. You can expect to catch sauger in Lake of the Woods, Kabetogama, Namakan and Rainy Lake, however.

Despite all of its attributes, the walleye will never be remembered as a great fighting fish. It does not leap like a bass or roll like a pike or turn sideways like a bluegill with heart.

Yet, the walleye is no slouch fish, either.

I'll admit, I've lost my share of walleyes "right at the boat" when the fish flopped, plunged or otherwise shook the hook. I'll never forget one walleye I lost because it cost Gary Roach and me a few thousand dollars of tournament money on Lake Darling. Until I lost that fish, I'd never heard Gary swear.

When hooked a hefty walleye will not tear madly about like a rainbow. Rather, it chooses to resist, making short but powerful runs back toward the depths

and flopping or swinging its head back and forth. So, don't get the wrong idea. Walleyes may not win any fighting awards, but neither do they surrender like a water-soaked log. Any big walleye will easily bust the line of an angler whose reel drag is set too tight.

While we profess to adore the walleye, we still haven't learned to call the fish by its right name.

Some folks insist on saying "walleye pike."

Good grief. A walleye has nothing to do with pike. Restaurants tend to be the biggest violators. The menu says walleye pike fillets. That's like offering pork horse steaks. If they don't know what it is, how can they cook it?

In Canada, the walleye is known as the "yellow pickerel." Why? Who knows? But, then, Canada is a foreign country.

The Walleye Sex Life

You probably haven't thought much about the sex life of a walleye. Too bad. It's pretty impressive. Happens on April nights. On gravel beds. Cool surroundings, 42-50 degrees. Not much courtship. More the merrier; group sex, sort of. No ties. When it's over, all swim their own way. The young fend for themselves, no problem. Slam, bam, thank you walleye.

Interestingly, in the world of fish, females tend to grow larger and faster than their male counterparts. Walleye are no different.

A male walleye seldom reaches a weight heavier than 5 pounds or lengths beyond 22 inches even if it lives to a ripe

old age. There are exceptions, however. One winter day of ice fishing at Minnesota's Northwest Angle, I caught a hefty walleye that was too weak to return to the water, despite repeated attempts to make it swim away. It weighed 7 pounds. I was sad about keeping the fish, thinking I'd killed a plump female only weeks away from spawning. Imagine my surprise when we filleted the fish only to discover it was a male!

However, most Minnesota lunkers, those walleyes of braggin' size are always big mamas.

What's a meal to a walleye?

Walleyes are meat-eaters, aquatic predators who prefer to attack prey that is alive, if only barely. Their most common natural food consists of small, young-of-the-year perch. Or when eating-size perch aren't abundant, food studies have shown that walleyes will switch to larvae of aquatic insects, such as the mayfly.

A walleye's food supply is what determines your own walleye fishing luck. Let's consider the fishing history of Mille Lacs. Some seasons it seems a walleye on the end of the line is more rare than reefs of gold. When this happens, most of us complain about the DNR and its poor handling of the walleye population. Stock Mille Lacs! They don't, of course.

The next year, bango, the hot bite is on. Everybody with a line in the water is catching walleyes. What happened? Well, nobody added more walleyes; they were there all along. What changed was

the walleye's food supply. An abundance of food makes fishing tough. A decline in young, bite-sized perch leads to a hot walleye bite. It happens every time.

Finding Walleyes

It's the hunt that makes walleye fishing so fascinating.

To catch em, first you've got to find 'em.

Too many fishermen with high hopes for walleyes try to fight the system. These anglers must like bad odds, such as hunting for needles in haystacks. It might be challenging but, hey, aren't we here to catch something?

If you want to catch walleyes, go to a walleye lake instead of a lake with walleyes in it.

Take the odds. Choose a lake to fish that has a reputation as a walleye producer. Granted, you've got a wide choice in Minnesota. But there are also a bunch of lakes that are not known walleye hotspots. When you're casting for walleyes in a danged good bass lake, you're in for a slow day, pal.

The best walleye seekers I know all have one skill in common: they know how to choose the best waters and the best time period for the fish they're after.

Creating your own list of good walleye lakes isn't difficult. The DNR offers walleye population data for every lake via the "Lake Find" feature on its website: www.dnr.state.mn.us. Local bait shops are happy to suggest their best walleye lakes.

Starting out to fish on a known walleye lake or river is half of the battle. The other half is… well, a little more difficult. It's called fishing.

Finding Walleye Hangouts

So where do you start fishing now that you've found the lake?

That depends on the time of year. Walleyes spawn in shallow water during April and early May in Minnesota. After spawning and as the weeks pass on into summer, the general rule is the walleyes gradually drop into deeper water.

There are expectations, of course.

Under the cover of darkness, walleyes may move back into shallow water, say 6 feet or less, even on the hottest days of July and August.

You will find walleyes hanging out in weed beds in less than 12 feet of water-

spring, summer or fall. One August day my brother Roger and I were casting huge jerk baits for muskies roaming weedy bays in Mille Lacs. Guess what we caught? We each landed 28-inch walleyes.

What are walleyes doing in the weeds? Following the food. Where you find the walleye's food, you'll find the walleyes.

Walleyes tend to be structure fish. A point. A reef. A sunken island. A pile of boulders. A sand flat. Any and all of these places may harbor walleyes on any given day in any given lake. Which one? There's not a walleye expert who can say with any accuracy without knowing more. Time of year? Wind direction? Many factors go into locating walleyes. Let's take a look.

Walleyes Love Wind

When the wind blows, the walleyes bite. There're no guarantees in fishing, but the wind and walleye connection is as close as it gets.

While walleyes tend to be nocturnal creatures, it's very possible to catch them in daylight, saving your nocturnal hours for more normal pursuits.

You can have the luxury of sunlight and catch walleyes, if you've got wind or dark water (tannic stained) or a feeding movement. A hungry walleye is very capable of ignoring bright sunlight while it feeds. Would it prefer less light? Probably, but a walleye eats first and hides second. You can learn that lesson in early season by casting jigs into 4 feet of water and catching walleyes in mid-day. They might bite better at sundown but don't rule out anything until you've tried it.

It was mid-day, high noon, when partner, Mark Bundgaard and I, were bouncing in a stiff walleye chop on a sand flat in less than 10 feet of water. We didn't know it but a walleye feeding binge was about to start, thanks to the sudden wind. When it was over, Mark had the largest walleye of his angling career, an 8-pounder on a jig-minnow in the boat. He's caught larger walleyes since, but you never forget feeding binges.

Walleyes tend to be clean bottom fish. That is, they prefer sand, rock or gravel sites or at least hard bottom. Again, there are expectations. The so-called "mud flats" of Mille Lacs are famed walleye hangouts in mid summer. But the flats

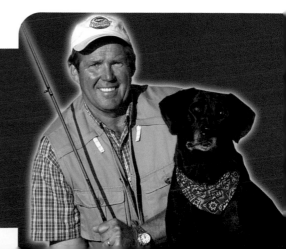

In all my years of fishing trips, one with my Dad stands out above all others. It would be my father's last fishing trip. He was battling cancer. That weekend was also Minnesota's walleye opener. No walleyes, but Dad caught a 12-pound northern pike.

are actually clay humps and they are quite hard, although covered with silt. At times during the summer, the Mille Lacs walleyes will go off the humps into truly pure, unadulterated soft mucky bottom. But their forays over mud are the exception not the rule.

In early season, walleyes looking for food also will stray into mud bays. Why? It's where the food is.

Walleyes By The Season

Just as the sun always rises in the east, Minnesota's walleye season always opens on the Saturday nearest May 15. Let's open the season and follow it through until winter once again caps the state's waters in ice.

Opening Day and the first two or three weeks of walleye fishing are typically a shoreline affair. Having completed spawning in the shallows, walleyes tend to hang around the rock, sand or gravelly shores in water seldom deeper that 15 feet. Usually less. If warming spring weather arrives early, this shallow period will be short.

Concentrations of male walleyes in early season can be spectacular, particularly where spawning rivers enter a lake. Seldom are the big mamas around.

Most of the male walleyes will run in the 1- to 2-pound range, maybe a few 3s.

Meanwhile, the larger females have already begun to disperse to their summer haunts and are recuperating from the stress of spawning. Hence, they are not where most of the fishermen are.

As the days go and the water warms, walleyes become more predictable. This happens in June.

If you're a lunker hunter, June fishing is more promising as the walleye can be found rather consistently in its usual hangouts—deep shoreline points, sunken islands, sandbars, rock bars. The fish producing depths range from about 15 to 30 feet. Remember, however, that not every walleye has moved. Shorelines with sharp drops of gravel or rock will continue to be productive, especially at dawn and dusk.

At that time of year—about mid-June—a practical depth to start fishing is about 20 feet. If that fails, move up or down in increments of 5-foot depths in trial and error fashion.

Sooner or later, if you're fishing typical summer hangouts, you should get a bite.

Summer Walleye Hangouts?

Today places where fish hang out are popularly called "structure." Your grand-daddy called them "hotspots."

Structure is an irregularity in a lake or river bottom, such as a sunken island, a sandbar, or so forth. A boulder or hole in a river would be structure. Fish usually hang around such structure. More specifically, fish tend to congregate near the "breaks" on the structure. A break is a sudden change of depth (see illustration).

For example, suppose a sandbar gradually deepens to 10 feet, then sharply drops down to 15 feet and then drops off again at 20 feet. There would then be two breaks on the sandbar, so to speak. One at 10 feet and another at 15 feet. A walleye

fisherman in early June would undoubt-edly start fishing at the point where the sandbar in 15 feet of water drops off to 20 or more feet. In May, you'd probably try the 10-feet "break" first.

Starting in mid-to-late June, most of the walleyes have gathered in their sum-mer haunts where they'll stay through much of the fishing season.

Some haunts are better than others. Sunken islands or humps in a lake are renowned walleye magnets, but you'll find there's a difference in sunken islands, particularly their cover and depth.

In mid-summer, walleyes tend to fre-quent the underwater humps with weedy tops, those that peak less than 20 feet under the surface. Those weed-free

humps or islands, which are devoid of weed or rock cover often are abandoned by walleyes. Or nearly so.

And then comes August.

August is a fine vacation month in Minnesota, unless you're expecting to taste some of that famous walleye fishing you've heard about. Time and again, Joe Blow, the visiting fisherman, brings his family to Minnesota in August, thinking he'll slip out and nab a few walleyes, too.

It's dangerous to generalize, but August fishing can be tough. Oh, yes, the water is warm and the walleyes are feeding. That's not the problem. The problem typically is an abundance of baby perch.

Late August and early September can

EDGE OF SUNKEN ISLAND

10 FT

20 FT.

30 FT.

walleyes

Walleye

mean fishing deep rock humps, 30 to 50 feet down. A live bait rig or 5/8ths jig works at those depths tipped with a minnow, leech or piece of night crawler. But it's slow fishing, because locating a walleye in deep water is more time consuming and difficult.

But let's not despair.

August can produce great walleye action in the right spots. I've enjoyed awesome August walleye fishing on Lake of the Woods and Rainy Lake. Where is a hunting question. Shallow 10-foot rock piles can be loaded or you'll have to fish deep 30-foot rocks to catch fish, you'll just have to try both.

Let's not forget the August potential of the Mississippi, Minnesota and St. Croix Rivers.

If you're thinking August is an impossible month to catch walleye, you didn't read it in these pages.

As September turns the leaves, the lakes also begin to turn, meaning the water temperature from top to bottom slowly becomes the same. By then, most of the visiting anglers have returned home. And many Minnesotans, themselves, have turned to the hunting seasons or the Vikings football schedule.

A walleye addict stays the course, however.

Some of the best fishing of the year can happen when autumn turns the shores to gold. It may not be as comfortable. Fall anglers seldom wear sunscreen; it's snowmobile suits and felt-pac boots, not T-shirts and tennis shoes.

On some lakes the walleyes become a shoreline fish again, hanging along the sharp drops that lead to deep water. Rock piles become alive again.

Full Moon Walleyes

Full moons have been associated with lots of strange behavior, werewolves and the like.

But not all of it's scary. Unless it's the size of the walleyes you can catch under a full moon.

Actually, full moons, anglers and big fish have a long relationship, ranging from sea to sea, blue marlin to largemouth bass.

Please include walleyes.

If you really want a chance for a big walleye, the autumn moon phases are your bible. When is the full moon coming? Make your plans to be on the water during a stretch of time, roughly, three days before and after the actual full moon.

This also is a night game.

"Clear full moon nights are better than cloudy ones. The light helps the big fish see to feed but it's not enough light for baitfish to escape," says Tommy Skarlis, one of Minnesota's pro-walleye anglers and full moon addict.

"Actually the best nights have a few passing clouds that change the light levels."

Most moonlight anglers troll rocky bars and weed lines with stick bait style lures, pulled on long lines 100 feet or so behind the boat. Water depths range from about 10 to 3 feet.

While a variety of lures are effec-

tive, the following are proven: floating Rapalas, Smithwick Rattlin' Rogue, Berkley Frenzy Diving Minnow.

Natural, gold and silver colors seem to work best, although any angler should experiment with color if the strikes are rare. Glow-in-the-dark baits also may work.

Best trolling speeds range from about 2 to 4 miles per hour. Again, vary your trolling speed until the walleyes say what they want.

In some Minnesota lakes, anglers will wade the shallows on full moon nights. Fishing guide, Brian "Bro" Brosdahl, of Cass Lake, looks for hard bottom shorelines with an incoming river or creek nearby.

"Shore fishing can be excellent," said Brosdahl, who uses neoprene waders. "I cast stickbaits and I've found that wall-

eyes sometimes will be surprisingly shallow."

Making false assumptions is a common pitfall in the hunt for walleyes. It's late July, right. We know the walleyes have gone to their deepwater summer haunts. We know because we've caught them in deep water, such as the "mud-flats" on Mille Lacs.

Who can argue with that?

However, the false assumption is that ALL the walleyes are deep.

One summer day, I motored out to the "mud-flats" of Mille Lacs in late July intending to find walleyes. Other fishermen already had the same idea. There were boats by the dozens drifting or trolling on the edge or top of the flats, which generally peak between 20 and 25 feet and drop off to 35 to 40 feet.

After an hour or so I hadn't had a

strike. And as far as I could tell, I wasn't alone. Why fight the system, I reasoned. Why not cast for northern pike that roam the lake's cabbage patches and bulrush beds?

So I motored back toward shore, switched tackle, and began casting a black and orange spinner bait in about 10 feet of water.

A few casts later, I knew I'd made the right decision. Catching northerns is better than catching nothing at all.

I had landed a couple of small northerns, 3-4 pounders, when suddenly, my lure was stopped by a vicious strike. A good northern, I thought.

Suddenly the big fish lunged and rolled near the surface, flashing its golden sides in the summer sun. I couldn't believe it. A 6-pound walleye. On a lure. In the weeds. In shallow water.

Let that be a lesson. Never say never. While the majority of walleyes may be found in predictable haunts, we have a lot left to learn. And that's the beauty of walleye fishing: the hunt never ends.

Walleyes And Rivers

We tend to forget our rivers in Minnesota. Good thing the walleyes haven't.

One of the most famous walleye hotspots is the Rainy River starting in late March when the Rainy turns free of ice. A vast population of pre-spawn walleyes move out of Lake of the Woods and enter the swift, dark waters of the Rainy literally from Baudette to International Falls. It's a jig fishing paradise, despite raw winds or ice floes that may still be around.

What more needs to be said about the walleye opportunities on the Mississippi River or the St. Croix or the Minnesota River? Each harbors plenty of walleye and sauger.

It may surprise you to know that wasn't always the case.

Once upon a time, the Mississippi River between Minneapolis and St. Paul was devoid of game fish. Why? Pollution had robbed the river of oxygen. Today, the Mississippi as it flows through the Twin Cities holds trophy walleyes that are protected by catch and release rules.

The lesson is simple. The pollution ended, now the fishing season on the Mississippi never ends.

Live Bait For Walleyes

When a fish hits an artificial lure—something made out of lead and feathers or molded in plastic or carved from wood—there's something special about the occasion. And every angler feels it.

Walleyes are quite catchable on artificial lures, particularly in shallow water. But once walleyes move deeper, the purist, the one who wouldn't stoop so low as to touch live bait, is apt to starve to death.

If you really want to catch walleyes, learn how to fish live bait. It's your No. 1 weapon. Actually, you have three big guns—minnows, night crawlers and leeches.

Once upon a time there was a fourth, salamanders. The first time I used a tiger

Weight-Forward Spinner. Usually tipped with a crawler, this rig works well for suspended walleyes. Cast it out, count while it sinks and then retrieve slowly. Experiment with different counts until you find the fish.

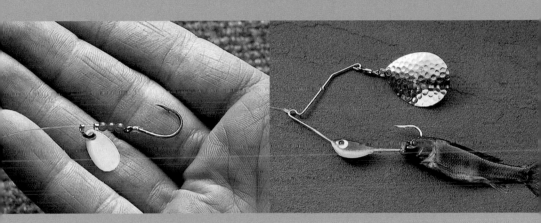

Flicker Blade. Instead of using a pre-tied spinner rig, just thread on a clevis and add a size 0 or 1 Colorado spinner blade (convex side forward). Then thread on some beads and tie on a bait hook.

Spin Rig. Tip this small, unskirted spinner-bait with a leech, half a crawler or a minnow. Because of its safety-pin design, it's a good choice for working weedbeds.

Weedless Rig. When slip-sinker fishing in light weeds or along a weed edge, substitute a bullet sinker for your egg or walking sinker. In denser weeds, you may want to replace your standard bait hook with a weedless hook (inset).

Floater Rig. To keep your bait above the bottom, rig it on a Phelps Floater or a floating jig head. Or thread a small float onto your line just ahead of the hook (inset).

⬥ hooking minnows for walleyes

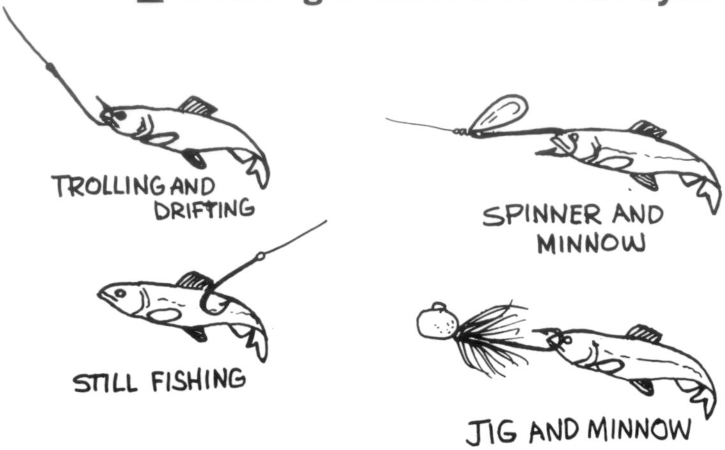

TROLLING AND DRIFTING

SPINNER AND MINNOW

STILL FISHING

JIG AND MINNOW

salamander for bait, it was inhaled by a six-pound walleye. Magic for big fish, I thought. They work but my success went downhill from there. Other anglers must have had the same experience because you don't hear much about salamanders.

The frog story is the same. Walleyes love frogs, but low frog populations have reduced their popularity as bait.

On the contrary, there seems to be no shortage of the Big Three.

Minnesota bait dealers annually sell countless dozens of minnows, night crawlers and leeches.

The most common minnow species, the fathead, are raised in small ponds, trapped and distributed by bait wholesalers.

The most common leech species, the ribbon leech, is trapped from certain ponds, marshes and bogs. Fish tend to dislike other leech species, including the large horse leech from which Leech Lake gets its name.

Most of the night crawlers sold in Minnesota, except those at roadside stands, are imported from Canada

where they are collected from golf courses and shipped to bait shops in refrigerated trucks.

Starting from opening day on, a serious walleye angler will carry all three baits. You never know the walleye's taste preferences of the day or, for that matter, of the hour.

Yes, minnows tend to be the best choice on opening day or in cold water, but don't tell that to my usual opening day partners, Uncle Ken and Uncle Charles Schara. They're worm devotees. They have extreme confidence in night crawlers. And, sure enough, Uncle Charles or Uncle Ken are apt to win the Schara family opener big fish pool.

About Minnows

If you want one bait to master, make it the minnow.

But which ones?

Let's keep it simple. Two choices: fatheads and spottail shiners.

Day in and day out, the fatheads—2- to 3-inches long—so commonly found in

bait shops will take walleyes from opening day to ice over. An old secret that's not so well kept anymore is the advantage of choosing female fatheads over the darker male fatheads. I've experimented enough to believe walleyes prefer the female fatheads. Why? I haven't a clue.

Shiners can perform magic in early season. A walleye that'll pass up fatheads will absolutely gorge itself on a spottail shiner so named for the black spot at the base of the tail.

Sometimes you learn that the hard way.

One opening weekend my brother Robert had a hot fishing hand on Lake Plantaganet. He was nailing nice walleyes at a rate much faster than anybody else, including me. And he was braggin' about it. Since I'm the older brother, this was almost too much to bear.

"Hey, bro'," I yelled over to Robert's boat, "what are they hitting?"

A very innocent question, I'd say. Bro' Robert kindly answered, "Chartreuse jig and minnow."

"Thanks," I said, quickly switching to a chartreuse jig and adding a fresh bait, a fathead minnow.

A few minutes later Robert landed another walleye; me, not a strike.

When the day was done, when Robert safely had braggin' rights, I learned "the rest of the story." When my sweet brother said jig and minnow, what he "forgot" to say was jig and SHINER. It was type of minnow, not the jig color that was the key.

Robert and I still laugh about his ploy (but I haven't forgiven him).

There's a third minnow that walleyes love, the redtail chub, but it's harder to find. If it's autumn and you can buy redtails, use 'em.

Minnows are used in many ways on the end of the line.

Most commonly, the minnow is fished alone, that is just attached to a hook lightly through the lips. Sometimes minnows are added behind spinners; sometimes added to lead head jigs. In winter, sometimes just a piece or half a minnow is utilized.

The proper way to hook a minnow depends on how it is being used:

For still-fishing with a bobber, lightly hook the minnow under the dorsal or back fin or through the lips.

For drifting and trolling, hook the minnow through the lips so that it follows naturally.

For spinners, the long-shanked spinner hook is weaved through mouth and gill and hooked lightly to keep the minnow from rotating behind the spinner.

For jigs, hook the minnow through the lips or behind the head or through both eyes so the minnow gives the appearance of being injured, swimming on its side (see Illustration).

About Night Crawlers

Called "garden hackle" by trout fishermen, the night crawler has become a walleye fooler supreme. Don't ask me why a walleye—miles from shore— would be looking for a night crawler in

the middle of a lake. But they are and that's all we need to know.

Chose plump, healthy night crawlers. Skinny, half-dead 'crawlers are less effective as are the regular earthworm, the smaller relative of the night crawler.

My walleye tournament partner, Gary Roach, always gave his night crawlers plenty of TLC. He believed in fresh bait and readily switched night crawlers if the bites slowed.

Night crawlers once were considered only a mid-summer walleye bait. But no more. A night crawler also works in a variety of presentations much like minnows, except for still-fishing under a bobber.

Slow trolling or drifting with a live bait rig are the best night crawler fishing methods, although a "piece" of night crawler added to a lead-headed jig often works well. Spinners also are designed with a "hook harness" to use on night crawlers.

Most of the time, a night crawler is hooked on the tip of the head and allowed to trail. Which end is the head? Don't know? Lay the night crawler on the boat seat. Whatever direction it crawls is the head end.

When using live bait rigs, many anglers also add something to their night crawlers. Air. Pumping a shot of air into a night crawler's "collar" makes the worm float. If done properly, the night crawler will puff up slightly, giving it extraordinary buoyancy. The air does not kill or appear to harm the

'crawler, but it does keep the bait floating higher off the bottom.

What's the advantage?

Aren't walleyes a bottom fish? Well, yes and no. Walleyes are known to suspend off the bottom at times. Sometimes as much as 10 feet or more. When suspended, a walleye will seldom move "down" to pick up your bait. But a walleye on the bottom will easily swim "up" to grab a meal. That's why it's often important to keep the bait floating slightly off the bottom. How high? It's impossible to know without trial and error.

The suspending nature of walleyes led to the development of "floating jigs" or "floating rigs." A floating jig looks like a regular lead-headed jig, except the "head" is made of cork or some other floating material. The floating rig is similar except the cork slips onto the line and against the hook, thereby floating the bait off the bottom. You can regulate the floating height by changing the length of your leader between the swivel and hook.

A jig and crawler is an effective combination. And a dozen 'crawlers will last longer because typically only one-half of the 'crawler is used at a time. The size or weight of jig depends on the water depth.

About Leeches

The name of the angler who discovered that leeches are deadly walleye bait has been lost to the waves of time.

For sure, he or she must have been the gutsy sort, being the first to reach into a slithering ball of leeches. Some people

would rather read their own obituary than touch a leech.

Now guess what?

The pointed end of the leech is its head and it swims in that direction. The rear of the leech has a "sucker" or suction end capable of attaching or clinging to your skin. But a leech is NOT a bloodsucker. Leeches do not feed on blood and bloodsuckers are not leeches.

Okay, so there's nothing pretty about a leech. But, lordy, can leeches catch walleyes.

The leeches may be hooked at either end, although most anglers slip the hook through the sucker-end. When bobber fishing, it's best to hook the leech in the middle.

Again, leeches may be fished much like minnows and night crawlers. In addition, leeches are effective any time during the walleye season, although they appear to be most effective when water temperatures hit above 60 degrees.

The discovery of leeches gave rise to a phenomenon called the "bobber brigade." These are anglers who fish for walleyes with a slip-bobber, a split-shot, small hook or jig and a lively leech. It's a deadly combination.

The use of the slip-bobber allows an angler to fish extremely deep while allowing the bait to be cast. The bobber or float slips freely on the fishing line until it hits a "bobber stop," a small knot or bead pinched on the line, which stops the bobber at a desired depth. Since the bobber stop passes through the rod guides, you

can cast or land a fish with a short line as the bobber slips toward the hook.

Choosing Hook, Line and Sinker

This is the business end of walleye fishing and very important. Almost any combination of good line (no more than 12-pound test), an adequate sinker to reach the bottom and a hook of proper size will suffice to catch a walleye.

River walleye fishermen do better with a "river rig," consisting of a 3-way swivel, a bell sinker and a hook.

Believe me, there's a difference. I was using the conventional live bait rig on the Mississippi River one spring while fishing buddy, Bob Nybo, a Red Wing river rat, went with the time-worn river rig. While we were fishing in the same boat, Nybo's better luck convinced me there was more than luck involved. I soon put together a river rig and started catching walleyes. Obviously the river's current was holding my bait too tight to the bottom. The river rig allows the bait to rise up where the walleyes are looking.

But undoubtedly the most popular and versatile terminal tackle used today is known as a live bait rig—a slip-sinker, a swivel and hook. Two popular designs by Minnesota tackle makers include the Lindy Rig by Lindy-Little Joe and the Roach Rig by Northland Tackle.

One rule is always use enough sinker weight to stay in touch with the bottom. Generally, a 1/4-ounce sinker will be adequate in water up to about 25 feet unless it's windy. Then, switch to a 1/2-

ounce weight. On windy days, when your boat will be drifting faster, you may find you'll also have to go to a heavier sinker. In shallow waters or calm days, a 1/8-ounce weight will work fine.

When in doubt, go heavy with the sinker since you release line when feeling the strike, the weight of the sinker has no bearing on what a walleye feels.

Stay in contact with the bottom. Know where you're at and you'll be a better walleye hunter.

But what length leader?

Most of the time a 36-inch live bait leader is sufficient for all situations. When the walleyes are finicky (you're not getting strikes), a smart angler will go to a longer leader, 4 to 10 feet long (and sometimes lighter 4-pound test line). I'm not sure why but there are days when a long leader will out-fish anything less.

A word about hooks. Hook sizes and colors are a personal choice, depending on the bait used. Normally, a hook size 4 is used for minnows, a size 6 for night crawlers and leeches. In recent years, the advantage of "circle" hooks has spread, especially in release situation where an angler wants to avoid deep hooking a fish. When used properly, a circle hook is seldom swallowed.

Colored and glow hooks also are in vogue, serving as an attractor.

Speed And The Strike

These are the two most common mistakes made by novice walleye-seekers. They troll or drift too fast and cannot recognize the walleye's soft "nonstrike."

Generally I don't think you can hurt your success by trolling too slowly. The need to move slow and still control the boat has led to the popular technique called "back trolling." It looks just like it sounds. The outboard is placed in reverse and the boat moves stern first instead of bow first. Fishermen who practice back trolling are easy to spot: their boats have large plastic flaps affixed above the transom on each side of the outboard.

These "flaps" serve one purpose: to keep waves from breaking over the transom. A bankroller's boat may look gaudy but the technique is very efficient. It's much easier to control the path of a boat that is being "pulled" and not "pushed" by the outboard. What's more, it's much easier to achieve slower trolling speeds since the boat is "pushing" more water ahead of the square stern compared to a pointed bow.

Pro-anglers also learned that controlling the boat from the bow seat is also effective, providing even more control in a reasonable walleye chop. Again, the idea is to present a fish-catching drift to unseen walleyes down below.

It is not necessary to back troll or front troll, if there's a pleasant wind drifting. Then, it's a matter of letting the breezes move the boat on, over or alongside walleye haunts. Use the outboard or electric to control your path or slow your drift.

In strong winds and heavy waves, it is almost impossible to back troll. To control drifting speed, use a drift sack. If that doesn't work, drop anchor.

Detecting A Strike

When bobber fishing, walleye bite is easily detected. Yesiree, the bobber goes down.

With conventional live bait rigs, beginners often miss the walleye's soft attack on minnows, night crawlers and leeches.

It's a non-strike really. You'll seldom feel a "jerk" so don't wait for one. Instead, the walleye strike is more like a light snag. You'll detect a gradually increasing tension on the line as if the bait had hooked on a soft tree branch. Sometimes it's a branch; usually it's a walleye.

For that reason, most fishermen fish walleyes with an open spinning reel while the bail is open to give line instantly. Your line then should be held by one finger or two fingers, which helps detect the growing line tension. Once the tension is felt, quickly drop your finger, giving line and adding slack. Let the walleye run with the bait, if it wants.

Then how long should you wait? That's a tough question. When you've had a strike, seconds seem like minutes. Count to 10 slowly and set the hook firmly. If you miss the fish, you might count to 20 on the next bite. If you counted to 10 and the walleye is landed with the hook already buried in its stomach, you know you can probably set the hook sooner on the next fish.

Not every strike ends with a walleye, of course. Sometimes they'll almost smack the bait, take line convincingly and then drop the hook. If that happens often in a day, some anglers will add a "stringer" hook, a hook that trails at the rear of the bait.

When a walleye drops the bait, it can mean you were slow to give slack.

Interestingly, a walleye's soft strike often disappears when trolling spinners. The flash or sound of the spinner must trigger aggression in a walleye. Same with crankbaits. When a walleye hits a Shad Rap, there's no doubt.

Casting For Walleyes

One opening day on the Minnesota-South Dakota border waters, TV angler Babe Winkelman and I headed for Big Stone Lake near Ortonville.

Babe had fished the lake many times before and knew of potential hotspots. We fished those places for several hours but they all proved to be "cold."

Finally, we happened to back troll along the edge of a wind-swept point, which had waves breaking into the shallows and muddying the waters. That meant the water wasn't much more than 3 to 4 feet deep. For no reason except a hunch, I reeled in and flipped a night crawler into the shallows along the edge of the muddy water.

Boom, I had a strike and landed a 2-pounder.

"That's the best news we've had all day," said Babe, who knew what to do.

Immediately, Babe used the outboard to hold us within casting distance of the windswept shallows. Two hours later we had a dozen plump walleyes, a two-man

limit, and won a friendly fishing contest with the locals.

If we had tried to back troll or drift over the shallows our luck probably would have suffered. Even a boat quietly drifting overhead easily spooks walleyes in 6 feet of water or less. In those cases, it's best to cast the bait, reeling it slowing back to the boat in hopes of a strike.

Walleyes On Jigs And Things

The walleye had absolutely no qualms about smashing food imitations, things like feathered hooks, plastic tails or painted plugs.

Jigs, lures, spoons, spinners—all have been known to take walleyes, sometimes more effectively than live bait.

Of those, the most famous artificial offering is the lead-headed jig. Two of the best jig fishermen I've ever known are Ray Ostrom and Dick Sternberg. What made them good was their ability to detect subtle strikes and to impart action to the jig at any depth. Both Ray and Dick could fish with jigs very effectively in waters of 20 feet or more while the rest of us tend to have better luck shallower water simply because the jig is much easier to fish.

The jig is used to imitate a minnow or a crayfish. That is, the jig is fished in such a way that it darts on the bottom, raising and falling, raising and falling.

Keep in mind, there are about as many jig head designs, as there are colors. This is because a jig head and hook shape may be designed for live bait, such as the popular Northland Fireball. Other jig models are made to secure and add a plastic body, grub or worm.

Several Minnesota jig makers, such as Bluefox, Lindy-Little Joe and Northland make various jig heads designed to stand on bottom, swim through vegetation, be weedless in brush or make noise when bounced.

Detecting A Jig Strike

The walleye, like the bass, tends to hit the jig when it is falling or immediately after it settles to the bottom. Knowing that, the trick is to detect the strike.

The key to detecting the strike is to make sure you maintain some tension on the line as the jig falls. If the jig falls on complete slack line, a strike may go unnoticed.

Seldom is a jig effective if you simply cast it out, let it sink and reel it in on a

Raven's tidbit

straight retrieve. You must impart action to the jig, which means you must lift and drop the jig with your rod tip using it like a band director's baton.

With tension on the line, the strike will come in the form of a "thunk" felt through the line and telegraphed to the rod handle and your hand. Or you may see the line will twitch slightly. The best jig anglers use their sensitive fingers and they watch the line. Feel or see something? Set the hook.

In many situations, a jig adorned with feathers or a power grub is all you need to catch a walleye, especially aggressive feeders. Most of the time, a jig's effectiveness is improved by adding a minnow, leech or piece of night crawler.

While live bait fishermen may be in the majority, anglers who cast or troll with crankbaits may win more tournaments. A walleye is no coward when faced with a tasty-looking crankbait.

Trolling or retrieving speed is somewhat less important. If a walleye wants it, it'll catch your crankbait. Usually the right speed is that which imparts or allows the lure to swim actively.

The strike, of course, is easily detected and the walleye is on immediately. Or off immediately.

Suspended Walleyes

This may be the last frontier of walleye fishing savvy. Not many years ago, nobody knew walleyes suspended in deep water. We just thought they were still on the bottom but not biting.

Now we know the famed bottom fish will go anywhere there's food even if that means suspended below schools of baitfish. This happens in large waters, Mille Lacs, Lake of the Woods and so forth but suspended walleyes also can be found in small lakes often those containing ciscoes or tullibees or lake shiners.

These baitfish will gather offshore in huge schools to feed on phytoplankton and zooplankton.

Catching suspended walleyes consists of trolling and covering vast areas of water with downriggers or trolling boards. Walleye pro, Tommy Skarlis, says he utilizes his fishing electronics to find clouds or swarms of bait. Once the bait schools are located, suspended walleyes are not far away.

Raven likes to jump off the dock in the backyard into the Rum River.

Skarlis said if he can see fish marks he notes the depth and chooses a crankbait that reaches the proper depth.

"Sometimes I'll stagger the depths at five-foot intervals to cover as much of the water column as possible," Skarlis explained.

In other situations, walleyes have been known to suspend away from a structure, say a 15-foot rock reef, while maintaining the 15-foot depth over say, 30 or 40 feet of water. When does that happen? The answer is found by that now famous trial and error method. If you're not contacting fish on the structure, they're either not hungry or they've suspended nearby.

What depth does XYZ crankbait swim? Check the lure box or consult the latest edition of a crankbait book where authors test and develop depth charts for all popular lure brands.

A Perfect Day?

Any time you land enough walleyes to fill a frying pan is cause for celebration. Day or night.

Veteran walleye hunters often look for gray, overcast skies with westerly winds. Typically, that's walleye catching weather. But don't be discouraged by bright, sunny days with calm waters. It might not be easy but walleyes are catchable then, too.

The best fishing weather often has nothing to do with sunny or overcast. The key word is: stable. A period of stable weather, say several days with moderate westerly or southerly winds is often the key to a good bite.

But whatever the weather. Don't give up. If you've ever tasted fresh walleye fillet, that's all you need to know.

Ice Fishing For Walleyes

Take what you know about summer wall-

▶ popular jigs

Feather jig

Short-shank jig with minnow

Curlytail jig

eye fishing, add a healthy scoop of patience, and you'll catch walleyes through the ice, too.

Winter walleye action even can be hot.

One day Mille Lacs guide, Ivan Burandt, put us on a huge school of walleyes that were biting like crazy at high noon. We were filming the outing for the Minnesota Bound television show. Unfortunately, I had scheduled too much travel that day.

Quickly, we caught enough small walleyes to do a story with Ivan, although he said bigger fish would show up later. "I can't stay," I replied, sadly.

In wintertime, it's not often you walk away from walleyes willing to bite.

Basically, the walleyes will be found in similar haunts, ranging from a depth of about 20 to 35 feet deep. Trial and error is the only way to find them. Only now it's more work, since you'll have to drill 6-inch holes through the ice that may be 12 inches or more in thickness. Usually more.

Minnesota's ice fishing guru, Dave Genz, preaches the ploy of drilling many holes before you begin fishing. For example, he'll drill a pattern of holes ranging in various water depths. Then, he'll start fishing the holes hoping to find the "hot" hole. Why drill so many? To reduce the noise and disturbance one you begin to fish. Winter fish might be sluggish but they can detect noise.

Keep quiet on the ice and you'll catch more.

Winter also neutralizes most of the elements. You have no wind or waves. You can't cast or troll, so there's not much need for fancy fishing gear. Most ice fishermen use small ice fishing "sticks." And fishing, itself is boiled down to a pure hook, line and sinker… and a small one at that.

While the ice fisherman is limited to fishing "vertically" through the ice, there are a few artificial lures available to the purist. The most popular are the Swedish Pimple, and Rapala's Balanced Jigging lure or Pilkki lure. Each may be fished alone or with a small minnow. The lures are designed to be pumped up and down, giving the action of an injured minnow. The action need not be vigorous. All fish in ice-cold water tend to be somewhat sluggish. They have no desire to chase something that appears hard to catch. In fact, if you don't dress properly for the cold, you will also begin to feel little sluggish.

It was Ivan Burandt who also showed me that silver hammered jigging spoons are very effective at times for walleyes or perch when tipped with a piece or head of a small fathead.

In Minnesota, the best winter walleye action starts with the first safe ice and continues into early January. After that the action becomes sporadic and winter gets long and sometimes dreary.

Hurry up opening day!

Trout

The Beau Brummels

When you're in a state famed for walleyes, it's difficult to think trout.

Yet, Minnesota's trout and salmon fishing rank as one of the state's greatest fishing success stories.

A century ago, Minnesota's picturesque southeast was an abused land with trout streams turned into muddy waters by eroded hillsides wrongly plowed for farming.

A half-century ago, Lake Superior's native lake trout populations were in rapid decline, eradicated by the combination of lamprey eels and excessive commercial netting.

A few decades ago, anglers depended solely on state hatcheries to supply "put and take" trout fishing.

Today, Minnesota's southeast corner has more miles of clear trout water flowing in scenic valleys through forested hillsides. Central Minnesota has a few gems, including one of the state's finest brown trout streams, Straight River.

Today, Lake Superior's lake trout populations are recovered and additional stocking appears unnecessary. In addition, several species of salmon have been added to the world's largest sea of freshwater to provide additional angling sport. The sea lamprey, which destroyed the lake trout fishing in Lake Superior, has been controlled with the use of selective eel larval toxicants.

Today, most of Minnesota's trout streams are harboring wild brown trout that sustain themselves naturally without the aid of stocking. The natural hatch is possible because landowners worked to control farmland pollution and soil erosion. Dedicated DNR fish managers worked diligently in the limestone bluff country to stabilize stream banks, create trout habitat and stimulate the return of natural trout spawning.

Minnesota's abundant number of coldwater lakes in the northeast region has led to a successful program of roughly 180 remote fishing lakes stocked with stream trout species, such as rainbow and brook trout. New fish toxicants and technical know-how have helped reclaim lakes for trout and each year the DNR stocks about 600,000 rainbows, browns, splake and brook trout to maintain the fishery. To maintain the trout and prevent the introduction of rough fish, anglers are not permitted to use live minnows in the designated trout lakes.

Where The Streams Are

Minnesota's trout streams are roughly located in the southeast, central and northeast portions of the state.

The southeast, a land of hardwood timbers, limestone bluffs and pastoral, Little Switzerland valleys, provides primarily brown trout fishing on self-sustaining streams, although hatchery trout are stocked where needed. A complete guide to southeast trout water is available from the DNR; *Trout Fishing Access* is a 100-page guide including maps. To order, call the DNR Information Center at 888-646-6367 (statewide) or 651-296-6157 (Twin Cities).

Brown trout also are the main quarry in north central Minnesota trout rivers, which wind sleepily amid the alder thickets and popple forests.

In the northeast, a land of spring-fed brooks, spruce swamps and timeless beaver dams, native brook trout abound in its forest-shrouded waters. Many of these small brooks are difficult to find in rugged, wilderness-like country. See DNR's list of *North Shore Trout Streams*.

Fly-fishing For Trout

My own angling teeth were first cut on Mississippi River bluegills followed by an immediate switch to brown trout at Livinggood's Springs.

Such a path of angling education is akin to jumping from 1st grade to post-graduate studies at Harvard. I didn't catch many trout in those early attempts, but I spooked the scales off a bunch of 'em.

Most novice anglers don't give a trout enough credit. They stomp up the bank and throw out a gob of worms big enough to choke a starved robin. They use monofilament line the size of baling twine tied to a shark hook. These folks could write the book, Fishing For Dummies. But, danged, if they don't some-

times catch a trout. A stocked fish, no doubt. Oh, I suppose a trout can make a mistake or be stupid at times, but I ain't seen it happen much.

No, trout tend to be pretty smart most of the time.

That's why somebody, a long time ago (Izaak Walton, maybe?), invented fly-fishing for trout. Come to think of it, a book publisher may have started fly-fishing as a way to sell books.

It seems about 8 out of every 10 fishing books written are about fly-fishing for trout. I don't know who's buying them all, but somebody must be. While it's not possible to adequately summarize the ins and outs of selecting rods, reels and fly lines. Or discuss gathering feathers and such for tying flies; let's eradicate a few false stereotypes. People who fish, but don't fly fish, tend to think that casting a fly rod is an angling peak they cannot climb.

This is a bunch of hooey.

If you can swing a flyswatter, you can learn to cast a fly rod. You can learn to drift a Hare's ear nymph or cast lightly a May fly dry.

If you will persevere and pay your dues, the skill and art of fly-fishing for

Raven's tidbit

trout is a wondrous adventure in angling. You will learn to match the hatch and sing in tune with a trout stream's song.

I think I know why fly anglers are such ravenous readers. It's such a high to fool a trout on feathers; the how-to books are like a drug.

Information about fly-fishing schools, lessons or trout guides are available from various Minnesota locales, such as local fly-fishing shops, Cabela's in Owatonna and Gander Mountain stores in Rochester.

Minnesota's Trout Unlimited chapters and Federation of Fly Fishing chapters are always willing to invite new members.

Longtime guide, Wayne Bartz, of Rochester, is the kind of fishing companion who relishes teaching as much as catching. He and I have spent several cherished days in southeastern streams, including an afternoon where we both caught nothing and enjoyed the experience.

Tom Helgeson, of Minneapolis, may be the consummate Minnesota fly angler. Years ago, he walked away from a successful newspaper career to seek out a living in fly-fishing circles. Tom now publishes a leading publication, *Midwest*

Fly Fishing magazine that is loaded with nifty information. To reach the magazine offices, call toll-free at 888-440-1628 or in the Twin Cities, 612-926-5128 or surf the Web at www.mwfly.com.

Lastly, there's one more reason why you may want to consider diving into the world of fly-fishing for trout. Trout eat flies. A bunch.

Trout Fishing Basics

Minnesota's trout are no different than anyplace else. They are suspicious, spooky and possess excellent eyesight. This means that any hooked offering sent to a trout should arrive naturally with the hook and line well camouflaged.

"Go light and small" is a key trout fishing phrase.

As a general rule, a trout will shy from fishing line heavier than 4-pound test. In extremely clear waters, it may be necessary to drop to 1-pound line to avoid the trout's sharp eyesight.

Go ahead, use 6-pound line if you want but you'll catch fewer fish.

The need for light line means you want a light or ultra-light action rod with a spinning or spin-cast reel. In trout fish-

We were taping a show for Minnesota Bound when my wife suggested Raven sit next to me.

The photographer said the dog was too black. "Do you have anything colorful to put on the dog?" he asked. I spotted a red farmer's handkerchief on a coat rack, tied the bandana around Raven's neck and a star was born!

Trout

ing, light and small also refers to everything from split-shot to your hooks, such as sizes 10, 12 or 14 for live bait.

Once you accept light line, small hooks and small lures, you've got half the battle won. I realize it takes luck to land a 3- or 4-pound trout on 2-pound line. But if you go armed to "horse" trout, your chances of fooling that 4-pounder are nil to begin with.

Trout streams and lakes are notoriously clear. Except for the riffles, you can see just about everything on the bottom. And if you don't see any trout in one stretch of stream, you might as well walk up to the next pool. Right?

Wrong, thunder foot.

Trout have imaginative hideaways. They can glide under banks, logs, rocks, moss, grass—places you'd swear weren't big enough to hide a dime.

Don't let your eyes deceive you. Besides that, whenever you can see a trout, chances are it can also see you.

It's always best to walk or wade upstream. Why? Because trout are facing upstream, too, which means you are approaching from behind the trout. When you approach a pool or run from the side, try to maintain a low profile.

Trout On Live Bait

In Minnesota, the popular baits for trout include small live minnows, night crawlers, earthworms, salmon eggs, grasshoppers, miniature marshmallows and canned corn (see photo). Yes, corn. Some people buy their bait in a supermarket instead of a bait shop.

Sometimes trout seemingly have no pride and will eat the same things a catfish might like, such as cutbait.

In my boyhood days, while I toyed with spinners and flies—and began to think of myself as a trout-fishing aristocrat—my father, Harlan, ventured to the Yellow River one day to fish the bridge hole. First, he used a piece of earthworm to catch a small chub. Then, he sliced a chunk of chub and slipped the meat on a small hook and plunked the whole thing into the deep bridge hole.

Wouldn't you know, Dad later came home with the fish of my dreams, a 23-inch brown.

He never let me forget how he caught that trout. And I haven't. Thus, I never sneer at one's choice of live bait.

Trout fishing purists are fine but they're not always smart.

My Uncle Bob Dickens was an accomplished fly fisherman who could handle a wet fly drift or make the perfect cast of a dry fly. But Uncle Bob never played the purist.

One gray, muggy morning, Uncle Bob and I were fishing trout in Waterloo Creek. He went to one pool upstream; I walked to another downstream. Suddenly, I heard him yell for me. He had had a good-sized brown take a swipe at his fly. And he wanted me to watch the next time he sent the fly into the big brown's lair. On the very next cast, the brown was on, a dandy 18-incher. I noted what fly Uncle Bob was using and

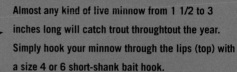

Garden worms probably account for more stream trout than any other type of natural bait. They will catch trout of any size. If you're targeting large trout, however, a nightcrawler is a better choice.

Almost any kind of live minnow from 1 1/2 to 3 inches long will catch trout throughtout the year. Simply hook your minnow through the lips (top) with a size 4 or 6 short-shank bait hook.

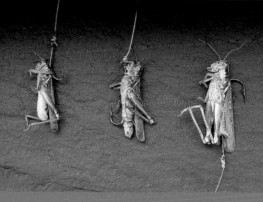

Grasshoppers, crickets and other terrestrial insects are commonly blown into streams, where they make an easy meal for trout. Even when no aquatic insects are hatching, trout will feed on terrestial forms.

Of all terrestrial insects, grasshoppers are most commonly used as bait. Grasshoppers and crickets can be hooked under the collar or threaded on using a size 6 to 10 long-shank, light-wire hook.

Even if the bait shop isn't open, you can still get some good trout bait at the corner grocery store. Trout are commonly caught on whole-kernel corn, cheese balls, marshmallows and even baked beans.

All trout and salmon feed on each others' eggs to some degree. So it's not surprising that fresh trout and salmon eggs make excellent stream-trout bait.

started rummaging through my own fly collection.

About then, it started to sprinkle. A few minutes later it was pouring rain.

Uncle Bob shuffled upstream to the next pool. Shortly, he yelled for me again. This time the trout was already hooked. He just wanted me to watch the fight. It was another nice brown, 14 or 15 inches long.

But I noticed something different. The second trout had been caught, not on a fly, but on a... yikes, night crawler.

Uncle Bob's idea of being trout smart is to notice things. He noticed the rain downpour had sent trickles of muddy water running into the clear trout water.

Seeing the muddy water, Uncle Bob started thinking like a trout. A trout might think the rain had swept food into the pool. Uncle Bob switched to live bait, a single, fat night crawler. On the first drift, his switch paid off.

Worm or night crawlers are basic trout baits, with minnows a close second. Live bait may be fished under a small bobber at times. Usually the idea is to drift the bait naturally, using a small splitshot about the size of a BB to keep the bait down. The hook should be hidden or buried in the bait as much as possible.

A small hook buried under the collar of a grasshopper and allowed to drift through a pool of unsuspecting trout is "real" fly-fishing.

The trout's strike often is not vicious. The bait, tumbling slowly in the current, will merely stop. You may feel a slight

⚑ hooking live baits for stream trout

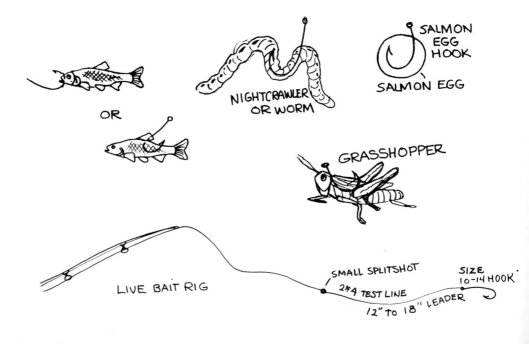

OR

NIGHTCRAWLER OR WORM

SALMON EGG HOOK

SALMON EGG

GRASSHOPPER

LIVE BAIT RIG

SMALL SPLITSHOT
2#4 TEST LINE
12" TO 18" LEADER
SIZE 10-14 HOOK

tug as the trout returns to its lair to finish the meal. It's time to set the hook.

Fishing Lakes For Stream Trout

Along the North Shore, a number of deep, cold lakes, have been stocked with rainbow trout or brook trout largely on a put and grow basis. Many of these remote lakes require long hikes in bush country to reach, which means you're apt to be alone except for the trout.

Stream trout stocked in lakes can be a puzzling fish to catch. Assuming a stable environment, a rainbow might be found in almost every location, near shore, near islands, near drop-offs or suspended near nothing.

To a trout, structure is based more on water temperature than anything else. That's why a trout—in a clear, cold lake—may indeed use all sides and all depths of its watery home.

A popular technique is to troll or drift, covering as much water as possible and experimenting with depths. With any luck at all, you'll soon discover that a particular shore or bay or point may produce more strikes than other areas.

A popular ploy with fly anglers is to utilize float tubes or light portable pontoon floats to explore the remote lakes. A float tube is easier to tote than a canoe. A novice in a float tube may take a few minutes to learn how to paddle with feet flippers but it's worth the effort.

You might also want to try casting a "bubble." A bubble is a modified float or bobber and the system works well in lakes. It's designed to cast with spinning gear and to retrieve slowly. Trailing behind the "bubble" is a light leader and your choice of trout flies. In other words, the bubble system allows you to cast a light fly without relying on a fly rod.

While flies and nymphs are the fly angler's weapons of choice, there are times when flies or hardware (spinners and such) simply are ineffective.

When that happens, one of my favorite trout methods is to employ an ultra-light spinning rod with a slip-bobber rig akin to that used for walleyes. Only the business end of the line will be different. I tie on extremely small, 1/64 or 1/80th ounce marabou jigs. A split-shot is pinched on the line about 24-inches above the jig.

When the outfit is cast, the split-shot pulls the jig down to where it is suspended mere inches off the bottom. Wave action or by jiggling the rod, I make the tiny jig vibrate.

Trout can't resist.

Trout Spoons And Spinners

Aside from flies and live bait, a trout angler is apt to employ a vast selection of "hardware" to fool a trout.

Spinners, spoons, and small trout crankbaits are part of the arsenal. In most cases, the smallest sizes made are best for trout.

Artificial lures work equally well in lakes or streams. In flowing waters, most artificials are cast downstream or across the current and reeled upstream… imitating the swimming action of a minnow. Live baits, of course, are cast

upstream or across the current and allowed to drift downstream.

In lakes, artificials may be trolled or cast. To add weight to a lure for trolling, place an adequate sinker about 4 feet ahead of the lure. A habitual troller may go to lead-core line or purchase "downriggers" to keep the lure at extreme depths.

Excessive trolling speed generally isn't critical. In fact, trout tend to be gullible for fast-moving lures. If you give a trout too much time to examine your false meal, its sharp eyes may detect something…well, fishy.

Minnesota's Brookies

Many streams in Minnesota's northeast corner, those with a steady supply of cold water, are occupied by native brook trout, whose coloration is stunning.

Brookies, measured by trout standards, may be the easiest of all Minnesota trout species to catch. The downside is they reach heavyweight sizes. In the boondocks streams, a 10-incher is a "nice one."

Yet, there is something very special about brookies. So beautiful. So willing to play the role of a trout, taking flies, eating worms, living in untainted places.

As a result, the brook trout has its own fraternity of addicts, those anglers who enjoy out-of-the way creeks and bushy streams far from the maddening crowds.

Clouds of mosquitoes and jungles of alder bushes sufficient enough to discourage a bull moose guard many of Minnesota's brookie haunts.

The brook trout addict won't be denied, however. Armed with a short fly rod or ultra-light outfit, he'll charge through the boondocks with his trusty box of tied flies, spinners or can of worms.

I once joined a brookie zealot as the mosquitoes and black flies helped carry us over windfalls and spruce swamps to a small, grassy creek no bigger than a street gutter. There was no place to swing a fishing rod using normal contortions of the body. With a bit of ingenuity, it was possible to swing your fishing line reasonably close to the water.

The brookie addict guide soon wandered off to an even thicker part of the stream where even more mosquitoes were waiting.

Suddenly, he began to whoop and holler.

First I figured the mosquitoes had pushed him toward the early stages of

Raven's tidbit

insanity. Yet, he sounded happy. I charged through the underbrush to find him. He was on his knees in a praying position. He was holding aloft with two hands a 13-inch brook trout as if the fish was a gift from heaven. He was nuts. With joy.

Many brook trout streams and creeks are marked on maps of the Superior National Forest. However, the many beaver dams that also hold trout are unknown except to the hiking angler who finds them.

Once located, brookies are gullible for live bait, such as worms or night crawlers. Grasshoppers work great if you can catch them. There are usually plenty of mosquitoes available, if you can thread them on a hook.

The Splake Story

In the late 1970s, DNR fisheries managers settled on a "new" fish to turn Minnesota's many coldwater lakes into fishing hotspots. This is the story of splake—a hybrid cross between a female lake trout and male brook trout.

With parents like that, splake are beautiful specimens.

Splake rarely reproduce. As a result, the state's splake fishing program is dependent on Crystal Spring Trout Hatchery where all of the splake for stocking are raised. Lakes are stocked in the fall, often with the use of floatplanes. Although splake are catchable whenever the season is open, winter is often productive, as the fish tends to be a bottom dweller and will hit small jigs bounced near the bottom. Usually splake are willing biters, feeding on insect hatches in summer months and dead minnows or jigging spoons in winter. Live minnows are forbidden in most trout lakes.

Splake also are noted for swimming close under the ice or, in summer, at shallow depths of 5 to 15 feet. A water temperature in the mid-60s is ideal.

In a splake lake, the average size is about 10 to 14 inches. A lunker is 18 inches or more.

To find lakes stocked with splake, check the list of DNR's managed trout lakes available on DNR's website www.dnr.state.mn.us.

Lakers Of Inland Waters

If it wasn't for ice fishing, Minnesota's lake trout might rank as the state's most overlooked sport fish.

Raven likes to pull Ron's daughter Laura on her Rollerblades.

Trout

For most of the summer fishing season, the deep-dwelling lake trout are difficult to find and almost as difficult to catch. In cold-water periods, lake trout are found at more reasonable depths. However, when the best lake trout action is possible, spring and fall, the season is often closed. Consequently, most lake trout diehards wish for a late spring. The colder the water for the May fishing opener, the greater the chance for lake trout action in the BWCAW or other northeast lakes.

In the fall, lakers move onto reefs to spawn and are easily caught, but Minnesota's lake trout typically ends in late September before the spawning run begins.

Although lake trout are not as "line shy" as other trout, it's still a good idea to use light line, 4- to 6-pound test.

In early season, lakes often are caught on live minnows, such as shiners, trolled along the rocky reefs. Other live baits are less effective.

The best artificial lures may have different shapes or designs but they'll almost always be white or silver in color. White jigs, silver spoons and silver-blue plugs are good choices. Sometimes plugs and spoons of fluorescent red are worth trying. Airplane jigs are effective.

As the lake surface temperatures rise, lake trout descend to the cooler depths to feed on smelt, tullibees, whitefish, herring and other deep-water prey fishes. You'll note the lake trout's eating preferences are composed of fish that are silvery in color. Hence, lures of the same color are effective for mid-summer fishing.

During the summer, the lake trout will roam in depths from 30 to more than 100 feet deep. When lakers are deep the problem is reaching them with a lure presentation that's effective.

Heavy sinkers, weighing several ounces, will take the lure down but then depth control become difficult. And if you do catch a laker, reeling in the fish along with heavy sinkers is like pulling in a bucket.

Some anglers use wire line or lead core line to reach the depths but those aids also take some of the sport out of landing a fish.

Downrigging For Lakers

The best way to reach deep lake trout is with a system of one or more downriggers.

A downrigger is simply a giant reel of cable attached to heavy lead ball. Your fishing line is snapped to the ball and lowered to whatever depth you want (see illustration).

The lure may be set to trail behind the ball, usually 5 to 10 foot distances.

When a lake trout strikes, the impact releases your fishing line from a release clip on the ball and you're free to play the fish.

Downriggers are an added expense but definitely worth the advantage if reaching lake trout is your game. A couple of fishing buddies, Jay Anderson and Jim Cook, routinely used downriggers to

▼ downriggers for trout

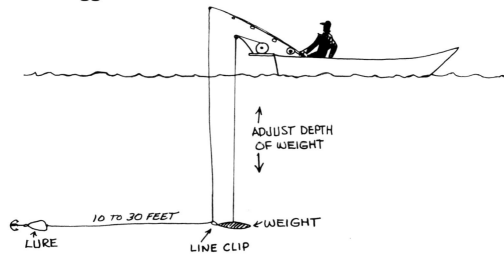

ADJUST DEPTH OF WEIGHT

10 TO 30 FEET

LURE

LINE CLIP

WEIGHT

catch mid-summer lake trout when other methods simply were ineffective.

By the way, downriggers aren't only valuable for lake trout fishing. Walleye anglers on Mille Lacs and Lake of the Woods have found downriggers are the right tool when depth control is important for reaching suspended walleyes with crankbaits.

Catching Winter Lake Trout

Winter is lake trout season. More lakers are likely taken through the ice in Minnesota than in any other season.

An angler's winter mobility also has improved success. Obviously, the use of snowmobiles and 4-wheelers has opened access to snowbound lakes.

In the motorless BWCAW, lake trout anglers have turned to sled dog teams or cross-country skis to reach lake trout haunts deep into the wilderness. Few lake trout hotspots are really isolated anymore.

Winter angling for lakers still presents unique problems, however. How do you

find them when the search is slow, one hole at a time?

Clearly, the easy hunt is to hire a guide or tag along with others who've fished the lake before in wintertime.

Key lake trout spots are often deep holes. Look for high rock walls, which may be a key to deep water close to shore. Plan on drilling lots of holes because this is a search that tests trial and error.

Shoreline drops or deep water holes between islands are often good places. Lake trout normally don't roam much; therefore, trout hotspots once found will be good winter after winter.

Lake trout are scavengers as well as predators. As a result, many ice anglers used dead bait with good results. Smelt, ciscoes, lake herring—kept frozen until ready to use—are popular. In most cases, the dead bait is threaded on special hooks. The best depth to fish is also found by trial and error. Start near the bottom and work up until you contact fish.

Lake trout seem to be slow eaters. Use patience when you detect a bite. Often

minutes will pass before the laker had consumed the bait. Remember, you're dealing with slow motion in such cold water. If you set the hook too soon, you'll set into nothing.

Some of most effective artificial lures for winter fishing include airplane jigs, bucktail jigs and sonar jigs.

White, silver or fluorescent red colors usually work best. The airplane jig is so named because it has wings. When the lure is pumped gently up and down, the airplane jig tends to "fly" in a circle. You'll know when a lake trout strikes. It's a bang.

Sonar jigs flutter and vibrate, imitating a minnow on its deathbed. Bucktail jigs are often tipped with white pork rind strips or pieces of live bait—a slice of cisco or chub meat.

All of these artificial lures require your constant attention since their action is dependent on your pumping action at the other end of the line.

Conventional rods and reels are best for winter lake trout because of the depths of 100 feet or more that might be required.

In addition, lakers are real battlers under the ice and you may need a good

ice fishing lake trout

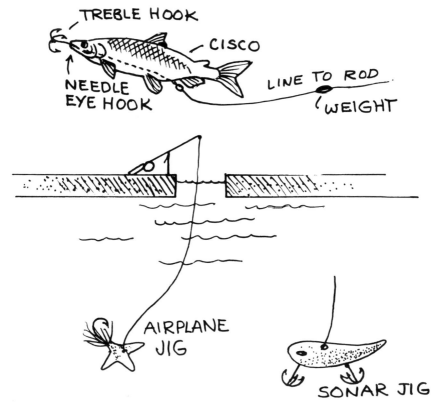

reel to give line fast. That's difficult to do when your fishing line is wrapped on an ice fishing stick.

One of my favorite days of lake trout fishing began on a bitter cold morning when Ely mushers, Stan Passananti and David Day, hitched their dog teams to lead our Minnesota Bound television crew into the winter bound BWCAW.

Destination: Knife Lake, home of the Root Beer Lady, the late Dorothy, and home to lake trout.

The 20-mile run from Moose Lake to Knife had its usual dog team glitches but nothing serious. The enthusiasm of sled dogs is amazing. As my friend, Bob Cary, once noted, the dogs are born to pull.

We began fishing not far from the island where the Root Beer Lady lived in seclusion most of her adult life. Although seclusion isn't quite the right word. In the summer, hundreds of canoeists would stop by to say hello and drink Dorothy's homemade root beer. When Dorothy passed away, folks in Ely rescued her cabins and created a Dorothy Molter Museum on the outskirts of Ely.

With the dogs anchored (and sleeping soundly) on Knife Lake, we quickly drilled a few holes and dropped lines into about 30 to 40 feet of water, using frozen herring for bait. Ten minutes later, a line indicator moved and soon the first plump laker was flopping at our feet.

For the next 90 minutes, we were in lake trout euphoria. I tied on a white airplane jig (no bait) and quickly caught two lakers, including the largest of the day, an 8-pounder.

We were so busy catching fish; the 10-below outside temperature seemed warm. Of course, it was warm... for our team of dogs.

North Shore Steelhead

Aside from muskies, no Minnesota fish stirs the emotions of fishermen like the steelhead in the North Shore streams. Sadly, the steelhead has been a troubled fish of late as populations of wild steelhead are at low levels.

The DNR and North Shore anglers are trying hard for a steelhead comeback. Wild or unmarked steelhead must be released until the population recovers. Stocked steelheads, which are fin-clipped, also have special protective regulations.

The steelhead is a rainbow trout that lives most of the year in Lake Superior. Come spring, the fish migrates up the snow-swollen streams along the North Shore to spawn.

The steelhead's movements into the streams give anglers a chance to match wits with a fish of exceptional beauty, grace and strength. As such, the steelhead is considered a true fishing trophy, regardless of size. The average size steelhead taken is about 3 pounds but 6 pounds are common and fish exceeding 10 pounds are taken every spring.

Most of the steelhead action starts in early April and continues into early June. However, the best fishing normally goes from mid-April to mid-May.

Trout

There are 59 streams on the North Shore that attract steelhead. However, the amount of stream available to the fish depends on the location of natural barriers, such as waterfalls. And the steelhead fishing season depends on how long the snow run-off continues. For once the stream flow begins to fade the migration run of steelhead ends quickly.

A migrating steelhead spends an average of about 10 days in a stream before completing spawning and returning to Lake Superior. The young steelheads, after hatching, spend from 2 to 3 years in the stream before moving to the lake.

To the spring steelhead fisherman, the stream's water temperature holds the important key to success. For as the temperature reaches the 40-degree mark, the intensity of the spawning movement and the activity of the steelhead increases.

But no matter what the temperature, steelhead fishing will challenge all of your angling skills. About the time you think you're an "expert," you'll get skunked the next time out.

It's important to "read" the stream, looking for deep runs, places where the steelhead may pause on its tough travels upstream. Once you catch or locate a fish in a particular spot, chances are that particular stretch will always hold a steelhead. Many veteran steelheaders do nothing but fish from "spot" to "spot," ignoring the waters in-between.

Steelhead fishing requires much different equipment than conventional angling. To do it right, you need a stout 8-foot to 9-foot fly rod with a single action or automatic fly reel. If you don't know how to cast a fly rod, don't worry. The fly rod is not used in that way. The bait or lure is not cast but "swung" much like you'd swing a bobber and worm with a cane pole.

Nor do you use fly line. Rather, fill the fly reel with 8- to 12-pound test line. Now don't forget chest waders or hip boots. Wading is very necessary in steelhead fishing and the water is too cold to use tennis shoes.

The steelhead fisherman's arsenal includes spawn bags (salmon eggs clustered in a net sack), single salmon eggs, steelie puffs or sponge balls (imitate a cluster of spawn and yarn flies) (see illustration).

The basic drifting rig or terminal tackle includes a swivel, 12- to 20-inch leader and a No. 4 salmon-egg type hook with a turned eye. A short 3 to 6 inch drop line, tied to the swivel, is used to attach split-shot weights.

The amount of weight depends on the strength of the current. It's best to add just enough splitshot to keep the bait "ticking" along the bottom rocks.

It's important to remember that the steelhead really is not in an aggressive feeding mood. They seldom will chase any bait for any distance. A strike is made more out of reflex action than hunger.

Thus, your bait must almost hit the trout on the nose before you'll get a strike, then the strike won't normally come as any jolt.

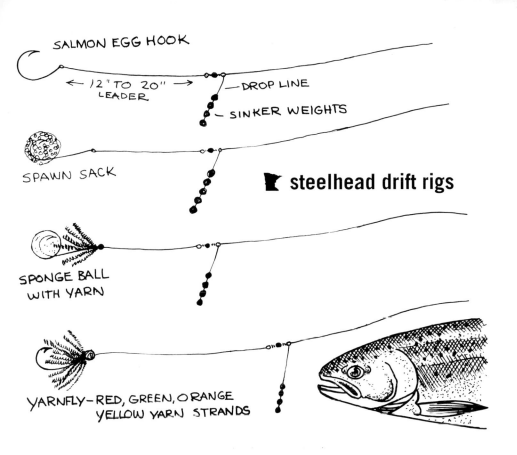

SALMON EGG HOOK

← 12" TO 20" → LEADER

—DROP LINE

— SINKER WEIGHTS

SPAWN SACK

steelhead drift rigs

SPONGE BALL WITH YARN

YARNFLY—RED, GREEN, ORANGE YELLOW YARN STRANDS

Rather, your bait will merely pause or stop. Then, set the hook immediately. It may be a rock, a snag or the current, but set the hook anyway. It also could be a steelhead.

Because the bait must pass so closely to a steelhead, one drift through a deep run or pool is not indication of steelhead's presence. Be sure to make many drifts through a likely looking spot before moving on.

Early in the steelhead season, spawn bags are the most productive bait. The actual eggs give off a scent, of course, which travels ahead of the sack. This is beneficial when the steelhead streams are murky and high. As the streams clear,

sponge balls or yarn flies become effective. Generally, the clearer the water, the smaller the bait.

Sponge balls and yarn are made up of red, red-orange and yellow colors, resembling actual spawn. Some yarn fly tiers occasionally add green or white yarn to the fly. As the name indicates, the yarn fly is made up of actual yarn tied in a bundle on a hook with a snell knot and trimmed to look like a cluster of trout eggs.

You can also add one strand of yarn to a spawn bag or sponge ball to serve as an attractor and help hide the hook shank.

Don't expect to master the art of steelhead fishing on your first attempt.

Successful steelheading requires a sensitive touch and an understanding of stream fishing. And both only come through practice. The beginner should probably start with actual spawn bags, which are available at bait stores along the North Shore.

Once you hook a steelhead, hang on. The fish will likely leap, roll and streak downstream, using the powerful force of the current to its advantage. Rather than try to stop a surging trout, it's best to follow the fish downstream if possible. Chances are, the steelhead will stop once

it reaches a pool where you can resume the battle with better odds for success.

The steelhead can be beached or netted. But don't try to scoop up a steelhead that still had some fight. I tried that once on a nice steelhead that fishing partner, Ron Weber, had on the line.

Weber, the man who introduced the Rapala to American anglers after discovering the lure in Duluth, was a diehard steelhead angler. Ron took his fishing very seriously, having developed a steelhead addiction in his younger days growing up on the North

how to drift fish

Angle your cast upstream to (A) the closest part of a likely riffle or run. Hold your rod tip high as your bait drifts, keeping the line taut until the bait is well downstream of your position. Make several drifts through the same zone and then reel up and make (B) a slightly longer cast at the same angle. Repeat the procedure until the entire riffle or run has been thoroughly covered (C and beyond).

Shore. Ron even went steelhead fishing on his honeymoon.

So there was Ron, battling this giant of a steelhead and hoping I could help with the landing net. The moment I scooped with the net, the steelhead streaked.

In an instant, the fish raced right between my legs. A split-second later, it was off.

I remember standing there, entwined in limp fishing line and wearing a sad face.

Ron was wearing a sad face, too.

Fishing Lake Superior

A half century ago, Lake Superior was a fishing desert. It was awesome to look at but lousy to fish.

Lake Superior was Minnesota's version of a dead sea. Excessive commercial netting and the stupidity of shippers who built the St. Lawrence Seaway that allowed the invasion of the sea lamprey from the Atlantic Ocean had decimated its once famed population of lake trout.

When the lampreys reached Lake Superior, they preyed on and killed the largest lake trout. Meanwhile, the nets of commercial fishermen were uncontrolled. Other game fish, such as steelhead (migratory rainbow trout) also fell victim to the blood-sucking lampreys.

When the lake trout population collapsed, so did the commercial fishing.

And sport fishing also disappeared.

In the 1960s and 70s, however, fisheries scientists achieved a breakthrough in the control of alien lampreys. A lampricide was developed that would selectively kill the young lampreys in the

streams where they hatch without harming fish life.

Gradually, the lamprey population was knocked back. Never eliminated but severely controlled.

Since then, Lake Superior has been on a slow comeback, thanks to massive trout stocking, led by the U.S. Fish and Wildlife Service plus fisheries agencies in Minnesota, Michigan, Wisconsin and Canada.

Fish by the millions—lake trout, rainbows, browns and several salmon species were stocked over the years. And now the comeback is largely complete. Minnesota's fisheries scientists believe Superior lake trout can expand on their own without additional stocking.

Today, Minnesota's share of Lake Superior harbors more lake trout than prior to the lamprey eel invasion. In other words, the angling future on Lake Superior is now. And more anglers are beginning to discover the "new" hotspot, trolling out on the big lake or casting from shore.

Keep in mind, Lake Superior is not your everyday fishing lake. This is a cold ocean, one capable of sinking ocean-going vessels. Common sense and boating know-how are important. Venturing far from shore without a compass, a marine radio and other safety gear is, well, stupid.

Fortunately, it isn't necessary to boat far out into the lake to find fish. Nor is it usually necessary to fish deep. Throughout most of the fishing season, trout and

Trout

salmon are catchable within 30 feet of the surface.

Superior Fishin' Savvy

There are several ways to pursue trout in the company of Lake Superior.

You can cast from Lake Superior's shores for lake trout or rainbows or salmon on any given day, weather permitting. The water goes deep and cold very fast on Minnesota's North Shore, which means a lake trout or salmon can be comfortable cruising the shore within your casting range. Try casting trout spoons and spinners.

In springtime, when the snows melt and the streams along the North Shore roar to life, the spring spawning run of rainbow trout (steelhead) begins to

appear in places like Knife River, Devils Track, Lester, Sucker.

The migrating native rainbows, also known as steelhead, are catchable, although closely protected by DNR. Check the fishing regulations. Populations of steelhead have been in decline for reasons still unclear. Hatchery-raised steelheads also are in the streams and are identified by its clipped adipose fin.

In the meantime, a new strain of rainbow seems to be making a go in Superior.

Fishing Kamloops

Originally stocked in 1972, the kamloop trout, which is a rainbow hybrid, has been an unabashed success in Lake Superior. While the average size runs in the 3 to 6 pound range, kamloops 28 inches long and weighing more than 10 to 12 pounds are roaming the lake and swimming up North Shore streams.

Kamloops also seem to be catchable for much of the year, starting in January as the fish gather near stream mouths. Starting in March and April, the hybrid rainbow congregates in streams to feed on smelt and other baitfish. When in the river mouths, kamloops will take spinners or spoons or spawn sack rigs drifted with the current. Slip bobber rigs also work with wax worms for bait, fished on small jigs.

The fall months, starting in late September, also are excellent for kamloops as the trout follow migrating salmon and lake trout to shore regions. Spoons, such as Little Cleos and Luhr Jensen

Trout

Krocodiles, are effective when casting from shore.

Upward of 100,000 yearling kamloops are stocked every year along the North Shore, of which roughly 10 percent survive to adulthood.

Trolling Gitchee Gumee

You're lucky. This is a great time to go trolling for lake trout or salmon on Minnesota's side of Lake Superior. Why? Because there's something to catch.

In the spring of 1969, I remember driving the North Shore of Lake Superior and wondering why not a boat could be seen on the lake. And this was on a calm day. Only later did I learn that Lake Superior was more like Lake Inferior in the mind of sport anglers. Smelt netters and steelheaders gathered on the shores of Lake Superior, but the lake's famed lake trout were more rare than skinny dippers.

Now the lake trout are back.

And catchable. From large charter boats. Or large private fishing boats. Or even small fishing boats—if you watch the weather and the waves.

Trolling for lake trout is possible along Minnesota's North Shore from Duluth Harbor to Grand Portage and beyond. To keep it simple, you can troll spoons with 100-foot flat lines or you can add weights or divers to troll at greater depths. Serious trollers also utilize downriggers.

The best trolling depths vary with the sun and the weather and the lake's water temperature. In early season, lake trout may be caught at depths of 20 feet or less. As the water warms, lake trout may hang at depths of 30 to 40 feet or more.

For newcomers, the best trolling method is to run parallel to shore, zigzagging in and out in search of fish locations. Vary the trolling depth of each line until the "hot depth" is determined. Watch fishing electronics.

Once a gathering of lake trout is located, troll in a figure 8 pattern over the area.

Spoons are popular but stickbaits, such as Jointed Rapalas and Bomber Long A models, are effective in early season. When the water warms to about 45 degrees, spoons tend to be most productive, although there are no hard, fast rules.

If you're a novice at trolling, the fastest lesson for learning is to hire a charter boat and ask questions. Most charter captains are anxious to share the joy of fishing on Superior. There's plenty of room out there for everybody.

Weather is a big factor on Lake Superior. When in doubt, ask for forecasts. The best winds for fishing tend to be westerly or southerly.

A strong east or nor'easter often means a poor day of fishing. And, for sure, a rough one, too.

Trout Lakes

County/City/Town	Species	County/City/Town	Species
Aitkin County		Cash***	LT
Blue	RB	Cherokee***	LT
Taylor*	BT, RT	Chester*	BRW
Townline (Loon)*	BT	Clearwater***	LT
Anoka County		Crooked***	LT
Cenaiko*	BT, RT	Crystal***	LT
Becker County		Daniels***	LT
Bad Medicine	RT	**Cook County**	
Hanson*	RT	Davis***	LT
Meadow	BRW	Duke*	BT
Beltrami County		Duncan***	LT
Benjamin*	RT	Dunn***	LT
Carlton County		Esther*	RB, SPL
Corona*	RT	Extortion*	SPL
Carver County		Fay***	BT, LT
Courthouse*	BT, RT, BRW, LT	Feather*	BT
Cass County		Fern, West***	LT
Diamond*	RT	Fern***	LT
Hazel*	RT	Flour	LT
Little Andrus (Snowshoe)*	BT	French***	LT
Margeret*	RT	Frost***	LT
Marion*	BT	Gabimichigani***	LT
Perch*	BT	Gadwall* ***	BT
Roosevelt	LT	Gillis***	LT
Tepee*	RT	Gneiss***	LT
Willard*	RT	Gogebic* ***	BT
Clearwater County		Gordon***	LT
Long, South	RT	Greenwood	LT
Wapatus (Island)*	RT	Gunflint	LT
Cook County		Howard***	LT
Alder***	LT	Jap* ***	LT
Alpine***	LT	Jasper ***	LT
Alton***	RT, LT	Jim	LT
Bat***	LT	Junco*	BT
Bath*	BT	Karl***	LT
Bearskin, East***	LT	Kemo	LT
Bearskin, West	LT	Kimball*	RB, BRW
Bench* ***	BT	Kingfisher***	LT
Bingshick* ***	BT	Leo*	RB, SPL
Birch	RT	Lima*	BT
Blue Snow***	LT	Lizz* ***	BT
Bogus*	SPL	Loft*	BT
Boys* **	BT	Long Island***	LT
Carrot*	BT	Loon	LT
		Magnetic***	LT
		Maraboeuf	LT

Trout lakes list

*designated trout lake   **special regulations   ***located in BWCAW

Brook Trout = BT   Rainbow Trout = RT   Splake = SPL   Brown Trout = BRW   Lake Trout = LT

County/City/Town	Species	County/City/Town	Species
Margaret*	BT, RT	Thompson*	RT, BRW
Mavis* ***	BT	Thrasher*	BT, SPL
Mayhew, Little	LT	Thrush* **	BT, SPL
Mayhew	LT	Topper* ****	BT
Meditation* ***	BT	Town***	LT
Mesaba***	LT	Trip*	BT
Mink*	RT, SPL	Trout, Little***	LT
Misquah***	LT	Trout	RT, LT
Missing Link* ***	BT	Turnip* **	BT
Monker	BT	Tuscarora***	LT
Moose***	LT	Vale* ***	BT
Moosehorn*	SPL	Vernon***	LT
Moss	LT	Wee* ****	BT
Mountain***	LT	Wench* ***	BT
Muckwa*	RT	Winchell***	LT
Mulligan* ***	BT	Wine***	LT
Musquash*	SPL		
North Shady*	BT	**Crow Wing County**	
North	LT	Allen*	RT
Olga*	SPL	Big Trout	LT
Olson*	BT	Mallen Mine Pit*	BT
Owl	LT	Manuel Mine Pit*	RT
Pancore (Lost)*	BT, SPL	Martin Mine Pit*	BT, RT
Partridge***	LT	Pennington Mine Pit*	BT
Pemmican* ***	BT	Pleasant*	BT
Peter***	LT	Portsmouth Mine Pit*	BT, RT
Pike, West***	LT	Sagamore Mine Pit*	BT
Pine Mountain*	BT	Section 6 Mine Pit*	BRW
Pine***	LT	Snoshoe Mine Pit*	BT
Pine*	RT, SPL	Strawberry*	RT
Popular	RB, LT	Yawkey Mine Pit*	RT
Portage, Little*	BT		
Portage*	SPL	**Dakota County**	
Powell***	LT	LacLavon	RT
Ram* ****	RT, LT		
Red Rock***	LT	**Hennepin County**	
Rog* ***	BT	Christmas	RT
Rose***	LT	Little Long	RT
Saganaga, Little***	LT		
Saganaga***	LT	**Hubbard County**	
Sea Gull***	LT	Blacksmith*	RT
Shoe*	LT	Blue	RT
Sled*	BT	Crappie*	RT
Snipe***	LT	Newman*	RT
Sock* ***	BT		
South***	LT	**Itasca County**	
State***	LT	Bee Cee*	RT
Surber*	BT	Bluewater	LT
Swan***	LT	Canisteo Pit	LT
Talus*	RT	Caribou	LT
		Erskine*	BT, RT
		Kremer*	SPL, BRW
		Larson*	RT, SPL
		Larue Mine Pit	RT

Trout Lakes

County/City/Town Species		County/City/Town Species	
Lucky*	BRW	Judd*	RT, SPL
Moonshine*	RT	Kekekabic, Little***	LT
Nickel*	RT	Kekekabic***	LT
Pokegama	LT	Knife, Little***	LT
Tioga Mine Pit*	RT	Knife***	LT
Trout	LT	Lake of the Clouds***	LT
Lake County		Lunar***	LT
Ahmakose***	LT	Makwa***	LT
Ahsub* ***	BT	Missionary***	LT
Amoeber***	LT	Neglige* ***	BT
Balsam	BT	Norway*	BT, SPL
Bean*	RT, SPL	Ogishkemuncie***	LT
Bear*	RT, SPL, LT	Ojibway	LT
Beaver Hut*	BT	Peanut*	BT
Beetle*	BT	Rabbit***	LT
Benson*	SPL	Raven***	LT
Bone*	RT, SPL	Scarp (Cliff *	RT
Cherry***	LT	Section 8*	BT
Conchu* ***	BT	Sema***	LT
Cramer Homestead	BT	Shoofly*	BT
Cross Cut	BT	Skull* ***	BT
Cypress***	LT	Snowbank***	LT
Dan*	BT	Sonju*	BRW
Divide*	RT	Steamhaul*	BT, SPL
East*	BT	Steer*	BT
Echo*	RT, SPL	Strup***	LT
Eikela*	BT	Thomas***	LT
Ennis*	BT, LT	Tofte*	RT, SPL
Ester***	LT	Tommy	BT
Explorer***	LT	Topaz***	LT
Finn Pond	BT	Trapper*	BT
Found* ***	BT, RT	Twenty Three	BT
Fraser***	LT	Unnamed (Pear)*	BT
Gijikiki***	LT	Weapon	BT
Glacier Pond 1*	RT	Wisini***	LT
Glacier Pond 2*	BT, RT	**Meeker County**	
Goldeneye*	BT	Mud, Little	RT
Gypsy*	BT	**Olmsted County**	
Hanson***	LT	Foster-Arend**	BT, RT, BRW
Hare	RT	**Otter Tail County**	
Highlife	BT	Bass*	RT
Hogback*	RT	**Pine County**	
Holt***	LT	Grindstone	RT, BRW, LT
Homestead	BT	**St. Louis County**	
Ima***	LT	Alruss* ***	BT, RT
Indian*	BT	Briar*	RT
Jouppi*	BT		

Trout lakes list
*designated trout lake   **special regulations   ***located in BWCAW
Brook Trout = BT   Rainbow Trout = RT   Splake = SPL   Brown Trout = BRW   Lake Trout = LT

Trout Lakes

County/City/Town	Species	County/City/Town	Species
Burntside	LT	Miners Mine Pit*	BT, RT
Camp 4*	BT, RT	Mirror*	BRW
Ceda *	RT	Mukooda	LT
Chant*	BT, RT	Norberg*	RT
Clearwater (Clear)*	RT	Normanna*	BT
Cruiser	LT	Oyster***	LT
Cub*	BT	Pickerel*	BT, RT
Deepwater*	BRW	Regenbogen*	LT
Dry, Little*	SPL, BRW	Spring Hole*	BT
Dry*	SPL, BRW	St. James Mine Pit*	BT, RT
Elbow, Little*	RT	Takuchich***	LT
Embarrass Mine Pit*	BT, RT	Trout, Big***	LT
Fat***	LT	Trout, Little	LT
Gun***	LT	Trygg* ***	BT
Hanson*	SPL	Upper Twin Ponds*	RT
High*	BT, RT, SPL		
Jammer (James)*	RT	***Stearns County***	
Judson Mine Pit*	RT	Big Watab	RT, BRW
Kinney Mine Pit	RT	***Washington County***	
Lac La Croix***	LT	Square**	RT
Loaine (Sand)*	RT		
Louis (Jacob)* ***	BT, RT		

Largemouth Bass

Largemouth Bass

Bucket Mouth

The Minnesota largemouth bass is an unsung superstar.

In fact, a largemouth bass is a success story of its own. No hatcheries. No stocking. And except for a few lakes, no special protections. The largemouth is a survivor and a provider of wonderful fishing enjoyment to state anglers.

Thanks to this amazing fish, Minnesota now has bassin' boys. Today, mature, responsible men and women go dingy over the fish. They ride in $30,000 bass boats; wear bass clothes and bass patches, cast bass rods, reels and baits. They compete in bass tournaments, and if some gizmo promises more bass, they buy it.

Here's what's interesting: the best thing that ever happened to a Minnesota largemouth is more folks wanting to catch it. Now we have bass clubs and bass fans paying attention to the fish and its future.

Down south where the bass is king, the good ol' boys think of Minnesota and bass a bit like they view Texans. Texans wear big cowboy hats, but they got no cows. Minnesota has water, they figure, but no thinkin' bass would live where the water freezes. Well, the good ol'boys are dead wrong. Many times I've been in famed bass waters down south, just wishing I was back on Minnetonka or Calhoun or a thousand other Minnesota bass lakes.

By almost any measure, Minnesota has excellent largemouth fishing. It's a fact that used to be a secret. No more.

It was a bass fishing enthusiast from Fergus Falls, who in the early 1970s launched the first organized bass fishing club in the state. Lynn Schultz, who called himself the "phishin' pharmacist," started the North Star Bassmasters Club and Minnesota quickly entered the era of bass fishing tournaments and bass hoopla.

The first bass fishing tournament in the state was held on Lake Minnetonka in the early 1970s. Both smallmouth and largemouth were legal catches and live bait was allowed. Some of Minnesota's best fished the 2-day contest, including Al Lindner, Ted Capra and the like. I competed and finished high enough to win back my entry fee.

Gary Roach, who is now famed as Mr. Walleye, won the event with a heavy stringer of smallies caught with leeches, making him Minnesota's first bass tournament champion.

Since then, Minnesota's largemouth bass has steadily gained admirers. You'll find bass widely distributed in the waters of Minnesota, except in northeast lakes where smallmouth normally take the place of its largemouth relative.

Despite their many differences, some anglers still confuse the two basses. The largemouth is most readily identified by the rather distinct lateral line along its sides: that and its big mouth. The corners of a largemouth's jaw extend past the eye, whereas the smallmouth's jaws do not.

Largemouth Bass

The smallmouth is also more golden in color and its eyes have a reddish hue.

Smallies and largemouth are both in the sunfish family, but you'll find them in different habitats. Largemouth fare best in weedy lakes or the back channels of rivers. The smallmouth is more at home in rock-strewn lakes and rocky rivers.

Of the two, the largemouth bass is most versatile. It can tolerate waters that are murky or clear, warm or cold, unpolluted or polluted. It will live in farm ponds, giant reservoirs or den room aquariums. It will roam in 3-foot shallows or 20-foot drop-offs. It'll smack a hundred different lures or baits in a day. Or none at all. Or it'll nail one lure of one color and refuse all the rest. That's the key to the popularity of the largemouth bass. Every fishing trip is a new ball game. You can chase walleyes with leeches day in and day out and probably have success. Not so with Mr. Bass.

Bass Patterns

So—if you want to discover the magnetism of bass fishing, prepare for an adventure. Bass anglers call it "finding the pattern."

The "pattern" is that unknown combination of habitat, lure, color, speed, and timing that will produce bass on any given day. And it's that daily search for the pattern that makes bass fishing so interesting.

This facet of bass fishing is never more apparent than in a tournament. Tournaments have been praised and criticized in debates over the propriety of competitive fishing. But fishing for money has proven one thing: the bass is the toughest competitor of all.

I've watched some of the best bass fishermen in the country gather on the same waters. You'd expect they would all take limits with the winner determined by who lucked into the biggest fish. But that's not the way it works.

On the same day, some of the "pros" will fill the boat; others will take a few and still others get skunked outright. The next day, the results may be the opposite.

Why? It's the pattern. The pattern changes. The bass may move. They may want something flashy or something dull. They may want something fast or something slow. They might be energetic; they might be lazy. Who knows? But the fisherman who discovers the pattern is the one who beats the largemouth bass.

fishing paw-tner

Everybody already knows one pattern: that bass tend to be sunrise and sunset fish, that they are feeding and therefore catchable. Who hasn't heard about the lone angler who paddles quietly into the silent lily pads on an early morn, armed with live frogs and lots of hope? Like some solitary watchman, he waits for the telltale gurgling sound of a lunker bass, slurping a meal near the grassy banks. Ever so gently, almost in slow motion, he pitches the wiggly frog into the fading ripples. And… boom. In a flash, the gaping jaws of a largemouth sweep in the defenseless frog and the fight is on.

That's the classic image of bass fishing. Go early or go late, otherwise forget it.

There is some truth to that. But bass fishermen these days don't suck their thumbs waiting for the sun to rise or set. Bass can be caught at any time of the day. Or night for that matter. It's just a matter of; you guessed it, finding the pattern.

Bass Lifestyles

Minnesota's bass fishing season—when the fish become legal catches—does not usually open until the last days of May. By then, the bulk of the bass spawning is well underway.

During spawning the male bass is protective of the nest and attacks almost anything that comes near. Thus, the male is vulnerable to the hook. Without paternal protection, marauding bluegills or perch quickly eat the young bass or the eggs. Fortunately, the bass is quite prolific. It is not necessary and no one expects every bass nest to be successful. If a few are protected as much as possible, a lake's bass supply will be plentiful.

In Minnesota, bass spend spring, summer and fall in water less than 20 feet deep. On any given day, you'll find bass in 2 feet of water or 20 feet of water on the same lake. But as a rule of thumb, concentrate your search for bass in water less than 20 feet. This is because in most Minnesota lakes the weed line—that point where aquatic vegetation quits growing for lack of sunlight—is between 10 to 20 feet (see illustration on next page).

Remember also that the bass is a cover freak. Cover means places to hide, stalk, lurk, rest or lollygag. Cover includes aquatic vegetation (cabbage, milfoil, lily pads), trees, docks, brush, boulders or overhanging bank grass.

I've had many wonderful fishing companions over the years, but Raven is the best one with four legs.

Largemouth Bass

If a bass has cover, the water depth is almost immaterial. A contented bass has no qualms about living in extremely shallow water. I know that's hard to imagine on bright, sunshiny days when your brows sweat just thinking about being outside. You'll want to believe that every fish in the lake is down in the cool, dark depths, hiding from the sun.

Not so folks. You might fish the shallows on just such a day; those bass are not gone.

Where Bass Lurk

On a typical bass lake in Minnesota, you'll run into one of two types of cover structures. You'll find lakes with emergent bulrushes, cattails or other above water vegetation on the shallow flats or bays up to depths of about 5 feet. Beyond 5 feet, you're apt to find no weed growth or very sparse bunches. Think about that. If the bass seeks out

cover, what choice does the fish have but to live within those 5-foot depths or less where the cover exists?

In other bass lakes, you find the usual shallow water emergent vegetation, along with a band of underwater or submerged vegetation growing out into depths of 10 to 20 feet of water, depending on the water's clarity. The bass then have a wider choice of locations. They may at times move up into the shallow flats to feed. Then, they'll retreat, moving back to the safety of deeper water and dense vegetation, often lingering on the outside edges.

At first glance, you might think that fishing lakes with less cover would be more productive, since the bass has fewer places to hide. That's not necessarily so. Those lakes may also have much smaller bass populations that are concentrated in a small area or in many small areas. In that situation, they also can be hard to

 **where to find largemouth bass**

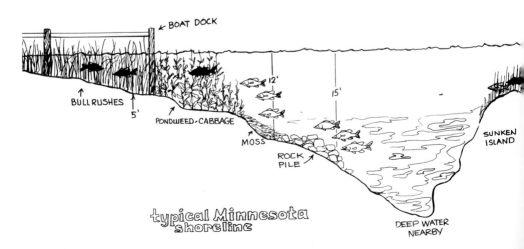

BOAT DOCK

BULL RUSHES

5'

PONDWEED-CABBAGE

MOSS

12'

15'

ROCK PILE

SUNKEN ISLAND

typical Minnesota shoreline

DEEP WATER NEARBY

find. The best bass lakes are those with an abundance and variety of cover. You'll have more area to fish, but there'll be more fish to find.

So you can see that bass fishing in Minnesota is largely a shallow water game. The aquatic weeds or the weed line (where vegetation stops growing) is as attractive structure to bass as drop-offs are to walleyes.

Bass anglers rely on their eyes more than those seeking other fish. Yet, a sonar depth finder is handy. It is not always possible to tell where the weeds stop (or start) by looking at a lake's surface. A depth finder will show such things clearly. If you still have trouble visualizing the weed line, drop floating buoy markers along the edge. Then cast or troll along those markers.

Of course, when the weeds stop growing, that means something in the underwater environment has changed. Usually, it's the depth. That means there's a drop-off or a change in bottom. In other words, structure. The bass is a fish whose behavior and haunts are regulated by structure.

But for bass, there's still another form of structure on almost every Minnesota lake. Man-made structure—boat docks, channels, marinas, bridge pilings, you name it. On some lakes there are so many docks lining the shore that bass anglers need look no further. To a bass, a boat dock is nothing but handy cover with shade.

How To Fish Milfoil

The invasion of milfoil into Minnesota waters prompted a major change in bass fishing technique. Milfoil grows on the surface in a mat of brittle, clingy weeds. Underneath, the milfoil looks like a giant forest with tall trunks and heavy tops.

Since milfoil grows in deeper water, entire bays become blanketed and impossible to penetrate with lures, except for heavy weedless jigs. When milfoil arrived, most bass anglers cursed the alien weed. But not anymore.

"Although it's not popular to say, Eurasian milfoil is one of the best things that ever happened to Minnesota's largemouth bass population. It provides cover and shelter that never before existed," notes Chip Leer, a pro bass guide.

Indeed, bass fishing in Lake Minnetonka seemed to boom with the advent of milfoil. Other species, such as crappies and bluegills, also seemed to grow to larger average sizes. One theory is milfoil gave more advantage to predators than the native cabbage (pondweed) and, thus, fewer fish lived to become stunted.

While milfoil is still too "new" to Minnesota lakes to claim the alien infestation is harmless or beneficial, there seems to be little doubt the bass have enjoyed the new cover. But there's still those thick mats covering bassy haunts. What to do?

Aside from casting to the edge with jig-worms, spinner-baits, Carolina rigs or crankbaits, the best way to reach bass amid the milfoil is to penetrate the jungle. This is best done with a 5/8th to 1-ounce skirted jig with a brushy weed guard. The jig is normally tipped with

Largemouth Bass

pork rind or plastic worm, or something like the Berkley power craws.

The jig is dropped vertically through the top mat of milfoil or tossed to holes and pockets and allowed to sink to the bottom. When the jig reaches the bottom, jiggle or bounce it for a second or two. If a bass is present, you'll feel the "thunk." Set the hook and horse the fish out of the milfoil fast.

Jigging milfoil holes is a tedious method, however. Plus, there is so much milfoil that theoretically, one could jiggle jigs for hours and never be in bassy haunts. In other words, some milfoil spots are better than others.

Said Leer, "The best milfoil beds occur over structure, such as break lines, gravel beds or rocks. Think of milfoil as the roof over a really good spot."

Bass pro, Karl Kleman, says green milfoil tends to hold fish more than plants that are brown and dying. "I find the outer edges of milfoil are most productive in early morning and late evening or on overcast days. When the sun hits, bass move deeper into the milfoil mat."

Kleman said once his jig hits bottom he "shakes" it and raises the jig a few inches and shakes it again. Next, he raises the jig 3-5 feet and drops it back down.

"I watch the line for twitches or limpness that indicates a bass hit the bait on the way down," he said.

Keep this in mind; bass tend to school under milfoil. Sometimes it's possible to catch two or more bass from the same hole in the milfoil.

Bass On Live Bait

Allow me to reveal a prejudice: I think it's a shame to take bass with live bait. It wouldn't bother me if they outlawed the use of frogs, minnows, night crawlers, and leeches for bass fishing.

This is an easy prejudice for me to sustain because I never keep a bass. And it's much easier to release a bass taken on artificials compared to the gut hooks you use with night crawlers for bait. Yet, to be fair, to some folks, bass fillets are good eatin' and it matters not if the fish has swallowed the hook.

There's another reason for my lack of enthusiasm for live bait bass fishing. To catch a largemouth on fake bait is what makes the whole thing challenging. The very nature of the bass forces any serious bass angler to sharpen his or her skills, if one is limited to artificials.

A skilled bass addict must acquire casting marksmanship and know how to effectively work an arsenal of lures. One must develop a sense of touch to master plastic worm fishing, for example. Live bait compromises these skills. A bass is a push over for a night crawler.

In the spirit of sport, I encourage bass beginners to strive toward the exclusive use of artificials. Sure, there are times when the ONLY way to catch a bass is with live bait, particularly in cold-water periods and following cold fronts. So what? So what if you get skunked sticking with artificials? It's more important how you caught your bass, rather than how many you caught. I think the fishing fraternity often forgets that.

Please understand I'm not accusing live bait anglers of being morons or meat hogs. The tradition of pitching live frogs to unsuspecting bass is a proven, respectable method of bass fishing. I've done plenty of it and I can't remember when I ever had a lousy time.

Bass On Artificials

Your choice of bass ammo is infinite. No fish has stretched the imagination of lure inventors like the largemouth. You can fill three tackle boxes and still find enough "new" to warrant another box.

The same can be said of rods and reels. A bass angler never has enough rods and reels. Each is readied to do battle with a different pattern in mind. The average bassin' man's rod has a rather stout butt and medium flexible tip.

Most bass lures weigh 1/4th of an ounce or more. To adequately cast lighter lures, tube jigs or top waters, you'll have to add another rod with more flexible tip.

The most popular choice in reels is a free-spool casting reel, although many anglers prefer a medium-sized open spinning reel instead. In reality, most of us carry both bait casting and open-faced spinning outfits.

If you're avoiding bait casting reels because of the danger of backlashes, it's time to suck it up. Put some brains in your thumb. Practice in the backyard. If you intend to climb the angling ladder of memorable experiences, you'll have to master a bait cast reel. Actually, it's easier than saying Abu Garcia.

Raven is an outside dog, but has a warm, cozy bed in Ron's kitchen.

Largemouth Bass

Choosing fishing line for Minnesota bass fishing involves making some subjective judgments. In most fishing situations, 10-pound test is adequate. The late Harlow Ellsworth, the Park Rapids "hawg" hunter, would have choked on his spinner-bait skirt if he heard that. Harlow was strictly a big bass fisherman. He went with big lures on big line, 20-pound test or more. He didn't want any fish of a lifetime breaking off in the bulrushes.

Today, bass anglers not only have heavy monofilament, but also may choose from many so-called "super lines" with hi-tech fibers or processing that makes them small in diameter, but nearly unbreakable, such as Spiderwire and Berkley's Fireline. These are best used in tough cover, such as docks and wood. Fireline is especially sensitive for use with plastic worms or vertical jigging when "feel" is important to detect strikes.

Best Bass Lures

If we dumped all the bass lures into a pile and sorted them into general categories, we'd end up with six piles: plastic worms,

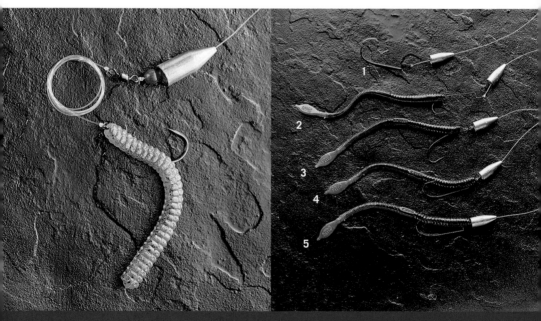

⯈ how to rig plastic worms

Carolina Rig: Thread a 1/4- to 1-ounce bullet sinker and a glass or plastic bead onto your line and attach a barrel swivel. Tie on an 18- to 36-inch leader of lighter mono and attach a worm hook. Push the hook into a buoyant worm and out the side, leaving the point exposed.

Texas Rig: (1) Thread a bullet sinker onto your line and tie on a worm hook. (2) Insert the point of the hook into the head, push it in about 1/2 inch and bring it out the side. (3) Push the hook all the way through the bait so only the hook eye protrudes at the head. (4) Rotate the hook 180 degrees. (5) Push the hook into the bait; the hook point should almost come out the other side and the bait should hang straight.

crankbaits, spinner-baits, spoons, flip-pin' jigs and top water lures.

If you had but one to choose, which would it be?

Most bassin' veterans would probably say the plastic worm. This chunk of plas-tic is the greatest bass catching invention since the live frog. The bass angler who can't fish a plastic worm is like a bird that can't fly. You won't get very far.

Properly rigged, the plastic worm is the most weedless lure available. Prop-erly fished, it will take bass when most everything else fails.

The worm itself comes in a variety of shapes and colors. Some have straight tails, some curly. Some have legs, some don't. And so forth. Pick what you like. They all work.

Color can be important. Any assort-ment should include the colors black, blue, purple, grape and green or combi-nations. You'll probably discover that black, purple and grape work best in most situations. In murky water, how-ever, green is often effective. And in clear water, blue may be best.

The best color of the day is discovered by trial and error. That's why it's important to have an assortment of worm colors.

The most common method of hook-ing a plastic worm is called "Texas rig," (see illustration) which includes a cone-shaped slip sinker and a specially designed worm hook.

Other worm rigs includes the jig-worm method, which features a bare lead-headed jig with a worm threaded on

the jig hook. No sinker is required with the jig-worm. The jig-worm is not entirely weedless and is best used on the edges of weed beds or in rocks.

A plastic worm tossed into the water is rather useless unless it is given the cor-rect action. Most lures provide their own bass-fooling gyrations. The plastic worm needs your help.

This is how it's done. With the worm properly rigged, cast it toward the waters of your choice and let it sink. Hold the rod at a 10 o'clock position (straight up is noon) and reel in the clack. Now slowly raise the rod to 11 o'clock and pause. By raising the rod, you've lifted the worm slightly off the bottom. Drop the rod again, reel in the slack and repeat.

Basically, you're "pumping" the worm back to the boat, letting it rise and fall, rise and fall over the bottom, through the weeds, brush piles or what-ever. You can literally cast the plastic worm into any kind of garbage you find and it won't "snag."

The bass almost always inhales the worm while it's falling. At a strike, you won't hear bells, parades or snapping rods. You won't hear anything. And you won't feel anything unless you're alert. I can only describe the feel of a bass strike on a plastic worm as a "deadening thunk" or "tic," telegraphed up the monofilament.

Also watch the line where it enters the water. When the bass strikes, you may see the line jump or twitch. At that moment, drop the rod forward, reel in the slack and slam the rod back to set the hook. All of that should take about one second.

Some fishermen like to let the bass run with the worm for a second or two. That's okay. But underwater filming has proven that the bass inhales the entire worm on the initial strike. Bass don't have big mouths for nothing.

A modification of the Texas worm rig is one called the "Carolina Rig." The only difference is the sinker placement. On the Texas worm rig, the sinker slides to the hook. On a Carolina Rig, the sinker is pinched to the line roughly 30 inches above the hook. This rig allows the floating worm to rise up from the bottom in a "do-nothing" mode. You can slowly "walk" the rig across the bottom until its time to re-cast.

One day on Lake Minnetonka, bass fishing champ, Mark Fisher and I enjoyed a hey-day catching plump, smallmouth bass on Carolina worm rigs cast to a deep, but bare rock hump. In the right situation, nothin's finer than the Carolina.

Pig 'N Jig Savvy

One of the great all-time bass baits also has an all-time great name: pig 'n jig.

The "pig" is a piece of real pork rind or a plastic replica and the "jig" is a heavy, skirted lead head with a weed guard designed for pitching in the most god awful, snaggy places, such as brush piles, under docks, milfoil beds.

In truth, there's probably never been a pig 'n jig that a bass wouldn't eat. I caught the largest bass of my life, a 13-

pounder, in Mexico's El Salto Lake, on a pig 'n jig.

A jig without the pig is normally called a flippin' jig. It's the same design except it's adorned with a plastic worm or power craw. The flippin' part of the name comes from the way the lure is pitched into tight cover spots or holes in weed beds. The key to good flippin' is accuracy and a quiet entry for the lure, so as not to spook a bass in shallow cover.

Next to the plastic worm, mastering the flippin' jig and the pig 'n jig should be high priority if you wanna be in the bassin' fraternity.

Crankbaits For Bass

Crankbaits are so named because you cast them out and crank 'em in. That's bassin' slang. If you saw a crankbait, you'd call it a lure or plug. And you'd be correct, too.

Crankbaits, trolled or cast, are ideal in combination with the new super lines. For example, Berkley Fireline slices or cuts the water with less resistance than monofilament; therefore your lure may run 2 to 6 feet deeper. Increased sensitivity of the new lines also telegraphs signals to the rod handle if the crankbait is vibrating correctly or is fouled by weeds.

Most of the crankbaits designed for bass have the appearance of lures that are fat or pregnant. They come in wild colors and in various designs. Some run shallow, 1 to 3 feet. Others go slightly deeper, 3 to 5, 5 to 7, 7 to 10, 10 to 12 or 12 feet and even deeper. The size of the lure's plastic lip determines the depth the lure is designed to run. You'll want to have an assortment. Sometimes you'll be fishing the deep outside edge of a weed bed, so you'll need a lure that dives quickly and stays deep. Other times, you may want to crank a bait that runs shallow over top of sunken weed beds. Get the picture?

I'm not convinced there is any standout or No. 1 color among crankbaits. The color that works for the day may be several or may be one shade. Only the bass can tell you.

When do you use crankbaits? There is no one perfect time. The type of water will determine if the use of crankbaits is even possible.

The best use of crankbaits is for testing unfamiliar bass haunts. A crankbait covers water in a hurry. If you nab a bass or two, the rule is cover the same water with a plastic worm or jig 'n pig and so forth. Sometimes the reverse is applicable. When a school of bass quits hitting a worm, show 'em a crankbait.

Consider the crankbait as part of the arsenal you'll want ready when solving the bass catching pattern of the day.

Crankbait Tuning

Sooner or later, your lure will start acting strange in the water. It won't dive or run straight. It'll roll to one side or the other. And if you increase speed, that crankbait will pop right out of the water when it should be swimming straight and digging deeper.

The problem? The lure needs tuning.

Note which way the lure tracks, right or left? Grab a needle nose pliers and bend the eye of the lure in the opposite direction. Careful now, you don't have to bend much. If the lure is running left, for example, gently bend the eye to the right. Test in the water and adjust accordingly.

Bass 'N Spinner-Baits

The spinner-bait is the shallow water version of a crankbait, so to speak. It's a good lure for locating bass because it can be fished more rapidly than flippin' jigs or Texas rigged worms.

The most interesting question is: Why does a bass inhale a spinner-bait? Nothing in nature looks like it: An L-shaped piece of wire, a spinning blade or two and a plastic skirt covering a weighted hook.

Mann's 20+
(deep diver)

Rapala Shad Rap
(medium runner)

Bagley Balsa B2
(shallow runner)

Largemouth Bass

You'd need a wild imagination to think a spinner-bait resembles anything edible.

Yet, who wants to argue with Mr. Bass? Bass are fools for spinner-baits. Since we're on the subject, northern pike and smallmouth bass also have a fetish for the strange lure.

In many ways, the spinner-bait is the perfect lure for the novice. Cast it out and bring it back in. Slow or fast. Doesn't matter. Or, give the spinner-bait some action by letting it swim and sink, swim and sink. Keep in mind, the spinner-bait is primarily a shallow water lure, most effective at less than 10-foot depths. To use a spinner-bait in deeper water, say 15 feet, the process is slow. Spinner-baits will catch fish at those depths but probably not as effectively as crankbaits.

A spinner-bait has another advantage. It's almost totally weedless, despite its looks. It'll come through the thickest bulrushes or cabbage tops with few hang-ups. The same is not true of milfoil, however.

Properly weighted, the spinner-bait—when pulled through the water—should ride vertically. A poorly designed model will turn or roll. Get your money back.

Spinner-baits are made with single, upturned jig hook, adorned with a plastic skirt. What color? The usual rule is go white or black in clear water; chartreuse or orange and other bright colors are best in stained or dinghy water.

You can customize a spinner-bait by adding a pork rind, twister tail or plastic worm to trail behind the hook (see illustration on page 141). When bass seem to be striking short, it might be good to add a second hook, a trailer behind the primary hook.

More Bass Weapons

While weedless spoons have declined in popularity, bass still love a Johnson Sil-

popular trailers

Pork Eel

Plastic Frog

Curlytail grubs

Pork Frog

SPINNER BAIT
ADD PORK RIND, OR
PLASTIC WORM
TO HOOK

customize a spinner bait

SILVER SPOON   PORK RIND

ver Minnow or the new spoon designs from Rapala or Northland Tackle.

You can fish the spoon like a lure, retrieving steadily. Or fish it like a plastic worm, letting it hop and fall through holes in a weed bed. Spoons are most effectively when adorned with a plastic skirt, pork rind or plastic tails.

While spoons have been around a long time, I became a real believer the day I shared a boat with legendary basser, Bill Dance, who nailed a 20-pound limit using only a spoon and a piece of Uncle Josh pork.

It just proves we anglers tend to chase the hot lure headlines. Even a lure that's been around awhile can still catch fish.

Magic Of Top Waters

Despite its oversized and gaping jaws, a largemouth bass is most famous for inhaling its meals off the water's surface. You name it, frogs, dragonflies, injured minnows; a bass seems to take special pleasure in eating prey in such a vulnerable position.

The late Harlow Ellsworth swears one morning he saw a big mama bass snatch a red-winged blackbird right off a lily pad. "First there was a bird there, then a swirl and no bird," Harlow told me. And it probably happened. Biologists have found baby muskrats and ducklings in bass bellies. Possibly even beer cans.

Generally top water fishing is best in early morning and late evening or on windless days when the water's surface is calm. Your popping, gurgling or sputtering top water lure may then get the attention it deserves from Mr. Bass.

No doubt the first surface lure ever invented to fool a bass looked like a frog. Today, the floating frog, built in weedless fashion, remains one of the favorites. Twitch it, jerk it or retrieve steadily amid the bulrushes or over the lily pads. Very few bass on the prowl can resist.

Other surface baits were designed to imitate injured minnows, such as the Smithwick Devilshorse or Frenzy Popper. There are many designs. Some make noise; others jiggle on surface. Still others, such as the floating-model Rapala, weren't necessarily designed to be a top water bait. Yet, the floating Rapala is extremely effective when it's twitched to dive momentarily, and then allowed to return to the surface. Watch out!

One of my favorite surface baits is known as the "buzz-bait." Actually, a buzz-bait is merely a modified spinnerbait with a spinning blade designed to sputter on the surface as it's retrieved. It's

also strictly a shallow water lure and most effective in water less than six feet deep or buzzed over sunken weed beds.

Talk about excitement. When a bass decides to gobble a buzz-bait, it's either a quiet slurp or one giant explosion. Witnessing a buzz-bait strike is so much fun, I sometimes use the buzz-bait even when I'd catch more fish with a different lure.

Still, a buzz-bait has one more advantage. On average, the lure can "call up" bigger bass than almost any other shallow lure.

If I had my druthers, I'd take every bass on the top. That's not realistic, of course. Fact is, ranked against other bass

fishing methods; top water fishing may produce the fewest bass.

Fewest fish, but most fun? Sometimes that's not a bad tradeoff.

Avoiding Bass Shutouts

No matter what lure is thrown (even the great plastic worm), there are two elements that can neutralize the most skilled bass angler: cold fronts and strong winds. Bass seem more sensitive to these elements than most other fish. A cold front is a weather phenomenon usually associated with high blue, cloudless skies and chilly breezes out of the northwest.

Biologists can't say why, but a severe

cold front can turn bass off almost completely for 72 hours. They move into heavy cover and seem to sulk. Under that condition, your best bet is to downsize. Try a 4-inch plastic worms (most are 6 to 8 inches long) or use live bait. And fish extremely slowly. A cold front means you're begging a bass to bite.

Wind is seldom a bass angler's friend.

Wind may rock your favorite weed bed. It can ruin top water action. It sabotages boat control. In my experience, bass under whitecaps get a case of lockjaw. Or maybe it's just my negative attitude. If you want to catch bass in the wind, you'd better believe you're doing the right thing. That said, I have seen times when wind and waves sweeping across a point of underwater weed beds seemed to stimulate a feeding binge.

Wind also is a nemesis to the plastic worm fisherman. Since line watching and feel are important, the wind—billowing your monofilament or super line—disrupts such communication and concentration.

If possible, cast downwind when fishing plastic worms in wind. You'll maintain some sense of feel. Or better yet,

throw a spinner-bait or crankbait, lures that make their own action and basically hook their own fish.

Cold water temperatures will slow bass down. Sometimes way down. That explains why few largemouth are caught through the ice. A bass in winter seems to like lah-lah land.

A couple of final bassin' thoughts: you can peak in the shallows of any clear water bass lake in Minnesota and conclude that I'm crazy. You won't see a bass. And you'll swear there's never a bass in less than 3 feet of water.

But if you checked out those same shallows over the course of 24 hours, you wouldn't say that. I've seen shallow flats change in one hour from fishless to being alive with keeper-sized bass.

Know this: bass have definite movement and feeding patterns. I can't predict them nor can I explain why a bass changes from a negative to a positive feeding mode. But of this I'm certain: feeding times do occur.

And one last word. Master the joy of catching bass on plastic. Once you do, you'll not only understand the national craze over bass fishing, you'll join in.

Bronze Beauty

Aaaah, the smallmouth bass; the fish so very good for your angling soul.

Smallies have it all. Feisty, muscular, sleek, sporting, the fish of finned perfection.

Chase the smallmouth and the quest will take you to Minnesota's wildest and most scenic garden spots. The famed waterways of the Boundary Waters Canoe Area Wilderness; the island maze of Rainy or Kabetogama or Lake Vermilion.

And a few not so wild. You can catch smallmouth in the heart of downtown Minneapolis under the traffic-laden bridges crossing the Mississippi River or the busy waters of Lake Minnetonka.

I remember wading for smallmouth bass along the banks of the Mississippi downstream from the Lake Street bridge. There I was, casting for this perfect fish while the morning rush hour traffic hummed overhead. It was kind of nifty... pulling in scrappy smallmouth that were lurking amid the urban masses.

Although smallmouth bass are native to Minnesota, today the fish is more widespread because of successful stocking efforts around the start of the 20th century. Smallies were first a river fish, but also thrive nicely in lake systems.

Smallies are willing targets throughout Minnesota's fishing season, except wintertime when, like its largemouth cousin, the fish is seldom caught.

Early season means shallow bass action on topwaters and spinner-baits; summer means tubeworms or crank-baits and autumn means deep jig fishing and lunkers.

When the dog days hit the lakes, you can almost always count on Minnesota's rivers to yield smallies.

Smallmouth fishing offers its own addictive qualities. First, it's a fish with a huge fighting heart: charging to the surface or plunging into the deep.

With a fly rod and popper, you can have tired arms after a day of floating the St. Croix or the Upper Mississippi or the Rum or the Zumbro or the Cannon or, well, the list goes on.

On light tackle, a 1-pound smallie will challenge your fish landing talents to the limit.

Generally, the smallie angler will use lighter tackle because smallmouth lures tend to be smaller than those for largemouth bass. A medium light spinning rod or casting outfit will suffice along with line weights in the 6- or 8-pound category. Heavier line will shorten your casting distance with light lures.

In addition, smallmouth are usually associated with relatively clear water, requiring the use of smaller diameter lines. Despite their fighting strength, smallmouth can usually be handled on light tackle. Unlike largemouth bass, smallies tend to hang around rock piles rather than brush piles.

Speaking of rocks: smallmouth are to rocks what leaves are to trees. They'll always be together. Or almost always. I've caught smallmouth in bulrushes and cabbage (pondweed) patches also.

Smallmouth Bass

low haunts and let it lay. Smallmouth, which tend to roam amid the rocks, will usually find it within a short time.

My buddy Gary Roach won Minnesota's first-ever bass tournament by simply flipping a leech into the shallows, using a splitshot for weight. A curious fish, the smallies that were roaming the shallow soon took the bait. Gary was watching the whole thing with the aid of Polarized sunglasses.

Using Artificial Lures

Smallmouth bass rely heavily on their eyesight to find food. So the most effective artificial lures are those that attract attention without speeding through the smallie's hangouts.

One of the smallmouth's favorite natural meals is crayfish. On Woman Lake, I've caught nice smallmouth whose lips and noses were bloodied and bruised from chasing crayfish into the rocks.

It follows that artificial lures that simulate or resemble crayfish are very effective. Tube jigs or power craws or crankbaits of brown, black, brown-orange or yellow are excellent choices.

Why not live crayfish?

To prevent the spread of rusty crayfish into Minnesota waters, it's illegal for bait

But these two aquatic plant species normally grow in hard sand bottoms and rock is often present in the form of boulders or stones about the size of a lumberjack's fist.

Owing to the smallmouth's rocky environment, its natural food diet consists almost totally of crayfish, minnows and insects.

Successful live baits for smallmouth include leeches and night crawlers along with shiner minnows. You can fish all three baits on the usual live bait rig, featuring a splitshot or 1/8- to 1/4-ounce slip-sinker, swivel and size 8 hook. You can vary the length of your monofilament leader, but 2- to 4-foot lengths are adequate. No steel leader, please.

When fishing live bait, smallmouth tend to act like bluegills. They like slow moving tidbits. A smallmouth might chase a fast moving night crawler, but they tend to inhale stationary bait or fall to the tantalizing wiggles of a leech. Often the ideal technique is to cast the leech or minnow into the smallie's shal-

Acme Kastmaster

Mepps Black Fury

shops to sell crayfish. While it's legal to use crayfish for live bait, the crayfish bait must be captured in the water you are fishing and may not be transported to other waters.

Lures that imitate crayfish are just about as good as the real thing anyway.

Granted, it's risky pitching jigs into rock-strewn bottoms, unless you arm yourself with snagless models which, surprisingly, are just that—snagless.

One day in the BWCAW, Bob Cary of Ely, Minn. pulled a sly ploy, casting a 1/16th ounce jig tipped with a white strip of pork rind. The combination really attracted lots of smallmouth, all of which made Bob hoot and holler as his catch for the day began to exceed mine.

Bob Cary, Ely's resident philosopher, author and all-around canoe paddler, is one of my favorite fishing companions. Except for the aforementioned trip, Bob always let me catch the most and the biggest. That's what he said anyway.

He once led me to West Lake in the BWCAW where we enjoyed nothing but the finest smallmouth action. While I didn't possess one of Bob's jig-worm concoctions, when the day ended I was comfortably ahead in numbers and weight (at least that's how I remember this story). My own lure of choice was a topwater, which on that day wasn't doing much. Afraid of suffering a rare defeat at the hands of Cary, I switched to a smallmouth basic, the Vibrax spinner. Size 1 or 2 spinners are about perfect for smallies. With size 3 spinners, the number of bass caught may decline, but you may catch larger ones. At least that's been my experience. Spinners with plain or dressed hooks both work fine.

I've found that smallmouth like a No. 2 gold blade spinner with a fox squirrel tail dressing on a single hook. Why a single hook? Less snags from a practical viewpoint. The other reason sounds like braggin. But I've had such fantastic luck with spinners that the treble hook becomes a burden when catching and releasing dozens of bass in a day.

I'll never forget that great day of smallie fishing with Bob. But I'll never duplicate it again. Bob said we were in West Lake. Later when I looked at a map, there must be one hundred "West" Lakes in the BWCAW-Quetico area.

Smallmouth make for good memories.

I'll never forget muskie fishing with a Suick, a wood lure about 8 inches long, when what should nail it but a 4-pound smallie.

Small crankbaits also belong in any smallmouth bass angler's tackle box.

Floating models work ideally as topwater or subsurface lures when cast over shallow reefs or rocky shorelines. Diving crankbaits are ideal for sharp shoreline breaks or sunken rock piles and reefs.

To a smallmouth, color counts.

One day on Lake of the Woods with Ron Weber, the man who found the original Rapala in Duluth, Minnesota, Ron was testing a new-colored Rapala that is best described as bathroom blue. The smallmouth bass absolutely would not leave the lure alone. Near as we could tell, color was the key because other Rapalas of a different color did not work as well.

It's important to experiment with color when chasing the smallmouth. I've seen times, for example, when a copper colored spinner blade on a small jig and spinner vastly out-performed the usual silver or chrome spinner blade. The old adage: dark days, dark lures; bright days, bright lures often holds true for smallies.

Let's not forget spinner-baits for smallmouth.

There was a time when I pooh-poohed spinner-baits for smallies but not any more. I spent a wonderful day drifting down the St. Croix with river addict, Tim Holschlag, although we weren't expect-

ing much. The river that day was running high and swift. Tim, a veteran river guide, suggested I cast a large chartreuse spinner-bait. Keeping my mouth shut, I didn't want to say that would have been my last choice.

I chose not to debate Tim, however. He is totally addicted to smallmouth, founding Minnesota's Smallmouth Alliance, an organization devoted to securing the future of smallmouth fishing.

A few casts later, Tim's first choice became my first choice. Seeking to escape the current, the big St. Croix bass were tucked tight to the bank, waiting to ambush bait drifting by, including the spinner-bait. We were on our way to a memorable day on the St. Croix.

Jigs For Smallies

When smallmouth aren't looking up, they're looking down. Down at jigs. A swimming jig—tipped with a plastic worm, tube or grub or enlivened with live bait is a major player in the game of smallmouth.

A jig obviously imitates minnows and/or crayfish and no smallmouth need know more.

The largest smallmouth of my fishing

my first rod 'n' reel

career (so far) was caught on a 1/8th ounce jig, tipped with a squirmy leech. Another Ely character, Roger Skraba, a BWCAW guide, was in the other end of the canoe. We had the Minnesota Bound television cameras rolling when Roger set the hook on a beauty, a 21-inch, deep golden smallmouth shaped like a football. I was happy for Roger but also very envious. I'd never caught a smallie near that size.

A few minutes later, fishing the same deep rock pile, I felt a strike and leaned into my own fantasy. The camera crew, Bob Crippa and Mark Ambrose, zoomed their cameras and moved in for the fight. And, oh, what a battle it was.

When the smallmouth finally surfaced, my knees went weak. I didn't want to tip the canoe, but I couldn't land that bass soon enough. Why? "It's a 22-incher," Roger shouted, measuring her. "Probably 7 pounds or so."

We'll never know. Moments later, she was released.

To summarize, a smallmouth arsenal consists of jigs, spinner-baits, crankbaits and topwater lures. Let's not forget plastic worms. One day bass fishing champ, Mark Fisher and I pulled out a few hefty smallies on Lake Minnetonka using the Carolina Rig and short floating worms that we cast to deep rock shelves.

Finding Smallies

The key to any lure's success is where it is used, of course.

In Minnesota's northeast region, where the smallmouth bass abounds in vast waterways, rocks and trees surround the lakes.

But lotsa rocks.

Rocks on the shoreline, rocks in the shallows and rocks in the depths. There's rock everywhere in lakes on the historic Glacial Shield. Since smallmouth like rocks, does that mean the smallmouth are everywhere?

You really didn't think the answer would be that simple, did you?

No, there are rocks and then there are rocks.

You could cast both arms off, fish in rocks every minute, and never catch a smallmouth. That's because the smallies like some rocks better than others.

In the northeast lakes, the smallmouth is seldom a deepwater fish, meaning

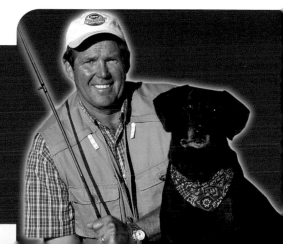

Many fishing rods and reels have passed through my hands since the day my first, a Mitchell combo, arrived, but there'll never be a more cherished rod and reel. It will now be preserved forever in Minnesota's Fishing Hall of Fame.

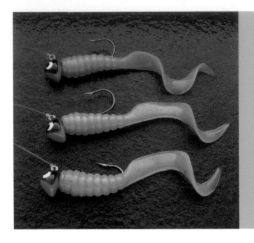

deeper than 20 feet. Normally, smallmouth hang out on or near shallow area bays, sunken islands, reefs, underwater points or shoreline flats. The more rocky the shallows, the more smallmouth on top or on the edge.

There are miles of rock-strewn shorelines that look good. But don't start casting yet. Look for the right rock first. Giant slabs of granite or boulders the size of cars seldom offer the right smallmouth habitat. It's tempting to cast to every rock, but such an exercise gradually teaches you about which rocks hold bass.

In early season smallmouth fishing, the key is to find shallows with bottoms scattered with rock interspersed with sand. Ideally, the rocks range from about fist-size to basketball size. Rock shorelines that drop quickly into deep water are a poor bet. The best smallmouth spots are those with the right rocks scattered on points or flats that extend a ways into the lake. You'll find smallies lurking amid the rocks because that's where the food is, too.

Shallow bays of sand, interspersed with a few boulders, with tree trunks and branches along the water's edge also are hotspots, particularly during the spawning time. Such bays can be checked out easily, since the bass often can be seen cruising against the light sand background. Active smallmouth nests, which show up as large, round white spots on the bottom, also are easily spotted.

I once hit a smallmouth lake on the Gunflint Trail on the 4th of July. To my surprise the smallies were active in the shallows. Moving quietly into sandy coves and bays, I could almost pick out the smallmouth I intended to catch. They were easily spooked, however, in the crystal clear waters. But with long casts and 4-pound test line, I managed to catch and release more than 75 bass in about five hours.

From mid-to-late-summer, smallmouth will frequent deeper water, such as sunken islands, reefs and flats scattered with small boulders in roughly 10 to 20 feet of water. Smallies often hang out where the bottom itself fades from view. Visual references are, of course, quite dependent on the clarity of the water.

Your ability to identify good smallmouth habitat will determine your fishing success. If you intend to simply cast toward rocks, you'll wear out both arms.

One small rock island with 30 to 40 feet of water on all sides will not be productive.

When fishing unknown water, start at the shallowest part of the lake where there's an abundance of rock-covered islands and humps. In fact, think in terms of what crayfish and minnows will like. Like other predator fish, where you find the food, you'll find the smallmouth.

Further south in Minnesota, the smallmouth's haunts are somewhat different. There are fewer rocks and more lake vegetation and sand. Still, where you do find rocks you'll probably find the smallmouth, preferably the deep sunken islands that may top out 15 to 20 feet below the surface. Generally, you'll have to fish deeper, 25 to 30 feet or more, and fish with live bait, such as leeches, for more success. Earlier in the season, shallow rock and sand humps, like those found on Lake Minnetonka, are worked effectively with live bait or artificials.

Rivers For Smallies

Of all the ways to catch a smallmouth in Minnesota, floating a river may be one of the best.

And it's getting better.

In recent years, I've caught or witnessed the catching of smallmouth of 20 inches or more in the Mississippi, the Rum, the St. Croix and other Minnesota streams. Believe me, a smallmouth longer than 20 inches is a whopper anywhere in the country.

In the last decade, DNR fisheries managers have worked to improve smallie habitat on state rivers and special slot

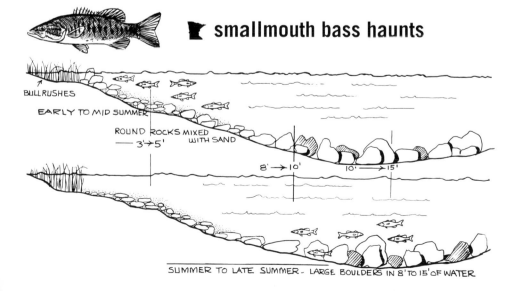

▼ smallmouth bass haunts

BULLRUSHES

EARLY TO MID SUMMER

ROUND ROCKS MIXED
— 3'→5' WITH SAND

8' → 10'

10' → 15'

SUMMER TO LATE SUMMER - LARGE BOULDERS IN 8' TO 15' OF WATER

limit regulations have improved bass sizes considerably. It's common now to tangle with 15- to 18-inch smallies on the St. Croix or the Upper Mississippi and it wasn't always that way.

One of the largest river smallmouth I know of weighed close to 8 pounds (unofficially) and was caught out of the St. Croix at Stillwater by a fisherman whose wife wouldn't let him hang a stuffed fish in the house. Since he couldn't have it mounted; he prepared his catch for the frying pan, thereby consuming what was probably a new state record.

Dan Gapen, a lover of fishing rivers,

was the first to show me the untapped potential of smallmouth fishing on Minnesota's rivers. Gapen and I floated the upper stretches of the Mississippi, above the Twin Cities. Gapen later worked hard as a citizen to encourage legislation to implement state laws to guard the riverbank from excessive development.

My appreciation for rivers was also boosted by a couple of river nuts and entrepreneurs, Minnesota's "canoe guys." Bill Plantan and Dave Frink are so enthused about river fishing they created a whole new product: the River Ridge Custom Canoe, a craft specifically designed for angling stability and comfort (www.riverridgecustomcanoes.com).

How stable?

Minnesota Bound's senior television producer/videographer, Joe Harewicz, was the ultimate test. A former linebacker, weighing 250 pounds, Joe has rolled hours of tape, holding a $25,000 camera on his shoulder, and never tipped a River Ridge. On the contrary, Joe has spilled over in conventional canoes.

The canoe guys are more than canoe makers, however. They are river explorers who appreciate every chance to float downstream to an ever-changing scenario of things to see and catch.

River smallmouth fishing offers more than new scenery around each bend. River fish tend to be less susceptible to weather changes, such as cold fronts. High or muddy water may make rivers unfishable; on the other hand, high but clear rivers may still produce good fishing.

Rivers also can be read, which means locating smallmouth is easier—if you can read the river's map. Rivers normally aren't exceptionally deep, so the bass don't have any choice but to stay relatively shallow.

River smallmouth tend to hang out in deep rock riffles, in pools or holes and on the edge of river eddies. These features are readable, thanks to the river's current.

A riverbank also has a message to give, especially in the slow moving stretches of river. There's a stretch of the St. Croix, for example, that features a long stretch of mud banks and sandbars with short stretches of rock outcrops. Generally, you can forget about fishing the mud. You'll find the smallmouth among the rocks. Take note, when the rock bank ends so does the bass fishing.

Reading a river also includes taking the easiest path through the rapids or riffles by following the "V" sign of current. Keep looking ahead, too. In a river, it's best to be prepared if you need to take a different path. Don't let a river surprise you.

Casting In Rivers

The presence of current will dictate where you cast and how you retrieve a lure or bait. If you don't adjust for current, your lure never seems to go where you wanted it to go. Or it won't go sink. Or it sinks too fast.

Thanks to loyal fans and Gander Mountain stores, Raven and her seven puppies raised $80,000 for the conservation group, "Pheasants Forever". The donations were used to preserve a 700-acre wildlife area in Minnesota.

Making the right casts solves these current ills. The key is to cast across or slightly upstream and allow the lure to work the fishy water as the current swings it downstream. In other words, try to use the current as an aid instead of a detriment.

If you really want to get snagged, cast directly upstream. Unless your lure floats, the current will quickly pull your hooks deep into the rocks. The only time I cast directly downstream in a rapids or deep run is when I'm using small spinners or floating crankbaits.

River pools can be fished in about any direction, unless there's a current or eddy. In that case, make the casts against the current. Smallmouth may be found at both the head and tail end of the pool.

In hunt for smallmouth, the only time rivers are not a wise choice is when its banks are full of swift and cold floodwater. Even a gentle river can be deadly with high water conditions.

The best river fishing usually begins mid-summer and continues into autumn when the river levels are normal or below normal. The current is readable and friendly and the bass hang out in predictable river haunts.

Aside from heavy rains, weather elements that impact smallmouth in lakes are often not as noticeable in rivers. Cold fronts, wind and temperature changes seem to be less important as far as angling success. In rivers, the constant mixing of water ensures that the temperature of river water is pretty much the same from top to bottom.

Best River Lures

Tube jigs, spinner-baits, floating lures, topwater poppers and jig-spinner combinations are a few of river angler's best smallmouth weapons.

Colors that are effective in lakes also seem to work in rivers.

By far the strangest lure color pattern I've ever used was called "clown" and it was offered by Rapala. Suffice it to say, a "clown" Rapala sorta looked the part, a lure with makeup on.

The reason I remember the clown Rapala, a floating model, is because it caught so many smallmouth. One day the canoe guy, Bill Plantan, nailed a 21-incher on a clown, casting right where I was going to cast. Sadly, the clown color has been discontinued; now my favorite is the chartreuse, floating Rap.

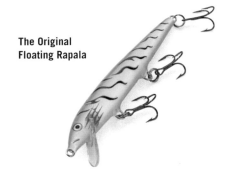

The Original Floating Rapala

If you've never floated a Minnesota river, please be my guest. The smallie fishing might be slow but it'll never be dull. A river is a trip in itself, a trip back in time, a trip around the bend, a trip along nature's original moving sidewalk.

Rivers constantly change, season-to-season, week-to-week. But one thing stays the same. Rivers always harbor smallmouth to catch.

Muskie/Northern

The Toothy Critters

Minnesota's muskies and northern pike are eating machines.

Each is shaped like a camouflaged torpedo with gaping jaws and rows of sharp teeth. Each is swift, deadly and, in their young life, even cannibalistic.

As an efficient predator, muskies and pike function as opportunists. They not only attack out of hunger. They'll attack if a prey looks weak or vulnerable.

While muskies and pike are freshwater versions of *Jaws*, they are not man-eaters. They will not attack swimmers or water skiers. Well, rarely. I know of one incident in Minnesota where a boy swimming in Lake Rebecca was cut by the teeth of a striking muskie.

Now any fisherman who jabs his fingers in the mouth of a muskie or northern is merely asking for a bloodied hand. Note how the teeth angle backwards. Once between the jaws, there's no escape, poor suckers.

While the two toothy predators have many similarities, there also are a few important differences.

Muskies strictly eat prey that's alive and seldom, if ever, gulp an easy meal of dead bait. On the other hand, northern pike will take the living and the dead, acting like a scavenger if it looks edible.

It is their willingness to attack, however, which makes muskies and northern pike near and dear to an angler's heart.

Of the two, the northern is the most popular and has the most widespread population. It is also considered easier to catch.

The muskie, on the other hand, is native to only a limited number of lakes and rivers. With the addition of stocked muskie lakes, Minnesota's muskie waters have about doubled to 80 lakes, including more than 20 lakes within the Twin Cities. More than one Lake Calhoun angler has watched as 40-inch muskie cruise by with impunity. As everyone knows, the muskie is stubborn, suspicious, moody and plain damned hard to catch.

Who's Who?

Muskie and northern pike are often confused in an angler's hand.

It's important to know the difference because muskies are often mistaken for northern pike and killed illegally. On most lakes, a muskie cannot be kept unless it's more than 40 inches long!!!

Obviously, muskies and northern pike are closely related. Both are members of the Pike family and may interbreed, resulting in a hybrid or tiger muskie.

Yet there are distinct differences between the two.

A northern has a more pointed snout and its body is dark, with light markings. By comparison, a muskie has a flat nose with a silvery body, with dark, bar-like vertical markings.

Remember, northern pike has light marks on a dark body, the muskie the opposite (see illustration on page 63).

The northern is "lighter" in another way. It never grows to the sizes reached by muskies. In Minnesota, a 20-pound

CURLY CABBAGE

BROADLEAF CABBAGE

CABBAGE

Northern pike have dark greenish sides with rows of oval shaped, cream colored spots. The tail has dark spots and the lobes are rounded

Muskies have dark spots or bars on light greenish to silvery sides. Or they may be unspotted. The tail has smaller spots, or no spots, and sharper lobes.

pike is becoming increasingly rare, while the same-sized muskie is becoming more abundant.

In fact, the number of 50-inch plus muskies roaming the state's waters may be at an all-time high, thanks to a rigorous catch and release ethic launched 30 years ago by Muskies, Inc. Now release of muskies is the rule rather than the exception all over muskie country.

Minnesota hopes to do the same thing for northern pike, using special regulations to allow more time for pike to grow before being caught and killed. It can be done. A few Minnesota lakes are capable of producing giant pike. Time is all they need.

Finding Muskies And Northerns

Both fish are designed for life in the aquatic jungles. They are camouflaged to melt into vegetation where they can lie in wait and ambush some unsuspecting meal. With one swift flip of a tail, a pike or muskie can hit 25 to 30 miles per hour in an instant.

Both fish also are known to frequent deep-water haunts away from weedy shallows or sunken islands. A pike is considered a cool water fish by biologists, meaning it prefers a cooler range of water temperatures. For that reason, pike may be difficult to find in mid-summer.

In the hunt for pike or muskies, it helps to know key signs of habitat. One of those is an aquatic plant known as "cabbage" or "pondweed." It is a member of the plant family, Potamogeton. You'd be wise to learn to identify cabbage (see illustration on page 162).

Thick beds of cabbage, ideally located around points or shoreline drop-offs, are excellent places to hunt for muskies and northern pike. You'll find the same vegetation also harbors largemouth bass, bluegills, perch and even walleyes.

With so much food in the shallows, that'll explain why muskies and pike are there. To eat. These are eating machines, remember?

Muskies also hang around points, rock piles or reefs or sandy flats with only a smattering of weedy cover.

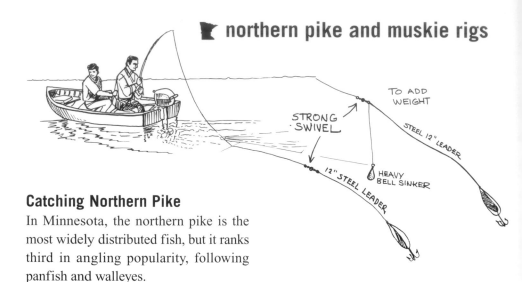

northern pike and muskie rigs

TO ADD WEIGHT

STRONG SWIVEL

STEEL 12" LEADER

12" STEEL LEADER

HEAVY BELL SINKER

Catching Northern Pike

In Minnesota, the northern pike is the most widely distributed fish, but it ranks third in angling popularity, following panfish and walleyes.

Generally, fishing for northerns is good in early season, declines in mid-summer and is best when late summer turns to autumn. The peak of pike action seems to begin as the days of September flow into October.

In the fall, northerns go on a feeding binge to fatten up for winter. Big pike move into the shallows, following bait-fish and become recklessly hungry. This begins after the first cold snap or when the nights turn cool and the days are Indian summer.

Yes, plenty of northerns can be taken at other times of the season. On live bait. By trolling, spoons, plugs and spinner-baits. A jig and minnow is also effective on pike. Generally, however, big pike catches happen come autumn.

By far the most common method of taking northern pike in Minnesota is with live bait (see illustration on page 165).

A medium or medium-heavy action rod will serve you well—spinning, spin-casting or casting types. Monofilament of 10 or 12 pound test will be sufficient,

providing you know how to handle an ornery fish. Northerns are tremendously strong and powerful swimmers. They'll leap, roll or flop on the end of the line like a wild puppet.

If you don't feel comfortable with 12-pound line, by all means go to heavier monofilament. In most cases, it will not hurt your success. Northern generally are not line shy. In fact, they fear nothing in their world, except each other.

Steel leader or wire leaders are impor-tant, however.

The famous dentures of northern and muskies are quite capable of slicing the toughest monofilament without losing a stroke. What about the super lines? Ha. They haven't made a super line yet that a pike can't cut in one swipe.

A 6- or 12-inch leader—single or woven wire—will help put your mind at ease. However, there are times when you should take your chances. The action of some lures, such as the Rapala, are badly impaired by the weight or stiffness of a wire leader.

Leader Smarts

The only time a steel or wire leader is important is when you are fishing for toothy pike and muskies. Unfortunately, many anglers think a steel leader is a must at all times just in case a pike might hit. "You betcha, you don't want to lose the lure or the fish, don't you know."

Uff-dah.

Your goal is to present any bait or lure as natural as possible. Rarely can that be accomplished with a thick leader ahead of the lure. In fact, a leader can hurt a lure's fish catching motion. So –if pike and muskies aren't the goal, skip the leader.

Live Bait For Pike

The usual live bait for northern pike consists of one kind of minnow—large suckers 4 to 8 inches long. Generally, the larger the bait, the larger the fish you might catch.

Live suckers are fished in several ways: hooked through the lips to be cast and retrieved or still-fished on the bot-

tom. You may want to use a larger bobber, allowing a lightly hooked sucker to swim below to entice a pike. For those anglers who insist on using jumbo bobbers, the size of softballs, now's your chance. You'll need a fairly large bobber to keep the sucker from swimming away.

A slip bobber rig works best. Chances are you'll be fishing in water from 10 to 20 feet deep.

Then, it's a waiting game. Waiting for the bobber to suddenly plunge. When it does go down, you'll have to wait some more. Northern pike tend to act like cats, preferring to play with their victims before gorging. Often, a northern will hit and run considerable distances with the large minnow still within its jaws. Then the pike will pause and resume swimming. That pause usually means the minnow is headed for the pike's stomach. Then strike. And hang on.

Trolling For Pike

Dunking sucker minnows is a lunker

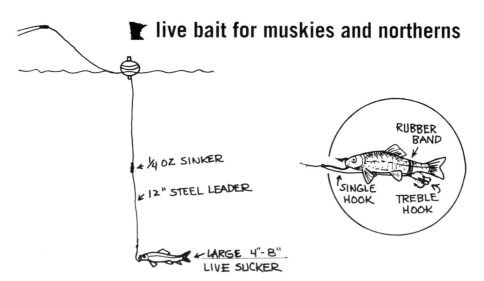

▶ live bait for muskies and northerns

¼ OZ SINKER

12" STEEL LEADER

RUBBER BAND

SINGLE HOOK   TREBLE HOOK

LARGE 4"-8" LIVE SUCKER

pike technique. But you need the patience of a young oak tree. And some of us don't have it.

Trolling is the next best thing. It's effective, yet a shade more active than watching bobbers float.

Trolling for pike isn't rocket science. Flip a lure out behind the boat, start the outboard and cruise back and forth along the outer edges of the weedy shores or outside edges of weed beds.

A trolled spinner-bait is very effective alongside weed edges or through light cabbage patches.

Don't forget spoons. The Daredevle spoon—red and white, what else?—it's all you need. For decades, the Daredevle has meant northern pike fishing. For good reason. The spoon was danged effective and still is.

Today, there's a whole new batch of pike spoons featuring realistic paint jobs or holographic effects. Someday the new lifelike spoons may make us forget the ol' red n' white. We'll wait and see what the pike have to say about that.

Trolling speed is important. While you can troll too slowly, seldom can you troll too fast. The minimum speed required is that which gives your lure an attractive swimming action or enough speed to rotate the spinners.

Sometimes the faster you troll, the more strikes you'll get. It's called speed trolling and it can be done with a spoon, for example, trolled literally behind the boat's prop wash.

A northern is capable of swimming 30 miles per hour for short bursts. If a pike wants your spoon or lure bad enough, it'll catch it.

Casting For Pike

Let there be no doubt, northerns are attracted to flashy things. That's good. We can cast flashy things.

While casting represents more work, and perhaps less efficiency, the caster has a much greater arsenal of shiny objects to attract the pike. And, in my opinion, the casting angler has more fun when a strike connects.

Casting also covers the water more thoroughly. You can hit weed bed pockets, edges, banks, the places where pike like to ambush. Weedless lures and spoons are an important part of the arsenal. Topwater lures, including buzzbaits, will make your day if the pike are present.

Pike seem to like spinner-baits, espe-

"Muskie Mania"

cially the colors of white, orange and black. Truth be told, a pike on the prowl would hit pink and mauve, too. Spinnerbaits also are weedless in nature and can be cast into the thicket weeds and bulrushes.

And what about lily pads? Lily pads are not the first choice of discriminating anglers. Don't get me wrong. Fields of lily pads do hold fish, but other aquatic vegetation does better. For one thing, the pads are associated with soft, mucky bottom, the kind that few fish seek out.

If lily pads are the only vegetation available, fish them. Since the northern has no choice, it won't be far away. The one time the lotus or lily pad fields may produce excellent fishing is in the late fall. Then, the mud bottom, absorbing the sun's last faint rays of heat, may maintain slightly higher water temperatures. Enough to attract prey fish. Remember, where you find food, you find northern pike.

One of the top lures discovered by northern pike addicts is a combination of artificial and live bait—the jig and minnow. Troll a jig and minnow slowly or cast and retrieve slowly. Edges of weed lines or deepwater rock humps are ideal pike haunts.

Northern pike have no qualms about smacking surface lures, yet many fishermen seldom try. Topwater fishing for any fish is pure, unadulterated angling excitement. Northerns hit with such velocity that they'll often miss their target.

On Rainy Lake, the huge and picturesque lake shared by Minnesota and Ontario, I was fishing topwater plugs for muskies on a warm, sleepy August afternoon when a northern pike made a believer out of me.

As the plug twitched noisily across the silent surface, the water suddenly exploded. An 11-pound northern shot skyward like a missile. Only it hadn't missed. The plug, a Mud Puppy, was stuck in the jaw and the fight was on.

I finally landed the pike, but I'd already had my fun. The strike was worth a day of thrills.

Fly-casting For Pike

A fly rod with a northern pike on the end of the line is a wonderful match up.

It may explain why streamer flies were invented.

I wrote my first book, "Muskie Mania," not because I was any kind of muskie fishing expert, but because any fish that could make a man tremble with excitement could also make a man write a book, I figured.

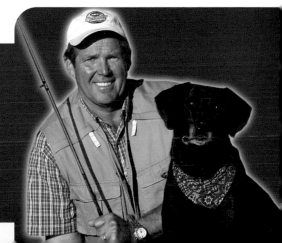

holding a pike

The proper way to hold a northern is to squeeze gently but firmly around the back of the head and gill covers. Use long-nosed pliers to remove the hooks. Never stick your fingers under the gill covers and into the gills. The gill rakers on a northern are like sharp teeth.

Pike love the slow, pulsating motion of feathered hooks. Indeed, when spoons and other hardware fail, a huge streamer fly will make a pike open its mouth.

Early season when pike are shallow is best for fly-fishing, although a white or black streamer (a 6- to 8-inch strip of rabbit fur or feathers) cast to any mid-summer weed bed may be attacked.

The added attraction of fly-casting to pike is the fight. Even a small pike—a hammerhandle, if you will, can put up enough fight to make a fly rod throb.

Holding A Pike

The proper way to hold a northern is to squeeze gently but firmly around the back of the head and gill covers. Use long-nosed pliers to remove the hooks. Never stick your fingers under the gill covers and into the gills. The gill rakers on a northern are like sharp teeth.

Please, don't grab a northern pike by the eye sockets. It can blind the fish. Even if you intend to keep the pike, the fish deserves more respect than to be held by the eyeballs. Nothing deserves to be held by the eyeballs.

Preserving Pike

Let's have a little heart to heart chat here. You want big pike to catch? It's up to you.

Over the decades, state anglers have pretty much over-kept the northern pike. In some cases, the DNR allowed over-populations of pike, which resulted in lakes full of hammerhandles (pike the size of hammer handles).

Minnesota's pike are now on the comeback trail. We now have a number of lakes with new pike rules, requiring pike of certain sizes to be released. If we follow the rules, in time, Minnesota will see an increase of trophy pike, 20-pounders or more.

If some of us cheat, we'll always have hammerhandles.

Catching Muskies

"In all of freshwater, there is no other fish like it.

Muskie!

Even the sound of its name has urgency, a sense of excitement. To experienced muskie hunters, the name symbolizes boldness, strength, jaws of needle-like teeth, obstinacy, gigantism. And—to many of the same veterans—the name also means ultimate frustration.

To others the muskie is a secretive fantasy, a torpedo-shaped cross between a slinky alligator and a cunning women, a fish that lurks in watery depths, seldom to be seen."

The foregoing is an excerpt from my first fishing book entitled, *Muskie Mania*, published in 1977. I use those words again to introduce the muskie because the fish hasn't changed a bit. A muskie still plays with your mind.

The fish remains Minnesota's most cherished trophy. Cherished, because seldom are muskies caught by cheap luck. You usually have to pay your dues. Again and again. It's a fever. If muskie anglers were smart, they'd throw away their tackle after catching the first muskie. None of us do, of course. We merely sink deeper into the depths of Esox passion.

The really good news is that Minnesota, season after season, has become a better place to go muskie fishing. The fish has been successfully introduced into more waters. Stocking efforts have expanded. And the fish attracted a collection of serious addicts known as *Muskies, Incorporated*, an organization that has promoted and financed muskie conservation and propagation practices.

Muskies are found in about 80 lakes and rivers in the state. No special stamp is required to fish muskies, although pike spearing is not permitted on many lakes designated as muskie water.

While pike spearing is a traditional pastime in Minnesota, the practice clashed with efforts to release muskies. Spearers can accidentally harpoon muskies mistaken for northern pike. Today, conflicts between spearers and muskie anglers are declining, as key lakes are off-limits. The number of pike spearing enthusiasts also has declined drastically in the last 20 years.

Muskie Lifestyles

Like the northern pike, the muskie is a fish of the aquatic jungles.

In fact, both species will share the same waters, although muskies often will not fare well in lakes with high northern populations. The muskie is one of the last fish to spawn. Hence, young muskies get a late start in life and are vulnerable targets to other predators, including young pike.

That may be nature's version of fair play, however. For muskies are voracious meat-eaters. According to nature's plan, the avid meat-eaters must have population controls one-way or the other. As a result, muskie populations seldom are "dense." A population of 1 or 2 muskies per acre of water is considered high.

The low density of muskies is another reason why it seems so difficult to catch one. It takes a lot of searching when you're looking for a couple of needles in the proverbial haystack.

Once located, the muskie—if presented with the right bait in the right way—will open its mouth just like any other mortal fish. So—don't think they're impossible to catch. They're not. They're just more difficult.

The key to muskie success is hard work and patience.

Consider Chan "Doc" Cotton, the "Muskie Man" of Minnesota's Leech Lake, which is famous for its muskies. Doc Cotton once landed 108 legal-sized muskies in one summer of fishing. His goal was to catch only 100. Wow, just lucky? Yes and no. But luck isn't enough to achieve those kind of muskie numbers. Doc simply paid his dues with one big secret: He never gave up.

Most if Minnesota's muskies are the

"true" muskie as compared to the hybrid muskie, which is a cross between a northern pike and a true muskie.

The hybrid, which is fast growing, has been stocked in a number of lakes, including several in the Twin Cities region. It's often called the "tiger muskie" because of its brilliant stripes or markings on each side of the body.

If you catch a tiger or hybrid, you'll probably think it's a true muskie because its fight and size are similar.

When fishing in the Park Rapids region, you may also catch a "silver muskie" or "silver pike." It is a rare species and considered to be a mutant of the northern pike. The silver pile has bright silvery-sides and plain dark back.

True muskies, themselves, will vary in coloration. Some will have dark vertical stripes, others light stripes and still others will be steel gray or silver-colored. Many fisheries scientists believe a muskie is a muskie, but the color variations are simply due to the environmental differences from lake to lake or watershed to watershed.

No matter what the muskie looks like, when you hook one you'll know it.

They are spectacular fighters; striking viciously and then exploding like a crazed tarpon. A muskie's fight may be shorter than that of a large northern, but a muskie's battle is more intense. They've been known to leap into boats... and out again.

So go prepared.

The muskie is one of the few Min-

nesota sport fish that requires special gear if you're going to fish seriously. You're in the heavyweight division now. A muskie rod is about as limber as a pool cue. For good reasons: muskie anglers use big lures and it's important to set the hook. You need a stout rod to handle both.

A typical muskie rod has a stout butt and stiff tip action with a length ranging from 5 1/2 to 7 feet, depending on personal preference. While you can fish muskies with open face spinning or spincast (closed face) reels, the only practical reel is the free-spool casting reel.

For line, heavy monofilament, braided Dacron or the new super lines are common choices. Line weights range from 20 to 50 pounds plus 12-18 inch braided steel or wire leader. Swivels and snaps are in the 100-pound test range. The leaders, snaps and swivels—the business end of your muskie tackle—is very important. Don't look for bargains. Buy the best. Don't underestimate the power of an ornery muskie.

If there's a weak link someplace, a hooked muskie will find it.

Trolling For Muskies

Some fishermen get their kicks out of tossing giant sucker minnows into muskie haunts. It's effective. The sucker usually is floated by a fat bobber or trolled in a harness of hooks.

But in one man's opinion, chasing muskies with sucker minnows is like getting married without a honeymoon. You're missing all the fun.

Muskies will gladly smash an artificial lure when they're in the right mood. You can troll that lure or cast it. Either way, you're in for a good time.

Trolling is considered the most efficient method of taking a muskie. Since muskies are usually widely scattered, trolling enables you to cover more water in less time.

Yet, trolling is not as popular as casting largely because you never know if the muskie follows. However, trolling is effective early to late season. And if you're on unfamiliar water, trolling may be the fastest way to see what's happening. For example, the vast sand flats of Mille Lacs and Leech Lake are difficult to cast and cover much water.

The most popular trolling baits include bucktails and crankbaits.

Trolling speed is seldom critical. What a muskie sees, what a muskie wants, it'll take in a burst of 30 miles per hour swimming speed. As a general rule, troll at a speed that offers the best swimming action to whatever lure you select.

Muskie trolling techniques include the use of trolling boards to help spread the lines. Popular trolling lures behind boards include in-line bucktail spinners or large spinner-baits.

Muskie guide, Chip Leer, also trolls topwater prop-style lures behind boards at an early morning or late evening ploy. The topwater lure is placed so it sputters on the surface about 25 feet behind the trolling board.

Leer said his favorite trolling outfit consists of 6 1/2- to 7-foot rods with a soft tip. His line is 25 to 30 pound test monofilament, such as Berkley Big Game. For a trolling leader, length is important. Leer uses a 36-inch single strand wire with a cross-lock snap and ball bearing swivel.

While many huge muskies have fallen to trolling ploys, the technique also has its disadvantages. Pinpoint trolling accuracy is difficult, especially following weed lines or inside turns where muskies often lurk. Snagging weeds gets old fast.

Casting For Muskies

One of the most exciting moments in all of freshwater angling is seeing a huge muskie follow inches behind your lure. The event is commonly called "a follow."

Afraid of little or nothing in its watery world, a curious muskie will cruise a short distance behind a lure as it's being retrieved to the boat or shore.

Raven's tidbit

The alert muskie angler will watch for a follow, which best explains why Polaroid sunglasses are an absolute must in a muskie addict's arsenal. You don't want to miss a follow. Knowing the fish is there means you might have a chance to catch it. And if you don't, well, having a muskie follow is almost as exciting as actually catching one.

And guess what? If you cast long enough in muskie water, sooner or later, it'll happen. Suddenly, there'll be something big following your lure like a puppy on a leash. Then, one of two things will happen. The muskie will strike, opening its huge jaws and inhaling your lure right at the boat or it'll pause at boat side, look up at you and slowly sink out of sight.

In the meantime, you will be babbling nonsense while your knees quiver like aspen leaves in a windstorm.

That alone is why I prefer casting. You can't weigh a muskie follow, you can't put a muskie follow on the wall or in a record book, but you'll receive the kind of thrill that has united generations of us in the spirit of fishing.

In reality, most of us who fish muskies will both cast and troll in our quest to find the elusive one.

Depth control is important and it's achieved with the lure's design or by the speed the lure when retrieved. Some days muskies tend to look up, some days, down. While I'm a fan of topwater lures, I'm also guilty of casting surface baits when sub-surface lures would produce more action. Why? Well, witnessing a surface strike by a muskie is like sitting in the eye of a waterspout. Spectacular is another good word.

But some days it doesn't happen.

If muskies aren't looking up, other lure types such as bucktails or diving plugs or jerkbaits are the proper choice. Which is best? That question is only answered by the muskie.

In Minnesota, the muskie angler who casts must tolerate exhausted arms, tired shoulders and sore hands. Casting is work. But it's fun, too. You must keep telling yourself that or you'll quit too soon.

But muskie casters tend to be eternally inspired. Larry Anderson, who guided the waters of Lake of the Woods for decades, always insisted there is but one

Raven likes to fly and rides in the back seat of the airplane.

Muskie/Northern

unbreakable muskie rule: *It Only Takes One Cast.*

However, we don't know if the one cast is your first or your 10,000th.

What To Cast

A beginning muskie angler need only acquire three, maybe four, muskie lures for his or hers casting debut. The lures are: a bucktail spinner, a diving plug, a jerkbait and a topwater lure.

A bucktail is a muskie angler's workhorse. It will fool muskies from opening day to the last day. If you can only afford one, make it a black bucktail with a silver spinner blade. Why? Well, it works. On any given day, a different presentation might be better, but day-in and day-out the bucktail will catch a muskie. As the old-timers are fond of saying, "Any lure color is good as long as it's black." If you want a variety of bucktails, add the colors of yellow, white, red, and purple.

While you provide the casting and retrieving power, the bucktail does the rest of the work. How fast? Fast or slow, depending on the whims of the muskie.

Noted muskie guide, Ted Roos, who knows Cass Lake like nobody else, is a booster of small, single blade bucktails, which he cranks back to the boat as fast as possible.

"When a muskie sees my bucktail flying by, I don't want to give it time to think. Either strike now or forget it," Ted explained one day. It works.

In a typical day of muskie fishing, a bucktail is one lure that never should be overlooked.

Casting Plugs

A diving plug is the caster's tool for fishing at depths greater than five feet. Most plugs provide their own wobble or wiggle action. Popular colors include perchgreen, silver and yellow-black.

A diving plug is effective in almost any situation, including weed bed edges, sharp drop-offs or ripped though sparse vegetation. Usually there's no finesse with a lure. Reel as fast as you can or reel and pause, reel and pause repeatedly.

A muskie typically hits the plug from the side and the collision is often quite impressive. Nevertheless, it's important to set the hooks hard. A muskie's strong jaws may otherwise grip the lure without being hooked. If you don't set, a muskie is apt to simply open its tight jaws and the lure (and hooks) go free.

Jerking Jerkbaits

On a tackle shelf, a class of lures known as jerkbaits look like nothing to buy. Most of them don't do anything in the water by themselves. Yet, jerkbaits may symbolize muskie fishing more than any other lure.

A typical jerk bait looks like a small baseball bat with treble hooks. But it's also fished as the lure's name implies. You jerk it. Yes, cast and jerk. Jerk rhythmically and watch the lure dodge from side to side like a very sick sucker that's too weak to swim straight.

If it looks like an easy meal, that's exactly what a muskie wants.

When the attack comes, you'll often see it because jerkbaits generally swim

A personal favorite is Poe's Giant Jackpot

less than five feet deep. Again, set the hook hard.

The downside of jerkbaits is the lure's weight, which makes it easier for a muskie to toss with a jump. I've lost more big muskies on jerkbaits than any other lure. While I'm not proud of that fact, it's also true I've hooked more muskies on jerkbaits than anything else.

So what have I learned? Maintain sharp hooks on your jerkbaits. Start sharpening the hooks the first time they come out of the box.

As you might expect, the best jerkbait color includes black, either black back and white belly or all black. Sometimes cream-colored or perch-colored jerkbaits also are effective. In dark-stained or dinghy muskie water the splashy, vivid lures—painted colors that belong in a clown's parade, will attract strikes when natural colors will not.

Please don't think you have to be realistic in the eyes of a muskie. A muskie thinks of only one thing: If it's swimming, it might be edible.

Topwater Tactics

It's not often an angler witnesses unabridged terror. Wanna see absolute violence? Unabashed jaws?

Cast a topwater plug to an ornery muskie.

If I had but one muskie lure to choose, it would float.

Years ago, a muskie nut, Billy Collins, showed me an old lure nobody made anymore. It was called "Muskie Magic." It was a piece of non-descript wood painted an ugly brown. Billy swore the old lure was magic. He was right. The old lure darted and dashed, slurped and sloshed on the surface like a sick sucker. Watching the lure was akin to waiting for an explosion of dynamite.

That old lure has seen its better days, but the concepts remains alive and well. Muskie pro, Bob Mehsikomer, has boated dozens of muskie monsters on topwater. One of his favorites (and mine) is the Jackpot Lure, which resembles a giant-sized Zara Spook.

There are many topwater designs, of course. Some sputter; some flutter. Some dart; some splash. Any topwater will work on any given day. You simply must have faith. When a muskie is looking up, as they say, life doesn't get much better.

A topwater can be fished in various ways; whatever your imagination concocts in the forms of jerks and pauses. As a general rule, don't worry about color. Seldom is the color of a topwater bait critical because of the muskie's angle of view. When in doubt, you guessed it, throw black.

Muskie nut, Lloyd Bolter, performed one of the best days of topwater fishing I've ever witnesses.

Bolter was casting a black Globe and landed three muskies, the largest going about 26 pounds. His technique was to retrieve the Globe as fast as he could, full tilt, no pausing, no stopping.

The collision of muskie and Globe was awesome.

When Bolter landed the third muskie of the day, he was done. His lure was wrecked beyond repair.

Muskies At Night

Fishing at night isn't for everybody. The slightest line tangle becomes a major problem. You can't see. The simplest tasks become complicated—even with a flashlight.

Yet, muskies do feed at night, especially in moonlight and they'll smack a topwater plug with all the gusto of an NFL linebacker. Trolling also is an effective method. More than one night angler on Mille Lacs, trolling for walleyes, has been awarded with a gigantic muskie.

Most muskie sages believe your chances of nabbing a really huge muskie is best at night. I suppose they're right. I still prefer to see what I catch.

If you catch a lunker some night, tell me about it in the morning.

Releasing Muskies

Now what happens when you catch one? How do you handle a fish that might be four feet long or more? Especially one with a mouthful of needle teeth and swinging treble hooks?

How do you grab a muskie?

Very carefully, my friends, very carefully. A muskie with a mouthful of hooks can be very dangerous. I know. One day I was demonstrating the proper release technique to John Clark, who was on his way to muskie addiction.

"Here's how you release a muskie," I declared as John awaited the expert's demonstration.

When the demonstration was over, the expert had two scars on a finger: one where the hook went in, a second where it came out. To be safe, use a hook-out device. Use a net or cradle to handle the fish, especially large muskies.

Muskies should only be netted with a muskie-size net. One day I tried to net a 20-pound muskie for Larry Bollig using a small net designed for walleyes. Of course, the muskie got away, flopping out of the too-small net and swimming away. Now Larry and I think that was probably a 30-, maybe 40-pounder.

The Gospel Of Release

If you're new to muskie fishing, here's the deal. This ain't no food catching expedition. Sure, a muskie might be good to eat but that doesn't mean we're cooking 'em up. Of all the fish in freshwater, the muskie is better at being a trophy than a meal in a frying pan. Trophy

muskies are rare and always have been. They are slow to grow and even slower to replace.

For those reasons, anglers who love muskies preach the gospel of catch and release. A child must wait 16 years before getting a driver's license. It takes the same amount of time for a muskie to reach 50 inches.

If you choose to fish for muskies, set a goal. Once that's reached set another goal. And so forth. Those muskies that don't measure up should be released. Don't kill it just to impress your friends.

With the advent of graphite replicas, any huge muskie can be released but remembered in graphite on the wall.

The greatest contribution you can make to the future of your own fishing is to release trophy fish. Think about it.

In life, they say, what goes around comes around. Someday I might catch the one you released. Think of the joy you passed on.

But someday you may catch the big one I let go.

Catfish, Carp and Others

Bewhiskered And Becareful

On an angler's social ladder, Minnesota's bewhiskered fishes—the catfish and bullheads—are often viewed near the bottom rung.

If you catch trout or walleyes and the like, you must be an angler of class, brains and sophisticated piscatorial articulation.

But if you fish for catfish or bullheads, you are, well, paddling with one oar.

Remember, you read it hear first. This is crude, angling class warfare. Walleye anglers being smarter than bullhead casters is an awful way to be thinking. It reeks to high heaven... like, well, good catfish bait.

Now hear this... the only folks who are allowed to ridicule the grand sports called catfishin' or bullheadin' are the ones who've done it. And they ain't about to tell you the truth because they don't want to see you sorry sweet smellers out there coolin' your feet in river mud.

This catfishin' ain't no fun at all.

There you be. A hot August night; the sky darker than the inside of a tire. The river gurgles on by. Tree frogs and whippoorwills make an awful racket. At your side is new fishing tackle; a fresh cut willow stick. You bait the hook with a gob of sun-stroked stinkin' something and plunk it out there. And, like a fool, you smell your fingers. A putrid odor rushes up your nose and stays there for two hours.

Fun, huh?

Suddenly. Lollapalooza! Your fishing line streaks for the far bank, threatening to take your favorite willow stick with it. You rear back and hang on, waiting for the next powerful lunge as a channel catfish leans the other way.

Now tell me, that doesn't sound fun at all, does it? Absolutely not. Some fish may fight with more style, but none have more determination than Minnesota's two species of catfish, the flathead (also called mudcat) and the more common, channel catfish. These sporty critters are found in the state's biggest rivers, the Mississippi, the St. Croix, the Minnesota, the Red River and the St. Louis. There are also cats lurking in the Horseshoe Chain near Richmond. Of these, the Red River is considered the mecca of cat fishing.

Sadly, most Minnesotans don't have a clue about the joys of cat fishing. The DNR says only about 1 percent of all anglers chase cats.

What about the bullhead?

Well… eerr… to tell the truth, the bullhead fights slightly harder than a freshwater clam. It eats anything, including bare hooks, and it can live without water longer than a camel. It's fair to wonder how seeking bullheads can be called fishing. Even with a loose definition.

Save that question for the folks in Waterville, Bullhead Capitol of Minnesota (And danged proud of it)

Hard to believe, but thousands of normal people go fishing for bullheads. And they catch 'em, of course. And, good grief, they eat 'em.

Is it possible they know something bullhead skeptics and belittlers do not?

The Truth About Cats And Bulls

Catfish and bullheads are members of the same fish family, noted for scaleless skin, chin whiskers and sharp needle-like spines on their pectoral and dorsal fins. Lots of folks think the chin whiskers are poisonous filaments. But that's not true. The whiskers merely act like another set of senses to help locate food.

The fin spines do have mild poison glands, which make a puncture rather painful. That's why you should be careful when handling the bewhiskered fishes.

The real truth is Minnesota harbors some of the nation's classic catfish rivers—the Mississippi, the Red, the Minnesota, the St. Croix along with plenty of good bullheadin' lakes.

Catfish and bullheads will, indeed, eat just about anything from meat to potatoes. That leaves your choice of baits rather open.

The flathead cat, the largest catfish species in the state, is much more per-

snickety, however. Whatever it eats must be alive first. No exceptions.

Channel cats and flatheads normally are considered a river fish. The two species often may be found in the same haunts, although the flathead tends to be extremely nocturnal in its feeding habits. Channel cats seem to be more opportunistic. If it smells good, let's eat. Sunrise and sundown periods still are probably best for channel cats.

special people

Channel cats and flathead cats represent the sportier side of the bewhiskered fish family.

The channel cats have neater appearance with a bluish back, irregularly spotted sides and forked tail. Whereas, the flathead cat looks mean with permanent evil grin, brown-gray funky color and a fat, square-ended tail.

Channel cats and flatheads also are an excellent eating fish, if you don't let their looks bother you.

Die-hard cat fishermen don't. Their nights or days on the mud-banked rivers are seldom dull and never boring. What excitement the big cats can't provide, a six-pack or two can.

Both fish hang out in the pools and sluggish waters or around sandy wing dams and spooky-looking logjams that quiver endlessly in the current.

The best time of the season to hit these spots is when the heat of summer has reached its peak in the lazy days of August. By then the rivers have pulled back to shallow riffles and deep holes, exposing handy sandbars to sit on while you ponder the universe.

One of my favorite channel cat baits is rotten shrimp, sold in bait shops wherever good cat fishing exists. Night crawlers, cut bait (chopped up suckers or chubs) chicken livers, blood sausage… anything with a lip-curling odor will attract channel cats.

Don't know if it's true but I was once told about a farmer who lost a fine sow during the furrowing season. Rather than let it go to waste, he dragged it to a place just upstream from one of his favorite cat fishing holes and let it ripen for a few weeks. They say when he finally returned there were so many catfish in that hole below the pig he could scoop'em out with a dip net.

I believe it.

Catfish bait can be still-fished or drifted with the current. For sure, you won't have any doubts about a strike. The channel catfish is one of the hardest striking fish in freshwater. It simply hits with a bang.

Channel cats also will smash artificial lures when they're in the mood. I've taken cats on crayfish-looking jigs when fishing for walleyes.

Nocturnal Flatheads

By far the best way to catch flatheads is

Fishing companions always seem to be special people. In one way or another. In a boat, a fishing partner may talk of secret wishes, troubles, illness, worries. It's a bonding moment.

to fish at night with large chubs or suckers. Sometimes a super-gob of night crawlers, stuffed in a wad on a large 6/0 to 9/0 hook also works well. All baits are fished in the bottom with a heavy sinker.

Then, it's a matter of patience. Once the big cats make a move the evening could get downright exciting. If not, the only thing you've got to lose is a little sleep.

Bullhead Strategies

While most fish feed at sunrise and sunset, I don't think the bullhead knows what time it is.

Or gives a dang.

Bullheads are more commonly fished in lakes, although they survive nicely in rivers and sewer lagoons.

The good folk of Waterville will probably chuckle about that… all the way to the bank.

Many of the lakes in southern Minnesota are shallow and fertile, an ideal combination to raise tons of bullheads, simply and easily. And that's how the fish is caught, too.

Almost any fishing outfit will do, any line, any hook, any bait. Worms, night crawlers, commercial stink-baits are the favorites. Fish from a boat or the shore.

Bottom fishing—plunking the bait smack-dab on the bottom—is a typical ploy. Some anglers use bobbers to hold the bait only slightly off the bottom. Whatever turns you on.

By now, you must be wondering what all the fuss is about. If bullheads can't fight, if they're not big, if they hit any-

thing, if they're tricky to hold without getting jabbed, why bother, huh?

Ready for the brutal truth?

'Cause bullheads are delicious to eat. And that's no bull. Skinned with entrails removed, a bullhead is nothing but firm white meat with an easily removed backbone.

A platter of deep-fried golden bullhead filets is awesome. A mug of cold beer helps, too.

Some folks say bullhead is better eatin' than walleye. They're the ones who drink beer during the Bullhead Days Parade in Waterville.

Carp And Others

Miscellaneous Bites

In some Minnesota waters, fishing is like gambling. You're never sure about what's on the other end of the line.

The Mississippi and St. Croix Rivers are famed potluck fishing holes. A high school chum, Don Koenig and I, once caught nine different species in the Mississippi River, despite fishing for only bluegills and using earthworms for bait. As I recall the lineup went like this: bluegills, crappies, redhorse sucker, largemouth bass, sheepshead, channel catfish, dogfish, sauger and walleye.

Fishing surprises swim anywhere.

Many winter walleye anglers have hooked "good fish" only to discover their anticipated trophy was a burbot or eelpout. Actually that's not bad. Walker, Minn. has put itself on the winter map with its annual burbot bash.

A fella named Ken Bresley started the

fight to the finish

One of the strongest fighting fish in freshwater is the much maligned carp. A carp on the end of fishing line is often your equal.

eelpout contest because he was bored with Walker's empty streets all winter. He also liked to have company when he was in the mood to bend elbows.

Another strange catch often shows up when largemouth bass anglers pitch a plastic worm: the bowfin. Also known as the dogfish with a long eel-like tail and dark spot. Dogfish apparently don't have much of a taste. I've never known one to appear in a frying pan. Most anglers are

happy when the bowfin is unhooked and swimming away.

One of the strongest fighting fish in freshwater is the much maligned carp. Yes, carp have created extensive destruction of our fishing waters since they were imported from Europe more than a century ago. Yes, they muddy the water. Yes, they'll never win a beauty contest.

But a carp on the end of fishing line is often your equal. Every summer carp fans gather below the Mississippi River dam in Coon Rapids to celebrate a Carp Fest of sorts. Carp ain't going away so you might as well fish for 'em and catch 'em. In Europe, the carp is so revered as a game fish; most are released to fight again another day. Carp are most easily caught with natural bait, if kernels of canned corn, boiled potatoes or gobs of bread dough can be called "natural." Night crawlers and earthworms also are effective.

Fish the bait on the bottom, using a light slip-sinker or none at all and with or without a small bobber.

Carp normally roam in shallows in mud bottom bays of lakes or the backwaters, pools of rivers.

Bow and arrow fishing for carp also is popular in the spring when carp move into shallow creeks to spawn or otherwise root in the shallows. That's another nice thing about carp fishing. There's no limit and the season is always open.

The Silvers Are Running

Among Minnesota's "second class" fishes, the one that gets the most respect is the white bass, also called the silver or striped bass. However, its popularity is not based on size or fighting skills.

Rather, the white bass has a penchant for committing suicide on a hook.

Starting in early May, large schools of white bass roam the waters of Minnesota's St. Croix and Mississippi Rivers. When the "stripers" start "running"—moving in large schools just below the surface—the fishing action can be gangbusters, a term which means a fish on almost every cast. They'll hit

Raven's tidbit

minnows as well as spinners, small jigs and small plugs.

August and September are also prime times.

The surest sign that the white bass are running is found in the air. In the form of gulls. When the hulls are seen in great bunches, circling over and diving into the water, you can bet that a school of white bass have gone into a feeding frenzy. The gulls hand around for the scraps, the prey fish crippled by the storming white bass.

In other times, white bass will be found around the slack water in the St. Croix and Mississippi, most notably below the locks and dams.

White bass are quite eatable but are best smoked.

The Ugly Eelpout

The eyes beholding an eelpout or burbot will be hard pressed to find much beauty. A bullhead looks downright glamorous compared to an eelpout.

I once interviewed John Galles, of S. St. Paul; on the day he was honored for catching a new state record eelpout, a 19-pound beauty.

"What's it like to have your name in the record book for an eelpout," I asked. John paused with his answer.

"What do you think," he said, finally.

If an eelpout is ugly to look at, it must be ugly in every way, right?

Wrong, pout breath.

Get this: The eelpout's beauty is in the eating.

The fish is correctly known as a burbot. It's the only fresh water member of the codfish family from whence cod liver oil is extracted.

The burbot has scaleless skin like a bullhead, a long dorsal fin like a dogfish and a tail like a monkey. That is, it is capable of wrapping its tail around an angler's arm, momentarily raising the question of who caught whom.

Walleye anglers most often mistakenly catch eelpout in the wintertime because the pout begin spawning on rock reefs where walleye, too, may be lurking. Eelpout also have respectable eating habits, feasting on minnows, rather than slurping its food like a carp.

Thanks to Walker's Eelpout Festival, a growing number of folks have learned the eelpout is no slouch in a frying pan. A

Raven came into my life a 7-week old puppy from Oak Ridge Kennels in Northfield, MN. I did some training, but most of Raven's good manners are thanks to pro-trainer, Tom Dokken.

Catfish, Carp and Others

filet of eelpout is firm, white and boneless. Prepared side by side with walleye—believe it or not—you might fail the taste test.

One winter day, I convinced the late Swede Carlson, the legendary Warroad bush pilot, to add a few eelpout filets to a lunch of walleyes he was about to fry up on an ice shack stove.

Swede wasn't particularly enthusiastic about my suggestion but he finally said he would, although he insisted on frying all the walleye first so as not to taint it.

Swede even agreed to take a tiny taste of eelpout.

"Not bad," he grumbled.

"Tastes just as good as walleye, doesn't it? I queried.

Swede grunted. He didn't say yes and he didn't say no.

The Ancient Fishes

If you fish with minnows much for walleyes, northern pike, crappies, bass, you'll also catch a dogfish. It's an unwritten rule.

More properly called a bowfin, the fish is most easily identified by its rounded tail, a long continuous dorsal fin and large circular scales.

The bowfin or dogfish also has another distinguishing feature: It's the only one of its kind, the sole survivor of an early primitive family of fishes.

Minnesota waters harbor two other primitive fishes, the longnose and shortnose gars, which look similar except for the length of their long jaws which are heavily armed with teeth.

Anglers seldom catch gar by hook and line because the jaws are bone hard and narrow. But you never know. I caught two gars on the St. Croix River one afternoon, using a small spinner intended for smallmouth bass.

These ancient fish species aren't much to brag about and their fighting heart isn't exactly praiseworthy. At most, the prehistoric fishes can give you a sense of history, possibly explaining why the cave men carried clubs not fishing rods.

Minnesota's Largest Fish

You might know. Minnesota's largest fish won't look at a shiner minnow. It won't chase a Rapala. It won't suck in a dry fly.

Nope, the lake sturgeon eats like a vacuum cleaner, sucking up critters too small to put on a hook. All of which means Minnesota's largest fish isn't caught too often.

Probably a good thing. The lake sturgeon will grow to weights exceeding 200 pounds. With a lot of patience and a gob of night crawlers, the big fish are possible to catch. The two best-known sturgeon waters include the Rainy River and the St. Croix River. I've heard horror stories from some of the St. Croix river rats who tell of hooking sturgeon longer than boats, of battling the huge beasts for hours.

Minnesota also has a smaller species, called the shovelnose sturgeon, commonly found in the St. Croix, Mississippi and Minnesota Rivers. It rarely weighs more than 6 pounds, however. And is seldom caught on hook and line.

Catfish, Carp and Others

More Oddities

A hook really is nothing more than a customized spear. But, lordy, can it bring in a host of strange things. Like suckers and redhorse—fishes with mouths shaped like the end of a vacuum cleaner hose.

And others. Sheepshead, silvery fish with humpbacks; madtoms, miniature bullheads; buffalofish, quillback carp-suckers; gizzard shad; mooneyes; tulli-bee. And don't forget the whitefish, creatures of deep water that in the right mood will take dry flies off the surface.

Those are just a few of the odd catches that might show up on a fishing hook in Minnesota.

The rare paddlefish is one oddity that you can't legally keep. It's snagged in rivers more often than caught. The paddlefish has a nose that looks like the handle of a canoe paddle with a tail that looks a lot like a shark.

Paddlefish don't bite, however.

Just so you know, there are sharks that bite in Minnesota. They swim under the Mall of America at Underwater Adventures.

Fishing Waters

Tristan Publishing, Inc., believes that the following charts are accurate; however, we cannot guarantee or accept liability for their accuracy. The reader should contact the Minnesota DNR to verify the accuracy of the charts.

Name	Nearest Town	Public Access	Acres	Max. Depth	Fish Species
Aitkin					
Aitkin	Libby	Yes	487	35	BLH, BC, B, LMB, NP, SUN, W, YP
Anderson	Tamarack	No	86	16	BLH, BC, YP
Bachelor	Aitkin	No	53	47	BLH, BC, B, LMB, NP, SUN, RKB, YP
Ball Bluff	Jacobson	Yes	159	78	BLH, BC, B, LMB, NP, SUN, RKB, W, YP
Bass	Aitkin	No	27	38	BLH, BC, B, LMB, NP, SUN, W
Bass	McGregor	No	86	42	BC, B, LMB, NP, SUN
Bass	McGregor	Yes	57	58	BC, B, LMB, NP, SUN, RKB, YP
Bass	Swatara	No	111	42	BC, B, LMB, NP, SUN, YP
Bay	Jacobson	No	65	36	BLH, NP, SUN, YP
Bear	McGrath	No	131	60	BLH, BC, B, LMB, NP, SUN, YP
Bible	Hill City	No	19	45	BC, B, LMB, NP, SUN, RKB, YP
Big Pine	Cutler	Yes	614	78	BLH, BC, B, LMB, NP, SUN, RKB, SMB, W, YP
Big Sandy	McGregor	Yes	6526	84	BLH, BC, B, LMB, NP, SUN, RKB, W, YP
Black Shadow	Aitkin	No	17	60	BLH, BC, B, NP, SUN
Blackface	Jacobson	Yes	172	18	BLH, B, LMB, NP, SUN, YP
Blind	Aitkin	Yes	370	17	BLH, BC, B, NP, SUN, YP
Blue	Aitkin	Yes	47	106	B, LMB, NP, SUN, RBT, YP
Boot	Jacobson	No	78	67	BLH, BC, B, LMB, NP, SUN, YP
Brown	McGregor	No	80	28	BLH, BC, B, LMB, NP, SUN, YP
Carlson	Aitkin	No	N/A	23	BLH, BC, B, NP, YP
Cedar	Aitkin	Yes	1769	105	BLH, BC, B, LMB, M, NP, SUN, RKB, W, YP
Cedar	McGrath	No	232	18	BLH, BC, B, LMB, NP, SUN, W, YP
Chamberlin	Hill City	No	10	24	BLH, B, LMB, NP, SUN, YP
Clear	Glen	Yes	562	24	BLH, BC, B, LMB, NP, SUN, RKB, W, YP
Cutaway	McGregor	Yes	113	24	BLH, BC, B, NP, SUN, RKB, YP
Dam	Aitkin	Yes	642	48	BLH, BC, B, LMB, NP, SUN, RKB, W, YP
Davis	McGregor	No	42	21	BLH, BC, B, NP, SUN, W, YP
Diamond	Aitkin	Yes	73	26	BLH, BC, B, NP, SUN, W, YP
Dogfish	Aitkin	No	29	85	BLH, BC, B, LMB, NP, SUN, YP
Douglas	Tamarack	No	75	39	BLH, BC, B, NP, SUN, YP
Dummer	Aitkin	No	31	33	BC
Elm Island	Aitkin	Yes	522	25	BLH, BC, B, NP, SUN, RKB, W, YP
Esquagamah	Palisade	Yes	853	31	BLH, BC, B, LMB, NP, SUN, RKB, W, YP
Farm Island	Bennettville	Yes	2054	56	BLH, BC, B, LMB, NP, SUN, RKB, W, YP
Fleming	Palisade	Yes	296	15	BLH, BC, B, LMB, NP, SUN, YP
Four	Aitkin	Private	121	31	BLH, BC, B, LMB, NP, SUN, W, YP
French	Palisade	Yes	137	37	BLH, BC, B, NP, SUN, RKB, W, YP
Glacier	Libby	Private	133	60	BLH, BC, B, LMB, NP, SUN, RKB, W
Gregg	Garrison	No	31	18	BLH, NP, YP
Gun	Palisade	Yes	730	44	BLH, BC, B, LMB, NP, SUN, RKB, W, YP
Hammal	Aitkin	Yes	373.7	44	BLH, BC, B, LMB, NP, SUN, RKB, YP
Hanging Kettle	Aitkin	Yes	302	35	BLH, BC, B, LMB, NP, SUN, RKB, W, YP
Hanson	Aitkin	Yes	135	42	BLH, BC, B, LMB, NP, SUN
Hay	Jacobson	Yes	106	32	BLH, BC, B, NP, SUN, YP
Hickory	Aitkin	Yes	197	32	BLH, BC, B, LMB, NP, SUN, RKB, W, YP
Hill	Aitkin	No	26	67	BLH, BC, B, LMB, NP, SUN, YP

Fishing Waters

Name	Nearest Town	Public Access	Acres	Max. Depth	Fish Species
Hill	Hill City	Yes	907	48	BLH, BC, B, LMB, NP, SUN, RKB, W, YP
Holy Water	Hill City	No	77	56	BLH, NP, SUN, YP
Horseshoe	Aitkin	No	53	26	BLH, BC, B, LMB, NP, SUN, W, YP
Horseshoe	Tamarack	Yes	237	12	BLH, BC, B, NP, SUN, W, YP
Island	Tamarack	Private	243	25	BLH, BC, B, NP, SUN, YP
Jenkins	Palisade	No	111	38	BLH, BC, B, LMB, NP, SUN, W, YP
Little Ball Bluff	Jacobson	Yes	34	49	BLH, BC, B, LMB, NP, SUN, RKB, YP
Little McKinney	Swatara	Carry In	21	9	BLH, BC, B, NP, SUN, YP
Little Pine	Aitkin	Yes	220	44	BLH, BC, B, LMB, NP, SUN, RKB, W, YP
Little Turtle	Aitkin	Yes	11	46	B, NP
Lone	Aitkin	Yes	448	60	BLH, BC, B, LMB, NP, SUN, RKB, W, YP
Long	Glen	Yes	415	116	BLH, BC, B, LMB, NP, SUN, RKB, W, YP
Long	Palisade	Yes	34	42	BLH, SUN
Loon	McGregor	Yes	33	21	BKT, RBT
McKinney	Swatara	No	60	33	BLH, BC, B, NP, SUN, RKB, YP
Minnewawa	McGregor	Yes	2512	21	BLH, BC, B, LMB, NP, SUN, W, YP
Monson	Glen	No	47	28	BLH, B, LMB, NP, SUN, YP
Moulton	Emily	Yes	258	24	BC, B, NP, SUN, W, YP
Nord	Aitkin	Yes	411.5	29	BLH, BC, B, LMB, NP, SUN, W
Pickerel	Aitkin	No	87	34	BLH, BC, B, LMB, NP, SUN, W, YP
Pine Island	Aitkin	No	60	8	BLH, SUN
Pine	Finlayson	Yes	372	28	BC, B, LMB, NP, SUN, W, YP
Portage	McGregor	Yes	316	18	BLH, BC, B, NP, SUN, YP
Rabbit	Glen	Yes	214	51	BLH, BC, B, LMB, NP, SUN, RKB, YP
Raspberry	Aitkin	No	21	23	BLH, B, NP, SUN, YP
Rat	Palisade	Yes	405	21	BLH, BC, B, LMB, NP, SUN, W, YP
Remote	McGregor	Yes	132	47	BLH, BC, B, NP, SUN, YP
Ripple	Aitkin	Yes	556	39	BLH, BC, B, LMB, NP, SUN, RKB, W, YP
Rock	McGregor	Yes	317	13	BLH, BC, B, LMB, NP, SUN, YP
Round	Aitkin	Yes	N/A	25	BLH, NP
Round	Aitkin	Yes	633	59	BLH, B, LMB, NP, SUN, RKB, W, YP
Round	Garrison	Yes	767	125	BC, B, LMB, NP, SUN, RKB, SMB, W, YP
Round	McGregor	Yes	186	52	BLH, BC, B, LMB, NP, SUN, RKB, W, YP
Round	Tamarack	Yes	577	27	BLH, BC, B, LMB, NP, SUN, W, YP
Savanna	McGregor	Yes	91	23	BLH, BC, B, NP, SUN, RKB, YP
Section Ten	Aitkin	Yes	421	17	BLH, BC, B, LMB, NP, SUN, RKB, W, YP
Section Twelve	Aitkin	Yes	156	40	BLH, BC, B, LMB, NP, SUN, RKB, W, YP
Sheriff	Lawler	Yes	85	80	BC, B, LMB, NP, SUN, W, YP
Shumway	Tamarack	Yes	68	23	BLH, BC, NP, SUN, RKB, W, YP
Sissabagamah	Aitkin	Yes	365	37	BLH, BC, B, LMB, NP, SUN, RKB, W, YP

KEY			
BKT=Brook Trout	LAT=Lake Trout	RKB=Rock Bass	W=Walleye
BLH=Bullhead	LMB=Largemouth Bass	SGR=Sauger	WC=White Crappie
BC=Black Crappie	M=Muskie	SMB=Smallmouth Bass	WHB=White Bass
B=Bluegill	NP=Northern Pike	SPT=Splake	YP=Yellow Perch
BRT=Brown Trout	PKS=Pink Salmon	SUN=Sunfish	
CAT=Catfish (Channel and Flathead)	RBT=Rainbow Trout	TM=Tiger Muskie	

Fishing Waters

Tristan Publishing, Inc., believes that the following charts are accurate; however, we cannot guarantee or accept liability for their accuracy. The reader should contact the Minnesota DNR to verify the accuracy of the charts.

Name	Nearest Town	Public Access	Acres	Max. Depth	Fish Species
Spirit	Bennettville	Yes	530	49	BLH, BC, B, LMB, NP, SUN, RKB, W, YP
Starry	Emily	Private	78	23	BLH, BC, B, LMB, SUN, YP
Starvation	McGregor	Private	66	32	BLH, BC, B, NP, YP
Sugar	Glen	Yes	398	45	BLH, BC, B, LMB, NP, SUN, RKB, W, YP
Sunset	Aitkin	Private	253	43	BLH, BC, B, LMB, NP, SUN, RKB, W, YP
Swamp	Glen	Yes	273	5	BLH, NP, SUN, YP
Sweetman	Glen	No	24	32	BC, B, LMB, SUN, YP
Taylor	Aitkin	No	50	47	BLH, B, LMB, NP, SUN, YP
Taylor	Hill City	Yes	52.3	84	BKT, RBT
Thornton	Deerwood	No	215.6	21	BLH, BC, B, LMB, NP, SUN, YP
Townline	Aitkin	No	173	69	BLH, BC, B, LMB, NP, SUN, YP
Townline	Palisade	No	61	40	BC, B, LMB, NP, SUN, YP
Turner	McGregor	Yes	61	21	BLH, BC, B, NP, SUN, YP
Vanduse	Jacobson	Yes	230	27	BLH, BC, B, LMB, NP, SUN, RKB, YP
WakeField	Jacobson	No	148	69	BLH, BC, B, NP, SUN, W, YP
Waukenabo	Palisade	Yes	644	38	BLH, BC, B, LMB, NP, SUN, RKB, W, YP
Wilkins	Palisade	Yes	372	39	BLH, BC, B, LMB, NP, SUN, RKB, W, YP
Wolf	Tamarack	Yes	168	31	BLH, BC, NP, YP
Anoka					
Burns	Elk River	No	91	18	BLH, SUN, YP
Cenaiko	Coon Rapids	Yes	29.2	36	BKT, BLH, SUN, RBT, SMB, W, WC
Centerville	Centerville	Yes	455	19	BLH, BC, B, LMB, NP, SUN, W, YP
Coon	Soderville	Yes	1259.2	27	BLH, BC, B, LMB, NP, SUN, W, WC, YP
Crooked	Andover	Yes	117.5	26	BC, B, LMB, NP, SUN, SGR, SMB, W, YP
East Moore	Fridley	Yes	28	22	BLH, BC, B, CAT, LMB, NP, SUN, W, YP
East Twin	Elk River	Yes	158	68	BLH, BC, B, LMB, NP, SUN, YP
Fawn	Stacy	Yes	70.5	23	BC, B, LMB, NP, SUN, YP
Fish	East Bethel	Yes	332	10	BLH, BC, B, SUN
George	St. Francis	Yes	495	32	BLH, BC, B, LMB, NP, SUN
Golden	Circle Pines	Yes	57.2	25	BLH, BC, B, LMB, NP, SUN
Ham	Ham Lake	Yes	174	22	BLH, BC, B, LMB, NP, SUN, YP
Island	Wyoming	Yes	66.7	22	BLH, BC, B, LMB, NP, SUN, W, WC
Laddie	Spring Lake Park	Yes	77	4	BLH, BC, B, LMB, SUN
Linwood	Wyoming	Yes	559	42	BLH, BC, B, LMB, NP, SUN, W, WC, YP
Loch Ness	Blaine	Yes	14	16	BLH, BC, B, NP, SUN
Martin	Wyoming	Yes	234	20	BLH, BC, B, LMB, NP, SUN, W, WC, YP
Moore	Fridley	Carry In	108	22	BLH, BC, B, CAT, LMB, NP, SUN, W, YP
Norris	St. Francis	Yes	55.3	21	BLH, BC, B, LMB, NP, SUN, YP
Otter	White Bear Lake	Yes	332	21	BLH, B, NP, SUN
Peltier	Centerville	Yes	465	18	BLH, BC, B, LMB, M, NP, W, YP
Reshanau	Centerville	Yes	336	16	BLH, BC, B, NP, WC, YP
Spring	Spring Lake Park	No	60	18	BLH, B, LMB, SUN, W, WC, YP
West Moore	Fridley	Yes	80	5	BLH, BC, B, LMB, NP, SUN, YP
Becker					
Acorn	Frazee	Yes	125	55	BLH, BC, B, LMB, NP, SUN, W, YP
Bad Medicine	Ponsford	Yes	799	84	BC, B, LMB, NP, RBT, RKB, W, YP

Fishing Waters

Name	Nearest Town	Public Access	Acres	Max. Depth	Fish Species
Bass	Ponsford	Yes	178	28	BLH, BC, B, LMB, NP, SUN, RKB, W, YP
Bass	Snellman	Yes	135	48	BLH, BC, B, LMB, NP, SUN, W, YP
Bass	White Earth	Yes	123	50	BLH, B, LMB, NP, SUN, YP
Beseau	Lake Park	Yes	226	27	BLH, BC, B, NP, SUN, W, YP
Big Cormorant	Audubon	Yes	3421	75	BLH, BC, B, LMB, NP, SUN, RKB, SMB, W, YP
Big Sugar Bush	Richwood	Yes	472	42	BLH, BC, B, LMB, NP, SUN, W, YP
Blueberry	Osage	Yes	69	47	BLH, BC, B, LMB, NP, SUN, W, YP
Boot	Two Inlets	Yes	348	109	BC, B, LMB, NP, SUN, RKB, W, YP
Boyer	Lake Park	Yes	310	26	BLH, B, LMB, NP, SUN, W, YP
Buck	Detroit Lakes	No	91	15	BLH, BC, B, LMB, NP, SUN, W, YP
Buffalo	Richwood	Yes	376	38	BLH, BC, B, NP, SUN, RKB, W, YP
Canary	Lake Park	Yes	61	25	BLH, BC, B, LMB, NP, SUN, YP
Cotton	Rochert	Yes	1720	28	BLH, BC, B, LMB, NP, SUN, RKB, W, YP
Dead	Frazee	No	274	19	BLH, B, NP, SUN, RKB, W, YP
Detroit	Detroit Lakes	Yes	3083	89	BLH, BC, B, LMB, M, NP, SUN, RKB, W, YP
Dinner	Park Rapids	Yes	57.2	32	BLH, BC, B, LMB, NP, SUN, RKB, W, YP
Eagle	Frazee	Yes	308	29	BLH, BC, B, LMB, NP, SUN, RKB, W, YP
East LaBelle	Lake Park	Yes	146	19	BLH, BC, B, NP, SUN, W, YP
Elbow	Waubun	Yes	1001	76	BLH, BC, B, LMB, NP, SUN, RKB, W, YP
Eunice	Audubon	Yes	325	30	BLH, BC, B, LMB, NP, SUN, RKB, W, YP
Floyd	Detroit Lakes	Yes	1212	34	BLH, BC, B, LMB, NP, SUN, RKB, W, YP
Fox	Detroit Lakes	Yes	135	24	BLH, BC, B, LMB, NP, SUN, RKB, W, YP
Green Water	Ponsford	No	81	57	BLH, B, LMB, NP, SUN, RKB, W, YP
Hanson	Rochert	Yes	32.5	29	RBT
Height of Land	Detroit Lakes	Yes	3520	21	BLH, BC, B, LMB, NP, SUN, W, YP
Hernando DeSoto	Lake Itasca	No	130	22	SUN, W
Hungry	Frazee	Yes	240	60	BLH, BC, B, LMB, NP, SUN, W, YP
Hungry Man	Two Inlets	Yes	91	21	BLH, BC, B, LMB, NP, SUN, W, YP
Ice Cracking	Ponsford	Yes	331	73	BLH, BC, B, LMB, NP, SUN, RKB, W, YP
Ida	Lake Park	Yes	580	20	BLH, BC, B, LMB, NP, SUN, RKB, W, YP
Island	Snellman	Yes	1142	38	BLH, BC, B, NP, SUN, RKB, SMB, W, YP
Johnson	Detroit Lakes	No	161	30	BLH, BC, B, NP, SUN, W, YP
Juggler	Ponsford	Yes	365	78	B, LMB, NP, SUN, RKB, SMB, W, YP
Kane	Park Rapids	Yes	24	52	BLH, B, NP, SUN, YP
Leif	Audubon	Yes	488	26	BLH, BC, B, LMB, NP, SUN, RKB, W, YP
Little Bemidji	Ponsford	Yes	275	58	BLH, BC, B, LMB, NP, SUN, RKB, W, YP

KEY BKT=Brook Trout BLH=Bullhead BC=Black Crappie B=Bluegill BRT=Brown Trout CAT=Catfish (Channel and Flathead) LAT=Lake Trout LMB=Largemouth Bass M=Muskie NP=Northern Pike PKS=Pink Salmon RBT=Rainbow Trout RKB=Rock Bass SGR=Sauger SMB=Smallmouth Bass SPT=Splake SUN=Sunfish TM=Tiger Muskie W=Walleye WC=White Crappie WHB=White Bass YP=Yellow Perch

Fishing Waters

Tristan Publishing, Inc., believes that the following charts are accurate; however, we cannot guarantee or accept liability for their accuracy. The reader should contact the Minnesota DNR to verify the accuracy of the charts.

Name	Nearest Town	Public Access	Acres	Max. Depth	Fish Species
Little Cormorant	Audubon	Yes	924	34	BLH, BC, B, LMB, NP, SUN, W, YP
Little Floyd	Detroit Lakes	Yes	205	34	BLH, BC, B, LMB, NP, SUN, RKB, W, YP
Little Long	Wolf Lake	Yes	11	28	BC, B, LMB, NP, SUN, W, YP
Little Sugar Bush	Richwood	Yes	202	29	BLH, BC, B, LMB, NP, SUN, W, YP
Little Toad	Frazee	Yes	345	65	BLH, BC, B, LMB, NP, SUN, RKB, W, YP
Long	Detroit Lakes	Yes	357	61	BLH, BC, B, LMB, NP, SUN, RKB, W, YP
Many Point	Ponsford	Yes	1737	92	BLH, BC, B, LMB, NP, SUN, RKB, W, YP
Marshall	Audubon	Yes	159	21	BLH, LMB, NP, SUN, W, YP
Maud	Audubon	Yes	547	32	BLH, BC, B, LMB, NP, SUN, RKB, W, YP
Meadow	Detroit Lakes	Yes	70	72	BLH, BC, B, BRT, LMB, NP, SUN, RBT, W, YP
Melissa	Detroit Lakes	Yes	1831	43	BLH, BC, B, LMB, NP, SUN, RKB, W, YP
Middle Cormorant	Lake Park	Yes	360	40	BLH, BC, B, LMB, NP, SUN, RKB, W, YP
Mill	Detroit Lakes	No	171	10	BLH, BC, B, LMB, NP, SUN, YP
Morrison	Lake George	No	63	30	LMB, SUN, YP
Munson	Detroit Lakes	Yes	123	26	BLH, BC, B, LMB, NP, SUN, W, YP
Muskrat	Detroit Lakes	Yes	67	18	BLH, BC, B, LMB, NP, SUN, W, YP
Net	White Earth	Yes	213	47	BLH, BC, B, LMB, NP, SUN, RKB, W, YP
Pearl	Detroit Lakes	Yes	236.8	54	BLH, BC, B, LMB, NP, SUN, W, YP
Perch	Detroit Lakes	Yes	40	38	BLH, BC, B, NP, SUN, RKB, YP
Pickerel	Detroit Lakes	Yes	332	74	BLH, BC, B, LMB, NP, SUN, RKB, W, YP
Pike	Waubun	No	120	50	BLH, B, LMB, NP, SUN, RKB, W, YP
Reeves	Detroit Lakes	No	81	43	BLH, BC, B, NP, SUN, YP
Rice	Callaway	Yes	177	23	BLH, BC, B, LMB, NP, SUN, W, YP
Rock	Detroit	Yes	1048	18	BLH, BC, B, LMB, NP, SUN, W, YP
Rossman	Lake Park	Yes	241	20	BLH, BC, B, LMB, NP, SUN, YP
Round	Ponsford	Yes	1087	69	BLH, BC, B, LMB, NP, SUN, RKB, W, YP
Sallie	Detroit Lakes	Yes	1246	50	BLH, BC, B, LMB, NP, SUN, RKB, W, YP
Sand	Lake Park	Yes	197	19	BLH, BC, B, LMB, NP, W, YP
Sauer	Detroit Lakes	Yes	212	39	BLH, BC, B, CAT, LMB, NP, SUN, W, YP
Shell	Snellman	Yes	3140	16	BLH, BC, B, LMB, NP, SUN, RKB, W, YP
Shipman	Osage	Yes	56	55	BLH, BC, B, LMB, NP, SUN, YP
Sieverson	Snellman	Yes	77	35	BLH, BC, B, LMB, NP, SUN, W, YP
South Twin	Detroit Lakes	Yes	139	37	BLH, BC, B, LMB, NP, SUN, YP
Stakke	Lake Park	Yes	450	15	BLH, B, YP
Straight	Osage	Yes	423	63	BLH, BC, B, LMB, NP, SUN, RKB, SMB, W, YP
Strawberry	White Earth	Yes	1522	40	BLH, BC, B, LMB, NP, SUN, RKB, SMB, W, YP
Tamarack	Rochert	Yes	1431	17	BLH, BC, B, LMB, NP, W, YP
Toad	Osage	Yes	1666	29	BLH, BC, B, LMB, NP, SUN, RKB, W, YP
Town	Frazee	Yes	106	15	BC, B, NP, SUN, YP

Name	Nearest Town	Public Access	Acres	Max. Depth	Fish Species
Turtle	Lake Park	Yes	147	73	BLH, BC, B, LMB, NP, SUN, RKB, W, YP
Two Inlets	Two Inlets	Yes	578	60	BLH, BC, B, LMB, NP, SUN, RKB, W, YP
Upper Cormorant	Lake Park	Yes	856	29	BLH, BC, B, LMB, NP, SUN, W, YP
Waboose	Ponsford	Yes	231.5	14	BLH, BC, NP, SUN, W, YP
White Earth	White Earth	Yes	2079	120	BLH, BC, B, LMB, NP, SUN, RKB, SMB, W, YP
Wolf	Wolf Lake	Yes	1445	16	BLH, NP, W, YP
Beltrami					
Andrusia	Cass Lake	Yes	1510	60	BC, B, LMB, M, NP, SUN, RKB, W, YP
Balm	Solway	Yes	512	33	BLH, BC, B, LMB, NP, SUN, RKB, W, YP
Bass	Turtle River	Yes	76	59	BLH, B, LMB, NP, SUN, YP
Beltrami	Bemidji	Yes	543	50	BLH, BC, B, LMB, NP, SUN, RKB, W, YP
Bemidji	Bemidji	Yes	6420	76	B, LMB, M, NP, RKB, W, YP
Benjamin	Blackduck	Yes	29.6	128	RBT
Big Bass	Bemidji	Yes	380	17	BLH, BC, B, LMB, NP, SUN, W, YP
Big Rice	Cass Lake	Carry In	618	13	BLH, BC, B, LMB, NP, SUN, RKB, W, YP
Big	Bemidji	Yes	3533	35	BLH, BC, B, LMB, M, NP, SUN, RKB, W, YP
Black	Turtle River	No	246	42	BLH, BC, B, LMB, NP, SUN, RKB, W, YP
Blackduck	Blackduck	Yes	2596	28	BLH, B, NP, SUN, RKB, W, YP
Bootleg	Bemidji	No	267	30	BLH, BC, B, NP, SUN, RKB, YP
Buck	Cass Lake	No	271	40	BLH, BC, B, LMB, M, NP, SUN, RKB, W, YP
Bullhead	Kelliher	No	44	17	BLH
Buzzle	Solway	No	189	83	BLH, BC, B, NP, SUN, RKB, YP
Campbell	Puposky	Yes	475	25	BLH, BC, B, LMB, NP, SUN, RKB, W, YP
Carr	Bemidji	No	29	30	BLH, BC, LMB, NP, SUN, RKB, W, YP
Carter	Tenstrike	No	30	69	BLH, B, LMB, NP, SUN, RKB, W, YP
Cass	Cass Lake	Yes	15596	120	BLH, BC, B, LMB, M, NP, SUN, RKB, SMB, W, YP
Clearwater	Leonard	Yes	1008	65	BLH, BC, B, LMB, NP, SUN, RKB, W, YP
Deer	Bemidji	Yes	262	42	BLH, BC, B, LMB, NP, SUN, RKB, W, YP
Dellwater	Bemidji	Yes	198.3	29	BLH, B, NP, SUN, RKB, YP
Fox	Turtle River	No	148	19	BC, B, LMB, NP, SUN, RKB, W, YP
Gilstad	Blackduck	Yes	294	55	BLH, BC, B, NP, SUN, RKB, W, YP
Grant	Wilton	Yes	207.9	92	BLH, BC, B, LMB, NP, SUN, RKB,
Gull	Tenstrike	Yes	2243	23	BLH, BC, B, LMB, NP, SUN, RKB, W, YP
Gull	Turtle River	Yes	114	20	BLH, BC, B, NP, SUN, RKB, YP
Hagali	Nebish	No	89	27	BLH

KEY	BKT=Brook Trout	LAT=Lake Trout	RKB=Rock Bass	W=Walleye
	BLH=Bullhead	LMB=Largemouth Bass	SGR=Sauger	WC=White Crappie
	BC=Black Crappie	M=Muskie	SMB=Smallmouth Bass	WHB=White Bass
	B=Bluegill	NP=Northern Pike	SPT=Splake	YP=Yellow Perch
	BRT=Brown Trout	PKS=Pink Salmon	SUN=Sunfish	
	CAT=Catfish (Channel and Flathead)	RBT=Rainbow Trout	TM=Tiger Muskie	

Fishing Waters

Tristan Publishing, Inc., believes that the following charts are accurate; however, we cannot guarantee or accept liability for their accuracy. The reader should contact the Minnesota DNR to verify the accuracy of the charts.

Name	Nearest Town	Public Access	Acres	Max. Depth	Fish Species
Irving	Bemidji	Yes	613	19	BLH, BC, B, LMB, NP, SUN, RKB, W, YP
Island	Red Lake	Yes	368	14	BLH, BC, B, LMB, SUN, YP
Jackson	Bemidji	No	120	37	BLH, BC, NP, SUN, RKB, YP
Julia	Puposky	Yes	450	43	BLH, NP, SUN, RKB, W, YP
Kitchi	Pennington	Yes	1785	50	BLH, BC, B, LMB, NP, SUN, RKB, W, YP
Larson	Bemidji	No	178	49	BLH, NP
Little Bass	Bemidji	No	343	22	BLH, BC, B, LMB, NP, SUN, RKB, W, YP
Little Buzzle	Pinewood	Yes	68	40	BLH, BC, B, LMB, NP, SUN, RKB, YP
Little Gnat	Turtle River	No	33	30	BLH, BC, B, NP, SUN, W, YP
Little Rice	Cass Lake	Private	118	26	BLH, BC, B, LMB, NP, SUN, RKB, W, YP
Little Turtle	Puposky	Yes	464	25	BLH, BC, B, LMB, NP, SUN, RKB, W, YP
Long	Puposky	No	719	18	BLH, BC, B, LMB, NP, SUN, RKB, W, YP
Long	Turtle River	Yes	395.5	87	BLH, BC, B, LMB, NP, SUN, RKB, W, YP
Lost	Pennington	No	112	31	BLH, BC, B, LMB, NP, SUN, RKB, W, YP
Marquette	Bemidji	No	504	51	BLH, BC, B, LMB, NP, SUN, RKB, W, YP
Meadow	Turtle River	Yes	118	28	BLH, BC, B, NP, SUN, RKB, YP
Medicine	Tenstrike	Yes	446	44	BLH, BC, B, LMB, NP, SUN, RKB, W, YP
Miller	Bemidji	Yes	32	24	LMB, W, YP
Moose	Debs	No	117	61	B, LMB, NP, SUN, RKB, YP
Moose	Pennington	Yes	568	71	BLH, BC, B, LMB, NP, SUN, RKB, W, YP
Moose	Wilton	Yes	124	13	BLH, BC, B, LMB, NP, SUN, RKB, W, YP
Movil	Bemidji	No	923	50	BLH, BC, B, LMB, NP, SUN, RKB, W, YP
Myrtle	Debs	No	116	50	BLH, BC, B, LMB, NP, SUN, RKB, YP
Nelson	Tenstrike	Yes	29	30	BLH, BC, B, LMB, NP, SUN, YP
North Twin	Turtle River	Yes	313	59	BC, B, LMB, NP, SUN, RKB, SMB, W, YP
Pimushe	Pennington	Yes	1268	40	BLH, BC, B, LMB, NP, SUN, RKB, W, YP
Puposky	Bemidji	Yes	2142	20	BLH, NP, YP
Rabideau	Blackduck	Yes	577	112	BLH, BC, B, NP, SUN, RKB, W, YP
Red	Waskish	Yes	107832	18	BC, NP, SMB, W, YP
Sandy	Debs	Yes	100	72	BLH, BC, B, LMB, NP, SUN, RKB, W, YP
Sandy	Tenstrike	Yes	260	32	BLH, BC, B, LMB, NP, SUN, W, YP
Silver	Bemidji	Carry In	90	55	BC, B, LMB, NP, SUN
Silver	Nebish	No	72	45	BLH, NP, SUN, YP
South Twin	Bemidji	Yes	205	45	BLH, BC, B, LMB, NP, SUN, RKB, W, YP
Stocking	Bemidji	No	75	9	BLH, B, LMB, NP, SUN, RKB, W, YP
Stump	Bemidji	No	290	24	BLH, BC, B, LMB, M, NP, SUN, RKB, W, YP
Swenson	Bemidji	Yes	388	76	BC, B, LMB, NP, SUN, RKB, W, YP
Sylvia	Solway	No	186	38	B, LMB, NP, SUN, RKB, W, YP

Name	Nearest Town	Public Access	Acres	Max. Depth	Fish Species
Three Island	Turtle River	Yes	678	25	BLH, BC, B, LMB, NP, SUN, RKB, W, YP
Turtle River	Turtle River	Yes	1740.04	63	BLH, BC, B, LMB, NP, SUN, RKB, W, YP
Turtle	Bemidji	Yes	1436	45	BLH, BC, B, LMB, NP, SUN, RKB, W, YP
Upper Lindgren	Puposky	Yes	29	43	BLH, BC, B, NP, SUN, W, YP
Webster	Blackduck	Yes	47.6	15	BLH, B, LMB, YP
Whitefish	Pinewood	Yes	120	30	BLH, BC, B, NP, YP
Windigo	Cass Lake	Carry In	199	25	BLH, BC, B, LMB, NP, SUN, RKB, SMB, W, YP
Wolf	Bemidji	Yes	1094	57	BC, M, NP, RKB, W, YP
Benton					
Little Rock	Rice	Yes	1450	23	BLH, BC, B, CAT, NP, W, WC, YP
Mayhew	Mayhew	Yes	131	20	BLH, BC, B, NP, SUN, W, WC, YP
Big Stone					
Artichoke	Correll	Yes	1964	15.5	BLH, BC, B, LMB, NP, SUN, W, YP
Big Stone	Ortonville	Yes	12610	16	BLH, BC, B, CAT, NP, SUN, RKB, W, WHB, YP
East Toqua	Graceville	Yes	428	9	BLH, BC, B, NP, SUN, W, WC, YP
Eli	Clinton	Yes	139	5	BLH
Long Tom	Ortonville	Yes	133	15	BLH, BC, NP, W, YP
Long	Correll	Yes	335	10	BLH, BC, B, SUN, W, YP
Marsh	Correll	Yes	4500	5	BLH, BC, NP, SUN, W, WHB, WC, YP
N. Rockwell Slough	Clinton	Yes	392	13	BLH, SUN, W, YP
Swenson	Clinton	Yes	110	N/A	BLH
Blue Earth					
Ballantyne	Madison Lake	Yes	350	58	BLH, BC, B, LMB, NP, W, YP
Crystal	Lake Crystal	Yes	393	8	BLH, BC, B, NP, SUN, W, YP
Dorothy	Mankato	Yes	12	17	BLH, BC, B, NP, SUN, W
Duck	Madison Lake	Yes	282	25	BLH, BC, B, LMB, NP, SUN, W, WC, YP
Eagle Lake	Eagle Lake	Yes	150	5	BLH, B, SUN, WC
Eagle	Madison Lake	Yes	914	9	BLH, BC, NP, SUN, W, YP
George	Madison Lake	Yes	80	28	BLH, BC, B, NP, SUN, W, YP
Hiniker Pond	North Mankato	Yes	15	21	BC, B, NP, SUN, W, WHB, WC, YP
Ida	Amboy	Yes	120	8	BLH, BC, B, LMB, NP
Lions	Mankato	Yes	7	7	BLH, BC, B, CAT, LMB, NP, SUN, W
Loon	Lake Crystal	Yes	755	7	BLH, BC, B, NP, SUN, W, YP
Lura	Mapleton	Yes	1224	9	BLH, BC, B, LMB, NP, W, YP
Madison	Madison Lake	Yes	1113	59	BLH, BC, B, CAT, LMB, NP, SUN, W, WHB, WC, YP
Mills	Garden City	Yes	235	7	BLH, B, SUN
Troost Pond	Mankato	Yes	3	45	BLH, BC, B, LMB, WC
Brown					
Clear	New Ulm	Yes	281	7	BLH, BC, B, LMB, W
Hanska	Hanska	Yes	1773	16	BLH, BC, LMB, NP, W, YP
Sleepy Eye	Sleepy Eye	Yes	227	21	BLH, BC, B, LMB, NP, YP
Springfield	Springfield	Yes	5	15	BC, B, CAT, SUN, WC, YP
Wellner-Hageman	Sanborn	Yes	70	24	BLH, BC, B, CAT, SUN, W, YP

KEY			
BKT=Brook Trout	**LAT**=Lake Trout	**RKB**=Rock Bass	**W**=Walleye
BLH=Bullhead	**LMB**=Largemouth Bass	**SGR**=Sauger	**WC**=White Crappie
BC=Black Crappie	**M**=Muskie	**SMB**=Smallmouth Bass	**WHB**=White Bass
B=Bluegill	**NP**=Northern Pike	**SPT**=Splake	**YP**=Yellow Perch
BRT=Brown Trout	**PKS**=Pink Salmon	**SUN**=Sunfish	
CAT=Catfish (Channel and Flathead)	**RBT**=Rainbow Trout	**TM**=Tiger Muskie	

Fishing Waters

Tristan Publishing, Inc., believes that the following charts are accurate; however, we cannot guarantee or accept liability for their accuracy. The reader should contact the Minnesota DNR to verify the accuracy of the charts.

Name	Nearest Town	Public Access	Acres	Max. Depth	Fish Species
Carlton					
Bang	Sawyer	Yes	53	9	BLH, BC, B, LMB, SUN, YP
Bear	Atkinson	No	52.75	28	BC, SUN, YP
Bear	Barnum	Yes	91	31	BLH, BC, B, LMB, NP, SUN, W, YP
Big	Sawyer	Yes	507	25	BLH, BC, B, LMB, NP, SUN, W, YP
Blackhoof	Mahtowa	No	39	9	BLH, BC, B, NP, SUN, YP
Bob	Sawyer	Yes	82	30	BC, B, LMB, NP, SUN, W, YP
Chub	Carlton	Yes	311	28	BLH, BC, B, LMB, NP, SUN, RKB, W, YP
Coffee	Moose Lake	Carry In	68.5	53	BLH, BC, B, LMB, NP, SUN, RKB, W, YP
Cole	Wright	Yes	153.5	24	BC, B, LMB, NP, SUN, W, YP
Corona	Sawyer	Yes	24.5	30	BLH, RBT
Cross	Cromwell	Yes	100.8	23	BLH, BC, B, NP, SUN, W, YP
Eagle	Cromwell	Yes	380	35	BLH, BC, B, NP, SUN, RKB, W, YP
Echo	Moose Lake	Yes	104.5	47	BC, B, LMB, NP, SUN, RKB, YP
Eddy	Barnum	Yes	23	37	BC, B, NP, SUN, RKB, W, YP
Ellstrom	Mahtowa	No	31	13	BLH, BC, LMB, NP, SUN, YP
Fond du Lac	Fon du Lac	Yes	217	59	CAT, NP, RKB, SMB, W, YP
Graham	Holyoke	Carry In	34.2	21	BLH, BC, B, NP, SUN, YP
Hanging Horn	Barnum	Yes	408	80	BLH, BC, B, LMB, NP, SUN, RKB, SMB, W, YP
Hay	Wrenshall	Yes	215	16	BLH, BC, LMB, NP, SUN, YP
Knife Falls	Cloquet	No	61	32	B, CAT, RKB, SMB, W
Little Hanging Horn	Barnum	Yes	117	70	BC, B, LMB, NP, SUN, RKB, W, YP
Lower Island	Cromwell	Yes	281	22	BLH, BC, B, LMB, NP, SUN, RKB, W, YP
Moose	Moose Lake	Private	125	67	BC, B, LMB, NP, SUN, RKB, W, YP
Moosehead	Moose Lake	Yes	292	18	BC, B, NP, SUN, RKB, W, YP
Munson	Mahtowa	No	36	23	BC, NP, YP
Park	Mahtowa	Yes	375.8	16	BLH, BC, B, LMB, NP, SUN, RKB, W, YP
Sand	Barnum	Yes	123	27	BLH, BC, B, NP, SUN, YP
Soper	Holyoke	No	31	11	BLH, BC, NP, YP
Spring	Barnum	Yes	32	25	B, NP, SUN, YP
Tamarack	Wright	Yes	228	48	BLH, BC, B, NP, SUN, RKB, W, YP
Thomson	Thomson	Carry In	339	22	BLH, BC, B, CAT, NP, RKB, SMB, W, YP
Torch Light	Sawyer	Yes	134.8	14	BC, B, LMB, NP, SUN, W
Twentynine	Barnum	No	50	25	NP, YP
Upper Island	Cromwell	Yes	101	25	BLH, BC, B, NP, SUN, W, YP
Venoah	Carlton	No	77	25	BLH, B, LMB, NP, SUN, YP
Carver					
Ann	Chanhassen	Yes	116	45	BLH, BC, B, LMB, NP, SUN, YP
Auburn	Victoria	Yes	261	37	BLH, BC, B, LMB, NP, SUN, YP
Aue	Cologne	No	34	27	BLH, SUN, YP
Bavaria	Victoria	Yes	162	66	BLH, BC, B, LMB, NP, SUN, YP
Burandt	Dahlgren	No	93	24	BLH, BC, B, NP, WC, YP
Church	Victoria	Yes	12.3	54	BLH, BC, B, LMB, SUN, YP
Courthouse	Chaska	Yes	10	57	BKT, BLH, BC, NP, RBT, SPT, W, WC
Eagle	Young America	Yes	233	14	BLH, BC, B, LMB, NP, SUN, TM, W
Firemen's Clayhole	Chaska	Yes	8	23	BLH, BC, B, SUN
Goose	Dahlgren	Yes	394	10	BLH, BC, B, CAT, LMB, NP, SUN, YP
Grace	Chaska	Yes	55.9	22	BLH, BC, B, LMB, NP, SUN, YP
Hydes	Young America	Yes	214.7	18	BLH, BC, B, LMB, NP, W, YP
Lotus	Chanhassen	Yes	246	29	BLH, BC, B, LMB, NP, SUN, W, YP
Lucy	Chanhassen	No	92	20	BLH, BC, B, LMB, NP, SUN
Maria	Belle Plaine	Yes	176	6	BLH

Fishing Waters

Name	Nearest Town	Public Access	Acres	Max. Depth	Fish Species
Miller	Dahlgren	No	140	14	BLH, BC, B, WC
Minnewashta	Chanhassen	Yes	738	70	BLH, BC, B, LMB, NP, SUN, W, YP
Oak	Watertown	No	339	11	BLH, BC, B, LMB, NP, SUN, W, WC
Parley	Dahlgren	Yes	242	18	BLH, BC, B, LMB, NP, SUN, W, WC, YP
Piersons	Victoria	Yes	235	40	BC, B, LMB, M, NP, SUN, TM, YP
Reitz	Dahlgren	Yes	79.3	36	BLH, BC, B, LMB, NP, SUN, YP
Riley	Chanhassen	Yes	297	49	BLH, BC, B, LMB, NP, SUN, W, YP
Schutz	Victoria	No	105	49	BLH, BC, B, LMB, NP, SUN, YP
St. Joe	Chanhassen	Yes	14	52	BLH, B, LMB, NP, SUN
Steiger	Victoria	Yes	158.3	37	BLH, BC, B, LMB, NP, SUN, W, YP
Stone	Victoria	No	99.6	30	BLH, M, WC
Susan	Chanhassen	No	93	17	BLH, BC, B, LMB, NP, SUN, W
Swede	Watertown	Yes	376	12	BLH, BC, B, LMB, SUN, W
Tamarack	Victoria	Yes	24.4	82	BC, B, NP, SUN, YP
Turbid	Dahlgren	No	40	37	BLH, B, SUN
Virginia	Victoria	Yes	110	34	BLH, BC, B, LMB, NP, SUN, W, WC, YP
Waconia	Dahlgren	Yes	2996	37	BLH, BC, B, LMB, M, NP, SUN, W, WC, YP
Wassermann	Victoria	Yes	153	41	BLH, BC, B, LMB, M, NP, SUN, YP
Zumbra-Sunny	Victoria	Yes	162.3	58	BLH, BC, B, LMB, NP, SUN, YP
Cass					
Ada	Backus	Yes	974	60	BLH, BC, B, LMB, NP, SUN, RKB, W, YP
Agate	Nisswa	No	150	9	BLH, BC, B, LMB, NP, SUN, RKB, W, YP
Alice	Walker	Carry In	57	55	BC, B, LMB, NP, YP
Andrus	Outing	Yes	44	55	BC, B, LMB, NP, SUN, YP
Anoway	Walker	Carry In	22	45	BC, B, NP, SUN, RKB, YP
Baby	Hackensack	Yes	704.5	69	BLH, BC, B, LMB, M, NP, SUN, RKB, SMB, W, YP
Barnum	Hackensack	No	134	30	BC, B, LMB, NP, SUN, RKB, SMB, YP
Bass	Outing	Yes	213	55	BLH, BC, B, LMB, NP, SUN, RKB, W, YP
Bass	Pine River	No	93.4	28	BLH, BC, B, LMB, NP, SUN, RKB, YP
Bass	Walker	Yes	264	33	BLH, BC, B, LMB, NP, YP
Beuber	Backus	Yes	111	32	BLH, BC, B, LMB, NP, SUN, YP
Big Deep	Hackensack	Private	484	107	BLH, BC, B, LMB, NP, SUN, RKB, SMB, W, YP
Big Hanson	Walker	Carry In	17	95	BLH, NP, SUN, YP
Big Portage	Backus	Yes	918	23	BLH, BC, B, LMB, NP, SUN, RKB, W, YP
Big Rice	Remer	Yes	2832	5	B, NP, SUN, RKB, W, YP
Big Sand	Remer	Yes	736	23	BLH, BC, B, LMB, NP, SUN, RKB, W, YP
Birch	Hackensack	Yes	1284	45	BLH, BC, B, LMB, NP, SUN, RKB, W, YP
Birch	Remer	No	255	30	BC, B, LMB, NP, SUN, RKB, YP

KEY			
BKT=Brook Trout	**LAT**=Lake Trout	**RKB**=Rock Bass	**W**=Walleye
BLH=Bullhead	**LMB**=Largemouth Bass	**SGR**=Sauger	**WC**=White Crappie
BC=Black Crappie	**M**=Muskie	**SMB**=Smallmouth Bass	**WHB**=White Bass
B=Bluegill	**NP**=Northern Pike	**SPT**=Splake	**YP**=Yellow Perch
BRT=Brown Trout	**PKS**=Pink Salmon	**SUN**=Sunfish	
CAT=Catfish (Channel and Flathead)	**RBT**=Rainbow Trout	**TM**=Tiger Muskie	

Fishing Waters

Tristan Publishing, Inc., believes that the following charts are accurate; however, we cannot guarantee or accept liability for their accuracy. The reader should contact the Minnesota DNR to verify the accuracy of the charts.

Name	Nearest Town	Public Access	Acres	Max. Depth	Fish Species
Blackwater	Longville	Yes	722	67	BLH, BC, B, LMB, NP, SUN, RKB, SMB, W, YP
Blind	Manhattan Beach	Yes	82.2	20	BLH, BC, B, LMB, NP, SUN, YP
Bluebill	Hackensack	Yes	43.95	6.5	BLH
Boot	Pine River	No	53	14	BLH
Bowen	Backus	Yes	176	25	BC, B, LMB, NP, SUN, RKB, W, YP
Boxell	Longville	Yes	60	27	BC, B, LMB, NP, SUN, W, YP
Boy	Boy River	Yes	3186	45	BLH, BC, B, LMB, M, NP, SUN, RKB, W, YP
Broadwater Bay	Longville	Yes	714	47	BLH, BC, B, LMB, NP, SUN, RKB, SMB, W, YP
Brockway	Backus	Yes	85	17	BLH, BC, B, LMB, NP, SUN, RKB, W, YP
Carnahan	Longville	Yes	23.05	25	BC, NP, W
Cedar	Remer	Yes	19	28	BLH, B, LMB, NP, SUN, RBT, YP
Cedar	Walker	Yes	32.9	15	BLH, NP, SUN, YP
Cedar	Whipholt	Carry In	141	42	BLH, BC, B, LMB, NP, SUN, RKB, YP
Child	Longville	Yes	316	29	BLH, BC, B, LMB, M, NP, SUN, RKB, W, YP
Cooper	Longville	Yes	147.1	70	BLH, B, LMB, NP, SUN, RKB, W, YP
Crooked	Cass Lake	No	528	74	BC, B, LMB, NP, SUN, RKB, W, YP
Crystal	Akeley	Yes	197	40	BC, B, LMB, NP, SUN, W, YP
Cub	Hackensack	Yes	19	24	BLH
Dead Horse Slough	Remer	No	30	70	B, LMB, NP, SUN, RKB
Dead Horse	Pillager	Yes	17	39	BC, B, NP, W
Deep Portage	Backus	Yes	122.7	105	BC, B, LMB, NP, SUN, RKB, W, YP
Deep	Walker	No	21.6	62	BLH, NP, SUN, YP
Diamond	Walker	Yes	82	31	RBT
Donut	Outing	No	34	18	BLH, BC, B, LMB, NP, SUN, W
Egg	Outing	Yes	90	8	BLH, BC, B, LMB, NP, SUN, YP
Fifth	Walker	Carry In	45.6	60	BC, B, LMB, NP, SUN, RKB, YP
Fish	Hackensack	No	39	43	LMB, NP, SUN, YP
Five Point	Hackensack	Yes	219	37	BLH, BC, B, LMB, NP, SUN, RKB, W, YP
Four-One-Eight	Hackensack	No	12	45	B, LMB, SUN, W
Fourth	Walker	Yes	43.4	65	BLH, BC, B, LMB, NP, SUN, YP
Gadbolt	Walker	Carry In	69	15	B, LMB, NP, YP
George	Outing	Yes	720	20	BLH, B, NP, SUN, YP
Girl	Longville	Yes	406	81	BLH, BC, B, LMB, M, NP, SUN, RKB, W, YP
Grave	Remer	Yes	377	55	BC, B, LMB, NP, SUN, RKB, W, YP
Green Bass	Pillager	Yes	41	27	BLH, BC, B, LMB, NP, RKB, W
Gull	Nisswa	Yes	9418	80	BLH, BC, B, LMB, NP, SUN, RKB, W, YP
Gut	Hackensack	Yes	56	43	BC, B, NP, SUN, YP
Hand	Backus	Yes	269	57	BLH, BC, B, LMB, NP, SUN, RKB, W, YP
Hanson	Walker	No	29	28	BLH, NP, SUN, YP
Hardy	Brainerd	Private	95	26	BC, B, LMB, NP, SUN, PKS, YP
Hattie	Backus	No	484	30	BLH, BC, B, LMB, NP, SUN, RKB, W, YP
Hay	Backus	Yes	350	56	BLH, BC, B, LMB, NP, SUN, RKB, W
Hazel	Longville	Yes	12.3	38	RBT
Heffron	Longville	No	46.5	35	BC, B, LMB, NP, SUN, YP
Horseshoe	Backus	Yes	225	51	BLH, B, LMB, NP, SUN, RKB, W, YP
Horseshoe	Pine River	No	85	26	BLH, BC, B, LMB, NP, SUN, RKB, W, YP

Name	Nearest Town	Public Access	Acres	Max. Depth	Fish Species
Horseshoe	Whipolt	Yes	124	12	BLH, B, LMB, NP, SUN, W, YP
Hovde	Walker	No	131	26	BLH, LMB, W, YP
Howard	Akeley	No	365.3	60	BLH, BC, B, LMB, M, NP, SUN, RKB, W, YP
Hunter	Longville	Private	168	48	BC, B, LMB, NP, SUN, RKB, SMB, W, YP
Inguadona	Longville	Yes	1116	79	BLH, BC, B, LMB, M, NP, SUN, RKB, W, YP
Island	Longville	Yes	277	45	BLH, BC, B, LMB, NP, SUN, RKB, W
Island	Pontoria	Yes	176	40	BLH, BC, B, LMB, NP, SUN, RKB
IXL	Hackensack	No	102	40	BC, B, LMB, NP, RKB, W, YP
Jack	Walker	Yes	201	110	BLH, BC, B, LMB, NP, SUN, RKB, W, YP
Jackpine	Hackensack	Yes	141	6	BLH, BC, B, LMB, NP, SUN, YP
Johnson	Backus	Yes	75.2	55	BC, B, LMB, NP, SUN, RKB, W, YP
Johnson	Remer	No	33	20	BLH, BC, B, LMB, NP, SUN, RKB, YP
Kego	Longville	No	82	40	BLH, BC, B, LMB, NP, SUN, YP
Kerr	Hackensack	No	74	79	BLH, BC, B, LMB, NP, SUN, RKB, YP
Kid	Hackensack	Private	166.7	52	BC, B, LMB, M, NP, SUN, RKB, W, YP
Kidney	Outing	No	55	55	BLH, BC, B, LMB, NP, SUN, RKB, YP
Knight	Remer	No	105	17	BLH, BC, B, LMB, NP, SUN, RKB, YP
Larson	Hackensack	No	189	73	BC, B, LMB, NP, SUN, RKB, W, YP
Lawrence	Outing	Yes	230	71	BLH, BC, B, NP, SUN, RKB, W, YP
Leavitt	Outing	Yes	130	60	BKT, BLH, BC, B, LMB, NP, SUN, RKB, W, YP
Lee	Backus	Carry In	20	24	BLH
Leech	Walker	Yes	111527	150	BLH, BC, B, LMB, M, NP, SUN, RKB, W, YP
Lind	Backus	Yes	377	27	BLH, BC, B, LMB, NP, SUN, RKB, W, YP
Little Andrus	Outing	Yes	25	37	BKT
Little Bass	Outing	No	112	30	BLH, BC, B, LMB, NP, SUN, RKB, W, YP
Little Bass	Walker	Carry In	105.7	16	BC, B, LMB, NP, YP
Little Boy	Longville	Yes	1372	74	BLH, BC, B, LMB, M, NP, SUN, RKB, SMB, W, YP
Little Sand	Remer	Yes	403	12	BC, B, LMB, NP, SUN, RKB, W, YP
Little Swift	Remer	Yes	62	25	BLH, NP, SUN, YP
Little Thunder	Remer	No	70	47	BC, B, NP, SUN, RKB, W, YP
Little Thunder	Remer	Yes	270	72	BC, B, LMB, NP, SUN, RKB, YP
Little Twin	Cass Lake	No	40	30	BLH, NP, YP
Little Vermillion	Remer	No	133	55	BLH, BC, B, LMB, NP, SUN, RKB, YP
Little Webb	Hackensack	No	167.7	37	BC, B, LMB, NP, SUN, RKB, W, YP
Little Wolf	Cass Lake	Yes	490	24	B, M, NP, SUN, RKB, W, YP
Little Woman	Hackensack	No	30.8	14	BLH, BC, B, LMB, NP, SUN, RKB, W, YP
Lomish	Remer	No	282	15	BLH, B, LMB, NP, W, YP
Long	Backus	Yes	125	48	LMB, NP, SUN, RKB, W, YP
Long	Hackensack	Yes	209	37	BLH, BC, B, LMB, NP, SUN, RKB, W, YP

KEY			
BKT=Brook Trout	**LAT**=Lake Trout	**RKB**=Rock Bass	**W**=Walleye
BLH=Bullhead	**LMB**=Largemouth Bass	**SGR**=Sauger	**WC**=White Crappie
BC=Black Crappie	**M**=Muskie	**SMB**=Smallmouth Bass	**WHB**=White Bass
B=Bluegill	**NP**=Northern Pike	**SPT**=Splake	**YP**=Yellow Perch
BRT=Brown Trout	**PKS**=Pink Salmon	**SUN**=Sunfish	
CAT=Catfish (Channel and Flathead)	**RBT**=Rainbow Trout	**TM**=Tiger Muskie	

Fishing Waters

Tristan Publishing, Inc., believes that the following charts are accurate; however, we cannot guarantee or accept liability for their accuracy. The reader should contact the Minnesota DNR to verify the accuracy of the charts.

Name	Nearest Town	Public Access	Acres	Max. Depth	Fish Species
Long	Longville	Yes	926	115	BLH, BC, B, LMB, NP, SUN, RKB, W, YP
Long	Pillager	No	107	68	BC, B, LMB, NP, SUN, W, YP
Long	Remer	No	118	33	BLH, BC, B, NP, SUN, RKB, YP
Long	Walker	No	271	80	BLH, BC, B, LMB, M, NP, SUN, RKB, YP
Loon	Pequot Lakes	Yes	237	25	BLH, BC, B, LMB, NP, SUN, RKB, W, YP
Loon	Remer	No	32	14	B, SUN
Lost Pond	Remer	No	2	38	BLH, NP, YP
Lost	Hackensack	No	N/A	26	BLH, BC, B, LMB, NP, SUN, RKB, YP
Louise	Backus	Yes	45.9	26	BLH, BC, B, LMB, NP, SUN, YP
Lower Milton	Remer	Yes	65	47	BC, B, LMB, NP, SUN, RKB, YP
Lower Sucker	Cass Lake	Yes	585	35	BLH, BC, B, LMB, NP, SUN, RKB, W, YP
Lower Trelipe	Longville	Yes	602	32	BLH, BC, B, LMB, NP, SUN, RKB, W, YP
Lydick	Cass Lake	No	56	20	BLH, NP, YP
Mabel	Remer	Yes	165	14	BC, B, LMB, NP, SUN, RKB, W, YP
Mann	Hackensack	No	445	93	BC, B, LMB, M, NP, SUN, RKB, SMB, W, YP
Maple	Longville	No	N/A	45	BC, B, LMB, NP, SUN, RKB, YP
Margaret	Nisswa	Yes	222	26	BLH, BC, B, LMB, NP, SUN, RKB, W, YP
Margaret	Outing	Yes	14	49	BC, RBT
Marion	Outing	Yes	10	60	BKT
May	Walker	Yes	123	59	BLH, BC, B, LMB, M, NP, SUN, RKB, W, YP
Michaud	Outing	No	107	45	BLH, BC, B, LMB, NP, SUN, RKB, YP
Middle Sucker	Cass Lake	Yes	200	20	BLH, BC, B, LMB, NP, SUN, YP
Million	Walker	Carry In	18	20	LMB, W, YP
Mitten	Longville	No	108	28	BLH, BC, B, LMB, NP, SUN
Moccasin	Hackensack	Yes	243	95	BLH, BC, B, LMB, NP, SUN, YP
Morrison	Outing	Private	163	49	BC, B, LMB, NP, SUN, RKB, W, YP
Mule	Longville	Yes	456	47	BLH, BC, B, LMB, M, NP, SUN, RKB, SMB, W, YP
Mule	Outing	No	62	45	BLH, BC, B, LMB, NP, SUN, RKB
Norway	Pine River	Yes	524	12	BLH, BC, B, LMB, NP, SUN, RKB, W, YP
One	Backus	No	N/A	35	BLH, BC, B, LMB, NP, SUN, YP
Ox Yoke	Backus	Yes	166	42	BLH, BC, B, LMB, NP, SUN, RKB, W, YP
Paquet	Hackensack	Private	118	19	BLH, BC, B, NP, SUN, RKB, W, YP
Pavelgrit	Outing	No	18	25	YP
Perch	Backus	Carry In	12.8	39	RBT
Phelon	Remer	No	25	45	BLH, NP
Pike Bay	Cass Lake	Yes	4760	95	BLH, LMB, M, NP, SUN, RKB, W, YP
Pillager	Pillager	Yes	206	39	BLH, B, LMB, NP, SUN, RKB, W, YP
Pine Mountain	Backus	Yes	1567	80	BLH, BC, B, LMB, NP, SUN, RKB, W, YP
Pine	Whipholt	Yes	183	25	BLH, BC, B, LMB, NP, SUN, RKB, YP
Pleasant	Hackensack	Yes	1038	72	BLH, BC, B, LMB, NP, SUN, RKB, SMB, W, YP
Ponto	Backus	Yes	347	60	BLH, BC, B, LMB, NP, SUN, RKB, W, YP
Portage	Bena	Yes	1488	55	BC, B, LMB, NP, SUN, RKB, W, YP
Portage	Cass Lake	No	356	65	BC, B, LMB, NP, SUN, RKB, SMB, W, YP

Fishing Waters

Name	Nearest Town	Public Access	Acres	Max. Depth	Fish Species
Portage	Hackensack	Yes	279	84	BC, B, LMB, NP, SUN, SMB, W, YP
Primer	Longville	No	39	37	B, NP, SUN, YP
Rainy	Backus	No	129	29	BLH, BC, B, LMB, NP, SUN, RKB, W, YP
Rat	Walker	No	102	35	BLH, BC, B, LMB, NP, SUN, RKB, YP
Ray	Nisswa	Yes	136	27	BLH, BC, B, LMB, NP, SUN, W, YP
Rice	Longville	Yes	248	30	BLH, BC, B, LMB, NP, SUN, RKB, W, YP
Rock	Pillager	Yes	240	17	BLH, BC, B, NP, SUN, RKB, W
Roosevelt	Outing	Yes	1585	129	BC, B, LAT, LMB, NP, SUN, RKB, SMB, W, YP
Ruth	Brainerd	No	82	42	BC, B, LMB, NP, SUN, W
Sanborn	Backus	Yes	233	48	BLH, BC, B, LMB, NP, SUN, RKB, W, YP
Sand	Hackensack	Yes	134	54	BLH, BC, B, LMB, NP, SUN, RKB, W, YP
Sand	Longville	Yes	43	8	BLH, BC, B, LMB, NP, SUN, W
Shurd	Longville	No	54	67	BC, B, NP, YP
Silver	Longville	Yes	89.5	20	BC, LMB, NP, W, YP
Six Mile	Bena	Yes	1288	68	LMB, NP, SUN, RKB, W, YP
Sleepy Island	Bakus	Carry In	14	23	B, NP, YP
South Stocking	Longville	Carry In	34	44	BC, NP, SUN, YP
Spider	Pine River	Yes	85	17	BLH, BC, LMB, NP, SUN, W, YP
Spring	Remer	No	89	46	BC, B, NP, SUN, RKB, YP
Squeedunk	Woman Lake	No	19	35	BLH, NP, RKB, YP
Steamboat	Cass Lake	Yes	1775	93	BLH, BC, B, LMB, M, NP, SUN, RKB, W, YP
Stevens	Longville	Yes	105	63	BLH, BC, B, LMB, NP, SUN, YP
Stony	Hackensack	Yes	595	50	BC, B, LMB, NP, SUN, RKB, W, YP
Sugar	Remer	Yes	664	44	BLH, BC, B, LMB, NP, SUN, RKB, W, YP
Sullivan	Remer	No	40	50	B, LMB, NP, YP
Swift	Remer	No	352	52	BLH, BC, B, LMB, M, NP, SUN, RKB, W, YP
Sylvan	Backus	Yes	98	26	BLH, BC, B, LMB, NP, W, YP
Sylvan	Pillager	Yes	803	57	BLH, BC, B, LMB, NP, SUN, RKB, W, YP
Teepee	Whipholt	Yes	18.05	31	RBT
Ten Mile	Hackensack	Yes	4669	208	BC, B, LMB, NP, SUN, RKB, W, YP
Thiebault	Remer	No	40	19	BLH, NP, YP
Third	Walker	No	22	34	BLH, BC, B, LMB, NP, SUN, RKB, W
Thirteen	Cass Lake	Yes	470	50	BLH, LMB, NP, SUN, W, YP
Three Island	Longville	Yes	173	13	BC, B, LMB, NP, SUN, W, YP
Thunder	Remer	Yes	1330	95	BC, B, LMB, NP, SUN, RKB, SMB, W, YP
Tidd	Remer	Yes	60	75	BLH, B, NP, SUN, RKB, YP
Town Line	Longville	Yes	510	11	BC, B, LMB, NP, SUN, RKB, W, YP
Trillium	Hackensack	No	136	48	BC, B, LMB, NP, SUN, RKB, W, YP
Twin	Cass Lake	Carry In	170	5	BLH
Upper Gull	Nisswa	Yes	371	54	BLH, BC, B, LMB, NP, SUN, RKB, W, YP

KEY			
BKT=Brook Trout	LAT=Lake Trout	RKB=Rock Bass	W=Walleye
BLH=Bullhead	LMB=Largemouth Bass	SGR=Sauger	WC=White Crappie
BC=Black Crappie	M=Muskie	SMB=Smallmouth Bass	WHB=White Bass
B=Bluegill	NP=Northern Pike	SPT=Splake	YP=Yellow Perch
BRT=Brown Trout	PKS=Pink Salmon	SUN=Sunfish	
CAT=Catfish (Channel and Flathead)	RBT=Rainbow Trout	TM=Tiger Muskie	

Fishing Waters

Tristan Publishing, Inc., believes that the following charts are accurate; however, we cannot guarantee or accept liability for their accuracy. The reader should contact the Minnesota DNR to verify the accuracy of the charts.

Name	Nearest Town	Public Access	Acres	Max. Depth	Fish Species
Upper Milton	Remer	Yes	28	35	BC, B, NP, SUN, W, YP
Upper Sucker	Cass Lake	Yes	120	25	BLH, BC, B, NP, SUN, YP
Upper Trelipe	Longville	Yes	409	69	BLH, BC, B, LMB, NP, SUN, RKB, W, YP
Variety	Hackensack	No	145	29	BLH, BC, B, LMB, NP, SUN, YP
Vermillion	Remer	Yes	397	27	BLH, BC, B, LMB, NP, SUN, W, YP
Wabedo	Longville	Yes	1185	95	BLH, BC, B, LMB, M, NP, SUN, RKB, SMB, W, YP
Washburn	Outing	Yes	1554	111	BLH, BC, B, LMB, NP, SUN, RKB, W, YP
Webb	Hackensack	Yes	754	84	BLH, BC, B, LMB, NP, SUN, RKB, W, YP
Welch	Cass Lake	Yes	188	59	BLH, BC, B, LMB, NP, SUN, RKB, W, YP
Widow	Longville	Yes	180	46	BLH, BC, B, LMB, NP, SUN, RKB, W, YP
Willard	Backus	Carry In	7.4	39	RBT
Wilson	Remer	No	68	13	BC, B, LMB, NP, SUN, YP
Windy	Outing	Yes	94	29	BLH, BC, B, LMB, NP, SUN, YP
Winnibigoshish	Deer River	Yes	58544	70	BLH, B, M, NP, RKB, W, YP
Woman	Longville	Yes	4782	54	BLH, B, LMB, M, NP, SUN, RKB, SMB, W, YP

Chisago

Name	Nearest Town	Public Access	Acres	Max. Depth	Fish Species
Chisago	Chisago City	Yes	873	34	BLH, BC, B, LMB, NP, SUN, W, YP
Comfort	Wyoming	Yes	219	47	BLH, BC, B, LMB, M, NP, SUN, W, YP
East Rush	Rush City	Yes	1359	24	BLH, BC, B, LMB, M, NP, SUN, W, YP
Fish	Harris	Yes	306	57	BLH, BC, B, LMB, NP, SUN, W, YP
Goose	Stark	Yes	442	55	BLH, BC, B, LMB, NP, SUN, W, YP
Green	Chisago City	Yes	1714	32	BLH, BC, B, LMB, NP, SUN, W, YP
Horseshoe	Harris	Yes	197	53	BLH, BC, B, LMB, NP, SUN, WC, YP
Kroon	Lindstrom	Yes	192	30	BLH, BC, B, LMB, NP, SUN, W, YP
Linn	Lindstrom	No	180	15	BLH, B, NP, SUN
Little	Center City	Yes	159	23	BLH, BC, B, LMB, NP, SUN, W, YP
Little Comfort	Wyoming	No	36	56	BLH, BC, B, LMB, NP, SUN, W, YP
Little Horseshoe	Harris	No	36	43	BLH, BC, B, NP, SUN, YP
Mandall	Stark	No	38	26	BLH, BC, B, LMB, NP, SUN, W, WC, YP
Moody	Chisago City	No	35	48	BLH, BC, B, NP, SUN, YP
Neander	Harris	No	52	17	BLH, BC, B, LMB, NP, SUN, YP
North Center	Center City	Yes	725	46	BLH, BC, B, LMB, NP, SUN, W, YP
North Lindstrom	Lindstrom	Yes	137	29	BLH, BC, B, LMB, NP, SUN, W, YP
North Sunrise Pool	Stacy	Yes	577.6	6	BLH, BC, B, NP, SUN, W, YP
Ogrens	Center City	No	46	41	BLH, BC, B, NP, SUN
Peterson	Lindstrom	No	15	19	BLH, BC, B, SUN, YP
Pioneer	Center City	No	77	8	BLH, B, SUN
Rabour	Stark	No	48	43	BLH, BC, B, LMB, NP, SUN, W, YP
South Center	Lindstrom	Yes	835	109	BLH, BC, B, LMB, NP, SUN, W, YP
South Lindstrom	Lindstrom	Yes	499.4	34	BLH, BC, B, LMB, NP, SUN, W, YP
South Sunrise Pool	Stacy	Yes	489.5	7	BLH, BC, B, LMB, NP, SUN, W, YP
Spider	Lindstrom	Yes	163	9	BLH
Sunrise	Lindstrom	No	742	21	BLH, BC, B, LMB, NP, SUN, YP
West Rush	Rush City	Yes	1464	42	BLH, BC, B, LMB, M, NP, SUN, W, YP

Clay

Name	Nearest Town	Public Access	Acres	Max. Depth	Fish Species
Fifteen	Hawley	Yes	139	22	BLH, BC, B, LMB, NP, SUN, W, YP
Lee	Hawley	Carry In	134	36	BC, B, LMB, NP, SUN, W, YP

Fishing Waters

Name	Nearest Town	Public Access	Acres	Max. Depth	Fish Species
Silver	Hawley	Yes	114	39	BLH, BC, B, CAT, LMB, NP, W, YP
Tilde	Hitterdal	Yes	259	13	BLH, B, NP, W
Clearwater					
Bagley	Leonard	Yes	94	39	BLH, BC, LMB, NP, SUN, W, YP
Big LaSalle	Lake Itasca	Yes	221	48	BC, B, LMB, NP, SUN, RKB, W, YP
Cox	Bagley	Yes	43	30	BLH, NP, SUN, W
Daniel	Shevlin	No	61	27	BLH, BC, B, LMB, NP, SUN, RKB, YP
Deep	Clearbrook	Yes	46.7	76	B, LMB, NP, SUN, YP
Elk	Lake Itasca	Yes	271	93	B, LMB, M, NP, SUN, RKB, W, YP
Falk	Clearbrook	Yes	65	33	BLH, LMB, NP, SUN, W, YP
First	Bagley	Yes	58	36	BLH, BC, B, NP, SUN, RKB, W, YP
Glanders	Zerkel	Yes	39	35	B, NP, SUN, RKB, W, YP
Heart	Zerkel	Yes	206	55	BLH, BC, B, LMB, NP, SUN, RKB, YP
Hoot Owl	Waubun	Private	87	78	BLH, BC, B, LMB, NP, SUN, RKB, W, YP
Island	Zerkel	Yes	37.6	58	SUN, RBT
Itasca	Lake Itasca	Yes	1077	40	BLH, BC, B, LMB, NP, SUN, RKB, W, YP
Jackson	Zerkel	Yes	120	35	BLH, NP, SUN, YP
Johnson	Clearbrook	Yes	56.4	70	BLH, B, NP, SUN, W, YP
Lindberg	Clearbrook	Yes	88.2	19	BLH, BC, B, NP, SUN, W, YP
Little Bass	Elbow Lake	No	46	35	BLH, BC, B, LMB, NP, SUN, YP
Lomond	Bagley	Yes	91	42	BLH, BC, B, LMB, NP, SUN, RKB, W, YP
Lone	Bagley	Yes	68.8	70	BC, B, LMB, NP, W, YP
Long Lost	Zerkel	Yes	390	63	BLH, BC, B, LMB, NP, SUN, SMB, W, YP
Long	Clearbrook	Yes	48.3	36	B, LMB, NP, SUN, YP
Long	Lake Itasca	Yes	145	80	BLH, BC, B, LMB, NP, SUN, RBT, RKB, W, YP
Lower Camp	Elbow Village	Yes	33	27	BC, B, NP, SUN, RKB, W, YP
Mallard	Lake Itasca	Yes	98	17	BLH, B, LMB, SUN, YP
McKenzie	Zerkel	Yes	77	17	BC, NP, SUN, YP
Minerva	Alida	Yes	236	16	BLH, BC, B, LMB, NP, SUN, W, YP
Minnow	Bagley	Yes	102	24	BLH, BC, B, LMB, NP, W, YP
Ozawindib	Lake Itasca	Yes	151	80	BLH, BC, B, LMB, NP, SUN, W, YP
Peterson	Clearbrook	Yes	76.5	70	BLH, B, NP, SUN, YP
Pickerel	Itasca State Park	Yes	122.5	46	BC, B, LMB, NP, SUN, RKB, W, YP
Pine	Gonvick	Yes	1188	15	BLH, B, LMB, NP, SUN, W, YP
Rockstad	Zerkel	Yes	128	18	BLH, NP, SUN, YP
Second	Bagley	Yes	69	47	BLH, BC, LMB, NP, SUN, RKB, W, YP
Twin	Itasca	No	91	45	BLH, B, LMB, NP, SUN
Upper Rice	Shevlin	Yes	1689	13	BLH, NP, SUN, YP
Walker Brook	Shevlin	Yes	90	45	BLH, BC, B, LMB, NP, SUN, W, YP
Waptus	McKenzie	Yes	38	45	BC, NP, YP
Cook					
Abita	Grand Marais	Carry In	N/A	14	YP
Ada	Tofte	Carry In	22	13	NP
Alder	Grand Marais	Carry In	506	72	LAT, NP, SMB, W, YP
Allen	Grand Marais	Carry In	49	12	NP, SMB, W, YP

KEY			
BKT=Brook Trout	**LAT**=Lake Trout	**RKB**=Rock Bass	**W**=Walleye
BLH=Bullhead	**LMB**=Largemouth Bass	**SGR**=Sauger	**WC**=White Crappie
BC=Black Crappie	**M**=Muskie	**SMB**=Smallmouth Bass	**WHB**=White Bass
B=Bluegill	**NP**=Northern Pike	**SPT**=Splake	**YP**=Yellow Perch
BRT=Brown Trout	**PKS**=Pink Salmon	**SUN**=Sunfish	
CAT=Catfish (Channel and Flathead)	**RBT**=Rainbow Trout	**TM**=Tiger Muskie	

Fishing Waters

Tristan Publishing, Inc., believes that the following charts are accurate; however, we cannot guarantee or accept liability for their accuracy. The reader should contact the Minnesota DNR to verify the accuracy of the charts.

Name	Nearest Town	Public Access	Acres	Max. Depth	Fish Species
Alpine	Grand Marais	Carry In	839	65	LAT, NP, W
Alton	Tofte	Carry In	1039	72	NP, RKB, SMB, W, YP
Ambush	Grand Marais	Carry In	31	14	NP, YP
Aspen	Grand Marais	Yes	131	29	BC, NP, SUN, W, YP
Axe	Lutsen	Carry In	53	12	NP, W
Baker	Grand Marais	Carry In	24	10	NP, W, YP
Ball Club	Grand Marais	Yes	196	25	NP, W, YP
Banadad	Grand Marais	No	168	45	NP
Barker	Lutsen	Carry In	142	15	BC, NP, SUN, SMB, W, YP
Bat	Grand Marais	Carry In	80	110	LAT
Bath	Grand Marais	Carry In	29.7	23	BKT
Bear Club	Grand Marais	Carry In	29	11	NP, YP
Bearskin	Grand Marais	Yes	494	78	B, LAT, NP, SUN, SMB, YP
Beaver	Grand Marais	No	59	22	SUN
Bedew	Grand Marais	Yes	45	18	YP
Bench	Grand Marais	Carry In	26	16	BKT
Benson	Grand Marais	Carry In	32	5	YP
Big Snow	Tofte	No	49	12	NP, YP
Bigsby	Lutsen	Yes	89.5	4	NP, SMB, W, YP
Binagami	Grand Marais	Carry In	109	21	B, RKB, W
Bingshick	Grand Marais	No	44	37	BKT, SUN
Birch	Grand Marais	Carry In	246	69	BKT, LAT, RBT
Bogus	Grand Marais	Carry In	17.1	25	SPT
Bouder	Grand Marais	Carry In	136	17	M, NP, SUN, W, YP
Boys	Grand Marais	Carry In	24	13	BKT
Brandt	Grand Marais	Carry In	104	80	NP, YP
Brule	Grand Marais	Carry In	4617	78	NP, SMB, W
Bulge	Lutsen	Carry In	12	8	NP, W, YP
Bull	Lutsen	Carry In	57	33	NP, YP
Burnt	Tofte	Carry In	327	23	NP, W, YP
Calf	Lutsen	Carry In	15	18	YP
Cam	Lutsen	Carry In	60	57	NP, YP
Canoe	Grand Marais	Carry In	94.8	40	SUN, W, YP
Caribou	Grand Marais	Carry In	255	26	NP, W, YP
Caribou	Grand Marais	Carry In	452	65	NP, SMB, W
Caribou	Lutsen	Yes	728	30	BC, NP, SMB, W, YP
Carl	Grand Marais	No	59	22	NP, YP
Carrot	Grand Marais	Carry In	27	17	BKT
Cascade	Lutsen	Yes	415	17	NP, W, YP
Cash	Grand Marais	Carry In	76	58	LAT, YP
Cherokee	Tofte	Carry In	753	142	LAT, NP
Chester	Hovland	Carry In	50	35	BRT
Christine	Lutsen	Yes	195	7	B, NP, SUN, W, YP
Circle	Grand Marais	Yes	31	3	BKT
Clam	Tofte	Carry In	59	19	NP
Clara	Lutsen	Yes	410	15	NP, SUN, W, YP
Clearwater	Grand Marais	Yes	1325	130	LAT, SMB, YP
Clove	Grand Marais	Carry In	172	25	NP, SMB, W, YP
Copper	Grand Marais	No	34	52	NP
Cow	Lutsen	No	39	36	YP
Crab	Grand Marais	No	79	17	B, NP, RKB, W, YP
Crescent	Grand Marais	Yes	744	28	M, NP, SMB, W, YP
Crocodile	Grand Marais	Carry In	272	17	W, YP
Crooked	Grand Marais	Carry In	233	66	LAT, NP
Crow	Grand Marais	Carry In	37	6	NP, W, YP
Crystal	Grand Marais	Carry In	218	80	LAT, NP, SUN, W, YP
Cucumber	Grand Marais	Carry In	54	26	W, YP

Fishing Waters

Name	Nearest Town	Public Access	Acres	Max. Depth	Fish Species
Daniels	Grand Marais	Carry In	489	90	LAT, SMB, YP
Davis	Lutsen	Carry In	353	64	LAT, NP, YP
Dawkins	Grand Marais	Carry In	68	19	NP, W, YP
Deer Yard	Lutsen	Carry In	351.9	20	W
Devil Track	Grand Marais	Yes	1838	50	NP, SUN, SMB, W, YP
Devilfish	Hovland	Yes	395.6	40	W, YP
Devils Elbow	Grand Marais	Carry In	88.9	50	NP, SMB, W
Dick	Grand Marais	No	130	12	NP, SMB, W, YP
Dislocation	Grand Marais	Carry In	38	22	BRT, YP
Dogtrot	Lutsen	Carry In	22	12	NP, W, YP
Dugout	Grand Marais	Carry In	25	8	NP, W, YP
Duke		No			BKT
Duncan	Grand Marais	Carry In	481	130	LAT, SUN, SMB, YP
Dunn	Grand Marais	Carry In	90.3	60	LAT, SUN
Eagle	Grand Marais	Carry In	72	14	NP, W, YP
East Bearskin	Grand Marais	Yes	441	66	BC, LAT, NP, SUN, SMB, W, YP
East Dawkins	Grand Marais	No	48	15	NP, W, YP
East Fox	Tofte	No	19	18	NP, YP
East Kerfoot	Grand Marais	Carry In	11	26	SUN
East Otter	Grand Marais	No	46	15	BKT
East Pike	Hovland	No	496	40	NP, SMB, YP
East Pipe	Lutsen	Carry In	106	12	NP, W
East Pope	Grand Marais	Carry In	30	28	NP, SMB, W
East Twin	Grand Marais	Yes	172.6	19	W
Echo	Lutsen	Carry In	133	12	NP, SMB, W
Ecstasy	Tofte	Carry In	66	47	SUN, YP
Edith	Grand Marais	Carry In	10	44	NP, YP
Eggers	Grand Marais	No	15	N/A	BKT
Elbow	Grand Marais	Yes	437	9	NP, W, YP
Elbow	Tofte	Carry In	516	23	NP, W, YP
Elm	Tofte	Carry In	126	77	NP
Esther	Hovland	Yes	79	35	RBT, SPT
Everett	Grand Marais	No	46	55	SUN, YP
Extortion	Grand Marais	Carry In	20	N/A	SPT
Fag	Grand Marais	Yes	8	9	YP
Fault	Grand Marais	No	61	10	SUN
Fay	Grand Marais	Carry In	66	62	BKT, LAT, SUN
Feather	Tofte	Carry In	10	24	BKT
Fern	Grand Marais	No	57	65	LAT
Finger	Tofte	Carry In	177	14	NP, W, YP
Flame	Tofte	Carry In	55	22	NP, YP
Fleck	Lutsen	Carry In	31	5	NP, W, YP
Flour	Grand Marais	Yes	334.8	75	LAT, SUN, SMB, W, YP
Four Mile	Tofte	Yes	572	19.5	BC, NP, W, YP
Fox	Tofte	Carry In	36	5	NP, YP
Frear	Schroeder	Carry In	277	17	NP, W, YP
French	Grand Marais	Carry In	112	130	LAT, YP
Frost	Tofte	Carry In	236	88	LAT, NP
Gabimichigami	Tofte	Carry In	1198	209	LAT, NP, YP
Gadwell	Grand Marais	Carry In	21	52	BKT
Gaskin	Grand Marais	Carry In	346	82	NP, SMB, W

KEY			
BKT=Brook Trout	**LAT**=Lake Trout	**RKB**=Rock Bass	**W**=Walleye
BLH=Bullhead	**LMB**=Largemouth Bass	**SGR**=Sauger	**WC**=White Crappie
BC=Black Crappie	**M**=Muskie	**SMB**=Smallmouth Bass	**WHB**=White Bass
B=Bluegill	**NP**=Northern Pike	**SPT**=Splake	**YP**=Yellow Perch
BRT=Brown Trout	**PKS**=Pink Salmon	**SUN**=Sunfish	
CAT=Catfish (Channel and Flathead)	**RBT**=Rainbow Trout	**TM**=Tiger Muskie	

Fishing Waters

Tristan Publishing, Inc., believes that the following charts are accurate; however, we cannot guarantee or accept liability for their accuracy. The reader should contact the Minnesota DNR to verify the accuracy of the charts.

Name	Nearest Town	Public Access	Acres	Max. Depth	Fish Species
Gillis	Grand Marais	Carry In	570	180	LAT, NP, YP
Glenn	Grand Marais	Carry In	25	12	NP
Gneiss	Grand Marais	Carry In	239.9	70	LAT, NP, SUN, SMB, W, YP
Gogebic	Grand Marais	Carry In	70	61	BKT
Gordon	Grand Marais	Carry In	139	95	LAT, NP
Grace	Grand Marais	Carry In	391	16	NP, W, YP
Grandpa	Schroeder	Carry In	120	55	NP, SUN, YP
Granite Bay	Grand Marais	No	65	35	NP, SUN, SMB, W, YP
Granite	Grand Marais	Carry In	20	45	NP, W, YP
Greenwood	Grand Marais	Yes	2021	112	BKT, LAT, SUN, SMB, YP
Gull	Grand Marais	Yes	183	40	NP, SUN, SMB, W, YP
Gunflint	Grand Marais	Yes	4210	200	LAT, NP, SMB, W, YP
Gust	Grand Marais	Carry In	135	6	LMB, NP, SUN, W, YP
Ham	Grand Marais	Carry In	100	40	NP, SMB, W, YP
Hand	Grand Marais	Carry In	80	22	NP, W, YP
Handle	Tofte	Carry In	14	7	NP, YP
Henson	Grand Marais	Carry In	124.6	40	NP, SUN, YP
Hilly	Lutsen	Carry In	30	23	NP
Hog	Tofte	Carry In	127	7	NP, YP
Holly	Lutsen	Yes	69	6	SUN, W, YP
Homer	Lutsen	Yes	443	22	NP, W, YP
Honker	Grand Marais	No	46	34	BKT
Horseshoe	Grand Marais	Carry In	202	26	NP, SUN, SMB, W, YP
Howard	Tofte	Carry In	158	125	LAT, NP
Hungry Jack	Grand Marais	Yes	463.2	71	B, LAT, NP, SUN, SMB, SPT, W, YP
Iowa	Lutsen	Carry In	30	13	NP, YP
Iron	Grand Marais	Carry In	105	19	B, NP, RKB, W, YP
Jack	Tofte	Carry In	101	10	NP, W, YP
Jackal	Grand Marais	No	28	26	BKT, BRT, NP
Jap	Grand Marais	Carry In	146	60	LAT
Jasper	Grand Marais	Carry In	239	125	LAT, SMB, W
Jim	Grand Marais	Carry In	59	26	LAT
Jock Mock	Lutsen	Carry In	17	20	NP, SMB
John	Hovland	Carry In	169	20	NP, SMB, W, YP
Junco	Grand Marais	Carry In	45	5	BKT
Juno	Lutsen	Carry In	248	23	NP, W, YP
Karl	Grand Marais	Carry In	105	70	LAT, NP
Kelly	Tofte	Carry In	152	13	SUN, SMB, W, YP
Kelso	Tofte	Carry In	97	16	NP, YP
Kemo	Grand Marais	Carry In	184	65	LAT, SPT
Kimball	Grand Marais	Yes	79	16	BRT, RBT, SPT
Kingfisher	Ely	Carry In	35	42	LAT, W, YP
Kinogami	Lutsen	No	115	30	LMB, NP, SUN, W, YP
Kiowa	Grand Marais	No	32	29	SUN, YP
Kiskadinna	Grand Marais	Carry In	131.4	40	SUN
Lac	Grand Marais	Carry In	55	20	NP
Lantern	Grand Marais	Carry In	102	30	BKT
Larch	Grand Marais	Yes	130.7	14	NP, W, YP
Larry	Grand Marais	Carry In	10	4	NP
Leo	Grand Marais	Carry In	101.2	28	RBT, SPT, W
Lichen	Lutsen	Carry In	276	17	M, NP, W, YP
Lily	Lutsen	Carry In	22	51	NP
Lima	Grand Marais	Carry In	10	25	BKT
Little Caribou	Grand Marais	Carry In	58	18	NP, SMB, W, YP
Little Cascade	Lutsen	Carry In	267	9	NP, YP
Little Gunflint	Grand Marais	Carry In	95	16	NP, SMB, W, YP
Little Iron	Grand Marais	Carry In	82	18	B, NP, RKB, SPT, W, YP

Fishing Waters

Name	Nearest Town	Public Access	Acres	Max. Depth	Fish Species
Little John	Hovland	Yes	34	8	NP, W, YP
Little Mayhew	Grand Marais	Carry In	35	31	NP, YP
Little Saganaga	Tofte	Carry In	1575	150	LAT, NP, YP
Little Snow	Tofte	Carry In	27.7	11	NP, W
Little Trout	Grand Marais	Carry In	123	56	LAT
Lizz	Grand Marais	Carry In	30	30	BKT, SUN
Locket	Grand Marais	Carry In	16	15	NP
Loft	Hovland	Carry In	13	48	BKT
Long Island	Grand Marais	Carry In	864	85	LAT, NP
Long	Hovland	Carry In	140	24	NP, SUN
Loon	Grand Marais	Yes	1025	202	B, LAT, NP, RKB, SMB, W, YP
Lost	Hovland	No	67	10	BKT, SPT
Lower Cone	Lutsen	No	67	21	NP, SMB, W
Lower Trout	Grand Marais	No	149	6	NP, SMB, W, YP
Lum	Grand Marais	No	27	17	NP, YP
Lux	Grand Marais	No	47	21	NP, YP
Magnetic	Grand Marais	Carry In	431	90	LAT, SMB, W
Marabaeuf	Grand Marais	Carry In	N/A	55	LAT, NP, SMB, W, YP
Margaret	Hovland	Carry In	6	29	BKT
Mark		No			NP
Marsh	Tofte	Carry In	69	13	NP, YP
Marshall	Grand Marais	Carry In	51	16	NP, SMB, W, YP
Mavis	Grand Marais	Carry In	10	55	BKT
Mayhew	Hovland	Carry In	219	84	LAT, SUN, YP
McDonald	Grand Marais	Carry In	99	8	NP, SMB, W, YP
McFarland	Hovland	Yes	384	49	NP, SMB, W, YP
Meditation	Tofte	Carry In	28	31	BKT
Meeds	Grand Marais	Carry In	337	41	NP, W, YP
Merganser	Grand Marais	Yes	24	3	NP, SUN, YP
Mesaba	Tofte	Carry In	201	65	LAT, NP
Mid Cone	Lutsen	Carry In	73	30	NP, SMB, W
Midget	Tofte	Carry In	24	25	NP, YP
Mine	Grand Marais	Carry In	29	30	SUN
Mink	Grand Marais	Yes	57	15	BKT, BRT, RBT, SPT
Misquah	Grand Marais	Carry In	60	60	LAT
Missing Link	Grand Marais	Carry In	40	25	BKT
Missouri	Lutsen	Carry In	28	4	NP
Mistletoe	Lutsen	No	122	6	NP, W, YP
Mit	Grand Marais	Carry In	80	40	NP, W, YP
Monker	Grand Marais	Carry In	88	7	BKT
Moon	Grand Marais	Carry In	145	30	NP, SUN, W, YP
Moore	Lutsen	Carry In	53	8	B, NP, YP
Moose	Hovland	Carry In	1005	113	LAT, SMB, W, YP
Moosehorn	Hovland	Carry In	63	9	SPT
Mora	Tofte	Carry In	205	40	NP
Morgan	Grand Marais	No	82	46	BKT, NP, SUN, SPT
Morris	Grand Marais	Carry In	62	22	NP, SUN, SMB, W
Moss	Grand Marais	Carry In	254	86	LAT, SMB
Mountain	Grand Marais	Carry In	2088	210	LAT, SMB
Muckwa	Grand Marais	Carry In	41	25	RBT
Mulligan	Lutsen	Carry In	30	62	BKT, SUN

KEY			
BKT=Brook Trout	**LAT**=Lake Trout	**RKB**=Rock Bass	**W**=Walleye
BLH=Bullhead	**LMB**=Largemouth Bass	**SGR**=Sauger	**WC**=White Crappie
BC=Black Crappie	**M**=Muskie	**SMB**=Smallmouth Bass	**WHB**=White Bass
B=Bluegill	**NP**=Northern Pike	**SPT**=Splake	**YP**=Yellow Perch
BRT=Brown Trout	**PKS**=Pink Salmon	**SUN**=Sunfish	
CAT=Catfish (Channel and Flathead)	**RBT**=Rainbow Trout	**TM**=Tiger Muskie	

Fishing Waters

Tristan Publishing, Inc., believes that the following charts are accurate; however, we cannot guarantee or accept liability for their accuracy. The reader should contact the Minnesota DNR to verify the accuracy of the charts.

Name	Nearest Town	Public Access	Acres	Max. Depth	Fish Species
Musquash	Grand Marais	Carry In	140	26	SPT
Night Hawk	Grand Marais	Yes	18	11	NP, W
Nisula	Grand Marais	No	108	18	LMB, RKB, W
North Fowl	Hovland	Carry In	1020	10	NP, W, YP
North Shady	Grand Marais	Carry In	35	20	BKT, SUN, W, YP
North Temperance	Lutsen	Carry In	178	50	NP, W, YP
North	Grand Marais	Yes	2695	125	LAT, NP, SMB, W, YP
Northern Light	Grand Marais	Yes	433	7.5	NP, SUN, SMB, W, YP
Olga	Hovland	Carry In	N/A	45	BKT, SPT
Olson	Grand Marais	Carry In	34	18	BKT
One Island	Grand Marais	Carry In	19	25	NP, YP
Onion	Grand Marais	No	31	4	SUN, YP
Otter	Hovland	Carry In	75	11	NP
Owl	Tofte	Carry In	81	70	LAT, YP
Paddle	Grand Marais	Carry In	16	16	NP, SMB, W, YP
Pagoda	Tofte	Carry In	13	7	NP
Pancore	Tofte	Carry In	32	38	BKT, SPT
Parsnip	Grand Marais	No	27	25	LMB
Partridge	Grand Marais	Carry In	109	80	LAT, SUN
Pemmican	Grand Marais	Carry In	28	51	BKT
Peter	Tofte	Carry In	259	120	LAT
Peterson	Tofte	Carry In	88	15	NP, RKB, SMB, W, YP
Phoebe	Tofte	Carry In	625	25	NP, W, YP
Pickerel	Grand Marais	Carry In	40.5	13	NP, YP
Pierz	Grand Marais	Carry In	88	28	SUN
Pike	Grand Marais	Yes	810	45	NP, SMB, W, YP
Pine Mountain	Grand Marais	Carry In	103	30	BKT
Pine	Grand Marais	Carry In	87	34	BKT, B, RBT, SPT
Pine	Hovland	Carry In	2257	113	LAT, NP, SMB, W, YP
Pipe	Lutsen	Carry In	300	33	NP, YP
Pit	Grand Marais	Carry In	27	17	B, LMB, NP, YP
Poplar	Grand Marais	Yes	728	73	BC, LAT, LMB, NP, SMB, W, YP
Portage	Grand Marais	Carry In	145	55	SUN, SPT
Powell	Grand Marais	Carry In	51	75	LAT
Prayer	Grand Marais	Carry In	43	19	NP
Quiver	Grand Marais	Yes	19.1	25	NP, W, YP
Ram	Grand Marais	Carry In	67	40	LAT, RBT
Rat	Grand Marais	Carry In	56	5	SUN, SMB, YP
Rattle	Grand Marais	Carry In	45	30	NP, YP
Red Rock	Tofte	Carry In	353	64	BKT, LAT, NP, SMB, W, YP
Reward	Grand Marais	Carry In	21	14	NP, YP
Rice	Lutsen	Yes	182	10	NP, W, YP
Road	Grand Marais	Carry In	14	15	B, W, YP
Rocky	Grand Marais	Carry In	76	35	NP
Rog	Tofte	Carry In	51	40	BKT, SMB, W
Ron	Grand Marais	Carry In	10	20	NP, YP
Rose	Grand Marais	No	1315	90	LAT, SMB, W, YP
Round	Grand Marais	Carry In	145	45	NP, SMB, W, YP
Rove	Grand Marais	No	78	30	SUN, SMB, YP
Roy	Grand Marais	Carry In	61	45	NP
Ruby	Grand Marais	Carry In	15	10	NP, YP
Rudy	Grand Marais	Carry In	42	15	NP, SUN, YP
Rush	Grand Marais	Carry In	274	54	NP
Saganaga	Grand Marais	Yes	17593	280	LAT, NP, SMB, W, YP
Sawbill	Tofte	Carry In	765	45	NP, RKB, SMB, W, YP
Sea Gull	Grand Marais	Yes	4032	145	LAT, NP, SUN, SMB, W, YP
Shadow	Grand Marais	Carry In	14	23	SUN

Fishing Waters

Name	Nearest Town	Public Access	Acres	Max. Depth	Fish Species
Shoe	Grand Marais	Carry In	29.3	12	BKT, SPT
Shoko	Grand Marais	Carry In	52.9	25	NP, SUN, SMB, W, YP
Shrike	Grand Marais	No	26	11	NP, YP
Silver	Lutsen	No	22	6	NP, W, YP
Skidway	Grand Marais	No	18	8	NP, W, YP
Skipper	Grand Marais	Carry In	108	30	NP, W, YP
Slip	Lutsen	Carry In	22	18	NP, W, YP
Snipe	Grand Marais	No	112	90	LAT
Sober	Tofte	Carry In	12	18	NP
Sock	Grand Marais	Carry In	20	23	BKT
South Fowl	Hovland	Carry In	1440	10	NP, SMB, W, YP
South Temperance	Grand Marais	No	204	24	NP, SMB, W, YP
South	Grand Marais	Carry In	1190	140	BKT, LAT, SMB
Squint	Grand Marais	Carry In	18	23	W, YP
Squire	Lutsen	Carry In	82	7	NP, YP
Star	Lutsen	Carry In	120	13	NP, W, YP
State		No	52.1		LAT
Stem		Carry In	43	34	NP
Stevens	Hovland	Carry In	20	16	NP, YP
Stump	Hovland	Carry In	237	54	NP
Sunfish	Grand Marais	Carry In	80	25	SUN, YP
Surber	Grand Marais	Carry In	8	21	RBT
Swamp River	Hovland	Yes	305	10	NP, YP
Swamp	Grand Marais	Carry In	181	10	NP, W, YP
Swamp	Lutsen	Carry In	86	8	NP, YP
Swamper	Grand Marais	Carry In	50	9.5	NP, SUN, W, YP
Swan	Grand Marais	Carry In	180	122	LAT, NP, SMB, W
Tait	Lutsen	Yes	338	15	B, NP, SUN, W, YP
Talus	Grand Marais	No	18	22	RBT
Temperance River	Tofte	Carry In	36	11	NP
Tenor	Grand Marais	Carry In	20	11	NP, W, YP
Tepee	Grand Marais	Carry In	96	22	NP, YP
Thompson	Grand Marais	Carry In	18.4	12	BRT, RBT
Thrasher	Grand Marais	Carry In	27	27	SPT
Thrush	Grand Marais	Carry In	16	48	BKT
Timber	Tofte	Carry In	236	12	NP, W, YP
Tobacco	Lutsen	No	13	9	NP, YP
Tom	Hovland	Yes	576	35	NP, W, YP
Tomash	Lutsen	Carry In	96	5	W, YP
Toohey	Schroeder	Yes	406	11	NP, W, YP
Topper	Grand Marais	Carry In	38	28	BKT
Town	Grand Marais	Carry In	79	72	LAT
Trip	Lutsen	Carry In	13.3	19	BKT
Trout	Grand Marais	Carry In	257	77	BKT, B, LAT, RBT, YP
Tucker	Grand Marais	Carry In	168	42	NP, W
Turnip	Grand Marais	Carry In	18	30	BKT
Turtle	Lutsen	Yes	65	8	W
Tuscarora	Grand Marais	Carry In	833	130	LAT, NP, YP
Twelve	Grand Marais	Yes	15	21	NP
Two Island	Grand Marais	Yes	731	27	B, NP, SUN, SMB, W, YP
Upper Cone	Grand Marais	Carry In	86	55	NP, SMB, W

KEY				
BKT=Brook Trout	**LAT**=Lake Trout	**RKB**=Rock Bass	**W**=Walleye
BLH=Bullhead	**LMB**=Largemouth Bass	**SGR**=Sauger	**WC**=White Crappie
BC=Black Crappie	**M**=Muskie	**SMB**=Smallmouth Bass	**WHB**=White Bass
B=Bluegill	**NP**=Northern Pike	**SPT**=Splake	**YP**=Yellow Perch
BRT=Brown Trout	**PKS**=Pink Salmon	**SUN**=Sunfish	
CAT=Catfish (Channel and Flathead)	**RBT**=Rainbow Trout	**TM**=Tiger Muskie	

Fishing Waters

Tristan Publishing, Inc., believes that the following charts are accurate; however, we cannot guarantee or accept liability for their accuracy. The reader should contact the Minnesota DNR to verify the accuracy of the charts.

Name	Nearest Town	Public Access	Acres	Max. Depth	Fish Species
Vale	Grand Marais	Carry In	24	34	BKT
Vern	Lutsen	Carry In	142	42	NP, SMB, W
Vernon	Grand Marais	Carry In	233	101	LAT, NP, SMB, W
Vista	Grand Marais	Carry In	222	47	LAT, NP, W, YP
Vyre	Isabella	Carry In	24	4	NP, YP
Wampus	Grand Marais	Carry In	28	18	BC, B, NP, YP
Ward	Lutsen	Carry In	42	13	NP
Watap	Grand Marais	Carry In	202	45	SUN, SMB, W, YP
Weasel	Grand Marais	Carry In	6.5	20	BKT, SUN
Wee	Tofte	Carry In	13	34	BKT
Weird	Tofte	Carry In	33	6	NP, W, YP
Wench	Lutsen	Carry In	23.6	59	BKT
West Fern	Grand Marais	Carry In	75	60	LAT
West Kerfoot	Grand Marais	Carry In	24	15	B, LMB, SUN
West Pike	Grand Marais	Carry In	715	120	LAT, SMB
West Pipe	Lutsen	Carry In	17	6	NP
West Pope	Grand Marais	Carry In	71	14	B, NP, W, YP
West Twin	Grand Marais	Yes	137	37	W
Whack	Lutsen	Carry In	34	27	NP
Whale	Grand Marais	Carry In	21	10	NP, YP
Whip	Lutsen	Carry In	35	9	NP, YP
White Pine	Lutsen	Yes	342	10	B, NP, W, YP
Williams	Grand Marais	No	40	19	NP
Wills	Lutsen	No	76	6	NP, W, YP
Winchell	Grand Marais	Carry In	826	160	LAT, NP
Wine	Tofte	Carry In	257	65	LAT
Zephyr	Grand Marais	Carry In	122	40	NP, SMB, W
Zoo	Grand Marais	No	90	26	NP
Cottonwood					
Arnold's	Windom	Yes	133	13	BLH, BC, B, NP, SUN, W, WC, YP
Bean	Storden	Yes	190	12	BLH, BC, NP, SUN, W, YP
Bingham	Bingham Lake	Yes	259	10	BLH, BC, B, CAT, LMB, SUN, W, YP
Cottonwood	Windom	Yes	140	10	BLH, BC, B, CAT, LMB, NP, SUN, W, YP
Double	Storden	Yes	246	9	BLH, BC, NP, SUN, W, WC, YP
Eagle	Mountain Lake	Yes	120	8	BLH, NP, YP
Mountain	Mountain Lake	Yes	320	8	BLH, BC, B, LMB, NP, SUN, W, YP
Shoper-Bush	Jeffers	Carry In	20	15	BLH, BC, B, SUN, YP
Talcot	Dundee	Yes	678	6	BLH, BC, CAT, NP, SUN, W, YP
Wolf	Windom	Yes	N/A	N/A	BLH, YP
Crow Wing					
Adney	Cross Lake	Yes	304	27	BC, B, LMB, NP, SUN, RKB, YP
Agate	Crosby	No	184	25	BC, B, LMB, NP, SUN, RKB, W, YP
Allen	Outing	Carry In	50	46	RBT
Ann	Deerwood	No	42	46	BC, B, LMB, NP, SUN
Anna	Emily	No	122	19	BC, LMB, NP, SUN, YP
Arrowhead	Manhattan Beach	Yes	308	13	BLH, BC, B, LMB, NP, SUN, RKB, W, YP
Barbour	Garrison	No	51	54	BC, B, LMB, NP, SUN, RKB, YP
Bass	Crosby	No	72	12	BLH, BC, B, NP, SUN, YP
Bass	Jenkins	No	116	47	BLH, BC, B, LMB, NP, SUN, RKB, W, YP
Bass	Merrifield	Yes	309	24	BLH, BC, B, LMB, NP, SUN, W, YP
Bass	Merrifield	Yes	433	38	BLH, BC, B, NP, SUN, RKB, W, YP
Bass	Nisswa	No	36	18	BC, B, NP, SUN, YP
Bassett	Garrison	Yes	32	38	BLH, BC, B, NP, SUN, YP

Name	Nearest Town	Public Access	Acres	Max. Depth	Fish Species
Bay	Deerwood	Yes	2392	74	BLH, BC, B, LMB, NP, SUN, RKB, W, YP
Bertha	Jenkins	No	334	64	BLH, BC, B, LMB, NP, SUN, RKB, W, YP
Big Trout	Manhattan Beach	Yes	1342	128	BLH, BC, B, LAT, LMB, NP, SUN, RKB, SMB, W, YP
Black Bear	Trommald	Yes	220	48	BLH, BC, B, LMB, NP, SUN, RKB, W, YP
Black Hoof	Ironton	Yes	183	29	BLH, BC, B, LMB, NP, SUN, RKB, W, YP
Black	Deerwood	Yes	95	47	BLH, BC, B, NP, SUN
Blue	Emily	No	176	48	BC, B, LMB, NP, SUN, RKB, YP
Bonnie	Merrifield	No	63	42	BLH, BC, B, LMB, NP, SUN, YP
Borden	Garrison	Yes	957	84	BLH, BC, B, LMB, NP, SUN, RKB, SMB, W, YP
Bulldog	Pine Center	No	141	34	BLH, BC, B, LMB, NP, SUN, RKB, W, YP
Butterfield	Emily	No	142	23	BC, B, LMB, NP, SUN, RKB, YP
Butternut	Deerwood	No	29	34	B, LMB, NP, YP
Camp	Pine Center	Yes	478	42	BLH, BC, B, LMB, NP, SUN, RKB, W, YP
Carlson	Cuyuna	No	92	37	BLH, BC, B, NP, SUN
Cascade	Deerwood	No	44	24	BLH, B, NP, SUN
Casey	Cuyuna	Yes	51	39	BLH, BC, B, LMB, NP, SUN, YP
Clamshell	Jenkins	Yes	189	44	BLH, BC, B, LMB, NP, SUN, RKB, W, YP
Clark	Nisswa	Yes	343	31	BLH, BC, B, LMB, NP, SUN, W, YP
Clear	Jenkins	Yes	220	63	B, LMB, NP, SUN, RKB, W, YP
Clearwater	Deerwood	Yes	880	54	BLH, BC, B, LMB, NP, SUN, RKB, SMB, W, YP
Clinker	Crosby	Yes	84	35	BLH, BC, B, LMB, NP, SUN, RKB, YP
Crooked	Garrison	Yes	443	72	BLH, BC, B, LMB, NP, SUN, RKB, W, YP
Cross Lake	Cross Lake	Yes	1751	84	BLH, BC, B, LMB, NP, SUN, RKB, W, YP
Crow Wing	Fort Ripley	Yes	382	26	BLH, BC, B, LMB, NP, SUN, W, YP
Daggett	Cross Lake	No	225	23	BC, B, LMB, NP, SUN, RKB, W, YP
Dolney	Emily	Yes	271	16	BLH, BC, NP, SUN
Eagle	Fifty Lakes	Yes	358	36	BC, B, LMB, NP, SUN, RKB, W, YP
East Fox	Fifty Lakes	Yes	239	65	BLH, BC, B, LMB, NP, SUN, RKB, SMB, W, YP
East Twin	Cross Lake	No	N/A	28	BLH, BC, B, LMB, NP
East Twin	Nisswa	Yes	146	45	B, LMB, NP, SUN, W, YP
Eastham	Emily	No	76	22	BLH, BC, B, NP, SUN, YP
Edna	Nisswa	Yes	153	63	BLH, BC, B, LMB, NP, SUN, RKB, W, YP
Edward	Merrifield	Yes	2032	75	BLH, B, LMB, NP, SUN, RKB, W, YP
Emily	Emily	Yes	664	13	BLH, BC, B, LMB, NP, SUN, RKB, W, YP
Erskine	Pine Center	Yes	176	14	BLH, BC, B, LMB, NP, SUN, YP
Fawn	Cross Lake	No	73	24	BLH, BC, B, LMB, NP, SUN, YP

KEY	BKT=Brook Trout	LAT=Lake Trout	RKB=Rock Bass	W=Walleye
	BLH=Bullhead	LMB=Largemouth Bass	SGR=Sauger	WC=White Crappie
	BC=Black Crappie	M=Muskie	SMB=Smallmouth Bass	WHB=White Bass
	B=Bluegill	NP=Northern Pike	SPT=Splake	YP=Yellow Perch
	BRT=Brown Trout	PKS=Pink Salmon	SUN=Sunfish	
	CAT=Catfish (Channel and Flathead)	RBT=Rainbow Trout	TM=Tiger Muskie	

Fishing Waters

Tristan Publishing, Inc., believes that the following charts are accurate; however, we cannot guarantee or accept liability for their accuracy. The reader should contact the Minnesota DNR to verify the accuracy of the charts.

Name	Nearest Town	Public Access	Acres	Max. Depth	Fish Species
Fawn	Merrifield	Yes	117	24	BLH, B, LMB, NP, SUN, W, YP
Fawn	Nisswa	Yes	60	40	BLH, BC, B, LMB, NP, SUN, RKB, W, YP
Flanders	Cross Lake	No	60	16	NP, SUN, RKB, YP
Gilbert	Brainerd	Yes	369	45	BLH, BC, B, LMB, NP, SUN, RKB, YP
Gladstone	Nisswa	Yes	407	36	BLH, BC, B, LMB, NP, SUN, RKB, W, YP
Goodrich	Cross Lake	Yes	360	35	BLH, BC, B, LMB, NP, SUN, SMB, W, YP
Grass	Jenkins	Yes	44	40	BLH, B, LMB, NP, SUN, YP
Grave	Brainerd	No	157	13	BLH, BC, B, NP, SUN, YP
Greer	Cross Lake	Yes	353	36	BLH, BC, B, LMB, NP, SUN, RKB, YP
Half Moon	Merrifield	Yes	44	23	BLH, BC, B, LMB, NP, SUN, W, YP
Hamlet	Deerwood	No	276	88	BLH, BC, B, LMB, NP, SUN, RKB
Hanks	Garrison	Yes	161	45	BLH, BC, B, LMB, NP, SUN, RKB, W
Hartley	Brainerd	No	129	20	BLH, BC, B, LMB, NP, SUN, W
Hay	Ironton	No	38	19	BLH, BC, B, LMB, NP, SUN, YP
Holt	Garrison	No	154	29	BLH, BC, B, NP, SUN, RKB
Horseshoe	Cross Lake	Yes	888	56	BLH, BC, B, LMB, NP, SUN, RKB, W, YP
Horseshoe	Deerwood	No	N/A	30	BC, B, LMB, NP, SUN
Horseshoe	Merrifield	No	39.8	28	B, NP, SUN, YP
Hubert	Nisswa	Yes	1294	83	BLH, BC, B, LMB, NP, SUN, RKB, SMB, W, YP
Huntington Mine	Crosby	Yes	100	258	BKT, BC, B, BRT, LMB, SUN, RBT, YP
Indian Jack	Crosby	No	78	25	BLH, B, NP, SUN, YP
Island	Cross Lake	Yes	176	76	BLH, BC, B, LMB, NP, SUN, RKB, W, YP
Island	Emily	Yes	240	37	BLH, BC, B, LMB, NP, SUN, RKB, W, YP
Island	Jenkins	No	63	24	BLH, BC, B, LMB, NP, SUN, RKB, YP
Island	Trommald	Yes	129	36	BLH, BC, B, LMB, NP, SUN, W, YP
Jail	Pine River	Private	170	22	BLH, BC, B, LMB, NP, SUN, YP
June	Ironton	No	41	51	BC, B, NP, SUN, YP
Kego	Fifty Lakes	Yes	272	20	BLH, BC, B, LMB, NP, SUN, YP
Kenney	Garrison	No	99	55	BLH, BC, B, NP, SUN, RKB, W
Kimball	Jenkins	Yes	190	77	BC, B, LMB, NP, SUN, RKB, W, YP
Knieff	Deerwood	No	38	42	BC, B, NP, SUN
Larson	Deerwood	Yes	45	43	BLH, BC, B, NP, SUN
Little Bass	Cross Lake	No	92	49	LMB, NP, SUN, YP
Little Black Hoof	Riverton	Yes	58	13	BLH, BC, B, LMB, NP, SUN, RKB, YP
Little Emily	Outing	Yes	111	26	BC, B, LMB, NP, SUN, YP
Little Hubert	Nisswa	No	185	41	BLH, BC, B, LMB, NP, SUN, W, YP
Little Ox	Cross Lake	No	40	72	BLH, BC, B, LMB, NP, SUN, RKB, YP
Little Pelican	Breezy Point	Yes	283	34	BLH, BC, B, LMB, NP, SUN, RKB, W, YP
Little Pine	Cross Lake	Yes	387	36	BLH, BC, B, LMB, NP, SUN, RKB, W, YP
Little Rabbit	Riverton	Yes	170	30	BC, B, LMB, NP, SUN, YP
Little Round	Cross Lake	No	20	22	BLH, BC, B, NP, SUN
Little Star	Cross Lake	Yes	50	30	BLH, BC, B, LMB, NP, SUN, RKB, YP
Lizzie	Pine River	Yes	370	13	BLH, BC, B, NP, SUN, W, YP
Long	Deerwood	No	214	39	BLH, BC, B, NP, SUN, W, YP
Lookout	Crosby	No	219	16	BLH, BC, B, LMB, NP, SUN
Loon	Crosby	Yes	40	20	BLH, B, LMB, NP, SUN
Lougee	Merrifield	Yes	217	53	BLH, BC, B, LMB, NP, SUN, RKB, W, YP

Name	Nearest Town	Public Access	Acres	Max. Depth	Fish Species
Love	Nisswa	Yes	78	27	BLH, BC, B, LMB, NP, SUN, W, YP
Lower Cullen	Nisswa	Yes	512	39	BLH, BC, B, LMB, NP, SUN, RKB, W, YP
Lower Hay	Jenkins	Yes	685	100	BLH, BC, B, LMB, NP, SUN, RKB, W, YP
Lower Mission	Merrifield	Yes	698	27	BLH, BC, B, LMB, NP, SUN, RKB, W, YP
Lows	Emily	No	319	9	BLH, BC, B, NP, SUN, YP
Mahnomen	Crosby	No	253	25	BLH, BC, B, LMB, NP, SUN, RKB, W, YP
Mahnomen, Alstead	Ironton	No	267	525	BLH, BC, B, LMB, NP, SUN, RBT, W, YP
Mallen Pit	Riverton	Carry In	5	95	B, BKT, NP, SUN
Manuel Mine	Crosby	No			RBT
Maple	Garrison	No	60	23	BLH, BC, B, NP, SUN, YP
Markee	Merrifield	Yes	106	33	BLH, BC, B, LMB, NP, SUN, RKB
Mary	Emily	Yes	380	34	BLH, BC, B, LMB, NP, SUN, RKB, W, YP
Mayo	Pequot Lakes	Yes	155	22	BLH, BC, B, LMB, NP, SUN, W, YP
Middle Cullen	Nisswa	Yes	382	48	BC, B, LMB, NP, SUN, RKB, W, YP
Miller	Crosby	No	107	35	BLH, BC, B, LMB, NP, SUN, RKB, W
Miller	Garrison	Yes	108	48	BLH, BC, B, LMB, NP, SUN, YP
Mitchell	Emily	Yes	439	78	BLH, BC, B, LMB, NP, SUN, RKB, SMB, W, YP
Mollie	Merrifield	No	270	7	BLH, BC, B, W
Morroco Mine	Trommald	No	23	N/A	B, LMB, YP
Mud	Emily	Yes	84	28	BLH, BC, B, NP, SUN, YP
Nelson	Deerwood	No	310	12	BLH, B, NP, SUN, YP
Nelson	Jenkins	No	86	65	BLH, B, LMB, NP, SUN, RKB, W
Nisswa	Nisswa	Yes	207	23	BLH, BC, B, LMB, NP, SUN, RKB, W, YP
Nokay	Brainerd	Yes	660	42	BLH, BC, B, LMB, NP, SUN, RKB, W, YP
North Long	Merrifield	Yes	5998	97	BLH, BC, B, LMB, NP, SUN, RKB, W, YP
O'Brien	Cross Lake	Yes	188	49	BLH, BC, B, LMB, NP, SUN, W, YP
Ossawinnamakee	Ideal Corners	Yes	644	63	BLH, BC, B, LMB, NP, SUN, RKB, W, YP
Ox	Cross Lake	No	238	74	BLH, BC, B, LMB, NP, SUN, RKB, W, YP
Papoose	Outing	Yes	81	21	BC, B, LMB, NP, SUN, YP
Partridge	Garrison	Yes	184	42	BC, B, LMB, NP, SUN, YP
Pascoe	Trommald	No	113	12	BLH, BC, B, NP, SUN, W, YP
Pelican	Breezy Point	Yes	8253	104	BLH, BC, B, LMB, NP, SUN, RKB, W, YP
Pennington Mine	Ironton	Yes	57	259	BC, B, LMB, NP, SUN, RBT, YP
Perch	Baxter	Yes	270	40	BLH, BC, B, LMB, NP, SUN, W, YP
Perry	Crosby	Yes	144	23	BLH, BC, B, LMB, NP, SUN, W, YP
Pickerel	Emily	No	90	25	BC, B, LMB, NP, SUN, RKB, YP
Pig	Cross Lake	Yes	191	56	BLH, BC, B, LMB, NP, SUN, RKB, SMB, W, YP

KEY			
BKT=Brook Trout	**LAT**=Lake Trout	**RKB**=Rock Bass	**W**=Walleye
BLH=Bullhead	**LMB**=Largemouth Bass	**SGR**=Sauger	**WC**=White Crappie
BC=Black Crappie	**M**=Muskie	**SMB**=Smallmouth Bass	**WHB**=White Bass
B=Bluegill	**NP**=Northern Pike	**SPT**=Splake	**YP**=Yellow Perch
BRT=Brown Trout	**PKS**=Pink Salmon	**SUN**=Sunfish	
CAT=Catfish (Channel and Flathead)	**RBT**=Rainbow Trout	**TM**=Tiger Muskie	

Fishing Waters

Tristan Publishing, Inc., believes that the following charts are accurate; however, we cannot guarantee or accept liability for their accuracy. The reader should contact the Minnesota DNR to verify the accuracy of the charts.

Name	Nearest Town	Public Access	Acres	Max. Depth	Fish Species
Pine	Cross Lake	Yes	390	18	BLH, BC, B, LMB, NP, SUN, RKB, SMB, W, YP
Platte	Sullivan	Yes	1746	23	BLH, BC, B, LMB, NP, SUN, W, YP
Pleasant	Cross Lake	Yes	21	72	BKT, BC, NP, RBT, W
Pointon	Ironton	No	171	14	BLH, BC, B, LMB, NP, SUN, RKB, YP
Portage	Deerwood	No	120	57	BLH, BC, B, LMB, NP, SUN, RKB, YP
Portage	Garrison	Yes	274	37	BLH, BC, B, LMB, NP, SUN, RKB, W, YP
Portage	Ironton	No	28	31	BC, B, NP, SUN, YP
Portsmouth Mine	Crosby	Yes	121	395	BKT, RBT
Pug Hole	Emily	No	48	30	BLH, BC, B, LMB, NP, SUN, YP
Rabbit (East)	Cuyuna	Yes	638	337	BLH, BC, B, LMB, NP, SUN, RKB, W, YP
Rabbit (West)	Cuyuna	Yes	531	50	BLH, BC, B, LMB, NP, SUN, RKB, W, YP
Red Sand	Brainerd	Yes	502	23	BLH, B, NP, SUN, W, YP
Reno	Deerwood	No	175	9	BC, B, NP, SUN, YP
Rice	Brainerd	Yes	434	25	BLH, BC, B, LMB, NP, SUN, RKB, SMB, W, YP
Rock	Cross Lake	No	45	13	BC, B, NP
Roe Mine	Riverton	No	25	135	BC, B, LMB, NP, SUN, YP
Rogers	Emily	Yes	219	64	BC, B, LMB, NP, SUN, RKB, W, YP
Rose	Ironton	No	40	11	BLH, BC, SUN
Ross	Emily	No	487	30	BLH, BC, B, LMB, NP, SUN, RKB, YP
Round	Fort Ripley	No	137	13	BC, B, NP, SUN, RKB, W, YP
Round	Nisswa	Yes	1644	51	BLH, BC, B, LMB, NP, SUN, RKB, W, YP
Roy	Nisswa	Yes	271	26	BLH, BC, B, LMB, NP, SUN, RKB, W, YP
Rush	Cross Lake	Yes	891	105	BLH, BC, B, LMB, NP, SUN, RKB, SMB, W, YP
Rushmeyer	Deerwood	No	37	26	BLH, BC, B, LMB, NP, SUN, YP
Ruth	Emily	Yes	588	39	BC, B, LMB, NP, SUN, RKB, W, YP
Sagamore Mine	Riverton	Yes	314	210	BKT, B, LMB, NP, SUN, YP
Sand	Fifty Lakes	No	95	12	BLH
Scott	Garrison	No	155	49	BLH, BC, B, LMB, NP, SUN
Sebie	Fort Ripley	Yes	169	27	BLH, BC, B, LMB, NP, SUN, RKB, YP
Serpent	Crosby	Yes	1057	65	BLH, BC, B, LMB, NP, SUN, RKB, SMB, W, YP
Shirt	Deerwood	Yes	224	38	BC, B, LMB, NP, SUN, W
Sibley	Pequot Lakes	Yes	418	40	BLH, BC, B, LMB, NP, SUN, RKB, YP
Silver	Merrifield	Yes	214	23	BLH, BC, B, NP, SUN, YP
Smith	Garrison	Private	441	54	BC, B, LMB, NP, SUN, RKB, W, YP
Smokey Hollow	Outing	Yes	114	25	BLH, BC, B, LMB, NP, SUN, YP
Snoshoe Mine	Riverton	Carry In	8	85	BKT, BC, B, LMB, SUN, YP
Sorenson	Merrifield	No	73	46	BLH, BC, B, NP, SUN
South Long	Brainerd	Yes	1313	47	BLH, BC, B, LMB, NP, SUN, RKB, W, YP
Star	Cross Lake	Private	126	83	BC, B, LMB, NP, SUN, RKB, W, YP
Stark	Emily	Yes	215	66	BLH, BC, B, LMB, NP, SUN, YP
Stewart	Swanburg	Yes	240	40	B, LMB, NP, SUN, W
Strawberry	Pequot Lakes	Yes	16	41	RBT
Sullivan	Crosby	No	80	38	BLH, BC, B, LMB, NP, SUN
Taylor	Ossipee	No	36	32	BLH, BC, B, NP, SUN, YP
Trout	Emily	Yes	114	22	BLH, BC, B, LMB, NP, SUN, RKB, W, YP

Name	Nearest Town	Public Access	Acres	Max. Depth	Fish Species
Turner	Crosby	Yes	53	36	BLH, BC, B, LMB, NP, SUN, RKB, YP
Turtle	Garrison	Private	95	33	BLH, BC, B, LMB, NP, SUN
Twin	Emily	No	78	94	BLH, BC, B, LMB, NP, SUN, YP
Upper Cullen	Breezy Point	Yes	435	40	BLH, BC, B, LMB, NP, SUN, RKB, W, YP
Upper Dean	Emily	Yes	285	24	BLH, BC, B, LMB, NP, SUN, YP
Upper Hay	Jenkins	Yes	581	42	BLH, BC, B, LMB, NP, SUN, RKB, W, YP
Upper Mission	Merrifield	Yes	817	36	BLH, BC, B, LMB, NP, SUN, RKB, W, YP
Upper South Long	Brainerd	Yes	802	47	BC, B, LMB, NP, SUN, RKB, W, YP
Velvet	Cross Lake	No	160	29	BLH, BC, B, LMB, NP, SUN, RKB, W, YP
West Fox	Fifty Lakes	Yes	472	55	BLH, BC, B, LMB, NP, SUN, RKB, W, YP
West Twin	Nisswa	Yes	117	42	BLH, BC, B, LMB, NP, SUN, RKB, W, YP
Whipple	Baxter	Yes	410	25	BLH, BC, B, LMB, NP, SUN, YP
White Sand	Baxter	Yes	368	27	BLH, BC, B, LMB, NP, SUN, RKB, W, YP
Whitefish	Cross Lake	Yes	7370	138	BLH, BC, B, LMB, NP, SUN, RKB, SMB, W, YP
Whitefish	Garrison	Private	696	62	BLH, BC, B, LMB, NP, SUN, RKB, W, YP
Wise	Brainerd	Private	129	44	BLH, BC, LMB, NP, SUN, YP
Wood	Outing	No	81	38	BC, B, LMB, NP, SUN, W, YP
Yawkey Mine	Crosby	No			RBT
Young	Ossipee	No	57	21	BLH, BC, B, LMB, NP, SUN, YP
Dakota					
Alimagnet	Apple Valley	Carry In	89.2	11.5	BLH, BC, B, LMB, NP, SUN, W, YP
Byllesby	Cannon Falls	Yes	1435	50	BLH, BC, B, CAT, LMB, NP, SMB, W, WHB, WC, YP
Chub	Farmington	No	274	10	BLH, SUN
Crystal	Lakeville	Yes	280	37	BLH, BC, B, LMB, NP, SUN, TM, W, YP
Fish	Eagan	Yes	28.7	33.5	BLH, BC, B, LMB, NP, SUN, W, YP
Heine Pond	Eagan	Yes	7.4	30	BLH, BC, B, SUN, W, YP
Holland	Eagan	Yes	32.5	55	BLH, BC, B, BRT, LMB, NP, RBT, SUN
Keller	Lakeville	Yes	51	7	BLH, BC, B, NP, SUN
Lee	Lakeville	No	22	14	BLH, B
Marcott	Inver Grove Hgts.	No	19	27	BLH, B
Marion	Lakeville	Yes	560	21	BLH, BC, B, LMB, NP, SUN, W, YP
Orchard	Lakeville	Yes	234	33	BLH, BC, B, LMB, NP, SUN, TM, W, YP
Quigley	Eagan	Yes	11.3	19	BLH, BC, B, CAT, LMB, SUN, W
Rebecca	Hastings	Yes	77.3	15	BLH, BC, B, CAT, LMB, M, NP, SUN, SGR, W, WHB, WC
Rogers	Mendota Heights	Yes	99	8	BLH, B
Simley	Inver Grove Hgts.	Yes	N/A	17	BLH, BC, B, NP, SUN, YP
Spring	Hastings	Yes	1839	17	BC, B, CAT, NP, SGR, W, WHB, WC

KEY			
BKT=Brook Trout	**LAT**=Lake Trout	**RKB**=Rock Bass	**W**=Walleye
BLH=Bullhead	**LMB**=Largemouth Bass	**SGR**=Sauger	**WC**=White Crappie
BC=Black Crappie	**M**=Muskie	**SMB**=Smallmouth Bass	**WHB**=White Bass
B=Bluegill	**NP**=Northern Pike	**SPT**=Splake	**YP**=Yellow Perch
BRT=Brown Trout	**PKS**=Pink Salmon	**SUN**=Sunfish	
CAT=Catfish (Channel and Flathead)	**RBT**=Rainbow Trout	**TM**=Tiger Muskie	

Fishing Waters

Tristan Publishing, Inc., believes that the following charts are accurate; however, we cannot guarantee or accept liability for their accuracy. The reader should contact the Minnesota DNR to verify the accuracy of the charts.

Name	Nearest Town	Public Access	Acres	Max. Depth	Fish Species
Douglas					
Aaron	Millerville	Yes	545	16	BLH, BC, B, LMB, NP, SUN, W, YP
Agnes	Alexandria	Yes	137	31	BLH, BC, B, LMB, NP, SMB, YP
Andrew	Alexandria	Yes	946	83	BLH, BC, B, LMB, NP, SUN, RKB, W, YP
Anka	Ashby	No	139	10	BLH, NP, SUN, YP
Blackwell	Holmes City	Yes	307	42	BLH, BC, B, LMB, NP, SUN, W
Brophy	Alexandria	Yes	289	44	BLH, BC, B, LMB, NP, SUN, W, YP
Burgen	Alexandria	Yes	184	43	BLH, BC, B, LMB, NP, SUN, RKB, W, YP
Carlos	Alexandria	Yes	2520	163	BLH, BC, B, LMB, NP, SUN, RKB, W, YP
Chippewa	Brandon	Yes	1186	95	BLH, BC, B, LMB, NP, SUN, RKB, W, YP
Christina	Ashby	Yes	3978	14	BLH, B, NP, YP
Cook	Alexandria	No	95	50	BLH, BC, B, LMB, NP, SUN
Cowdry	Alexandria	Yes	238	52	BLH, BC, B, LMB, NP, SUN, RKB, W, YP
Crooked	Holmes City	Yes	153	35	BLH, BC, B, LMB, NP, SUN
Darling	Alexandria	Private	954	62	BLH, BC, B, LMB, NP, SUN, RKB, W, YP
Devils	Brandon	Yes	221	35	BLH, BC, B, LMB, NP, SUN, W, YP
Freeborn	Farwell	Yes	241	18	BLH, BC, B, LMB, NP, SUN, W, YP
Geneva	Alexandria	Yes	631	63	BLH, BC, B, LMB, NP, SUN, RKB, W, YP
Gilbert	Holmes City	Yes	204	17	BLH, LMB, NP, SUN, YP
Grants	Holmes City	Yes	171	60	BLH, BC, B, LMB, NP, SUN, W, YP
Grill	Alexandria	Yes	58	11	BLH, BC, B, LMB, NP, SUN, W, YP
Henry	Alexandria	Yes	159	32	BLH, BC, B, LMB, NP, SUN, SMB, W, YP
Hidden	Carlos	No	10	18	BLH, B, NP, SUN
Ida	Alexandria	Yes	4289	106	BLH, BC, B, LMB, NP, SUN, RKB, SMB, W, YP
Ina	Melby	No	202	48	BLH, BC, B, LMB, NP, SUN, RKB, YP
Indian	Garfield	Yes	76	38	BLH, BC, B, LMB, NP, SUN, YP
Irene	Miltona	Yes	630	44	BLH, BC, B, LMB, NP, SUN, W, YP
Jessie	Alexandria	No	105	26	BLH, BC, B, LMB, NP, SUN, W, YP
Latoka	Alexandria	Yes	776	108	BLH, BC, B, LMB, NP, SUN, RKB, W, YP
Le Homme Dieu	Alexandria	Yes	1744	85	BLH, BC, B, LMB, NP, SUN, RKB, SMB, W, YP
Little Chippewa	Brandon	Yes	270	24	BLH, BC, B, LMB, NP, SUN, W, YP
Lobster	Garfield	Yes	1308	65	BLH, BC, B, LMB, M, NP, SUN, RKB, W, YP
Long	Evansville	Yes	218	18	BLH, BC, B, LMB, NP, SUN, W, YP
Lottie	Alexandria	No	49	31	BLH, B, LMB, NP, SUN, W, YP
Louise	Alexandria	Yes	219	33	BLH, BC, B, LMB, NP, SUN, RKB, W, YP
Maple	Forada	Yes	815	78	BLH, BC, B, LMB, NP, SUN, RKB, W, YP
Mary	Alexandria	Yes	2371	40	BLH, BC, B, LMB, NP, SUN, RKB, W, YP
Mill	Alexandria	Yes	600	40	BLH, BC, B, LMB, NP, SUN, W, YP
Miltona	Miltona	Yes	5838	105	BLH, BC, B, LMB, M, NP, SUN, RKB, SMB, W, YP
Mina	Alexandria	Yes	424	123	BLH, BC, B, LMB, NP, SUN, RKB, W, YP

Name	Nearest Town	Public Access	Acres	Max. Depth	Fish Species
Moon	Brandon	Private	124	38	BLH, BC, B, LMB, NP, SUN, W, YP
Moses	Millerville	Yes	822	32	BLH, BC, B, LMB, NP, SUN, RKB, W, YP
Nelson	Alexandria	No	88	52	BLH, BC, B, LMB, NP, SUN
North Union	Alexandria	No	117	42	BLH, BC, B, LMB, NP, SUN, W, YP
Oscar	Holmes City	Yes	630	25	BLH, BC, B, LMB, M, NP, SUN, W, YP
Pocket	Lowry	Yes	275	40	BLH, BC, B, LMB, NP, SUN, W, YP
Rachel	Holmes City	Yes	496	65	BLH, BC, B, LMB, NP, SUN, W, YP
Red Rock	Kensington	Yes	708	22	BC, B, LMB, NP, SUN, W, YP
Round	Garfield	Yes	66	30	BLH, BC, B, LMB, NP, SUN, YP
Smith	Alexandria	Yes	575	30	BLH, BC, B, LMB, NP, SUN, W, YP
Stony	Alexandria	No	87	58	BLH, BC, B, LMB, NP, SUN, RKB, W, YP
Stowe	Brandon	Yes	366	14	BLH, BC, B, LMB, NP, SUN, W, YP
Turtle	Forada	Yes	220	21	BLH, BC, B, LMB, NP, SUN, W, YP
Union	Forada	Yes	104	45	BLH, BC, B, LMB, NP, SUN, W, YP
Vermont	Miltona	Yes	309	59	BLH, BC, B, LMB, NP, SUN, YP
Victoria	Alexandria	Yes	419	60	BLH, BC, B, LMB, NP, SUN, RKB, W, YP
Whiskey	Brandon	Yes	158	46	BLH, BC, B, LMB, NP, SUN, W, YP
Winona	Alexandria	Carry In	190	9	BLH, BC, B, LMB, NP, YP
Faribault					
Bass	Delavan	Yes	203	20	BLH, BC, B, LMB, NP, SUN, YP
Rice	Wells	Yes	266	4	BLH, YP
Fillmore					
Lanesboro Mill Pond	Lanesboro	Yes	5.8	10	BLH, BC, B, LMB, NP, SUN, SGR
Freeborn					
Albert Lea	Albert Lea	Yes	2654	6	BLH, BC, B, CAT, LMB, NP, SUN, W, WC, YP
Bear	Twin Lakes	Yes	1536	6	NP
Fountain	Albert Lea	Yes	534	14	BLH, BC, B, CAT, LMB, NP, SUN, W, WC, YP
Freeborn	Freeborn	Yes	2126	7	BLH, BC, SUN, WC
Geneva	Geneva	No	2214	8	BLH, SUN
Morin	Lanesboro	Yes	21	7	BLH, BC, B, SUN, W, WC, YP
Pickeral	Albert Lea	Yes	620	6	BLH, BC, B, SUN, WC, YP
Goodhue					
Clear	Hastings	No	198	7	BC, B, LMB, NP, SUN, WHB, WC, YP
Frontenac	Frontenac	No	34	5	BC, B, NP, SUN, WC, YP
Goose	Red Wing	Yes	157	5.7	BLH, BC, B, LMB, NP, SUN, SGR, W, WHB, WC, YP
Mississippi River	Cannon Falls	No	N/A	N/A	BC, B, CAT, LMB, NP, SUN, RKB, SGR, SMB, W, WHB, WC, YP
Pepin	Lake City	Yes	25060	60	BC, CAT, LMB, NP, RKB, SGR, SMB, W, WHB, WC, YP
Grant					
Barrett	Barrett	Yes	544	28	BLH, BC, B, LMB, NP, SUN, W, YP
Cottonwood	Donnelly	Yes	243	16	BC, B, LMB, NP, W
Elk	Hoffman	Yes	190	29	BLH, BC, B, LMB, NP, SUN, W, YP
Graham	Herman	Yes	131	7	BLH, NP

KEY			
BKT=Brook Trout	**LAT**=Lake Trout	**RKB**=Rock Bass	**W**=Walleye
BLH=Bullhead	**LMB**=Largemouth Bass	**SGR**=Sauger	**WC**=White Crappie
BC=Black Crappie	**M**=Muskie	**SMB**=Smallmouth Bass	**WHB**=White Bass
B=Bluegill	**NP**=Northern Pike	**SPT**=Splake	**YP**=Yellow Perch
BRT=Brown Trout	**PKS**=Pink Salmon	**SUN**=Sunfish	
CAT=Catfish (Channel and Flathead)	**RBT**=Rainbow Trout	**TM**=Tiger Muskie	

Fishing Waters

Tristan Publishing, Inc., believes that the following charts are accurate; however, we cannot guarantee or accept liability for their accuracy. The reader should contact the Minnesota DNR to verify the accuracy of the charts.

Name	Nearest Town	Public Access	Acres	Max. Depth	Fish Species
Lightning	Wendell	Yes	500	11	BLH, BC, LMB, NP, W, YP
Lower Elk	Hoffman	Yes	152	16	BLH, B, LMB, NP, SUN, W, YP
Mustinka River	Norcross	Yes	108	10	BLH, NP, W, WC, YP
Pelican	Ashby	Yes	3932	21	BLH, BC, B, LMB, NP, SUN, W, WC, YP
Pomme de Terre	Elbow Lake	Yes	1758	23	BLH, BC, B, LMB, NP, SUN, W, WC, YP
Thompson	Hoffman	Yes	150	22	BLH, BC, B, LMB, NP, SUN, W, YP
Hennepin					
Anderson	Bloomington	No	81.5	9	BLH, BC, SUN
Ardmore	Loretto	No	10	20	BLH, B, SUN
Arrowhead	Edina	Yes	22	7	BLH, B, SUN
Bass	Plymouth	Yes	174	31	BLH, BC, B, LMB, NP, SUN, W, WC
Boundary Creek	Osseo	Yes	11	8	BLH, BC, B
Brownie	Minneapolis	Yes	12.3	47	BLH, BC, B, NP, SUN, TM, W, YP
Bryant	Eden Prairie	Yes	161	45	BLH, BC, B, LMB, NP, SUN, TM, YP
Bush	Bloomington	Yes	172.2	28	BLH, BC, B, LMB, NP, SUN, TM, W, YP
Calhoun	Minneapolis	Yes	401	82	BC, B, LMB, M, NP, SUN, TM, W, YP
Cedar	Minneapolis	Carry In	169	51	BC, B, LMB, M, NP, SUN, W, YP
Champlin Mill Pond	Champlin	Yes	34	11	BLH, BC, B, NP, SUN, WC, YP
Christmas	Chanhassen	Yes	257	87	BLH, B, BRT, LMB, NP, SUN, RBT, W, YP
Crystal	Robbinsdale	No	78	39	BLH, BC, B, LMB, NP, SUN, TM, YP
Diamond	Minneapolis	Yes	115	5.8	BLH, BC, B, SUN
Diamond	Rogers	Yes	406	8	BLH
Dickey's	Long Lake	No	12	26	BLH
Dutch	Mound	Yes	159.5	45	BLH, BC, B, LMB, NP, SUN, YP
Eagle	Maple Grove	Yes	291.3	34	BLH, BC, B, LMB, M, NP, SUN, W, YP
Fish	Maple Grove	Yes	223	48	BLH, BC, B, LMB, NP, SUN, W, WC, YP
Gleason	Plymouth	Yes	142	16	BLH, BC, B, CAT, LMB, NP, SUN, W, WC, YP
Glen	Glen Lake	No	104	25	BLH, BC, B, SUN, WC
Hafften	Rockford	Yes	43	44	BLH, BC, B, LMB, NP, SUN, YP
Half Moon	Loretto	Yes	28.8	25	BLH, BC, B, LMB, NP, SUN, W, YP
Harriet	Minneapolis	Yes	335	87	BLH, BC, B, LMB, M, NP, SUN, W, YP
Haughey	Delano	No	48	23	BLH, BC, B, WC
Hiawatha	Richfield	Yes	53.5	33	BLH, BC, B, NP, SUN, YP
Hidden	Plymouth	Yes	9	28	BLH, B
Holy Name	Medina	Yes	65	7	BLH
Hyland	Bloomington	Yes	84.4	12	BLH, BC, B, LMB, SUN, TM, YP
Idlewild	Eden Prairie	Yes	15	9	BLH, BC, B, LMB, SUN
Independence	Maple Plain	Yes	844	58	BC, B, LMB, M, NP, SUN, W, YP
Jubert	Corcoran	No	64	41	BLH
Lake of the Isles	Minneapolis	Yes	109	31	BC, B, LMB, M, NP, SUN, W, YP
Langdon	Mound	Yes	144	38	BLH, BC, B, SUN
Libbs	Wayzata	No	23	8	BLH, BC, B, LMB, NP, SUN, W, YP
Little Long	Minnetrista	Yes	108.4	76	B, LMB, NP, SUN, RBT, YP
Lone	Minnetonka	Yes	22	27	BLH, BC, B
Long	Long Lake	Yes	261	33	BLH, BC, B, LMB, NP, SUN, W, YP
Lost	Osseo	No	20	6	SUN
Lydiard	Wayzata	No	32.8	52	BLH, BC, B, LMB, SUN
Medicine	Plymouth	Yes	886	49	BLH, BC, B, LMB, NP, SUN, W, WC, YP

Name	Nearest Town	Public Access	Acres	Max. Depth	Fish Species
Minnetoga	Minnetonka	Yes	15	27	BLH, BC, NP
Minnetonka	Mound	Yes	14004	113	BLH, BC, B, LMB, M, NP, SUN, RKB, SMB, W, WC, YP
Mitchell	Eden Prairie	Yes	112	19	BLH, BC, B, LMB, NP, SUN, WC
Mooney	Medina	No	118	10	BLH, BC, B, NP, SUN, YP
Nokomis	Minneapolis	Yes	204	33	BLH, BC, B, LMB, SUN, TM, W, WC, YP
Parkers	Plymouth	Yes	97.1	37	BLH, BC, B, LMB, NP, SUN
Peavey	Wayzata	Yes	9	63	BLH, B, SUN
Penn	Bloomington	Yes	31	7	BLH, BC, B, SUN, WC, YP
Peter	Loretto	No	46	68	BLH, BC, B, LMB, NP, SUN
Pike	Maple Grove	Carry In	57.73	22	BLH, BC, B, LMB, NP, SUN, YP
Pomerleau	Crystal	No	29.5	26	BLH, BC, B, LMB, SUN
Powderhorn	Minneapolis	Yes	10	20	BLH, BC, B, SUN
Rebecca	Rockford	Yes	254	30	BLH, BC, B, LMB, M, SUN, YP
Red Rock	Eden Prairie	Yes	92	16	BLH, BC, B, LMB, NP, SUN, YP
Rice	Maple Grove	Yes	314	11.5	BLH, BC, B, LMB, NP, SUN, WC, YP
Round	Eden Prairie	Yes	33	37	BLH, BC, B, LMB, M, SUN, W, YP
Ryan	Brooklyn Center	No	18	33	BLH, BC, B, NP, SUN
Sarah	Rockford	Yes	574	59	BLH, BC, B, LMB, NP, SUN, WC, YP
Schandell	Loretto	No	41	29	BLH, BC, NP
Schmidt	Plymouth	Yes	37	25	BLH, BC, B, LMB, NP, SUN
School	Long Lake	No	11	21	BLH
Shady Oak	Hopkins	Yes	85	35	BLH, BC, B, LMB, NP, SUN
Snelling	St. Paul	Yes	103	9.5	BLH, BC, B, CAT, NP, SUN, WHB, WC, YP
Spurzem	Medina	Yes	70	38	BLH, BC, B, LMB, NP, SUN, YP
Staring	Eden Prairie	Yes	155	16	BLH, BC, B, LMB, NP, SUN, WC, YP
Sweeney	Golden Valley	No	66	28	BLH, BC, B, LMB, NP, SUN, WC, YP
Taft	Richfield	Yes	12.4	45	BLH, BC, B, CAT, LMB, NP, SUN, W, WC, YP
Twin	Golden Valley	No	19	56	BLH, BC, B, LMB, NP, SUN
Twin	Robbinsdale	Yes	212	44	BLH, BC, B, LMB, NP, SUN, TM, W, YP
Weaver	Maple Grove	Yes	149.2	57	BLH, BC, B, LMB, NP, SUN, TM, YP
Webber	Minneapolis	Yes	2	5	BLH, B, SUN, YP
Whaletail	St. Bonifacius	Yes	558	25	BLH, BC, B, LMB, NP, SUN, WC, YP
Winterhalter	Medina	No	13	27	BLH, BC, B, NP, SUN
Wirth	Golden Valley	Yes	38	25	BLH, BC, B, LMB, NP, SUN, W, YP
Wolsfeld	Golden Valley	No	34	26	BLH, BC, B, NP, SUN, WC, YP
Houston					
Shamrock	Caledonia	Carry In	8	15	BC, B, LMB, NP, YP
South Fork	Lanesboro	Yes	30	15	BC, B, LMB
Hubbard					
2nd Little Gulch	Laporte	Carry In	13	41	BLH, NP, SUN, YP
Alice	Lake George	No	121	21	BLH, BC, B, NP, SUN, RKB, W, YP
Bad Axe	Emmaville	No	271	39	BLH, BC, B, LMB, M, NP, SUN, RKB, SMB, YP
Beauty	Park Rapids	Yes	54	53	B, LMB, NP, SUN, W, YP
Belle Taine	Nevis	Yes	1185	56	BLH, BC, B, LMB, M, NP, SUN, RKB, SMB, W, YP

KEY			
BKT=Brook Trout	**LAT**=Lake Trout	**RKB**=Rock Bass	**W**=Walleye
BLH=Bullhead	**LMB**=Largemouth Bass	**SGR**=Sauger	**WC**=White Crappie
BC=Black Crappie	**M**=Muskie	**SMB**=Smallmouth Bass	**WHB**=White Bass
B=Bluegill	**NP**=Northern Pike	**SPT**=Splake	**YP**=Yellow Perch
BRT=Brown Trout	**PKS**=Pink Salmon	**SUN**=Sunfish	
CAT=Catfish (Channel and Flathead)	**RBT**=Rainbow Trout	**TM**=Tiger Muskie	

Fishing Waters

Tristan Publishing, Inc., believes that the following charts are accurate; however, we cannot guarantee or accept liability for their accuracy. The reader should contact the Minnesota DNR to verify the accuracy of the charts.

Name	Nearest Town	Public Access	Acres	Max. Depth	Fish Species
Benedict	Benedict	Yes	440	91	BLH, BC, B, LMB, NP, SUN, RKB, TM, W, YP
Big Bass	Akeley	Yes	124	60	BC, B, LMB, NP, SUN, RKB, W, YP
Big Sand	Dorset	Yes	1659	135	B, LMB, M, NP, SUN, RKB, SMB, W, YP
Big Stony	Park Rapids	Yes	319	24	BLH, BC, B, LMB, NP, SUN, W, YP
Blacksmith	Park Rapids	Yes	37	45	RBT, W
Blue	Park Rapids	Yes	324	84	BLH, BC, B, LMB, NP, SUN, RBT, RKB, W, YP
Boulder	Dorset	Yes	360	28	BLH, BC, B, LMB, NP, SUN, RKB, SMB, W, YP
Cedar	Park Rapids	Yes	97.5	26	BLH, BC, B, LMB, NP, SUN, YP
Coon	Lake George	Yes	17.9	38	BC, B, SUN
Coon	Park Rapids	No	80	85	BLH, BC, B, LMB, NP, SUN, YP
Crappie	Lake George	Yes	15	73	RBT
Dead Horse	Nevis	Yes	39	9	NP
Dead	Dorset	Yes	292	34	BLH, BC, B, LMB, NP, SUN, YP
Deer	Nevis	Yes	155	9	BLH, BC, B, LMB, NP, SUN, W, YP
Duck	Hubbard	Yes	326	23	BC, B, LMB, NP, SUN, RKB, SMB, W, YP
Eagle	Park Rapids	Yes	411	77	BLH, BC, B, LMB, NP, SUN, RKB, W, YP
East Crooked	Nevis	Yes	365	96	BC, B, LMB, NP, SUN, RKB, SMB, W, YP
Eighth Crow Wing	Nevis	Yes	492	30	BC, B, LMB, NP, SUN, RKB, W, YP
Eleventh Crow Wing	Akeley	Yes	790	80	BLH, BC, B, LMB, NP, SUN, RKB, W, YP
Emma	Dorset	Yes	77	50	BLH, BC, B, LMB, M, NP, SUN, RKB, W, YP
Evergreen	Lake George	Yes	200	38	BC, B, NP, SUN, RKB, W, YP
Fifth Crow Wing	Nevis	Yes	392	35	BLH, BC, B, LMB, NP, SUN, RKB, W, YP
First Crow Wing	Hubbard	Yes	526	15	BLH, BC, B, LMB, NP, SUN, RKB, W, YP
Fish Hook	Park Rapids	Yes	1632	76	BLH, B, LMB, NP, SUN, RKB, SMB, W, YP
Fourth Crow Wing	Nevis	Yes	479	10	BLH, BC, B, LMB, NP, SUN, RKB, W, YP
Frontenac	Becida	Yes	204	16	BLH, BC, B, LMB, NP, SUN, RKB, W, YP
Garfield	Laporte	Yes	979	32	BLH, BC, B, LMB, NP, SUN, RKB, W, YP
George	Lake George	Yes	798	29	BLH, BC, B, LMB, NP, SUN, RKB, W, YP
Gillett	Lake George	Yes	28	49	BLH, BC, B, LMB, NP, SUN, W, YP
Gilmore	Dorset	No	91	54	BC, B, LMB, NP, SUN, RKB, W, YP
Grace	Bemidji	Yes	887	42	BLH, BC, B, LMB, NP, SUN, RKB, SMB, W, YP
Halverson	Halverson	Carry In	22	32	BLH, BC, NP, SUN
Ham	Nevis	Yes	178	22	BLH, BC, B, LMB, NP, SUN, RKB, W, YP
Hart	Guthrie	Yes	224	13	BLH, BC, NP, SUN, W, YP
Hattie	Lake George	Yes	259	39	BLH, BC, B, LMB, NP, SUN, RKB, W, YP
Hennepin	Becida	Yes	407	14	BLH, BC, B, LMB, NP, SUN, W, YP
Hinds	Park Rapids	Yes	294	36	BLH, BC, B, LMB, NP, SUN, RKB, YP
Horseshoe	Laporte	No	253	52	BLH, BC, B, LMB, NP, SUN, RKB, W, YP

Name	Nearest Town	Public Access	Acres	Max. Depth	Fish Species
Ida	Dorset	Yes	76	40	BC, B, LMB, NP, SUN, RKB, SMB, W, YP
Indian	Akeley	Yes	49	36	BLH, B, LMB, NP, SUN, W, YP
Island	Akeley	No	78	46	BLH, BC, B, LMB, NP, SUN, RKB, YP
Island	Nevis	Yes	212	32	BLH, BC, B, LMB, NP, SUN, RKB, W, YP
Island	Park Rapids	Yes	544	65	BLH, BC, B, LMB, NP, SUN, RKB, W, YP
Ivan	Park Rapids	No	24	35	BLH, BC, B, LMB, NP, SUN, YP
Kabekona	Laporte	Yes	2252	133	BLH, B, LMB, NP, SUN, RKB, SMB, W, YP
LaSalle	Becida	Yes	221	213	BC, B, LMB, NP, SUN, RKB, W, YP
Little Mantrap	Park Rapids	Yes	348	54	BC, B, LMB, NP, SUN, RKB, W, YP
Little Sand	Dorset	Yes	386	80	BC, B, LMB, M, NP, SUN, RKB, SMB, W, YP
Long	Park Rapids	Yes	1974	135	BLH, BC, B, LMB, NP, SUN, RKB, W, YP
Loon	Park Rapids	No	90	50	BC, B, LMB, NP, SUN, RKB, SMB, W, YP
Lord	Park Rapids	Yes	52	32	BC, B, NP, SUN, YP
Lower Bottle	Dorset	Yes	652	110	BLH, BC, B, LMB, M, NP, SUN, RKB, SMB, W, YP
Mantrap	Emmaville	Yes	1556	68	BLH, BC, B, LMB, M, NP, SUN, RKB, SMB, W, YP
Mary	Lake Itasca	Yes	55.8	41	BC, B, NP, SUN, RKB, W, YP
Middle Crooked	Nevis	No	294	33	BLH, BC, B, LMB, NP, SUN, W, YP
Midge	Bemidji	Yes	521	24	BLH, BC, B, LMB, NP, SUN, RKB, W, YP
Minnie	Lake George	Yes	76	16	BC, B, LMB, NP, SUN, RKB, W, YP
Moran	Park Rapids	Yes	95	15	BC, B, LMB, NP, SUN, YP
Mow	Akeley	Yes	100	34	BC, B, LMB, NP, SUN, RKB, W, YP
Nagel	Akeley	Yes	69	65	BLH, BC, B, LMB, NP, SUN, RKB, W, YP
Nelson	Laporte	Yes	33	19.5	B, LMB, NP, SUN, W, YP
Newman	Bemidji	Yes	39	63	RBT
Ninth Crow Wing	Akeley	No	227	65	BLH, BC, B, LMB, NP, SUN, RKB, W, YP
Owl	Nevis	No	85	26	BLH, BC, B, LMB, NP, SUN, YP
Paine	Lake George	Yes	259	6	BLH, B, LMB, NP, SUN, YP
Palmer	Park Rapids	Yes	142	21	BC, B, LMB, NP, SUN, RKB, W, YP
Peysenske	Park Rapids	No	195	14	BLH, BC, B, LMB, NP, SUN, RKB, W, YP
Pickerel	Park Rapids	Yes	311	26	BC, B, LMB, M, NP, SUN, RKB, W, YP
Plantagenet	Bemidji	Yes	2529	65	BC, M, NP, RKB, W, YP
Portage	Park Rapids	Yes	412	17	BLH, BC, B, NP, SUN, W, YP
Potato	Park Rapids	Yes	2100	87	BLH, BC, B, LMB, NP, SUN, RKB, SMB, W, YP
Schoolcraft	Park Rapids	Yes	116	37	BLH, B, LMB, NP, SUN, RKB, W, YP
Second Crow Wing	Park Rapids	No	181	35	BLH, BC, B, LMB, NP, SUN, RKB, SMB, W, YP

KEY			
BKT=Brook Trout	**LAT**=Lake Trout	**RKB**=Rock Bass	**W**=Walleye
BLH=Bullhead	**LMB**=Largemouth Bass	**SGR**=Sauger	**WC**=White Crappie
BC=Black Crappie	**M**=Muskie	**SMB**=Smallmouth Bass	**WHB**=White Bass
B=Bluegill	**NP**=Northern Pike	**SPT**=Splake	**YP**=Yellow Perch
BRT=Brown Trout	**PKS**=Pink Salmon	**SUN**=Sunfish	
CAT=Catfish (Channel and Flathead)	**RBT**=Rainbow Trout	**TM**=Tiger Muskie	

Fishing Waters

Tristan Publishing, Inc., believes that the following charts are accurate; however, we cannot guarantee or accept liability for their accuracy. The reader should contact the Minnesota DNR to verify the accuracy of the charts.

Name	Nearest Town	Public Access	Acres	Max. Depth	Fish Species
Seventh Crow Wing	Nevis	Carry In	254	42	BLH, BC, B, LMB, NP, SUN, RKB, W, YP
Shingobee	Akeley	No	160	40	BLH, BC, B, LMB, NP, SUN, RKB, YP
Sixth Crow Wing	Nevis	Yes	320	40	BLH, BC, B, LMB, NP, SUN, RKB, W, YP
Skunk	Park Rapids	Private	198	55	BC, B, LMB, NP, SUN, RKB, W, YP
Spearhead	Becida	Yes	172	81	BLH, BC, B, LMB, NP, SUN, RKB, W, YP
Spider	Nevis	Yes	544	96	BLH, BC, B, LMB, M, NP, SUN, RKB, W, YP
Stocking	Park Rapids	No	88	25	BLH, BC, B, LMB, M, NP, SUN, RKB, YP
Sweitzer	Park Rapids	Yes	93	10	BLH, BC, B, LMB, NP, SUN, YP
Tenth Crow Wing	Akeley	Yes	173	40	BLH, BC, B, LMB, NP, SUN, RKB, W, YP
Third Crow Wing	Hubbard	Yes	643	35	BLH, BC, B, LMB, NP, SUN, RKB, SMB, W, YP
Tripp	Nevis	No	145	65	BLH, BC, B, LMB, NP, SUN, YP
Twenty	Lake George	Yes	40	24	B, LMB, SUN, YP
Twenty-One	Laporte	Yes	28	51.5	B, LMB, NP, SUN, YP
Upper Bottle	Dorset	Yes	465	55	BC, B, LMB, M, NP, SUN, RKB, SMB, W, YP
Upper Twin	Menahga	Yes	225	12	BLH, BC, B, LMB, NP, SUN, RKB, W, YP
Waboose	Nevis	Yes	172	32	BC, B, LMB, NP, SUN, W, YP
West Crooked	Nevis	Yes	279	50	BC, B, NP, SUN, W, YP
Williams	Akeley	No	102	34	BC, B, LMB, NP, SUN, RKB, W, YP
Isanti					
Adams	Stanchfield	No	11.7	47	BLH, B, NP, YP
Baxter	Isanti	Yes	78	10	BLH, BC, B, LMB, NP, SUN, W, YP
Blue	Princeton	Yes	309	31	BLH, BC, B, LMB, NP, SUN, W, YP
Elms	Cambridge	Yes	53	26	BLH, BC, B, NP, SUN, YP
Fannie	Cambridge	Yes	366	33	BLH, BC, B, LMB, NP, SUN, W, YP
Florence	Cambridge	Yes	141	26	BLH, BC, B, LMB, NP, SUN, W, YP
Francis	Isanti	Yes	301	7	BLH, BC, B, NP, YP
Green	Princeton	Yes	802	28	BLH, BC, B, LMB, NP, SUN, W, YP
Krans	Grandy	No	42	31	BLH, B, LMB, SUN, YP
Little Stanchfield	Grandy	Yes	138	12	BLH, BC, B, LMB, NP, SUN, RKB, W, WC, YP
Long	Grandy	No	90	14	BLH, B, NP, SUN, YP
Long	Isanti	Yes	390	15	BLH, BC, B, LMB, NP, SUN, W, YP
Lory	Dalbo	Yes	212	21	BLH, BC, B, LMB, NP, SUN, W, YP
North Stanchfield	Princeton	Yes	143	11	BLH, BC, B, NP, W, YP
Skogman	Cambridge	Yes	226.2	36	BLH, BC, B, LMB, NP, SUN, W, YP
South Stanchfield	Princeton	Yes	398	17	BLH, BC, B, NP, SUN, W, YP
Spectacle	Cambridge	Yes	239.6	51.5	BLH, BC, B, LMB, NP, SUN, W
Typo	Stacy	Yes	295	6	BLH, BC, B, NP, SUN, W, WC
Itasca					
Alice	Bigfork	No	53	70	B, LMB, NP
Alice	Squaw Lake	Yes	37	65	BLH, BC, B, NP, SUN, RKB, W, YP
Allen	Marcell	No	56	25	BLH, BC, B, NP, SUN
Amen	Deer River	No	198	75	BC, B, LMB, NP, SUN, YP
Anderson	Bigfork	Private	274	110	BC, B, LMB, NP, SUN, W, YP
Ann	Bigfork	No	89	20	BLH, BC, B, NP, YP
Antler	Bigfork	Yes	306	90	BC, B, LMB, NP, SUN, RKB, W, YP
Arrowhead	Wirt	Yes	86	30	BC, B, LMB, NP, SUN, W, YP
Aspen	Bigfork	No	96	26	BLH, NP, YP
Baldy	Marcell	No	21	47	B, W

Name	Nearest Town	Public Access	Acres	Max. Depth	Fish Species
Ball Club	Ball Club	Yes	3936	85	BLH, BC, B, NP, SUN, RKB, W, YP
Balsam	Taconite	Yes	710	37	BLH, BC, B, LMB, NP, SUN, RKB, W, YP
Barcus	Bovey	No	63	15	BLH, B, LMB, NP, SUN, RKB
Bartlet	Bigfork	No	116	8	BLH, NP, YP
Barwise	Bovey	Yes	92	50	BC, B, LMB, NP, SUN, RKB, YP
Bass	Bigfork	No	64	45	B, LMB, NP, SUN, SMB, YP
Bass	Cohasset	Yes	2407	76	BLH, BC, B, LMB, NP, SUN, RKB, W, YP
Bass	Effie	Yes	117	65	B, LMB, NP, RKB, SMB, YP
Bass	Spring Lake	Yes	93	25	BC, B, LMB, NP, SUN, RKB, YP
Bass	Taconite	No	129	43	BLH, BC, B, LMB, NP, SUN, RKB, YP
Batson	Marcell	No	110	50	BLH, BC, B, LMB, NP, SUN, RKB, W, YP
Battle	Effie	Yes	199	15	BC, B, NP, SUN, RKB, W, YP
Bear	Nashwauk	Yes	339	16	BLH, BC, B, NP, SUN, RKB, W, YP
Beatrice	Side Lake	Yes	123	29	BC, B, LMB, NP, W, YP
Beauty	Goodland	Yes	217	31	BLH, BC, B, LMB, NP, SUN, W, YP
Beaver	Deer River	Yes	47	30	NP, RKB
Beaver	Marcell	No	50	30	BLH, BC, B, LMB, NP, SUN, YP
Bee Cee	Grand Rapids	Carry In	25	33	RBT
Bello	Marcell	Yes	493	58	BLH, BC, B, LMB, NP, SUN, RKB, YP
Bengal	Goodland	Yes	48	54	BLH, BC, B, LMB, NP, SUN
Bevo	Bigfork	No	53	40	BLH, BC, B, LMB, NP, SUN, YP
Big Diamond	Marble	Yes	122	31	BLH, BC, B, LMB, NP, SUN, YP
Big Dick	Marcell	Yes	249	20	BC, B, LMB, NP, SUN, RKB, YP
Big Fork River	Bigfork				M, NP, SMB, W
Big Horn	Grand Rapids	Carry In	34	23	B, LMB, YP
Big Island	Marcell	Yes	238	42	BC, B, LMB, NP, YP
Big Jack	Marcell	No	30	46	B, LMB
Big McCarthy	Nashwauk	Yes	110	45	BC, B, NP, SUN, YP
Big Ole	Marcell	Carry In	179	65	BC, B, LMB, NP, SUN, SMB, W, YP
Big Rainbarrel	Grand Rapids	No	20	44	LMB, YP
Big Rose	Bigfork	No	63	25	BLH, B, LMB, NP, SUN, YP
Big Sucker	Nashwauk	No	230	36	BLH, BC, B, LMB, NP, SUN, W, YP
Big Too Much	Talmoon	Yes	232	95	BC, B, LMB, NP, SUN, RKB, W, YP
Bird's Eye	Max	No	82	50	BLH, BC, LMB, NP, SUN, RKB, W, YP
Black Island	Marcell	Yes	107	59	BC, B, LMB, NP, RKB, SMB
Blackwater	Cohasset	Yes	674	N/A	BLH, BC, B, NP, SUN, RKB, W, YP
Blandin	Grand Rapids	Yes	449	38	BC, B, LMB, NP, SUN, RKB, W, YP
Blandin	Marcell	No	93	20	B, LMB, NP, SUN
Blind Pete	Bigfork	No	60	20	BLH, BC, NP, SMB, YP
Blind	Marcell	Carry In	46	106	B, LMB, NP, SUN, RKB, YP
Bluebill	Marcell	No	136	14	BLH, BC, B, NP, SUN, RKB, W, YP
Bluewater	Grand Rapids	Yes	364	120	BLH, B, LAT, LMB, SUN, RKB, SMB, YP
Bower	Nashwauk	Yes	89	35	BC, B, LMB, NP, SUN, W, YP
Bowstring	Deer River	Yes	9220	32	BLH, BC, B, NP, SUN, RKB, W, YP
Boy	Marcell	No	27	42	BLH, NP, W, YP
Bray	Nashwauk	Yes	196	44	BLH, BC, B, NP, SUN, RKB, W, YP
Brush Shanty	Bigfork	No	150	35	BC, B, LMB, NP, SUN, YP

KEY	BKT=Brook Trout	LAT=Lake Trout	RKB=Rock Bass	W=Walleye
	BLH=Bullhead	LMB=Largemouth Bass	SGR=Sauger	WC=White Crappie
	BC=Black Crappie	M=Muskie	SMB=Smallmouth Bass	WHB=White Bass
	B=Bluegill	NP=Northern Pike	SPT=Splake	YP=Yellow Perch
	BRT=Brown Trout	PKS=Pink Salmon	SUN=Sunfish	
	CAT=Catfish (Channel and Flathead)	RBT=Rainbow Trout	TM=Tiger Muskie	

Fishing Waters

Tristan Publishing, Inc., believes that the following charts are accurate; however, we cannot guarantee or accept liability for their accuracy. The reader should contact the Minnesota DNR to verify the accuracy of the charts.

Name	Nearest Town	Public Access	Acres	Max. Depth	Fish Species
Buck	Nashwauk	Yes	492	31	BC, B, LMB, NP, SUN, RKB, W, YP
Buckeye Pit	Coleraine	Yes	48	80	B, LMB, SUN, RBT, RKB, W, YP
Burns	Marcell	Yes	144	100	BC, B, LMB, NP, SUN, RKB, YP
Burnt Shanty	Marcell	Yes	182	35	BC, B, LMB, NP, SUN, YP
Burrows	Marcell	Yes	291	38	BC, B, NP, W, YP
Bustic	Bigfork	No	82	35	BLH, BC, B, LMB, NP, SUN, YP
Busties	Holyoke	Yes	237	44	BC, B, NP, SUN, W, YP
Button Bow	Togo	Yes	75	18	B, SMB, YP
Cameron	Bigfork	Yes	73	35	BLH, BC, B, LMB, NP, SUN, RKB, W, YP
Canisteo Pit	Coleraine	Yes	1338	311	BC, B, LAT, LMB, SUN, RBT, RKB, SMB
Caribou	Marcell	Yes	240	152	B, LAT, RKB, SMB, YP
Carlson	Grand Rapids	No	174.5	7	BLH
Carpenter	Marcell	Yes	31	52	LMB
Cavanaugh	Cohasset	No	67	48	BLH, BC, B, LMB, NP, SUN, W, YP
Cedar	Max	No	168	45	BLH, B, LMB, NP, SUN, RKB, W, YP
Charlotte	Grand Rapids	No	75	30	BC, B, NP, SUN, W, YP
Chase	Deer River	Yes	209	95	BC, B, LMB, NP, SUN, W, YP
Clarke	Cohasset	Yes	37	34	BC, B, NP, RKB, SMB, YP
Clear	Wirt	Yes	132	30	BC, B, LMB, NP, SUN, W, YP
Clearwater	Blackberry	No	128	16	BLH, NP, SUN, YP
Clubhouse	Marcell	Yes	210	90	BLH, BC, B, LMB, NP, SUN, RKB, YP
Connors	Bigfork	No	135	68	BLH, BC, B, LMB, NP, SUN, RKB, W, YP
Coon	Effie	No	324	30	BLH, BC, B, NP, SUN, YP
Coon-Sandwick	Bigfork	Yes	627	36	BLH, BC, B, LMB, NP, SUN, W, YP
Cottonwood	Deer River	Yes	105	42	BLH, BC, B, NP, SUN, RKB, YP
Crane	Grand Rapids	No	38	80	BLH, B, LMB, NP, SUN, YP
Crooked	Marble	Yes	418	60	BC, B, LMB, NP, SUN, W, YP
Crooked	Marcell	Yes	115	46	BC, B, NP, YP
Crooked	Talmoon	Yes	82	110	BLH, BC, B, NP, SUN, YP
Cropless	Goodland	No	32	9	BC
Crum	Togo	Carry In	18	14	LMB
Cut Foot Sioux	Squaw Lake	Yes	2851	78	BLH, BC, B, NP, SUN, RKB, W, YP
Cutaway	Bovey	Carry In	257	55	BLH, BC, B, LMB, NP, SUN, RKB, YP
David	Bigfork	Yes	53	30	BLH, BC, NP, SUN, W, YP
Day	Grand Rapids	Yes	34	40	BC, B, LMB, YP
Dead Horse	Marcell	Yes	97	30	BLH, BC, B, LMB, NP, SUN, RKB, W, YP
Decker	Blackduck	Yes	300	12	BLH, NP, SUN, YP
Deer	Deer River	Yes	4097	121	BLH, BC, B, LMB, M, NP, SUN, RKB, SMB, W, YP
Deer	Effie	Yes	1748	50	BC, B, LMB, NP, SUN, RKB, W, YP
Dixon	Squaw Lake	Yes	616	29	BLH, BC, NP, SUN, RKB, W, YP
Doan	Grand Rapids	No	89	40	BC, B, LMB, NP, RKB, W
Dock	Marcell	Yes	31	40	BC, B, LMB, W
Dode	Goodland	Carry In	84	25	BLH, BC, B, LMB, NP, SUN, YP
Dollar	Nashwauk	No	51	20	BLH, B, NP, SUN, YP
Dora	Wirt	Yes	447	18	BLH, BC, B, NP, SUN, RKB, W, YP
Duck	Effie	Yes	10	45	SMB
Duck	Marcell	Yes	17	15	B, LMB
Dunbar	Squaw Lake	Yes	254	30	BLH, BC, B, LMB, NP, SUN, W, YP
Eagle	Marcell	Yes	279	47	BLH, BC, B, LMB, NP, SUN, RKB, W, YP
East Smith	Marcell	Yes	145	38	BC, B, LMB, NP, SUN, YP
East	Bigfork	Yes	83	30	BC, NP, SUN, YP

Name	Nearest Town	Public Access	Acres	Max. Depth	Fish Species
East	Marcell	No	160	65	BLH, BC, B, NP, SUN, RKB, YP
Elizabeth	Marcell	No	193	42	BC, B, NP, SUN, YP
Erickson	Bigfork	No	26	70	B, LMB, NP, YP
Erskine	Effie	Yes	40	56	BKT, SPT
Fawn	Deer River	No	167	37	BLH, BC, B, LMB, NP, SUN, RKB, W, YP
Five Island	Effie	Yes	175	33	BC, B, LMB, NP, SUN, RKB, YP
Forest	Grand Rapids	Yes	37.7	31	BC, B, LMB, NP, SUN, RKB, W, YP
Forsythe	Cohasset	No	60	17	BLH, B, LMB, NP, SUN, W, YP
Fox	Marcell	No	280	75	BLH, BC, B, LMB, NP, SUN, RKB, YP
Gale	Bigfork	No	73	50	BC, B, LMB, NP, SUN, RKB, W, YP
Glove	Northome	Yes	14	12	BLH
Grass	Marcell	No	117	54	BC, B, NP, SUN, W, YP
Grave	Marcell	Yes	500	39	BLH, BC, B, LMB, NP, SUN, RKB, W, YP
Greenway Pit	Grand Rapids	Yes	72	295	BC, LMB, NP, RKB
Guile	Cohasset	Yes	103	60	BC, B, LMB, NP, SUN, YP
Gunderson	Talmoon	No	146	41	BLH, BC, B, LMB, NP, SUN, YP
Gunn	Marcell	No	342	39	BLH, BC, B, LMB, NP, SUN, RKB, YP
Gunn	Marcell	No	88	75	BC, B, LMB, NP, SUN, RKB, YP
Gunny Sack	Bigfork	No	78	13	BLH, BC, B, NP, SUN, RKB, W, YP
Hale	Grand Rapids	No	131	59	BLH, BC, B, LMB, NP, SUN, W, YP
Hale	Grand Rapids	Yes	142	60	BC, B, LMB, NP, SUN, RKB, YP
Hamrey	Alvwood	Yes	44	60	BLH, B, LMB, NP, SUN, YP
Hansen	Deer River	No	58	45	BLH, BC, B, NP, SUN, YP
Hanson	Bovey	No	74	66	BLH, BC, B, NP, SUN, RKB, YP
Harrison	Nashwauk	Yes	39	28	BLH, BC, B, NP, SUN, YP
Hart	Pengilly	Yes	325	55	BLH, BC, B, LMB, NP, SUN, RKB, W, YP
Hartley	Nashwauk	Yes	281	49	BLH, BC, B, NP, SUN, RKB, YP
Haskell	Bovey	No	86	52	BLH, B, LMB, NP, SUN, RBT, RKB, YP
Hatch	Marcell	No	243	88	BC, B, LMB, NP, SUN, RKB, SMB, W, YP
Hay	Grand Rapids	Yes	59	40	BLH, BC, B, LMB, NP, SUN, YP
Helen	Goodland	Yes	164	33	BLH, BC, B, LMB, NP, SUN
Herrigan	Togo	No	24	29	NP, YP
Highland	Marcell	Yes	102	38	BLH, BC, B, LMB, NP, SUN, RKB
Hill	Grand Rapids	Carry In	38	32	B, YP
Holland	Talmoon	Yes	19	45	BLH, BC, B, LMB, NP, SUN, YP
Holloway	Wirt	No	193	40	BLH, BC, B, LMB, NP, SUN
Holman	Bovey	Yes	146	65	BC, B, NP, RKB, YP
Homestad	Bigfork	No	26	51	BLH, B, NP, YP
Horsehead	Bigfork	No	76	16	LMB, SUN, YP
Horsehead	Nashwauk	Yes	19	40	BC, LMB, NP, YP
Horseshoe	Grand Rapids	No	141	11	BLH
Horseshoe	Marcell	Yes	127	60	BC, B, LMB, NP, SUN, SMB, W
Horseshoe	Marcell	No	270	25	BLH, BC, B, NP, SUN, RKB, SMB, W, YP
Ice	Grand Rapids	Yes	42	53	BLH, BC, B, LMB, NP, SUN, YP
Inkey	Coleraine	No	76	68	BC, B, LMB, NP, SUN

KEY			
BKT=Brook Trout	**LAT**=Lake Trout	**RKB**=Rock Bass	**W**=Walleye
BLH=Bullhead	**LMB**=Largemouth Bass	**SGR**=Sauger	**WC**=White Crappie
BC=Black Crappie	**M**=Muskie	**SMB**=Smallmouth Bass	**WHB**=White Bass
B=Bluegill	**NP**=Northern Pike	**SPT**=Splake	**YP**=Yellow Perch
BRT=Brown Trout	**PKS**=Pink Salmon	**SUN**=Sunfish	
CAT=Catfish (Channel and Flathead)	**RBT**=Rainbow Trout	**TM**=Tiger Muskie	

Fishing Waters

Tristan Publishing, Inc., believes that the following charts are accurate; however, we cannot guarantee or accept liability for their accuracy. The reader should contact the Minnesota DNR to verify the accuracy of the charts.

Name	Nearest Town	Public Access	Acres	Max. Depth	Fish Species
Island	Deer River	Yes	283	31	BLH, BC, B, LMB, NP, SUN, RKB, W, YP
Island	Grand Rapids	Yes	73	45	BC, B, LMB, NP, SUN, YP
Island	Marcell	No	19	65	LMB, SMB
Island	Northome	Yes	3088	35	BLH, BC, B, NP, SUN, RKB, W, YP
Island	Taconite	Yes	61	35	BLH, BC, B, LMB, NP, SUN, YP
Jack the Horse	Marcell	Yes	383	45	BLH, BC, B, LMB, NP, SUN, RKB, YP
Jay Gould	Cohasset	Private	426	33	BLH, BC, B, LMB, M, NP, SUN, RKB, SMB, W, YP
Jessie	Talmoon	Yes	1753	42	BLH, BC, B, LMB, NP, SUN, RKB, W, YP
Jingo	Bigfork	Yes	77	60	LMB, NP, SUN, YP
Johnson	Grand Rapids	Yes	492	88	BC, B, LMB, NP, SUN, RKB, SMB, W, YP
Johnson	Marcell	Yes	305	51	BC, B, LMB, NP, SUN, RKB, W, YP
Kelly	Bigfork	Yes	69	39	BC, B, NP, SUN, RKB, YP
Kennedy	Nashwauk	No	92	80	BC, B, LMB, NP, SUN, RKB, W, YP
King	Taconite	Yes	296	23	BLH, BC, B, LMB, NP, SUN, RKB, W, YP
Kremer	Grand Rapids	No	72	86	BRT, LMB, RBT, SPT
La Barge	Marcell	Yes	39	30	BLH, BC, B, NP, SUN, YP
La Croix	Talmoon	No	120	80	BC, B, LMB, NP, SUN, RKB, YP
Lac-A-Roy	Bigfork	Yes	74	30	NP, SUN, YP
Lake of Isles	Bigfork	Yes	68.6	48	NP, SUN, W, YP
Lammon Aid	Calumet	No	66	21	BLH, BC, B, LMB, NP, SUN, RKB, YP
Larson	Effie	Yes	198	177	BLH, NP, SUN, RBT, SPT, YP
Lauchoh	Bigfork	Yes	40	40	BLH, B, NP, SUN, YP
Lawrence	Taconite	Yes	395	32	BC, B, NP, SUN, RKB, SMB, W, YP
Leighton	Cohasset	No	229	63	BLH, B, LMB, NP, SUN, RKB, YP
Libby	Nashwauk	No	110	15	BLH, B, NP
Lind Pit	Grand Rapids	Yes	82	284	BC
Link	Bigfork	No	46	25	B, LMB, NP, SUN, YP
Little Ball Club	Deer River	Yes	132	30	BLH, BC, B, LMB, NP, SUN, RKB, W, YP
Little Bass	Cohasset	Yes	155	62	BLH, BC, B, LMB, NP, SUN, RKB, W, YP
Little Bass	Togo	No	30	72	BLH, NP, SUN, YP
Little Bear	Togo	Yes	142	35	BLH, BC, B, LMB, NP, SUN, W, YP
Little Bowstring	Deer River	Yes	319	33	BLH, BC, B, LMB, NP, SUN, RKB, W, YP
Little Cavanaugh	Cohasset	No	19	27	BLH, B, LMB, SUN, YP
Little Coon	Effie	No	68	123	BLH, BC, B, NP, SUN, YP
Little Cowhorn	Grand Rapids	Yes	166	12	BLH, NP, SUN, YP
Little Cut Foot Sioux	Deer River	Carry In	660	20	BLH, BC, B, NP, SUN, RKB, W, YP
Little Dead Horse	Marcell	No	77	30	B, LMB, NP, SUN, W, YP
Little Deer	Deer River	Yes	67	39	BLH, BC, B, LMB, NP, SUN, YP
Little Dick	Marcell	Yes	83	20	BLH, BC, NP, YP
Little Dixon	Squaw Lake	Yes	32	18	BLH, BC, NP, SUN, YP
Little East	Marcell	No	61	100	B, LMB, NP, RKB, YP
Little Flower	Goodland	Carry In	30	25	BLH, BC, B, LMB, NP, SUN, YP
Little Horn	Marcell	Carry In	31	68	LMB, W, YP
Little Island	Goodland	No	109	45	BLH, BC, B, LMB, NP, SUN, YP
Little Island	Marcell	Yes	61	35	BC, B, LMB, NP, SUN, YP
Little Jay Gould	Cohasset	Private	150	56	BC, B, LMB, NP, SUN, RKB, W, YP
Little Jessie	Deer River	Yes	637	50	BC, B, LMB, NP, SUN, RKB, SMB, W, YP
Little Long	Bigfork	Yes	26.1	29	BC, B, NP, RKB, YP

Name	Nearest Town	Public Access	Acres	Max. Depth	Fish Species
Little Long	Grand Rapids	Yes	253	61	BC, B, LMB, NP, SUN, RKB, W, YP
Little McCarthy	Nashwauk	No	70	24	BLH, BC, B, LMB, NP, SUN, RKB, W, YP
Little Moose	Effie	Yes	76	20	BLH, BC, B, LMB, NP, SUN, W, YP
Little Moose	Grand Rapids	Yes	271	23	BC, B, LMB, M, NP, SUN, RKB, W, YP
Little North Star	Marcell	No	54	43	BLH, BC, B, NP, SUN, RKB, W, YP
Little Otter	Marcell	No	53	35	B, LMB, W, YP
Little Ranier	Marcell	No	47	48	BLH, BC, B, LMB, NP, SUN, YP
Little Rice	Cohasset	Yes	162	32	BLH, BC, B, LMB, NP, SUN, RKB, W, YP
Little Sand	Calumet	Yes	213	44	BLH, BC, B, LMB, NP, SUN, RKB, W
Little Sand	Squaw Lake	Yes	361	19	BLH, BC, B, NP, SUN, RKB, W, YP
Little Smith	Marcell	No	27	35	BC, B, NP, YP
Little Split Hand	Grand Rapids	Yes	223	25	BLH, BC, B, LMB, NP, SUN, RKB, W, YP
Little Spring	Talmoon	No	133	10	BLH, BC, B, LMB, NP, SUN, YP
Little Too Much	Talmoon	No	67	60	BC, B, NP, SUN, RKB, W, YP
Little Trout	Grand Rapids	No	74	80	B, LAT, LMB, NP, SUN, RKB, SPT, YP
Little Turtle	Talmoon	Yes	475	29	BLH, BC, B, LMB, NP, SUN, RKB, W, YP
Little Wabana	Grand Rapids	Yes	104	57	BC, B, LMB, NP, SUN, RKB, W, YP
Little Whitefish	Wirt	No	152	15	YP
Little Winnibigoshish	Deer River	Yes	938	28	BLH, BC, B, LMB, M, NP, SUN, RKB, W, YP
Long	Bigfork	No	75	40	B, LMB, NP, RKB, SMB, YP
Long	Goodland	Yes	124	84	BLH, BC, B, LMB, NP, SUN, RKB, W, YP
Long	Grand Rapids	Yes	121	85	BLH, BC, B, NP, SUN, RKB, YP
Long	Grand Rapids	Yes	48	47	BC, B, LMB, YP
Long	Nashwauk	No	128	45	BLH, BC, B, NP, SUN, W
Long	Talmoon	Yes	93	72	BLH, BC, B, LMB, NP, SUN, RKB, YP
Loon	Cohasset	No	57	40	BC, B, LMB, NP, SUN, RKB, W, YP
Loon	Grand Rapids	Yes	235	69	BLH, BC, B, LMB, NP, SUN, RKB, W, YP
Lost Moose	Grand Rapids	Yes	101	N/A	B, LMB, NP, SUN, YP
Lost	Bigfork	Yes	88	27	BLH, BC, B, NP, SUN, RKB, W, YP
Lower Balsam	Taconite	No	283	29	BLH, BC, B, LMB, NP, SUN, RKB, W, YP
Lower Hanson	Bovey	No	82	75	BLH, BC, B, LMB, NP, SUN, RKB, YP
Lower Lawrence	Bovey	No	152	34	BLH, BC, NP, SUN, W, YP
Lower Panasa	Calumet	Yes	254	25	BLH, BC, B, LMB, NP, SUN, RKB, W, YP
Lower Spring	Marcell	No	15	15	BLH
Lucky	Grand Rapids	Carry In	12	44	BRT
Lundeen	Marcell	Yes	76	30	BC, B, NP, SUN, YP
Maple	Marcell	Yes	228	39	BC, B, LMB, NP, SUN, RKB, W, YP
Marie	Bigfork	No	47	48	BLH, B, NP, SUN, YP
Mary	Marcell	No	193	45	BC, B, LMB, NP, SUN, RKB, YP
May	Bigfork	No	63	15	LMB, NP, YP

KEY			
BKT=Brook Trout	**LAT**=Lake Trout	**RKB**=Rock Bass	**W**=Walleye
BLH=Bullhead	**LMB**=Largemouth Bass	**SGR**=Sauger	**WC**=White Crappie
BC=Black Crappie	**M**=Muskie	**SMB**=Smallmouth Bass	**WHB**=White Bass
B=Bluegill	**NP**=Northern Pike	**SPT**=Splake	**YP**=Yellow Perch
BRT=Brown Trout	**PKS**=Pink Salmon	**SUN**=Sunfish	
CAT=Catfish (Channel and Flathead)	**RBT**=Rainbow Trout	**TM**=Tiger Muskie	

Fishing Waters

Tristan Publishing, Inc., believes that the following charts are accurate; however, we cannot guarantee or accept liability for their accuracy.
The reader should contact the Minnesota DNR to verify the accuracy of the charts.

Name	Nearest Town	Public Access	Acres	Max. Depth	Fish Species
McAvity	Grand Rapids	Yes	137	29	BLH, BC, B, LMB, NP, SUN, RKB, W, YP
McKewen	Marcell	Yes	37.4	31	BC, B, NP
McKinney	Grand Rapids	Yes	115	34	BLH, BC, B, LMB, NP, SUN, YP
Middle Hanson	Bovey	Yes	65	32	BLH, BC, B, LMB, NP, SUN, RKB, YP
Mirror	Togo	Yes	105	45	B, LMB, NP, SUN, RKB, W, YP
Moon	Marcell	No	25	32	B, YP
Moonshine	Bovey	No	19	38	YP
Moonshine	Grand Rapids	Yes	25	68	RBT
Moore	Grand Rapids	Yes	74	60	B, LMB, RKB, YP
Moose	Bovey	Yes	62	11	BLH, BC, B, NP, SUN, RKB, YP
Moose	Deer River	Yes	1265	61	BC, B, LMB, M, NP, SUN, RKB, SMB, TM, W, YP
Moose	Northome	Yes	357	52	BLH, BC, LMB, NP, SUN, RKB, W, YP
Mosomo	Squaw Lake	Yes	29	30	W, YP
Moss	Marcell	Yes	21	15	B, LMB
Mountain Ash	Grand Rapids	No	107	16	BLH, BC, B, LMB, NP, SUN, YP
Mud	Deer River	No	99	31	NP, SUN, W, YP
Murphy	Grand Rapids	Yes	119	20	BLH, NP, YP
Napoleon	Bigfork	No	123	30	BLH, BC, B, LMB, NP, SUN, YP
Nashwauk	Nashwauk	Yes	144	53	BLH, BC, B, NP, SUN, RKB, YP
Natures	Squaw Lake	Yes	2158	6	BLH, BC, NP, SUN, W, YP
New	Goodland	Yes	63	22	BC, B, NP, YP
Nickel	Marcell	Yes	13.2	36.5	RBT
Noma	Wirt	Yes	55	47	BC, B, LMB, NP, SUN, W, YP
North Star	Marcell	Yes	1059	90	BC, B, LMB, M, NP, SUN, RKB, SMB, W, YP
North Twin	Marble	Yes	250	42	BC, B, LMB, NP, SUN, RKB, W, YP
Nose	Grand Rapids	Carry In	96	47	BC, B, LMB, NP, SUN, W, YP
No-ta-she-bun	Remer	Yes	238	45	BC, B, LMB, NP, SUN, RKB, W, YP
O'Brien	Nashwauk	Yes	900	63	BLH, BC, B, LMB, NP, SUN, RKB, W, YP
O'Brien Res. #4	Nashwauk	Yes	102	41.5	BLH, BC, B, LMB, NP, W, YP
O'Leary	Nashwauk	Yes	131	14	BC, B, NP, SUN, W, YP
O'Reilly	Taconite	Yes	202	79	BLH, BC, B, LMB, NP, SUN, RKB, YP
Orange	Marcell	Carry In	86	30	BC, B, LMB, M, YP
Otter	Bigfork	Carry In	164	17	BLH, NP, SUN, YP
Owen	Bigfork	Yes	257	34	BLH, BC, B, LMB, NP, SUN, SMB, W, YP
Ox Hide	Pengilly	Yes	121	40	BLH, BC, B, LMB, NP, SUN, RKB, YP
Pancake	Goodland	Yes	122	34	BLH, BC, B, NP, SUN, YP
Peterson	Talmoon	Yes	130	55	BLH, BC, B, LMB, NP, SUN, SMB, W, YP
Pickerel	Effie	Yes	293	70	BC, B, LMB, NP, SUN, RKB, SMB, W, YP
Pike	Marcell	No	33	75	BLH, B, LMB, NP, SUN, RKB
Pine	Marcell	No	72	44	B, LMB, NP, YP
Plantation	Bovey	No	76	35	BLH, BC, B, LMB, NP, SUN, RKB, YP
Pokegama	Grand Rapids	Yes	6612	112	BC, B, LAT, LMB, NP, SUN, RKB, SMB, W, YP
Poplar	Effie	No	97	50	BLH, BC, B, LMB, NP, SUN, RKB, YP
Portage	Inger	No	69	60	BLH, BC, B, NP, SUN, RKB, W, YP
Poverty	Deer River	No	62	40	BLH, BC, B, LMB, NP, SUN, SMB, YP

Name	Nearest Town	Public Access	Acres	Max. Depth	Fish Species
Prairie	Grand Rapids	Yes	1064	31	BLH, BC, B, LMB, NP, SUN, RKB, SMB, W, YP
Pughole	Grand Rapids	Yes	152	23	BC, B, LMB, NP, SUN, W, YP
Raddison	Bigfork	Yes	197	40	BC, B, LMB, NP, SUN, SMB, YP
Ranier	Marcell	No	83	45	BC, B, NP, SUN, W, YP
Rice	Blackberry	Carry In	N/A	4	BLH
Rice	Grand Rapids	Yes	857	68	BC, B, LMB, NP, SUN, RKB, YP
Ross	Marcell	No	51	35	B, LMB, YP
Round	Bigfork	Yes	502	40	B, LMB, NP, SUN, RKB, W, YP
Round	Blackberry	Yes	100	16	BC, LMB, NP, SUN, YP
Round	Effie	Yes	54	60	BC, LMB, NP, SUN, W, YP
Round	Squaw Lake	Yes	2828	24	BLH, BC, B, LMB, NP, SUN, RKB, W, YP
Ruby	Grand Rapids	Yes	243	88	B, LMB, NP, SUN, RKB, SMB, W, YP
Rush Island	Talmoon	Yes	296	32	BLH, BC, B, NP, SUN, RKB, W, YP
Sand	Grand Rapids	Yes	157	58	BC, B, LMB, NP, SUN, RKB, W, YP
Sand	Squaw Lake	Yes	4328	70	BLH, BC, B, NP, SUN, RKB, SMB, W, YP
Sand	Warba	No	118	36	BLH, BC, B, LMB, NP, SUN, W, YP
Sawyer	Bovey	Yes	140	15	B, LMB, NP, YP
Scooty	Nashwauk	Yes	160	75	BC, B, NP, SUN, RKB, W
Scrapper	Bovey	No	153	28	BLH, BC, B, LMB, NP, SUN, RKB
Shallow Pond	Alvwood	Yes	176	14	BLH, BC, B, LMB, NP, SUN, RKB, W, YP
Shallow	Warba	Yes	531	85	BLH, BC, B, LMB, NP, SUN, RKB, W, YP
Shamrock	Taconite	Yes	59	55	B, NP, W
Shine	Effie	No	70	45	BLH
Shoal	Grand Rapids	No	645	7	BLH, YP
Shoal	Nashwauk	Yes	286	77	BC, B, LMB, NP, SUN
Sioux	Squaw Lake	Yes	58	34	BLH, BC, B, NP, SUN, YP
Siseebakwet	Grand Rapids	Yes	1306	105	B, LMB, NP, SUN, RKB, W, YP
Skelly	Cohasset	No	57	35	BLH, B, NP, SUN, YP
Slauson	Marcell	No	106	40	BLH, BC, B, LMB, NP, SUN, RKB, YP
Smith	Grand Rapids	Yes	46	25	BLH, BC, B, LMB, NP, SUN, RKB, YP
Smith	Marcell	No	155	32	BC, B, LMB, NP, SUN, SMB, W, YP
Snaptail	Taconite	Yes	146	70	BC, B, LMB, NP, SUN, RKB, W, YP
Snowball	Calumet	Yes	146	38	BC, B, LMB, NP, RKB, W, YP
Someman	Nashwauk	No	62	13	BLH, BC, B, NP, SUN, RKB, YP
South Ackerman	Spring Lake	No	23	55	BLH, BC, B, LMB, NP, SUN, YP
South Fork	Nashwauk	No	56	22	BLH, BC, B, NP, SUN, RKB, W, YP
South Sturgeon	Chisholm	Yes	192	43	BLH, BC, B, NP, SUN, RKB, W, YP
South Sugar	Grand Rapids	Yes	88.5	36	BLH, BC, B, LMB, NP, SUN, RKB, W, YP
South Twin	Marble	No	179	40	BLH, BC, B, LMB, NP, SUN, RKB, W, YP
Spider	Marcell	Yes	1349	36	BLH, BC, B, LMB, M, NP, SUN, RKB, SMB, W, YP
Split Hand	Grand Rapids	Yes	1420	34	BLH, BC, B, LMB, NP, SUN, RKB, W, YP
Spring	Grand Rapids	Yes	27	60	BC, B, LMB, NP

KEY			
BKT=Brook Trout	LAT=Lake Trout	RKB=Rock Bass	W=Walleye
BLH=Bullhead	LMB=Largemouth Bass	SGR=Sauger	WC=White Crappie
BC=Black Crappie	M=Muskie	SMB=Smallmouth Bass	WHB=White Bass
B=Bluegill	NP=Northern Pike	SPT=Splake	YP=Yellow Perch
BRT=Brown Trout	PKS=Pink Salmon	SUN=Sunfish	
CAT=Catfish (Channel and Flathead)	RBT=Rainbow Trout	TM=Tiger Muskie	

Fishing Waters

Tristan Publishing, Inc., believes that the following charts are accurate; however, we cannot guarantee or accept liability for their accuracy. The reader should contact the Minnesota DNR to verify the accuracy of the charts.

Name	Nearest Town	Public Access	Acres	Max. Depth	Fish Species
Spring	Spring Lake	No	126	36	BLH, BC, B, LMB, NP, SUN, RKB, W, YP
Stingy	Nashwauk	Yes	378	25	BLH, BC, B, NP, SUN, RKB, W, YP
Sugar	Cass Lake	No	1585	22	BLH, BC, LMB, NP, SUN, RKB, W, YP
Sunken	Squaw Lake	Yes	55	35	BC, B, LMB, NP, SUN, YP
Sunrise	Marcell	Carry In	34	20	B, LMB, NP, SUN
Swan	Pengilly	Yes	2472	65	BLH, BC, B, LMB, NP, SUN, RKB, W, YP
Thirty	Nashwauk	No	114	14	BC, B, LMB, NP, SUN, YP
Thistledew	Togo	No	318	45	BC, B, LMB, NP, SUN, RKB, W, YP
Three Island	Marcell	No	76	28	BC, B, NP, SUN, W
Three Island	Marcell	Yes	235	66	B, LMB, NP, SMB, W, YP
Tioga Mine Pit	Cohasset	Yes	51	225	LMB, RBT, RKB, SPT
Trestle	Bovey	No	78	48	BLH, BC, B, LMB, NP, SUN, SMB
Trestle	Talmoon	Yes	96	35	BLH, BC, B, NP, SUN, YP
Trout	Coleraine	Yes	1890	135	BLH, BC, B, LMB, NP, SUN, RKB, SMB, W, YP
Trout	Grand Rapids	Yes	1753	157	BC, B, LAT, LMB, NP, SUN, RKB, SMB, SPT, YP
Turtle	Marcell	Yes	2052	137	BC, B, LMB, NP, SUN, RKB, SMB, W, YP
Twin	Goodland	Carry In	133	35	BLH, BC, B, LMB, NP, W, YP
Upper Hanson	Bovey	No	107	35	BLH, BC, B, LMB, NP, SUN, RKB, YP
Upper Panasa	Calumet	Yes	174	13	BLH, BC, B, NP, SUN, W, YP
Upper Spring	Spring Creek	No	17	20	BLH, B, YP
Virgin	Squaw Lake	Carry In	57	22	BLH, NP, YP
Wabana	Grand Rapids	Yes	2215	115	BC, B, LMB, NP, SUN, RKB, SMB, W, YP
Wagner	Northome	Yes	61	60	BLH, BC, NP, SUN, W, YP
Walters	Bigfork	Yes	117.5	19	BLH, B, NP, SUN, YP
Wasson	Taconite	No	415.1	67	BC, B, LMB, NP, SUN, RKB, SMB, YP
West Smith	Marcell	No	19	28	BC, B, NP, SUN, YP
West	Nashwauk	No	72	25	BLH, BC, LMB, NP, YP
White Swan	Bigfork	No	158	19	BC, B, LMB, NP, SUN, RKB, W, YP
Whitefish	Wirt	Yes	563	51	BLH, BC, LMB, NP, SUN, RKB, W, YP
Wilderness	Squaw Lake	Yes	25	25	BLH, NP, YP
Wilson	Togo	Yes	86	60	BC, B, LMB, NP, SUN, RKB, W, YP
Wirt	Wirt	No	32.5	25	BLH, BC, B, NP, SUN, YP
Wolf	Nashwauk	Yes	188	6	BC, B, NP, SUN, W, YP
Jackson					
Chandler	Southwest	Yes	83	8	BLH, SUN, YP
Clear	Jackson	Yes	415	9	BLH, CAT, NP, SUN, W, YP
Fish	Windom	Carry In	300	26	BLH, BC, B, CAT, LMB, SUN, SMB, W, YP
Heron	Lakefield	Yes	2845	5	BLH, B, NP, SUN, YP
Independence	Jackson	Yes	112	10	BLH, BC, B, LMB, SUN, W
Little Spirit	Jackson	Yes	572	8	BLH, BC, B, CAT, LMB, NP, SUN, W, WHB, YP
Loon	Jackson	Yes	679	9	BLH, BC, B, CAT, NP, SUN, W, YP
Pearl	Jackson	Yes	155	6	BLH, BC, B, CAT, NP, SUN, W, YP
Round	Round Lake	Yes	1024	9	BLH, BC, CAT, NP, W, WC, YP
Rush	Jackson	Yes	293	3	BLH, BC, NP, SUN, W, YP
Timber	Windom	Yes	198	8	BLH, BC, NP, W, YP

Name	Nearest Town	Public Access	Acres	Max. Depth	Fish Species
Kanabec					
Ann	Ogilvie	Yes	653	17	BLH, BC, B, CAT, LMB, NP, SUN, RKB, W, YP
Devils	Mora	No	58	19	BLH, B, NP, SUN, YP
Eleven	Kroschel	Yes	290	13	BLH, BC, B, LMB, NP, SUN, W, YP
Fish	Mora	Yes	407	8	BLH, BC, B, CAT, LMB, NP, SUN, W, WHB, YP
Five	Kroschel	Yes	42	32	BLH, BC, B, LMB, NP, SUN, YP
Knife	Mora	Yes	1266	15	BC, B, LMB, NP, RKB, W, YP
Lake Full of Fish	Mora	No	78	28	BLH
Lewis	Ogilvie	Yes	220	48	BLH, BC, B, LMB, NP, SUN, W, YP
Mora	Mora	No	63	24	BLH, BC, NP, SUN, YP
Pennington	Brunswick	No	119	25	BLH, BC, B, LMB, NP, SUN, YP
Pomroy	Quamba	Yes	422	11	BLH, BC, B, LMB, NP, SUN, RKB, W, YP
Quamba	Quamba	Yes	214	11	BLH, BC, B, LMB, NP, SUN, W, WC, YP
Kandiyohi					
Andrew	New London	Yes	814	26	BLH, BC, B, LMB, NP, SUN, W, YP
Bass	Spicer	Yes	52	31	BLH, BC, B, LMB, NP, SUN, W, YP
Bear	New London	No	133	21	BLH, B, LMB, NP, SUN, YP
Big Kandiyohi	Lake Lillian	Yes	2692	15	BLH, BC, B, CAT, NP, SMB, W, YP
Calhoun	Spicer	Yes	618	13	BLH, BC, B, LMB, NP, SUN, W, YP
Carrie	Atwater	Yes	81	26	BLH, BC, B, LMB, NP, SUN, W, YP
Diamond	Atwater	Yes	1565	27	BLH, BC, B, LMB, NP, SUN, W, YP
Eagle	Willmar	Yes	824	67	BLH, BC, B, NP, SUN, W, YP
East Solomon	Willmar	Yes	706	14	BLH, B, LMB, NP, SUN, W, YP
Elizabeth	Atwater	Yes	1054	9	BLH, BC, B, LMB, NP, SUN, W, YP
Elkhorn	Spicer	Yes	87	41	BLH, B, LMB, NP, SUN, W, YP
Ella	Atwater	Yes	136	12	BLH, BC, B, CAT, LMB, NP, W, WC, YP
Florida	Spicer	Yes	674	40	BLH, BC, B, LMB, NP, SUN, W, YP
Foot	Willmar	Yes	694	24	BLH, BC, B, CAT, LMB, NP, SUN, W, YP
Games	Sunburg	Yes	515	42	BLH, BC, B, LMB, NP, SUN, W, YP
George	Spicer	Yes	231	34	BLH, BC, B, LMB, NP, SUN, SMB, W, YP
Green	Spicer	Yes	5406	110	BLH, BC, B, LMB, NP, SUN, RKB, SMB, W, YP
Hefta	Sunburg	No	100	10	BLH
Henderson	Spicer	Yes	73	57	BLH, BC, B, LMB, NP, SUN, W, YP
Lillian	Lake Lillian	Yes	1149	7.8	BLH, BC, B, CAT, NP, SUN, W, WC, YP
Long	New London	Yes	286	46	BLH, BC, B, LMB, NP, SUN, W
Long	Willmar	Yes	1575	16	BLH, BC, B, LMB, NP, SUN, W, YP
Mud	New London	Yes	2318	14	BLH, BC, B, LMB, NP, SUN, W, YP
Nest	Spicer	Yes	945	40	BLH, BC, B, CAT, LMB, NP, SUN, SMB, W, YP
Norway	Sunburg	Yes	2344	33	BLH, BC, B, LMB, NP, SUN, W, YP
Point	Spicer	Yes	164	32	BLH, B, LMB, NP, SUN, W, YP
Ringo	Spicer	Yes	716	10	BLH, BC, B, LMB, NP, W, YP

KEY			
BKT=Brook Trout	**LAT**=Lake Trout	**RKB**=Rock Bass	**W**=Walleye
BLH=Bullhead	**LMB**=Largemouth Bass	**SGR**=Sauger	**WC**=White Crappie
BC=Black Crappie	**M**=Muskie	**SMB**=Smallmouth Bass	**WHB**=White Bass
B=Bluegill	**NP**=Northern Pike	**SPT**=Splake	**YP**=Yellow Perch
BRT=Brown Trout	**PKS**=Pink Salmon	**SUN**=Sunfish	
CAT=Catfish (Channel and Flathead)	**RBT**=Rainbow Trout	**TM**=Tiger Muskie	

Fishing Waters

Tristan Publishing, Inc., believes that the following charts are accurate; however, we cannot guarantee or accept liability for their accuracy. The reader should contact the Minnesota DNR to verify the accuracy of the charts.

Name	Nearest Town	Public Access	Acres	Max. Depth	Fish Species
Skataas	Willmar	No	197	11	BLH, BC, B, NP, SUN, YP
Swenson	Sunburg	Yes	109	14	BLH, BC, B, LMB, NP, SUN, W, YP
Wagonga	Willmar	Yes	1664	15	BLH, BC, NP, YP
Willmar	Willmar	Yes	435	14	BLH, BC, B, CAT, NP, SUN, W, YP
Kittson					
Bronson	Lake Bronson	Yes	335	29	BLH, B, LMB, NP, SUN, RKB, W, YP
Koochiching					
Bartlett	Northome	Yes	292	16	BLH, NP, YP
Clear	Gemmell	Yes	78	30	BLH, B, LMB, NP, W, YP
Dark	Gemmell	Yes	100	50	BLH, B, LMB, NP, W, YP
Little Fork River	Little Fork				M, NP, SMB, W
Moose	Littlefork	Yes	53	7	BC, NP, YP
Pine	Northome	Yes	10	44	BLH, YP
Rat Root	International Falls	No	1125	8	BLH, BC, NP, W, YP
Tuefer	Northome	Yes	42	52	BC, NP, SUN, W, YP
Lac Qui Parle					
Lac Qui Parle	Milan	Yes	5589	15	BLH, BC, B, CAT, NP, SUN, RKB, W, WHB, WC, YP
Lake					
Abinodji	Winton	Carry In	33	33	NP
Adams	Ely	Carry In	448	84	B, NP, RKB, W
Adventure	Winton	Carry In	45	10	NP, W, YP
Ahmakose	Ely	Carry In	38	68	LAT
Ahsub	Ely	Carry In	58	78	BKT, SMB
Alger	Isabella	Carry In	20	6	M, NP, W, YP
Alice	Ely	Carry In	1566	53	B, NP, RKB, W, YP
Alworth	Ely	Carry In	203	33	NP, RKB, W, YP
Amber	Ely	No	135	27	B, NP, RKB, W, YP
Amoeber	Ely	Carry In	386	110	LAT
Annie	Ely	Carry In	18	16	NP, SUN
Arkose	Ely	No	21	37	SUN, YP
Artlip	Isabella	No	60	4	SMB, W, YP
Ashdick	Ely	Carry In	100	50	LMB, NP, RKB
Ashigan	Ely	Carry In	189	59	SUN, SMB, YP
August	Isabella	Yes	228	19	B, NP, RKB, W, YP
Bald Eagle	Ely	Carry In	1238	36	BC, B, NP, RKB, W, YP
Balsam	Finland	Carry In	225	18	BKT
Basswood	Ely	Carry In	22722	111	BC, B, NP, SUN, RKB, SMB, W, YP
Bean	Silver Bay	Carry In	30	26	RBT, SPT
Bear	Silver Bay	Carry In	18	69	LAT, SPT
Beaver Hut	Isabella	Carry In	56	12	BKT, SUN, YP
Becoosin	Ely	Carry In	52	17	YP
Beetle	Isabella	Carry In	26.2	26	BKT
Benezie	Ely	Carry In	59	27	B, LMB, NP, RKB, YP
Benson	Finland	Carry In	18.7	36	SPT
Birch	Ely	Carry In	711	34	B, LMB, NP, RKB, SMB, W, YP
Blackstone	Ely	Carry In	13	14	NP, YP
Blesener	Finland	Carry In	18	11	BKT
Bluebill	Isabella	Carry In	42	5	NP, YP
Bog	Isabella	No	249	16	BKT, NP, W, YP
Bone	Tofte	Yes	46	51	RBT, SPT
Bonnie	Ely	Carry In	71	11	NP, SUN, YP
Boot	Ely	Carry In	209	83	NP, RKB, SMB, W
Browns	Ely	No	205	19	NP, W, YP
Bruin	Ely	Carry In	N/A	30	NP, RKB, YP
Bullet	Winton	Carry In	50	10	B, NP, RKB, W, YP
Bullfrog	Ely	Carry In	62	26	NP, YP

Fishing Waters

Name	Nearest Town	Public Access	Acres	Max. Depth	Fish Species
Bunny	Isabella	Carry In	39	6.5	NP, YP
Cache	Ely	Carry In	42	15	NP, SMB, W
Calico	Ely	Carry In	11	20	SUN, YP
Camp	Ely	Carry In	84	31	NP, SUN, W, YP
Canoe	Ely	Carry In	18	30	SUN, YP
Carol	Ely	Carry In	96	16	B, NP, RKB, W, YP
Cat	Isabella	No	39	21	BC, B, LMB, NP, W, YP
Cattyman	Winton	Carry In	17	9	NP, RKB, W, YP
Cedar	Ely	Yes	464	45	BC, B, LMB, NP, SMB, W, YP
Cherry	Ely	Carry In	147	90	LAT, W
Chipmunk	Isabella	No	27	4	NP, YP
Chow	Isabella	No	43	11	NP, YP
Christianson	Two Harbors	Yes	158	8	BC, NP, SUN, YP
Clam	Ely	Carry In	18	10	SUN, YP
Clear	Ely	Carry In	236	17	BC, B, NP, W, YP
Clearwater	Ely	Carry In	641	46	NP, YP
Cloquet	Finland	Yes	182.6	7	NP, W, YP
Coffee	Isabella	Carry In	129	11	NP, RKB, W, YP
Comfort	Isabella	Carry In	38	7	NP, W, YP
Conchu	Ely	Carry In	53	67	BKT, LMB, SPT
Cook County	Ely	Carry In	43	38	SUN
Cook	Tofte	Carry In	93	12	NP, YP
Cramer Homestead	Finland	Yes	23	22	SUN, YP
Cramer	Finland	No	62	4	NP, SUN, YP
Crooked	Ely	Carry In	7941	165	NP, RKB, SGR, W, YP
Crooked	Finland	Yes	283	18	M, SMB, W, YP
Cross River	Schroeder	Carry In	75	7	BC, NP, W, YP
Crosscut	Isabella	Carry In	12	16	BKT
Dam Five	Isabella	Carry In	95	38	LMB, SUN, W, YP
Dan	Winton	No	8.4	26	BKT
Delay	Isabella	Carry In	104	18	B, NP, SUN, RKB, SMB, W, YP
Denley	Babbitt	Carry In	42.2	21	NP
Dime	Isabella	No	3	18	YP
Disappointment	Ely	Carry In	867	54	LMB, NP, RKB, SMB, W, YP
Discovery	Ely	Carry In	30	22	B, YP
Divide	Isabella	Carry In	58	22	RBT, SPT
Dragon	Isabella	Carry In	72	15	BC, NP, RKB, W, YP
Dumbbell	Isabella	Yes	437	40	M, RKB, SMB, W, YP
Dunnigan	Isabella	Yes	86	14	B, RKB, SMB, W
Dutton	Ely	Carry In	33	80	YP
East Chub	Isabella	Yes	64	9	B, LMB, NP, SUN, RKB, W, YP
East	Schroeder	Carry In	71	18	BKT, YP
Echo	Finland	Yes	46	61	BKT, LAT, RBT, SPT
Eddy	Ely	No	122	95	LMB, NP, YP
Eighteen	Isabella	Carry In	99	12	W, YP
Eikala	Isabella	Carry In	8.8	33	BKT
Elixir	Isabella	Carry In	19	8	NP, YP
Ella Hall	Ely	Carry In	372	28	B, LMB, NP, SUN, RKB, SMB, YP
Elton	Ely	Carry In	123	53	NP
Ennis	Ely	Carry In	21	42	BKT, SPT
Ensign	Ely	Carry In	1408	30	NP, RKB, SMB, W, YP

KEY			
BKT=Brook Trout	**LAT**=Lake Trout	**RKB**=Rock Bass	**W**=Walleye
BLH=Bullhead	**LMB**=Largemouth Bass	**SGR**=Sauger	**WC**=White Crappie
BC=Black Crappie	**M**=Muskie	**SMB**=Smallmouth Bass	**WHB**=White Bass
B=Bluegill	**NP**=Northern Pike	**SPT**=Splake	**YP**=Yellow Perch
BRT=Brown Trout	**PKS**=Pink Salmon	**SUN**=Sunfish	
CAT=Catfish (Channel and Flathead)	**RBT**=Rainbow Trout	**TM**=Tiger Muskie	

Fishing Waters

Tristan Publishing, Inc., believes that the following charts are accurate; however, we cannot guarantee or accept liability for their accuracy. The reader should contact the Minnesota DNR to verify the accuracy of the charts.

Name	Nearest Town	Public Access	Acres	Max. Depth	Fish Species
Ester	Ely	Carry In	388	110	LAT, YP
Explorer	Winton	Carry In	52	75	LAT, YP
Fall	Winton	Carry In	2173	32	BC, B, NP, SUN, RKB, SMB, W, YP
Farm	Ely	Yes	1328	56	BC, B, LMB, NP, SUN, RKB, SMB, W, YP
Finn Pond	Isabella	No	4.1	4.5	BKT
Fish	Ely	Carry In	92	30	NP, YP
Fishfry	Isabella	No	18	7	W
Flash	Ely	Carry In	72.6	24	W
Flat Horn	Isabella	Carry In	56	13	NP, SUN, RKB, W, YP
Found	Ely	Carry In	58	38	SPT
Four	Ely	Carry In	655	25	B, NP, RKB, W, YP
Fourth McDougal	Isabella	No	14	26	NP, W, YP
Fourtown	Winton	Carry In	1902	25	B, NP, RKB, SMB, W, YP
Fran	Isabella	No	20	19	NP, YP
Frank	Isabella	No	18	5	NP, YP
Fraser	Ely	Carry In	811	105	LAT
Frog	Ely	Carry In	41.7	38	LMB, NP, YP
Fulton	Isabella	Carry In	39.7	17.5	BC, NP, W, YP
Gabbro	Ely	No	896	50	BC, B, NP, RKB, W, YP
Gander	Isabella	Carry In	112	7	NP, YP
Garden	Ely	Yes	670	55	BC, B, NP, RKB, W, YP
Gegoka	Isabella	Yes	159	10	NP, SUN, RKB, W, YP
Gerund	Ely	Carry In	98	85	NP
Gibson	Winton	Carry In	34	24	NP, W, YP
Gift	Ely	Carry In	38	35	NP, YP
Gijikiki	Ely	Carry In	103	70	LAT, YP
Glacier Pond 2	Ely	Carry In	5.7	32	BKT, RBT
Glacier Pond	Ely	Carry In	17.3	27	RBT
Goldeneye	Schroeder	Carry In	10.4	19	BKT
Good	Ely	Carry In	177	51	BC, B, LMB, NP, RKB, W, YP
Grass	Isabella	Carry In	24	9	BC, NP, SUN, YP
Greenstone	Ely	Carry In	345	72	B, NP, RKB, W, YP
Greenwood	Isabella	Yes	1300	7	NP, W, YP
Grouse	Isabella	Yes	112	11	B, NP, W, YP
Grub	Ely	No	43	31	LMB, SUN, SMB
Gypsy	Isabella	Carry In	16.4	18	BKT
Hanson	Ely	Carry In	284	100	LAT, NP
Hare	Schroeder	Carry In	55	18	BRT, YP
Harriet	Isabella	Yes	265	37	BC, NP, W, YP
Harris	Ely	Carry In	123	15	BC, B, LMB, M, SUN, W, YP
Hatchet	Winton	Carry In	126	40	NP, W, YP
Haven	Winton	Carry In	15	7	NP
Hide	Isabella	No	22	9	NP, YP
Highlife	Isabella	Carry In	20	23	BKT, B, SUN, YP
Hogback	Isabella	Yes	40	43	RBT, YP
Hoist	Isabella	No	113	6	NP, YP
Holt	Ely	No	106	73	LAT
Homestead	Isabella	Yes	42	7.5	LMB, YP
Horse	Ely	Carry In	681	25	B, NP, RKB, SMB, W, YP
Hula	Ely	Carry In	N/A	N/A	NP, SUN, YP
Ima	Ely	Carry In	772	116	B, LAT, NP, RKB, W, YP
Indiana	Ely	Carry In	153	26	B, NP, RKB, SMB, YP
Inga	Isabella	No	41	6	NP, YP
Insula	Ely	Carry In	2957	63	NP, RKB, W, YP
Isabella	Isabella	Carry In	1516	19	NP, RKB, W, YP
Island River	Isabella	Carry In	122	7	NP, W, YP

Fishing Waters

Name	Nearest Town	Public Access	Acres	Max. Depth	Fish Species
Jack	Isabella	No	42	5	NP, YP
Jasper	Ely	Carry In	154	25	B, LMB, NP, SUN, RKB, SMB, W, YP
Jenny	Ely	Carry In	102	93	NP, YP
Jewell	Ely	Carry In	N/A	55	NP
Jitterbug	Winton	Carry In	25	5	NP, YP
Johnson	Finland	Carry In	30.5	24	W, YP
Jordan	Winton	Carry In	136	66	NP, W, YP
Jouppi	Isabella	Carry In	7	19	BKT
Judd	Ely	Carry In	26	22	SUN, RBT, SPT
Kane	Two Harbors	No	110	17	B, NP, SUN, W, YP
Katherine	Finland	No	65.3	6	NP, YP
Kawishiwi	Tofte	Yes	400	12	NP, SUN, RKB, W, YP
Kek	Ely	Carry In	58	130	LAT, YP
Kekekabic	Ely	Carry In	1620	195	LAT
Kettle	Winton	Carry In	37	15	SUN, YP
Kitigan	Isabella	Carry In	69	8	B, LMB, NP, RKB, SMB, W, YP
Knife	Ely	Carry In	5254	179	LAT, NP, RKB, SMB, W, YP
Kowalski	Finland	No	13	32	NP, SUN, YP
Lake of the Clouds	Ely	Carry In	28	110	LAT, SUN
Langley	Two Harbors	No	14	4	NP, YP
Lax	Finland	Yes	296	35	BC, B, LMB, NP, SUN, W, YP
Legler	Two Harbors	No	52	3	NP, SUN, YP
Link	Ely	Carry In	37	34	NP
Little Gabbro	Ely	Carry In	154	26	NP, RKB, W, YP
Little Knife	Ely	Carry In	650	184	LAT, NP, RKB, SMB, W
Little Wilson	Schroeder	Yes	52.5	22	NP, W, YP
Lost	Schroeder	Carry In	81.5	16	NP, YP
Lunar	Ely	Carry In	58	60	LAT, SUN
Lupus	Isabella	Carry In	93	7	NP, YP
Madden	Ely	Yes	35	24	NP, YP
Makwa	Ely	No	143	76	LAT, NP, YP
Manomin	Winton	Carry In	403	18	NP, SUN, YP
Marble	Silver Bay	No	159	20	BLH, BC, NP, SUN, W, YP
Micmac	Finland	Carry In	132	20	NP, YP
Midas	Ely	Carry In	20	50	NP
Middle McDougal	Isabella	Yes	103	7	B, NP, W, YP
Mitawan	Isabella	Carry In	185	24	B, NP, RKB, SMB, W, YP
Moccasin	Isabella	Carry In	14.1	5	YP
Moose	Ely	Carry In	1211	65	B, LMB, NP, SUN, RKB, SMB, W, YP
Moose	Isabella	Carry In	207	6	B, NP, YP
Moosecamp	Winton	Carry In	190	16	B, NP, RKB, W
Mud	Ely	Carry In	179	16	NP, YP
Mueller	Ely	Carry In	24.3	36	NP, YP
Muskeg	Ely	Carry In	132	7	NP, YP
Muskrat	Ely	Carry In	24	18	W, YP
Nawakwa	Ely	Carry In	88	9	NP, YP
Neglige	Ely	Carry In	28	58	BKT, RBT
Newfound	Ely	Carry In	604	45	B, LMB, NP, SUN, RKB, SMB, W, YP
Newton	Ely	Carry In	500	47	BC, B, NP, RKB, SMB, W, YP
Nicado	Finland	Yes	14	18	NP
Nickel	Ely	Yes	24	10	W

KEY			
BKT=Brook Trout	**LAT**=Lake Trout	**RKB**=Rock Bass	**W**=Walleye
BLH=Bullhead	**LMB**=Largemouth Bass	**SGR**=Sauger	**WC**=White Crappie
BC=Black Crappie	**M**=Muskie	**SMB**=Smallmouth Bass	**WHB**=White Bass
B=Bluegill	**NP**=Northern Pike	**SPT**=Splake	**YP**=Yellow Perch
BRT=Brown Trout	**PKS**=Pink Salmon	**SUN**=Sunfish	
CAT=Catfish (Channel and Flathead)	**RBT**=Rainbow Trout	**TM**=Tiger Muskie	

Fishing Waters

Tristan Publishing, Inc., believes that the following charts are accurate; however, we cannot guarantee or accept liability for their accuracy. The reader should contact the Minnesota DNR to verify the accuracy of the charts.

Name	Nearest Town	Public Access	Acres	Max. Depth	Fish Species
Ninemile	Schroeder	Yes	296	40	NP, W, YP
Nipisiquit	Finland	Carry In	57	21	NP, W, YP
North McDougal	Isabella	Yes	273	13	NP, RKB, W, YP
Norway	Isabella	Carry In	12	19	BKT, SPT
Ogishkemuncie	Ely	Carry In	701	75	LAT, NP, W, YP
Ojibway	Ely	Yes	371	115	LAT, SMB
One	Ely	Carry In	876	57	B, NP, RKB, W, YP
Orchid	Isabella	Carry In	10	8	NP, YP
Organ	Schroeder	Carry In	38	7	NP, YP
Ottertrack	Ely	Carry In	1146	116	LAT, NP, RKB, SMB, W
Paco	Ely	Carry In	19	5	RKB
Parent	Ely	Carry In	326	50	NP, RKB, SMB, W, YP
Pear	Babbitt	Carry In	9.7	14	BKT
Peavey	Isabella	No	24	6	NP, YP
Perent	Isabella	Carry In	1800	28	NP, RKB, W, YP
Pickerel	Ely	Carry In	184	13	NP, RKB, SMB, W, YP
Pike	Isabella	Carry In	73.5	8	LMB, NP, YP
Portage	Ely	Carry In	69	45	NP, SMB
Quadga	Isabella	No	248	35	NP, SUN, RKB, W, YP
Rabbit	Ely	Carry In	104	105	LAT
Range	Winton	Carry In	82	19	BC, B, LMB, NP, SUN, RKB, YP
Rat	Isabella	Yes	7.1	6	NP, SUN, RKB, YP
Raven	Ely	Carry In	205	56	LAT, YP
Redskin	Isabella	Carry In	43.3	25	BKT
Round Island	Isabella	No	54	4	NP, W, YP
Sagus	Ely	Carry In	172	37	NP, W, YP
Sand	Isabella	Yes	476	11	NP, W, YP
Sandpit	Winton	Carry In	61	53	BC, B, LMB, NP, RKB, SMB, W, YP
Scarp	Isabella	Carry In	42	15	RBT
Section 29	Isabella	Yes	89	20	NP, RKB, W, YP
Section Eight	Isabella	Carry In	5	24	BKT
Section Twelve	Ely	Carry In	43	52	B, LMB, SUN, RKB, SMB, W, YP
Sema	Ely	Carry In	86	72	LAT
Shamrock	Isabella	Carry In	55	13	B, LMB
Shepo	Ely	Carry In	52	17	NP, W
Shoepack	Finland	No	54	11	NP, YP
Shoofly	Isabella	Carry In	9.8	25	BKT
Silver Island	Isabella	Carry In	1102	15	BC, NP, RKB, W, YP
Sink	Finland	No	16	22	NP, YP
Sister	Isabella	No	123	15	NP, W, YP
Skindance	Ely	No	58	52	NP, YP
Skull	Ely	Carry In	28	38	BKT, LMB
Slate	Isabella	Yes	294	7	B, NP, RKB, W, YP
Small	Isabella	No	19	5	NP, YP
Snowbank	Ely	Carry In	3303	150	LAT, LMB, NP, RKB, SMB, W, YP
Sonju	Finland	Carry In	39.5	8	BRT
Soup	Isabella	No	17	4	BKT
South Farm	Ely	Carry In	618	30	BC, B, NP, RKB, SMB, W, YP
South McDougal	Isabella	Yes	273	7	NP, W, YP
South Wigwam	Schroeder	Carry In	69	6	NP, W, YP
Spear	Isabella	No	8	4	BKT, YP
Spice	Ely	Carry In	24	27	NP, SUN, YP
Splash	Ely	Carry In	97	18	B, NP, RKB, W, YP
Spoon	Winton	Carry In	223	85	NP, RKB, YP
Square	Isabella	Carry In	127	7	NP, RKB, W, YP
Steamhaul	Isabella	Carry In	21	17	BKT, SPT
Steer	Isabella	Carry In	5	24	BKT

Fishing Waters

Name	Nearest Town	Public Access	Acres	Max. Depth	Fish Species
Stewart	Two Harbors	Yes	248	24	NP, SUN, W, YP
Stony	Isabella	No	227	4	NP, RKB, W, YP
Stub	Ely	No	90	20	BC, B, NP, W, YP
Sucker	Ely	Carry In	382	31	B, LMB, NP, RKB, SMB, W, YP
Sullivan	Two Harbors	Yes	52.8	7	B, NP, YP
Surprise	Isabella	Carry In	38	9	BC, LMB, NP, SUN, W, YP
Swallow	Isabella	Carry In	148	38	LMB, NP, RKB, W, YP
T (Tee)	Schroeder	Carry In	336	15	BC, NP, RKB, W, YP
Tanner	Isabella	No	52	8	BLH, M, RKB, YP
Tetagouche	Finland	Carry In	79	20	NP, YP
Thomas	Two Harbors	Yes	148	20	BLH, BC, B, LMB, NP, SUN, RKB, W, YP
Thomas	Winton	Carry In	1471	110	B, LAT, NP, RKB, W, YP
Three	Ely	No	881	37	B, NP, RKB, W, YP
Thunderbird	Schroeder	Carry In	101	18	NP, W, YP
Tickle	Ely	Carry In	43	61	SUN, YP
Tin Can Mike	Winton	Carry In	147	29	B, NP, RKB, SMB, W
Tofte	Ely	Yes	155	73	RBT, SPT
Tommy	Isabella	No	8	5	BKT
Topaz	Ely	Carry In	130	70	LAT, SMB
Totem	Ely	Carry In	15	19	NP, YP
Trader	Winton	Carry In	54	10	SUN, YP
Trappers	Isabella	Carry In	21	13	BKT
Triangle	Ely	Carry In	309	43	B, LMB, NP, RKB, SMB, W, YP
Trident	Ely	Carry In	90.1	14	B, NP, SUN, RKB, SMB, W, YP
Turtle	Ely	Carry In	337	10	NP, YP
Twenty Three	Finland	No	46	23	BKT, SUN, YP
Two Deer	Isabella	Carry In	43	7	LMB, NP, YP
Two	Ely	Carry In	481	35	B, NP, RKB, W, YP
Vera	Ely	Carry In	245	55	W, YP
Wadop	Isabella	No	36	9	NP, YP
Wanless	Isabella	Carry In	78	16	NP, YP
Watonwan	Isabella	Carry In	59	25	NP, W, YP
Weapon	Isabella	Carry In	12	4	BKT
Wedge	Ely	No	N/A	29	NP, YP
West Chub	Isabella	Yes	114	12	B, NP, SUN, YP
Whitefish	Tofte	Carry In	339	49	NP, W, YP
Wilson	Schroeder	Yes	622	53	NP, W, YP
Wind	Ely	Carry In	1009	32	B, LMB, NP, SUN, RKB, W, YP
Windy	Isabella	Carry In	450	39	NP, RKB, W, YP
Witness	Ely	Carry In	41	19	W, YP
Wood	Ely	Carry In	643	21	B, NP, SUN, W, YP
Wye	Isabella	Carry In	55	13	NP, W, YP

Lake Of The Woods

Name	Nearest Town	Public Access	Acres	Max. Depth	Fish Species
Lake of the Woods	Warroad	Yes	950400	38	BLH, BC, M, NP, RKB, SGR, SMB, W, YP
Rainy River	Baudette	Yes	N/A	N/A	NP, SMB, W, YP

Le Sueur

Name	Nearest Town	Public Access	Acres	Max. Depth	Fish Species
Clear	Lexington	Yes	268	18	BLH, BC, B, LMB, NP, SUN, W, YP
Dora	Kilkenny	Yes	760	6	BLH, BC, B, LMB, NP, W, WHB, YP

KEY			
BKT=Brook Trout	**LAT**=Lake Trout	**RKB**=Rock Bass	**W**=Walleye
BLH=Bullhead	**LMB**=Largemouth Bass	**SGR**=Sauger	**WC**=White Crappie
BC=Black Crappie	**M**=Muskie	**SMB**=Smallmouth Bass	**WHB**=White Bass
B=Bluegill	**NP**=Northern Pike	**SPT**=Splake	**YP**=Yellow Perch
BRT=Brown Trout	**PKS**=Pink Salmon	**SUN**=Sunfish	
CAT=Catfish (Channel and Flathead)	**RBT**=Rainbow Trout	**TM**=Tiger Muskie	

Fishing Waters

Tristan Publishing, Inc., believes that the following charts are accurate; however, we cannot guarantee or accept liability for their accuracy. The reader should contact the Minnesota DNR to verify the accuracy of the charts.

Name	Nearest Town	Public Access	Acres	Max. Depth	Fish Species
East Jefferson	Cleveland	Yes	700	37	BLH, BC, B, LMB, NP, SUN, W, WC, YP
Emily	St. Peter	Yes	235	37	BLH, BC, B, LMB, NP, SUN, W, WC, YP
Fish	Waterville	Yes	78	55	BLH, BC, B, LMB, NP, SUN, YP
Frances	Elysian	Yes	797	60	BLH, BC, B, LMB, NP, SUN, W, WHB, YP
German	Cleveland	Yes	899	51	BLH, BC, B, CAT, NP, SUN, W, WHB, YP
Gorman	Le Center	Yes	499	14	BLH, BC, B, LMB, NP, SUN, W, WHB, WC, YP
Greenleaf	Montgomery	Yes	293	18	BLH, BC, B, NP, SUN, W, YP
Horseshoe	Waterville	Yes	393	26	BLH, BC, B, LMB, NP, SUN, W, YP
Pepin	Montgomery	Yes	403	8	BLH, BC, NP, SUN, W, YP
Rays	Elysian	Yes	156.3	32	BLH, BC, B, LMB, NP, SUN, W, YP
Roemhildts	Mankato	Yes	72.5	60	BC, B, LMB, NP, SUN, YP
Sabre	Cordova	Yes	263	13	BLH, BC, B, LMB, NP, SUN, W, WHB, YP
Scotch	Cleveland	Yes	565	11	BLH, BC, SUN, W, WC, YP
Steele	Elysian	Yes	69.8	27	BLH, BC, B, LMB, NP, SUN, YP
Sunfish	Kilkenny	Yes	119	30	BLH, BC, B, LMB, NP, SUN, WC, YP
Tetonka	Waterville	Yes	1336	35	BLH, BC, B, CAT, NP, W, WHB, YP
Upper Sakatah	Waterville	Yes	881	12	BLH, BC, B, LMB, NP, W, WHB, WC, YP
Volney	Le Center	Yes	283	67	BLH, BC, B, CAT, NP, SUN, W, YP
Washington	Madison Lake	Yes	1487	51	BLH, BC, B, LMB, NP, W, WC, YP
West Jefferson	Cleveland	Yes	441	24	BLH, BC, B, LMB, NP, SUN, W, WHB, WC, YP
Lincoln					
Benton	Lake Benton	Yes	2857	9	BLH, BC, B, LMB, NP, W, WC, YP
Dead Coon	Arco	Yes	569	9	BLH, BC, NP, W, YP
Drietz	Ivanhoe	Carry In	74	4	BLH, YP
Hawksnest	Ivanhoe	Yes	282	8.7	BLH, YP
Hendricks	Hendricks	Yes	1557	12	BLH, BC, B, NP, SUN, W, WHB, YP
Oak	Ivanhoe	Yes	99	10	BLH, SUN, W, YP
Perch	Ivanhoe	No	224	18.5	BLH, B, LMB, NP, SUN, W, YP
Popowski	Ivanhoe	No	136	12	BLH, BC, LMB, W, YP
Porter	Porter	Yes	19	13	BLH, BC, B, LMB, NP, SUN
Shaokotan	Ivanhoe	Yes	995	10	BLH, B, NP, W, YP
Stay	Arco	Yes	224	7	BLH, NP, SUN, W, YP
Steep Bank	Hendricks	Yes	208	6.5	BLH, BC, NP, W, YP
Lyon					
Brawner	Russell	Yes	28	18	B, LMB
Clear	Russell	Yes	68	11	BLH, BC, B, LMB, SUN, W, YP
Cottonwood	Cottonwood	Yes	323	7	BLH, CAT, SUN, W, YP
East Twin	Florence	Yes	280	22	BLH, B, CAT, SUN, W, YP
Goose	Lynd	Yes	139	9	BLH, BC, W, YP
Island	Lynd	Yes	163	8	BLH, NP, SUN, YP
Lady Slipper	Cottonwood	Yes	247	11	BLH, B, SUN, W
Rock	Russell	Yes	439	7.2	BLH, BC, NP, SUN, W, YP
Sanderson	Florence	No	99	6	BLH, W
School Grove	Cottonwood	Yes	318	11	BLH, BC, CAT, SUN, W
West Twin	Florence	Yes	232	10	BLH, B, NP, W, YP
Wood	Russell	Yes	367	14	BLH, B, SUN, W, YP
Yankton	Balaton	Yes	387	8	BLH, BC, LMB, NP, W, WC, YP

Name	Nearest Town	Public Access	Acres	Max. Depth	Fish Species
McLeod					
Cedar	Cedar Mills	Yes	1924	8	BLH, BC, B, LMB, NP, SUN, W, YP
French	Hutchinson	No	94	23	BLH, BC, B, LMB, NP, SUN, W, YP
Hook	Hutchinson	Yes	327	18	BLH, BC, B, NP, SUN, W, YP
Marion	Brownton	Yes	594	12	BLH, BC, B, CAT, LMB, NP, SUN, W, WC, YP
Otter	Hutchinson	Yes	583	6	BLH, BC, B, CAT, NP, SUN, W, WC, YP
Round Grove	Stewart	Yes	307	7	BLH, BC, B, NP, SUN
Stahl's	Hutchinson	Yes	142	37	BLH, BC, B, LMB, NP, SUN, W, YP
Swan	Silver Lake	Yes	343	10	BLH, BC, B, CAT, LMB, NP, SUN, W, YP
Winsted	Winsted	Yes	376	12	BLH, BC, B, NP, SUN, W, WC, YP
Mahnomen					
Bass	Waubun	Yes	689	26	BC, B, LMB, NP, SUN, SMB, W, YP
Church	Mahnomen	Yes	167	19	B, NP, SUN
Island	Lengby	Yes	611	43	BLH, BC, B, LMB, NP, SUN, RKB, W, YP
Little Elbow	Waubun	Yes	158	18	BLH, BC, B, LMB, NP, SUN, W, YP
Little Vanose	Bejou	Yes	144	28	BLH, BC, B, NP, SUN, W
Lone	Ebro	Yes	107	22	BLH, B, NP, SUN, RKB, YP
McCraney	Nay-tah-waush	Yes	268	43	BLH, BC, B, LMB, NP, SUN, RKB, W, YP
North Twin	Nay-tah-waush	Yes	901	16	BLH, BC, B, LMB, NP, SUN, RKB, W, YP
Roy	Mahnomen	Yes	653	16	BLH, BC, B, LMB, NP, SUN, W, YP
Sargent	Nay-tah-waush	Yes	128	15	BLH, BC, B, LMB, NP, SUN, W, YP
Snider	Nay-tau-waush	Yes	632	29	BLH, BC, B, LMB, NP, SUN, RKB, W, YP
South Twin	Waubun	Yes	1000	29	BLH, BC, B, LMB, NP, SUN, RKB, W, YP
Tulaby	Waubun	Yes	773	43	BLH, BC, B, LMB, NP, SUN, RKB, W, YP
Marshall					
Florian Park	Stephen	Yes	50	23	BLH, BC, B, LMB, NP, SUN, RKB
Martin					
Amber	Fairmont	Yes	180	19	BLH, BC, B, CAT, SUN, W, WC, YP
Big Twin	Trimont	Yes	457	18	BLH, BC, B, LMB, SUN, W, YP
Bright	Ceylon	Yes	645	7	BLH, BC, CAT, NP, W, WC
Budd	Fairmont	Yes	222	23	BLH, BC, B, CAT, LMB, NP, W, WC, YP
Cedar	Trimont	Yes	710	7	BLH, BC, B, CAT, NP, SUN, W, WC, YP
Clam	Trimont	Yes	74	8	BLH, BC, NP, SUN, WC, YP
Clear	Ceylon	Yes	273	7	BLH, BC, B, CAT, NP, SUN, W, WC, YP
East Chain	East Chain	Yes	485	6	BLH, BC, CAT, NP, SUN, W, WC, YP
Fish	Odin	Yes	175	5.5	BLH, BC, NP, SUN, W, WC, YP
Fox	Sherburn	Yes	1041	20	BLH, BC, B, CAT, M, W, WC, YP
George	Fairmont	Yes	84	11	BLH, BC, B, CAT, LMB, NP, W, WC, YP
Hall	Fairmont	Yes	513	27	BLH, BC, B, CAT, NP, W, WC, YP
Iowa	Fairmont	Yes	812	9.4	BLH, BC, B, NP, SUN, W, WHB, WC, YP

KEY			
BKT=Brook Trout	**LAT**=Lake Trout	**RKB**=Rock Bass	**W**=Walleye
BLH=Bullhead	**LMB**=Largemouth Bass	**SGR**=Sauger	**WC**=White Crappie
BC=Black Crappie	**M**=Muskie	**SMB**=Smallmouth Bass	**WHB**=White Bass
B=Bluegill	**NP**=Northern Pike	**SPT**=Splake	**YP**=Yellow Perch
BRT=Brown Trout	**PKS**=Pink Salmon	**SPT**=Splake	
CAT=Catfish (Channel and Flathead)	**RBT**=Rainbow Trout	**SUN**=Sunfish	
		TM=Tiger Muskie	

Fishing Waters

Tristan Publishing, Inc., believes that the following charts are accurate; however, we cannot guarantee or accept liability for their accuracy. The reader should contact the Minnesota DNR to verify the accuracy of the charts.

Name	Nearest Town	Public Access	Acres	Max. Depth	Fish Species
Little Twin	Trimont	Yes	68	9	YP
Okamanpeedan	Ceylon	Yes	2294.3	6.5	BLH, CAT, NP, W, WC, YP
Perch	Truman	Yes	175	5	BLH, BC, NP, SUN, W, YP
Sisseton	Fairmont	Yes	140	19	BLH, BC, B, CAT, NP, SUN, W, WC, YP
South Silver	Fairmont	Yes	245	22	BLH, BC, B, LMB, NP, W, WHB, WC, YP
Temperance	Sherburn	Yes	176	5	BLH, NP, SUN, WC, YP
Wilmert	Fairmont	Yes	362	8	BLH, BC, B, W, WC, YP
Meeker					
Arvilla	Kingston	Yes	130	9	BLH, BC, SUN, W
Belle	Hutchinson	Yes	826	25	BLH, BC, B, LMB, NP, SUN, W, YP
Betty	Kimball	Yes	147.5	29	BLH, BC, B, CAT, LMB, NP, SUN, W, YP
Big Swan	Kingston	Yes	628	32	BLH, BC, NP, W
Clear	Watkins	Yes	497	18	BLH, BC, B, LMB, NP, SUN, W, YP
Dunns	Darwin	Yes	142	20	BLH, BC, B, LMB, NP, WC, YP
Erie	Darwin	Yes	182	34	BLH, BC, B, LMB, NP, SUN, W, YP
Francis	Kingston	Yes	921	17	BLH, BC, B, LMB, NP, SUN, W, YP
Goose	Corvuso	No	190	12	BLH, B, NP, W
Greenleaf	Litchfield	Yes	224	18	BLH, BC, B, LMB, NP, SUN, W, WC, YP
Hoff	Cedar	Yes	158	8	BLH, BC, NP, SUN, YP
Hope	Grove City	Yes	250	10	BLH, B, SUN, YP
Jennie	Dassel	Yes	1056	15	BLH, BC, B, LMB, NP, SUN, W, YP
Little Mud	Watkins	No	37	42	BLH, BC, B, LMB, SUN, RBT, SMB
Little Swan	Dassel	Yes	45	31	BLH, BC, B, LMB, NP, SUN, W, WC, YP
Long	Dassel	Yes	163	28	BLH, BC, B, LMB, NP, SUN, W, YP
Long	Grove City	Yes	771	11	BLH, BC, SUN
Manuella	Darwin	Yes	286	51	BLH, BC, B, LMB, NP, SUN, SMB, W
Maple	Dassel	No	133	7	BLH, B, YP
Minnie-Belle	Litchfield	Yes	545	49	BLH, BC, B, LMB, NP, SUN, W, YP
Mud	Kingston	No	100	26	BLH, BC, B, WC
Peterson	Grove City	Yes	127	15	BLH, B, NP, W
Richardson	Darwin	Yes	111	47	BLH, BC, B, LMB, NP, SUN, W, WC, YP
Ripley	Litchfield	Yes	558	18	BLH, BC, B, LMB, NP, SUN, W, YP
Round	Litchfield	Yes	263	8	BLH
Spring	Dassel	Yes	218	30	BLH, BC, B, LMB, NP, SUN, W, YP
Star	Litchfield	Yes	554	15	BLH, BC, B, NP, YP
Stella	Darwin	Yes	553	75	BLH, BC, B, LMB, NP, SUN, SMB, W, YP
Thompson	Cosmos	Yes	220	8	BLH, B, LMB, NP, YP
Washington	Darwin	Yes	2639	17	BLH, BC, B, LMB, NP, SUN, SMB, W, WC, YP
Willie	Litchfield	Yes	182	17	BLH, BC, LMB, NP, SUN, W, WC, YP
Wolf	Dassel	Yes	259	11	BLH, BC, B, LMB, NP, SUN, W, YP
Youngstrom	Litchfield	Yes	132	5	BLH, BC, B, NP, SUN, YP
Mille Lacs					
Black Bass	Onamia	No	26	23	B, LMB, NP, YP
Mille Lacs	Garrison	Yes	132516	42	BLH, BC, M, NP, SUN, RKB, SMB, W, YP
Ogechie	Vineland	No	410	6	BLH, BC, NP, SUN, RKB, W, YP
Onamia	Onamia	Yes	2142	10	BLH, NP, W, YP
Shakopee	Onamia	Yes	675	15	BLH, BC, B, LMB, NP, SUN, RKB, W, YP

Name	Nearest Town	Public Access	Acres	Max. Depth	Fish Species
Morrison					
Alexander	Randall	Yes	2763	64	BLH, BC, B, LMB, M, NP, SUN, RKB, SMB, W, YP
Alott	Little Falls	No	46	34	BLH, LMB, NP, SUN, W, YP
Cedar	Upsala	Yes	253	88	BLH, BC, B, LMB, M, NP, SUN, RKB, W, YP
Crookneck	Lincoln	Yes	168	22	BLH, BC, B, LMB, NP, SUN, RKB, W, YP
East Twin	Little Falls	No	20	35	BLH, LMB, NP, SUN, W
Fish Trap	Lincoln	Yes	1303	42	BLH, BC, B, LMB, NP, SUN, RKB, W, YP
Green Prairie	Randall	Yes	178	22	BLH, BC, B, LMB, NP, SUN, W, YP
Ham	Cushing	Yes	38	22	BLH, BC, B, NP, SUN, YP
Hannah	Sullivan	No	109	27	BLH, BC, B, LMB, NP, SUN, W, YP
Lagerquist	Cushing	No	30	49	BC, LMB, NP, SUN, YP
Long	Sullivan	Yes	120	35	BLH, BC, B, LMB, NP, SUN, W, YP
Peavy	Sullivan	Yes	123	63	BLH, BC, B, LMB, NP, SUN, W
Pelkey	Lil Falls	No	96	7	BLH, BC, B, NP, SUN, YP
Pierz	Genola	Yes	170	34	BC, B, LMB, NP, SUN, RKB, W, YP
Pine	Upsala	Yes	197	59	BLH, BC, B, LMB, NP, SUN, W, YP
Placid	Pillager	Yes	459	25	BC, B, NP, SUN, RKB, W, YP
Rice	Little Falls	Yes	323	8	BLH, NP, RKB, W, YP
Round	Harding	Yes	122	29	BLH, BC, B, LMB, NP, SUN, RKB, W, YP
Round	Pillager	Yes	95	18	BC, B, LMB, NP, SUN, W, YP
Round	Randall	Yes	121	20	BC, B, LMB, M, NP, SUN, W, YP
Shamineau	Motley	Yes	1626	52	BLH, BC, B, LMB, M, NP, SUN, RKB, W, YP
Stanchfield	Pillager	Yes	38	32	BC, B, LMB, NP, YP
Sullivan	Harding	Yes	1221	57	BLH, BC, B, LMB, NP, SUN, RKB, W, YP
Sylvan	Pillager	Yes	655	31	BLH, BC, B, LMB, NP, SUN, RKB, W, YP
Mower					
East Side	Austin	Yes	39	10	BLH, BC, B, LMB, SUN, SMB, WC, YP
Louise Mill Pond	Leroy	Yes	26	8	BLH, BC, LMB, SUN, SMB, WC
Mill Pond	Austin	Yes	19	17	BLH, BC, B, LMB, NP, SUN, RKB, SMB, WC, YP
Pine Lawn	Grand Meadow	Yes	6	8	BLH, BC, LMB, RKB, WC
Ramsey Mill Pond	Ramsey	Private	53	18	BLH, BC, B, LMB, NP, SUN, RKB, YP
Murray					
Bloody	Currie	Yes	248	9	BLH, BC, B, CAT, NP, SUN, W, YP
Buffalo	Dovray	Yes	124	8.5	BLH, BC, NP, W, YP
Corabelle	Iona	Yes	107	6	BLH, BC, NP, SUN, YP
Currant	Balaton	Yes	377	9.5	BLH, BC, SUN, W, YP
First Fulda	Fulda	Yes	179	7	BLH, BC, B, CAT, LMB, NP, SUN, W, YP
Fox	Currie	Yes	174	8.5	BLH, BC, NP, SUN, W, WC, YP
Lime	Avoca	Yes	338	7	BLH, CAT, NP
Louisa	Westbrook	Yes	298	8	BLH, BC, NP, W

KEY			
BKT=Brook Trout	**LAT**=Lake Trout	**RKB**=Rock Bass	**W**=Walleye
BLH=Bullhead	**LMB**=Largemouth Bass	**SGR**=Sauger	**WC**=White Crappie
BC=Black Crappie	**M**=Muskie	**SMB**=Smallmouth Bass	**WHB**=White Bass
B=Bluegill	**NP**=Northern Pike	**SPT**=Splake	**YP**=Yellow Perch
BRT=Brown Trout	**PKS**=Pink Salmon	**SUN**=Sunfish	
CAT=Catfish (Channel and Flathead)	**RBT**=Rainbow Trout	**TM**=Tiger Muskie	

Fishing Waters

Tristan Publishing, Inc., believes that the following charts are accurate; however, we cannot guarantee or accept liability for their accuracy. The reader should contact the Minnesota DNR to verify the accuracy of the charts.

Name	Nearest Town	Public Access	Acres	Max. Depth	Fish Species
Sarah	Garvin	Yes	1093	11	BLH, BC, B, NP, SUN, W, YP
Second Fulda	Fulda	Yes	60	5	BLH, BC, B, NP, W, YP
Shetek	Currie	Yes	3808	10	BLH, BC, CAT, NP, SUN, W, WC, YP
Smith	Currie	Yes	93	9	BLH, NP, YP
Summit	Hadley	Yes	77	7	BLH, BC, B, LMB, NP, SUN, W, WC, YP
Wilson	Lake Wilson	Yes	170	8	BLH, BC, SUN, W, YP
Nicollet					
Hallett	St. Peter	No	12	35	BC, B, LMB, SUN, YP
Nobles					
Bella	Worthington	Yes	182	14	BLH, BC, B, CAT, NP, SUN, W, WC, YP
East Graham	Fulda	Yes	604	8	BLH, BC, CAT, NP, SUN, W, YP
Indian	Round Lake	Yes	204	6	BLH, BC, CAT, NP, W, WC, YP
Kinbrae	Kinbrae	Yes	120	7	BLH, BC, NP, SUN, W, WC, YP
Ocheda	Worthington	Yes	1917	5	BLH, BC, NP, SUN, W, WC, YP
Okabena	Worthington	Yes	751.5	16	BLH, BC, B, CAT, LMB, NP, SUN, W, WC, YP
West Graham	Kinbrae	Yes	515	8	BLH, BC, CAT, NP, SUN, W, WC, YP
Olmsted					
Bear Creek	Chester	Yes	118	37	BLH, BC, B, CAT, LMB, SUN
Foster-Arend	Rochester	No	18	42	BKT, BLH, BC, B, BRT, CAT, SUN, RBT, W, WHB, WC, YP
Shady	Oronoco	Yes	191	13	BLH, BC, B, LMB, WC
Silver	Rochester	No	34	9	BLH, BC, B, CAT, LMB, NP, SUN, RKB, WC, YP
WR4 Pond	Rochester	No	39	24	SUN, SMB
WR6A Pond	Rochester	Carry In	70	22	SUN
Zumbro	Oronoco	Yes	606	43	BLH, BC, B, CAT, LMB, M, NP, SUN, SMB, WHB, WC, YP
Otter Tail					
Adley	Parkers Prairie	Yes	239	20	BLH, BC, B, LMB, NP, SUN, W, YP
Alice	Dent	No	47	39	BLH, BC, B, LMB, NP, SUN, YP
Anderson	Erhard	Yes	83	25	BLH, BC, B, LMB, NP, SUN, W
Anna	Underwood	Yes	538	55	BLH, BC, B, LMB, NP, SUN, W, YP
Annie Battle	Battle Lake	No	334	51	BLH, BC, B, LMB, NP, SUN, RKB, W, YP
Bass	Pelican Rapids	Carry In	26	43	BLH, B, SUN, RBT
Bass	Underwood	Yes	292	36	BLH, B, LMB, NP, SUN, W, YP
Bear	Perham	Yes	181	32	BLH, BC, NP, SUN, W, YP
Beers	Pelican Rapids	Yes	195	61	BC, B, LMB, M, NP, SUN, W, YP
Belmont	Clitherall	No	192	34	BLH, BC, B, LMB, NP, SUN, YP
Big McDonald #2	Dent	Yes	489	33	BLH, BC, B, LMB, NP, SUN, RKB, W, YP
Big McDonald	Perham	Yes	935	46	BLH, BC, B, LMB, NP, SUN, RKB, W, YP
Big Pine	Perham	Yes	4730	76	BLH, BC, B, LMB, NP, SUN, RKB, W, YP
Blanche	Ottertail	Yes	1268	64	BLH, BC, B, LMB, NP, SUN, RKB, W, YP
Block	Urbank	Yes	263	23	BLH, BC, B, NP, SUN, W, YP
Boedigheimer	Richville	Yes	176	26	BLH, BC, B, LMB, NP, SUN, RKB, W, YP
Buchanan	Ottertail	Yes	929	42	BLH, BC, B, LMB, NP, SUN, W, YP
Clear	Dalton	Yes	352	29	BLH, BC, B, LMB, NP, SUN, SMB, W, YP

Name	Nearest Town	Public Access	Acres	Max. Depth	Fish Species
Clitherall	Clitherall	Yes	2493	69	BLH, BC, B, LMB, NP, SUN, RKB, SMB, W, YP
Cow	Erhard	Carry In	16	33	LMB, NP, SUN, YP
Crane	Battle Lake	No	367	43	BLH, BC, B, LMB, NP, SUN, RKB, W, YP
Crystal	Pelican Rapids	Yes	1317	55	BLH, BC, B, LMB, NP, SUN, RKB, SMB, W, YP
Dayton Hollow	Fergus Falls	No	209	32	BLH, BC, B, CAT, NP, RKB, SMB, W, YP
Dead	Dent	Yes	7901	65	BLH, BC, B, LMB, NP, SUN, RKB, W, YP
Deer	Battle Lake	Yes	457	26	BLH, BC, B, LMB, NP, SUN, RKB, W, YP
Devils	Perham	Yes	314	67	BLH, BC, B, LMB, NP, SUN, W, YP
Donalds	Ottertail	Yes	168	43	BLH, BC, B, LMB, NP, SUN, RKB, W, YP
Eagle	Battle Lake	Yes	845	46	BLH, B, LMB, NP, SUN, RKB, W, YP
East Battle	Henning	Yes	1949	87	BLH, BC, B, LMB, NP, SUN, RKB, W, YP
East Leaf	Henning	Yes	404	47	BLH, BC, B, LMB, NP, SUN, RKB, W, YP
East Loon	Vergas	Yes	1048	105	BLH, BC, B, LMB, NP, SUN, RKB, W, YP
East Lost	Battle Lake	Yes	501	36	BLH, BC, B, LMB, NP, SUN, RKB, W, YP
East Silent	Dent	Yes	310	48	BC, B, LMB, NP, SUN, RKB, W, YP
East Spirit	Vergas	Yes	544	38	BLH, BC, B, LMB, NP, SUN, RKB, W
Eddy	Erhard	No	139	34	BLH, BC, B, LMB, NP, SUN, YP
Elbow	Battle Lake	Yes	189	46	BLH, BC, B, LMB, NP, SUN, W, YP
Elbow	Vergas	No	84	85	BLH, BC, B, NP, SUN, YP
Ellingson	Vining	Yes	138	19	BLH, BC, B, LMB, NP, SUN, W, YP
Ethel	Ottertail City	Yes	194	64	BLH, B, LMB, NP, SUN, W, YP
Fischer (Carroll)	Frazee	No	66	33	BLH, BC, B, NP, YP
Fish	Fergus Falls	Yes	888	14	BLH, BC, NP, W, YP
Fish	Parkers Prairie	Yes	435	17	BLH, BC, B, NP, W, YP
Fish	Pelican Rapids	Yes	261	69	BLH, BC, B, LMB, NP, SUN, RKB, W, YP
Fiske	Battle Lake	Yes	250	26	BLH, BC, B, LMB, NP, SUN, W, YP
Five	Vergas	No	224	77	BC, B, LMB, NP, SUN, RKB, W, YP
Fladmark	Erhard	Yes	55	45	BLH, BC, B, LMB, NP, SUN, YP
Franklin	Pelican Rapids	Yes	1336	48	BLH, BC, B, LMB, NP, SUN, RKB, W, YP
German	Underwood	Yes	71	46	BLH, BC, B, LMB, NP, SUN, W, YP
Graham	Frazee	No	210	34	BLH, BC, B, LMB, NP, SUN, W, YP
Grass	Pelican Rapids	Yes	70	21	BLH, BC, B, NP, SUN
Grunard	Vergas	Yes	117	37	BLH, BC, B, NP, SUN, W, YP
Hancock	Battle Lake	No	182	23	BLH, BC, B, LMB, NP, RKB, YP
Hanson	Ottertail	No	54	65	BLH, B, LMB, NP, YP
Head	Richville	Private	249	26	BLH, BC, B, LMB, NP, SUN, W, YP
Heilberger	Erhard	Yes	224	47	BLH, BC, B, LMB, NP, SUN, W, YP
Hoffman	South of Vegas	Yes	150	16	BLH, BC, B, LMB, NP, SUN, W, YP

KEY			
BKT=Brook Trout	LAT=Lake Trout	RKB=Rock Bass	W=Walleye
BLH=Bullhead	LMB=Largemouth Bass	SGR=Sauger	WC=White Crappie
BC=Black Crappie	M=Muskie	SMB=Smallmouth Bass	WHB=White Bass
B=Bluegill	NP=Northern Pike	SPT=Splake	YP=Yellow Perch
BRT=Brown Trout	PKS=Pink Salmon	SUN=Sunfish	
CAT=Catfish (Channel and Flathead)	RBT=Rainbow Trout	TM=Tiger Muskie	

Fishing Waters

Tristan Publishing, Inc., believes that the following charts are accurate; however, we cannot guarantee or accept liability for their accuracy. The reader should contact the Minnesota DNR to verify the accuracy of the charts.

Name	Nearest Town	Public Access	Acres	Max. Depth	Fish Species
Hoot	Fergus Falls	Yes	155	20	BLH, BC, B, LMB, NP, SUN, RKB, SMB, W, YP
Indian	Dalton	No	109	37	BC, B, LMB, SUN, YP
Iverson	Fergus Falls	Yes	54	18	B, SUN, W
Jacobs	Pelican Rapids	No	N/A	17	LMB, SUN
Jewett	Elizabeth	Yes	737	75	BLH, BC, B, LMB, NP, SUN, RKB, W, YP
Jim	Vergas	Yes	99	27	BLH, BC, B, LMB, NP, SUN, W, YP
Johannes	Dalton	No	120	46	LMB, NP, SUN, W, YP
Johnson	Dalton	Yes	338	32	BLH, BC, B, NP, SUN, W, YP
Jolly Ann	Dalton	Yes	256	89	BLH, BC, B, LMB, NP, SUN, W, YP
Leek (Trowbridge)	Vergas	Yes	609	76	BLH, BC, B, LMB, NP, SUN, W
Leon	Phelps	No	74	35	BLH, B, NP, SUN, YP
Little McDonald	Perham	Yes	1174	109	BLH, BC, B, LMB, NP, SUN, RKB, W, YP
Little Pelican	Vergas	Yes	345	25	BLH, BC, B, LMB, NP, SUN, RKB, W, YP
Little Pine	Perham	Yes	1969	63	BLH, BC, B, NP, SUN, RKB, W, YP
Lizzie	Pelican Rapids	Yes	4035	66	BLH, BC, B, LMB, NP, SUN, RKB, SMB, W, YP
Lone Pine	Richville	No	78	79	BLH, BC, B, LMB, NP, SUN, W, YP
Long	Dalton	Yes	350	88	BC, B, LMB, NP, SUN, W, YP
Long	Fergus Falls	Yes	756	73	BLH, BC, B, LMB, NP, SUN, RKB, W, YP
Long	Fergus Falls	No	76	29	BLH, BC, B, LMB, SUN, YP
Long	Ottertail	No	103	56	BLH, BC, B, LMB, NP, SUN, W, YP
Long	Underwood	No	198	24	BLH, BC, B, LMB, NP, SUN, W, YP
Long	Vergas	Yes	1273	128	BLH, BC, B, LMB, NP, SUN, RKB, W, YP
Long	Weetown	No	293	17	BLH, NP, SUN, YP
Maine (Round)	Maine	Yes	83	34	BLH, B, LMB, NP, SUN, W, YP
Marion	Richville	Yes	1664	62	BLH, BC, B, LMB, NP, SUN, RKB, W, YP
Middle Leaf	Ottertail	Yes	398	43	BLH, BC, B, LMB, NP, SUN, RKB, W, YP
Middle	Battle Lake	Yes	194	56	BLH, BC, B, LMB, NP, SUN
Moenkedick	Perham	No	64	35	BC, B, LMB, NP, SUN, RKB, W, YP
Molly Stark	Battle Lake	Yes	153	48	BLH, BC, B, LMB, NP, SUN, RKB, W, YP
Mule	Edward	No	45	31	BLH, BC, B, LMB, NP, SUN, YP
Murphy	Frazee	Yes	310	30	BLH, BC, B, LMB, NP, SUN, W, YP
Nitche	Perham	Yes	75.9	28	BLH, BC, B, LMB, NP, SUN, YP
North Lida	Pelican Rapids	Yes	5564	58	BLH, BC, B, LMB, NP, SUN, RKB, SMB, W, YP
North Ten Mile	Fergus Falls	No	745	14	BLH, BC, B, LMB, NP, SUN, RKB, W, YP
North Turtle	Underwood	No	1484	19	BLH, BC, B, LMB, NP, SUN, W, YP
Norway	Underwood	Yes	384	19	BC, B, LMB, NP, SUN, W, YP
Olaf	Pelican Rapids	Yes	143	61	BC, B, LMB, NP, SUN, W, YP
Orwell	Fergus Falls	Yes	782	25	BC, B, CAT, LMB, NP, SUN, RKB, SMB, W, YP
Otter Tail River	Fergus Falls	Yes	305	55	BLH, BC, B, LMB, NP, SUN, RKB, W, YP
Otter Tail	Ottertail	Yes	13725	120	BLH, B, NP, SUN, RKB, W, YP
Otter	Vergas	No	97	64	B, LMB, NP, SUN, W, YP
Paul	Perham	Yes	319	81	BLH, B, LMB, NP, SUN, RKB, W, YP

Name	Nearest Town	Public Access	Acres	Max. Depth	Fish Species
Pebble	Fergus Falls	Yes	169	62	BLH, BC, B, LMB, NP, SUN, RKB, W, YP
Pelican	Pelican Rapids	Yes	3986	55	BLH, BC, B, LMB, M, NP, SUN, RKB, SMB, W, YP
Pickerel	Dent	Yes	28	50	BLH, BC, B, LMB, NP, SUN, YP
Pickerel	Maine	Yes	829	78	BLH, BC, B, LMB, NP, SUN, RKB, SMB, W, YP
Pine (Reames)	Dent	No	67	33	BLH, BC, B, LMB, NP, SUN, YP
Pine	Dent	No	63	94	BC, B, LMB, NP, SUN, RKB, W, YP
Pleasant	Underwood	Yes	370	38	BLH, BC, B, LMB, NP, SUN, W, YP
Portage	Ottertail	Yes	265	49	BLH, BC, B, LMB, NP, SUN, W, YP
Prairie	Pelican Rapids	Yes	1016	22	BLH, BC, B, LMB, NP, SUN, RKB, W, YP
Rice	Vergas	Yes	350	8	BLH, BC, B, NP, SUN, W, YP
Rose	Dalton	No	103	37	BLH, BC, B, LMB, NP, SUN, YP
Rose	Vergas	Yes	1190	137	BLH, BC, B, LMB, NP, SUN, RKB, W, YP
Round	Amor	No	155	24	BLH, BC, B, LMB, NP, SUN, RKB, W, YP
Round	Dent	Yes	166	18	BLH, B, LMB, NP, SUN, W, YP
Round	Maine	No	73	14	BLH, B, SUN, W
Round	Ottertail City	Yes	262	36	BLH, BC, B, LMB, NP, SUN, RKB, W, YP
Rusch	Dent	No	98	32	BLH, B, LMB, NP, SUN, RKB, W, YP
Rush	Ottertail	Yes	5338	68	BLH, BC, B, LMB, NP, SUN, RKB, W, YP
Sand	Pelican Rapids	Yes	124	29	BLH, BC, NP, SUN, W, YP
Scalp	Frazee	Yes	243	90	B, LMB, NP, SUN, RKB, W, YP
Schuster	Perham	No	43	80	BLH, BC, B, LMB, NP, YP
Sewell	Dalton	Yes	338	52	BLH, BC, B, LMB, NP, SUN, W, YP
Shallow	Vergas	No	65.3	28	BLH, BC, B, LMB, NP, SUN, YP
Silver	Battle Lake	Yes	547	43	BLH, BC, B, LMB, NP, SUN, RKB, W, YP
Silver	Frazee	Yes	247	34	BLH, BC, B, LMB, NP, SUN, W, YP
Siverson	Vining	No	137	41	BLH, BC, B, LMB, NP, SUN, YP
Six	Frazee	Yes	188	140	BLH, BC, B, LMB, NP, SUN, RKB, W, YP
South Lida	Pelican Rapids	Yes	856	48	BLH, BC, B, LMB, NP, SUN, RKB, W, YP
South Turtle	Underwood	Yes	630	35	BLH, BC, B, LMB, NP, SUN, W, YP
Spitzer	Urbank	Yes	728	33	BLH, BC, B, LMB, NP, SUN, W, YP
Spring	Fergus Falls	No	47	22	BLH, NP, SUN, YP
Stalker	Underwood	Yes	1280	95	BLH, B, LMB, NP, SUN, RKB, W, YP
Star	Dent	Yes	4721	94	BLH, BC, B, LMB, NP, SUN, RKB, W, YP
Steenerson	Dalton	No	38	56	BLH, BC, B, LMB, NP, SUN, RKB, W, YP
Stuart	Vining	Yes	699	49	BLH, BC, B, LMB, NP, SUN, RKB, W, YP
Sunfish	Vergas	No	41	38	BLH, B, SUN

KEY			
BKT=Brook Trout	**LAT**=Lake Trout	**RKB**=Rock Bass	**W**=Walleye
BLH=Bullhead	**LMB**=Largemouth Bass	**SGR**=Sauger	**WC**=White Crappie
BC=Black Crappie	**M**=Muskie	**SMB**=Smallmouth Bass	**WHB**=White Bass
B=Bluegill	**NP**=Northern Pike	**SPT**=Splake	**YP**=Yellow Perch
BRT=Brown Trout	**PKS**=Pink Salmon	**SUN**=Sunfish	
CAT=Catfish (Channel and Flathead)	**RBT**=Rainbow Trout	**TM**=Tiger Muskie	

Fishing Waters

Tristan Publishing, Inc., believes that the following charts are accurate; however, we cannot guarantee or accept liability for their accuracy. The reader should contact the Minnesota DNR to verify the accuracy of the charts.

Name	Nearest Town	Public Access	Acres	Max. Depth	Fish Species
Swan	Fergus Falls	Yes	689	44	BLH, BC, B, LMB, NP, SUN, RKB, SMB, W, YP
Sybil	Vergas	Yes	706	74	BLH, BC, B, LMB, NP, SUN, RKB, W, YP
Tamarac	Pelican Rapids	Yes	392	11	BLH, BC, B, NP, SUN, RKB, SMB, W, YP
Ten Mile	Dalton	Yes	1411	51	BLH, BC, B, LMB, NP, SUN, RKB, SMB, W, YP
Tenter	Dent	No	83	63	BLH, BC, B, LMB, NP, SUN, W, YP
Tonseth	Erhard	No	156	27	BLH, BC, B, LMB, NP, SUN, W, YP
Torgerson	Dalton	No	144	40	BLH, BC, B, LMB, NP, SUN, YP
Twenty-one	Erhard	Carry In	122	47	BLH, BC, B, LMB, NP, SUN, YP
Twin	Amor	Yes	333	50	BLH, BC, B, LMB, NP, SUN, W, YP
Walker	Ottertail	Yes	540	29	BLH, BC, B, LMB, NP, SUN, RKB, W, YP
Wall	Fergus Falls	Yes	683	34	BLH, BC, B, LMB, NP, SUN, RKB, W, YP
West Battle	Battle Lake	Yes	5624	108	BLH, BC, B, LMB, M, NP, SUN, RKB, W, YP
West Leaf	Ottertail	Yes	684	55	BLH, BC, B, LMB, NP, SUN, RKB, W, YP
West Lost	Underwood	Yes	723	16	BLH, BC, B, LMB, NP, SUN, RKB, W, YP
West McDonald	Vergas	Yes	573	62	BLH, BC, B, LMB, NP, SUN, RKB, W, YP
West Silent	Pelican Rapids	Yes	328	58	BLH, BC, B, LMB, NP, SUN, RKB, W, YP
Wimer	Frazee	No	275	58	BLH, BC, B, LMB, NP, SUN, RKB, W, YP
Wolf	Dent	No	73	51	BLH, BC, B, LMB, NP, SUN, YP
Wright	Fergus Falls	Carry In	63	32	BLH, BC, B, LMB, NP, SUN, RKB, W, YP

Pennington
Red Lake River	Thief River Falls	Yes	135	18	BLH, BC, B, NP, SUN, RKB, W, YP

Pine
Bass	Finlayson	Yes	189.3	24	BLH, BC, B, LMB, NP, SUN, W, YP
Bass	Finlayson	No	30	12	BLH, BC, B, LMB, NP, YP
Big Pine	Finlayson	Yes	387	25	BLH, BC, B, LMB, NP, SUN, W, YP
Big Slough	Willow River	No	71	14	BLH, BC, B, NP, SUN, YP
Clear	Rutledge	No	23	39	BC, B, LMB, NP, SUN, YP
Close	Sturgeon Lake	No	36	37	BC, B, LMB, NP, SUN, YP
Cross	Pine City	Yes	942.8	30	BLH, BC, B, CAT, LMB, M, NP, SUN, SMB, W, WHB, WC, YP
Dago	Willow River	No	107	20	BLH, B, NP, W, YP
Devils	Pine City	No	18	80	BC, B, NP, SUN
Elbow	Finlayson	No	103	33	BLH, BC, NP, SUN, YP
Eleven	Sturgeon Lake	No	109	49	BLH, BC, B, LMB, NP, SUN, YP
First	Willow River	No	80	18	BLH, BC, B, LMB, NP, SUN, RKB, YP
Fish	Finlayson	No	82	18	BLH, BC, B, LMB, NP, SUN, YP
Five	Duxbury	No	22	14	BLH, BC, NP, YP
Fox	Willow River	Yes	239	14.5	BLH, BC, B, LMB, NP, SUN, YP
Grace	Duxbury	Yes	53	11	BLH, BC, B, LMB, NP, SUN, YP
Grass	Finlayson	No	84	7	BLH
Greigs	Hinckley	No	53.5	68	BLH, BC, B, LMB, NP, SUN, YP
Grindstone	Sandstone	Yes	526	153	BC, B, BRT, LAT, NP, SUN, RBT, RKB, SMB, YP
Hay Creek	Markville	Yes	88	10	BLH, BC, B, LMB, NP, SUN, YP

Fishing Waters

Name	Nearest Town	Public Access	Acres	Max. Depth	Fish Species
Headquarters	Nickerson	No	14	7	BLH, BC, B, NP, SUN, YP
Indian	Finlayson	No	73	15	BLH, BC, LMB, NP, SUN, YP
Island	Sturgeon Lake	Yes	510.2	42	BLH, BC, B, LMB, M, NP, SUN, RKB, W, YP
Keene	Hinckley	Yes	13	17	BLH, BC, B, LMB, NP
Kenney	Duxbury	No	15	15	B, NP, YP
Little Bass	Finlayson	No	16.4	28	BLH, BC, B, LMB, NP, YP
Little Island	Sturgeon Lake	No	34	20	BLH, BC, B, NP, SUN, W, YP
Little Mud	Rutledge	No	17	25	BLH, BC, B, LMB, NP, SUN, YP
Little Pine	Finlayson	No	75	17	BLH, BC, B, LMB, NP, SUN, YP
Little Tamarack	Duxbury	No	60	31	BLH, BC, B, LMB, NP, SUN
Long	Rutledge	Yes	75	24	BLH, BC, B, LMB, NP, SUN, W, WC
McCormick	Willow River	Carry In	54	17	BLH, BC, B, LMB, NP, SUN, YP
McGowan	Duxbury	Yes	21	24	BC
Net	Nickerson	No	136	15	BLH, BC, B, LMB, NP, SUN, YP
Oak	Duquette	Yes	442	20	BLH, BC, B, LMB, NP, SUN, W, YP
Passenger	Willow River	No	70	22	BLH, BC, B, LMB, NP, SUN, W, YP
Pickerel	Nickerson	Yes	53	10	BC, B, LMB, NP, SUN, YP
Pokegama	Pine City	Yes	1474	25	BLH, BC, B, CAT, LMB, NP, SUN, W, WHB, WC, YP
Razor	Cloverdale	No	100	36	BLH, BC, B, LMB, NP, SUN, YP
Rhine	Finlayson	No	111	8	BLH, BC, B, NP, SUN, YP
Rock	Markville	Yes	77	11	B, NP, SUN, W, YP
Rock	Pine City	No	82	32	BLH, BC, CAT, NP, SUN, WC
Rush	Sturgeon Lake	No	71.8	37	BLH, BC, B, LMB, NP, SUN, YP
Sand	Moos Lake	Yes	501	47	BLH, BC, B, LMB, NP, SUN, RKB, W, YP
Second	Willow River	No	44	25	BLH, BC, B, NP, SUN, YP
Stanton	Willow River	Yes	95	12	BLH, BC, B, LMB, NP, SUN, RKB, W, YP
Sturgeon	Sturgeon Lake	Yes	1405	40	BLH, BC, B, LMB, NP, SUN, RKB, W, YP
Tamarack	Duxbury	Yes	74.9	47	BC, B, LMB, NP, SUN, YP
Twelve	Sturgeon Lake	No	58	31	BLH, BC, B, LMB, NP, SUN, YP
Upper Pine	Finlayson	Yes	210	15	BLH, BC, B, LMB, NP, SUN, W, YP
Wilbur	Cloverdale	No	45	14	NP, YP
Pipestone					
Minett-Kranz	Ruthton	Yes	10	22.5	BLH, B, LMB, NP, YP
Split Rock	Pipestone	Yes	81	16	BLH, BC, B, CAT, LMB, NP, SUN, W, YP
Polk					
Badger	Erskine	Yes	353	19	BLH, BC, B, NP, SUN, YP
Cable	Mentor	Yes	143	14	BLH, BC, B, LMB, NP, SUN, YP
Cameron	Erskine	Yes	224	9	BLH, NP
Cross	Fosston	Yes	328	19	BLH, BC, B, LMB, NP, SUN, W, YP
Crystal	Erskine	No	102	30	BLH, BC, B, NP, SUN, YP
Hill River	McIntosh	Yes	96	60	BLH, B, NP, YP
Maple	Mentor	Yes	1477	14	BLH, BC, B, LMB, NP, SUN, W, YP
Perch	Gully	Yes	79	19	BLH, BC, B, NP, SUN, YP
Poplar	Lengby	Yes	75	23	BLH, BC, B, NP, SUN, RKB, YP
Sand Hill	Fosston	Yes	510	17	BLH, NP

KEY			
BKT=Brook Trout	**LAT**=Lake Trout	**RKB**=Rock Bass	**W**=Walleye
BLH=Bullhead	**LMB**=Largemouth Bass	**SGR**=Sauger	**WC**=White Crappie
BC=Black Crappie	**M**=Muskie	**SMB**=Smallmouth Bass	**WHB**=White Bass
B=Bluegill	**NP**=Northern Pike	**SPT**=Splake	**YP**=Yellow Perch
BRT=Brown Trout	**PKS**=Pink Salmon	**SUN**=Sunfish	
CAT=Catfish (Channel and Flathead)	**RBT**=Rainbow Trout	**TM**=Tiger Muskie	

Fishing Waters

Tristan Publishing, Inc., believes that the following charts are accurate; however, we cannot guarantee or accept liability for their accuracy. The reader should contact the Minnesota DNR to verify the accuracy of the charts.

Name	Nearest Town	Public Access	Acres	Max. Depth	Fish Species
Sarah	Erskine	Yes	352	27	BLH, BC, B, NP, SUN, W, YP
Spring	Lengby	Yes	136	35	BLH, BC, B, LMB, NP, SUN, RKB, W, YP
Store	Fosston	Yes	52	19	BLH, W, YP
Turtle	Fosston	Yes	545	12	BLH, NP, SUN, YP
Union	Erskine	Yes	734	83	BLH, BC, B, LMB, NP, SUN, W, YP
Whitefish	Fosston	Yes	226	18	BLH, BC, NP, SUN, RKB, W, YP
Pope					
Amelia	Villard	Yes	910	69	BLH, BC, B, LMB, NP, SUN, RKB, W, YP
Ann	Glenwood	Yes	356	14	BLH, B, NP, SUN, W
Emily	Hancock	Yes	2377	7	BLH, BC, B, CAT, LMB, NP, SUN, RKB, W, YP
Gilchrist	Sedan	Yes	321	24	BLH, BC, B, LMB, NP, SUN, W, YP
Grove	Sedan	Yes	379	31	BLH, BC, B, LMB, NP, SUN, YP
Johanna	Brooten	Yes	1584	10	BLH, BC, B, LMB, NP, SUN, W
Leven	Villard	Yes	283	33	BLH, BC, B, LMB, NP, SUN, W, YP
Linka	Sedan	Yes	197	50	BLH, BC, B, LMB, NP, SUN, W, YP
Minnewaska	Glenwood	Yes	7110	32	BLH, BC, B, LMB, NP, SUN, W, YP
Nelson	Glenwood	Carry In	403	9	BLH, NP, SUN, YP
Pelican	Glenwood	Yes	519	34	BLH, BC, B, LMB, NP, SUN, W, YP
Reno	Alexandria	Yes	3722	23	BLH, BC, B, LMB, NP, SUN, RKB, W, YP
Scandinavian	Terrace	Yes	424	49	BLH, BC, B, LMB, NP, SUN, W, YP
Signalness	Starbuck	Yes	39	14	BC, B, LMB, NP, SUN, W, YP
Villard	Villard	Yes	536	16	BLH, BC, B, LMB, NP, SUN, RKB, W, YP
Ramsey					
Bald Eagle	White Bear Lake	Yes	1268.5	36	BLH, BC, B, LMB, M, NP, SUN, W, YP
Beaver	St. Paul	Carry In	65	11	BLH, BC, B, CAT, LMB, NP, SUN, YP
Bennett	Roseville	No	23	9	BLH, BC, B, CAT, LMB, NP, SUN, W
Casey	White Bear Lake	Carry In	11.6	3.5	BLH, BC, SUN
Charley	North Oaks	No	33	21	BLH, BC, B, CAT, M, RKB, SMB, W, WHB, WC, YP
Como	St. Paul	Carry In	66.7	15.5	BLH, BC, B, CAT, NP, YP
Crosby	St. Paul	Carry In	48	19	BLH, BC, B, LMB, NP, SUN, YP
Deep	North Oaks	Yes	53	11	BLH, BC, B, CAT, LMB, M, NP, SUN, SMB, W, WHB, WC, YP
East Vadnais	Vadnais Heights	No	394	58	BLH, BC, B, LMB, NP, SUN, RKB, SMB, W, WHB, YP
Evergreen Ponds	Shoreview	Yes	18	18	BLH, BC, B, NP, SUN, WC, YP
Gervais	Little Canada	Yes	234	41	BC, B, LMB, NP, SUN, TM, W, YP
Goose	White Bear Lake	No	145	6	BLH
Island	Shoreview	Yes	59.64	11	BLH, BC, B, CAT, LMB, NP, SUN, TM, W, YP
Johanna	Arden Hills	Yes	213.1	43	BLH, BC, B, LMB, NP, SUN, W, YP
Josephine	Roseville	Yes	118	44	BLH, BC, B, LMB, NP, SUN, W, YP
Keller	Maplewood	Yes	72	8	BLH, BC, B, LMB, SUN, W, YP
Kohlman	Hancock	No	74	9	BC, B, SUN, W
Little Johanna	Arden Hills	No	18	28	BLH, BC, NP
Little Josephine	Roseville	No	10	25	BLH, B, NP, SUN, YP
Loeb	St. Paul	Yes	9.4	28	BLH, BC, B, CAT, LMB, NP, SUN, W
Long	New Brighton	Yes	183	30	BLH, BC, B, CAT, LMB, NP, SUN, W, WC, YP
McCarron	Roseville	Yes	68.1	57	BC, B, M, NP, SUN, W, YP

Fishing Waters

Name	Nearest Town	Public Access	Acres	Max. Depth	Fish Species
Owasso	Shoreview	Yes	384.1	37	BLH, BC, B, LMB, M, NP, SUN, W, YP
Phalen	St. Paul	Yes	198	91	BLH, BC, B, LMB, NP, SUN, SGR, W, WHB, YP
Pigs Eye	St. Paul	No	628	4	BC, B, CAT, LMB, NP, SUN, WHB, WC, YP
Pike	New Brighton	No	35	16	BLH, BC, B, LMB, NP, SUN, W, YP
Pleasant	North Oaks	No	585	58	BC, B, CAT, NP, SUN, RKB, SMB, W, WHB, YP
Silver (East)	North St. Paul	Yes	72	18	BLH, BC, B, LMB, NP, SUN, TM, W, YP
Silver (West)	Columbia Heights	Yes	69.5	47	BLH, BC, B, NP, SUN, W, YP
Snail	Shoreview	Yes	150	30	BLH, BC, B, LMB, NP, SUN, YP
Spoon	Maplewood	Yes	6.7	6	BLH, BC, B, NP, SUN
Sucker	Vadnais Heights	Yes	60.8	26	BLH, BC, B, LMB, NP, SUN, SMB, W, YP
Turtle	Shoreview	Yes	408.62	28	BLH, BC, B, LMB, NP, SUN, W, WC, YP
Twin	Little Canada	No	35.5	33	BC, B, LMB, NP, SUN, PKS, YP
Wabasso	Vadnais Heights	Yes	46.4	66	BLH, BC, B, LMB, NP, SUN, YP
Wakefield	Maplewood	Carry In	22.5	9.5	BLH, BC, SUN
West Vadnais	Vadnais Heights	Yes	216	9	BLH, BC, B, NP, SUN
Willow	White Bear Lake	No	N/A	5	BLH, B, LMB, M, SUN

Redwood

Laura	Walnut Grove	Yes	22	21	BLH, BC, B, LMB, NP, SUN, WC, YP
Redwood	Redwood Falls	Yes	64	11	BLH, BC, B, NP, SUN, W, WC

Renville

Allie	Buffalo Lake	Yes	451	12	BLH, BC, B, CAT, NP, SUN, W, YP
Preston	Buffalo Lake	Yes	670	11	BLH, BC, B, LMB, NP, SUN, W, YP

Rice

Cannon	Faribault	Yes	1591	15	BLH, BC, B, CAT, LMB, NP, W, WHB, WC, YP
Cedar	Faribault	Yes	804	42	BLH, BC, B, LMB, NP, SUN, W, WC, YP
Circle	Lonsdale	Yes	624	14	BLH, B, LMB, NP, SUN, W, YP
Cody	Montgomery	No	257	14	BLH, BC, B, LMB, NP, W, YP
Dudley	Faribault	Yes	124.9	60	BLH, BC, B, LMB, NP, SUN, WHB, YP
Fox	Shieldsville	Yes	308	47	BLH, BC, B, LMB, NP, W, WHB, WC, YP
French	Faribault	Yes	816	56	BC, B, M, NP, SUN, W, WHB, WC, YP
Hunt	Shieldsville	Yes	159.7	27	BLH, BC, B, LMB, NP, SUN, W, YP
Lower Sakatah	Waterville	No	310	7	BLH, BC, B, LMB, NP, W, WHB, YP
Lyman	Northfield	No	8	7	BLH, BC, B, SUN, WC
Mazaska	Shieldsville	Yes	685	50	BLH, BC, B, LMB, NP, SUN, W, WHB, YP
Phelps	Montgomery	Yes	299	8	BLH, BC, B, LMB, NP, W, YP
Rice	Shieldsville	No	323	6.7	BLH, BC, B, LMB, NP, SUN, W, WC, YP
Roberds	Shieldsville	Yes	625.4	43	BLH, BC, B, CAT, NP, SUN, W, WHB, WC, YP

KEY			
BKT=Brook Trout	**LAT**=Lake Trout	**RKB**=Rock Bass	**W**=Walleye
BLH=Bullhead	**LMB**=Largemouth Bass	**SGR**=Sauger	**WC**=White Crappie
BC=Black Crappie	**M**=Muskie	**SMB**=Smallmouth Bass	**WHB**=White Bass
B=Bluegill	**NP**=Northern Pike	**SPT**=Splake	**YP**=Yellow Perch
BRT=Brown Trout	**PKS**=Pink Salmon	**SUN**=Sunfish	
CAT=Catfish (Channel and Flathead)	**RBT**=Rainbow Trout	**TM**=Tiger Muskie	

Fishing Waters

Tristan Publishing, Inc., believes that the following charts are accurate; however, we cannot guarantee or accept liability for their accuracy. The reader should contact the Minnesota DNR to verify the accuracy of the charts.

Name	Nearest Town	Public Access	Acres	Max. Depth	Fish Species
Shields	Shieldsville	Yes	872	42	BLH, BC, B, LMB, NP, SUN, W, YP
Union	Little Chicago	Yes	403	10	BLH, BC, B, LMB, NP, SUN, YP
Wells	Faribault	Yes	634	4	BLH, BC, B, CAT, LMB, NP, W, WHB, WC, YP

Rock
Hills	Hills	Yes	10	12	BLH, BC, B, CAT, LMB, NP, W
Luverne Pit	Luverne	Yes	10	7	BLH, BC, B, LMB, W, WC
S. Mound Springs	Luverne	Carry In	19	7.5	BLH, BC, CAT, LMB, SUN, YP

Roseau
Hayes	Wannaska	Yes	180	28	BLH, BC, B, LMB, NP, SUN, YP

St. Louis
Aerie	Alborn	Yes	139	37	BLH, BC, B, LMB, NP, SUN, W, YP
Agassa	Ely	Carry In	55	9	W, YP
Agawato	Crane	Carry In	39	58	YP
Agnes	Ely	Carry In	984	30	NP, RKB, SGR, SMB, W, YP
Agnes	Ray	Yes	32	18	BLH, NP, YP
Alden	Duluth	No	180	29	BC, B, NP, SUN, RKB, SMB, W, YP
Alruss	Ely	Carry In	29	48	BKT, RBT, SPT
Amundsen	Crane	No	100	18	NP, YP
Angleworm	Ely	Carry In	144	11	NP, W, YP
Anne	Cotton	Yes	8	27	BC, B, LMB, NP, YP
Armstrong	Ely	Yes	389	33	BC, B, LMB, NP, SUN, RKB, SMB, W, YP
Arthur	Ely	No	67	19	B, NP, RKB, W, YP
Ash	International Falls	Yes	669	25	BC, B, NP, SMB, W, YP
Astrid	Buyck	Yes	109	30	NP, SUN, RKB, W, YP
Auto	Virginia	Yes	88	29	BC, B, LMB, NP, W, YP
Ban	Orr	Yes	380	10	BC, B, LMB, NP, SUN, RKB, SMB, W, YP
Barrs	Duluth	No	117	23	BLH, BC, B, NP, SUN, RKB, W, YP
Bass	Biwabik	Yes	149	35	BLH, BC, B, LMB, NP, SUN, RKB, W
Bass	Ely	Carry In	174	36	BC, B, LMB, NP, SMB, W, YP
Bass	Soudan	No	242	18	BC, B, LMB, NP, SUN, RKB, SMB, YP
Bassett	Fairbanks	Yes	442	21	BLH, BC, B, NP, SUN, RKB, W, YP
Bear Island	Babbitt	Yes	2351	62	BC, B, LMB, NP, SUN, RKB, SMB, W, YP
Bear Trap	Ely	Carry In	122	38	NP, SUN, W
Bearhead	Tower	Yes	674	46	BC, B, LMB, NP, SUN, W, YP
Beartrack	Crane Lake	Yes	168.6	55	SUN, YP
Beast	International Falls	Yes	81	66	NP, SMB
Beaver	Ely	Carry In	93	4	LMB, NP, SUN, YP
Bergen	Fredenberg	No	62	30	BC, B, CAT, NP, SUN, W, YP
Big Bear	Two Harbors	Yes	130	15	BLH, NP, SUN, W, YP
Big Moose	Ely	Carry In	1032	23	NP, RKB, SMB, W, YP
Big Rice	Ely	Carry In	420	5	NP, YP
Big Rice	Tower	Yes	N/A	5	NP, YP
Big Rosendahl	Cook	No	44	9	YP
Big	Ely	Carry In	1789	22	NP, SUN, RKB, SMB, W, YP
Big	Hoyt Lakes	Carry In	805	30	NP, RKB, W, YP
Birch	Babbitt	Yes	5628	25	BC, B, NP, SMB, W, YP
Bird	Hoyt Lakes	Carry In	16	15	BC, B, NP
Black Duck	Orr	Yes	1185	30	BC, B, NP, SUN, SMB, W, YP
Black	Cook	No	118	8	BC, B, LMB, NP, SUN, W, YP
Blackwood	Cromwell	Yes	27	26	BLH, BC, B, LMB, NP, SUN, RKB, YP
Blueberry	Babbitt	No	53	14	YP

Name	Nearest Town	Public Access	Acres	Max. Depth	Fish Species
Blueberry	Ely	No	127	6	BC, B, NP, SUN, SMB, W, YP
Boot	Ely	Carry In	313	27	NP, RKB, W, YP
Boot	International Falls	Yes	56	25	M, YP
Bootleg	Ely	Carry In	340	26	B, LMB, NP, SUN, RKB, YP
Boulder	Duluth	Yes	3881.6	18	BLH, BC, NP, SUN, RKB, W, YP
Boulder	Ely	Carry In	238	51	NP
Briar	Rollins	Yes	70	21	BLH, RBT
Buck	Tower	Carry In	228	19	NP, W, YP
Burns Pit	Eveleth	No	20	95	B, LMB, NP, SUN, YP
Burntside	Ely	Yes	7139	126	B, LAT, NP, SUN, RKB, SMB, W, YP
Cadotte	Fairbanks	Yes	325	18	B, NP, SUN, W, YP
Cameron	Cotton	Yes	162.1	27	BC, B, LMB, NP, SUN, RKB, SMB, W, YP
Cameron	Duluth	No	70.4	17	BLH
Camp A	Buhl	Yes	15	31	BKT, RBT
Carey	Hibbing	Yes	139	13.5	BC, B, NP, SUN, W, YP
Caribou	Duluth	Yes	546	21	BLH, BC, B, LMB, NP, SUN, RKB, W, YP
Carlson	Orr	No	116	8	BC, NP, RKB, YP
Cedar Island	Biwabik	No	185	20	BLH, BC, B, CAT, NP, SUN, RKB, W, YP
Cedar	Aurora	Yes	32	51	RBT
Cedar	Biwabik	No	63	30	BC, NP, YP
Central	Central Lakes	No	75	19	BLH, B, NP, SUN, YP
Chad	Ely	Carry In	266	18	B, LMB, NP, RKB, YP
Chant	Ely	Carry In	15	37	BKT, RBT, SPT
Chase	Ely	Carry In	17	15	YP
Chub	Orr	No	124	15	W, YP
Clear	Buhl	Yes	112.2	24	BLH, BC, B, LMB, NP, SUN, YP
Clear	Ely	No	119	24	BC, B, LMB, NP, W, YP
Clearwater	Chisholm	No	72	30	BC, B, NP, W
Clearwater	Duluth	Yes	14.6	25	RBT
Coe	Biwabik	Yes	51	22	BC, B, NP, SUN, RKB, YP
Colby	Hoyt Lakes	Yes	539	30	BC, B, CAT, LMB, NP, RKB, W, YP
Cold	Babbitt	No	18	17	NP, YP
Comstock	Whiteface	Yes	443	30	BLH, BC, B, NP, SUN, W, YP
Coo	Ely	Carry In	20	25	NP, YP
Cooks	Duluth	No	93	19	BLH, BC, B, NP, SUN, W, YP
Coon	Hibbing	Yes	100	9	BLH, BC, B, LMB, NP, SUN, W, YP
Coxey Pond	Ely	Carry In	204	14	B, LMB, NP, SUN, SMB, YP
Crab	Ely	Carry In	541	57	NP, SUN, RKB, SMB
Crane	Crane Lake	Yes	3088	80	BLH, BC, B, NP, RKB, SGR, SMB, W, YP
Crellin	Buyck	Yes	N/A	25	YP
Crooked	Brookston	No	99.4	35	BLH, BC, B, LMB, NP, SUN, YP
Cruiser	Ray	Yes	115	91	LAT, YP
Crystal	Cotton	No	34	54	B, NP, RKB, YP
Cub	Ely	Yes	8	39	BKT
Cummings	Ely	Carry In	1121	41	B, NP, SUN, RKB, SMB, YP
Dark	Buhl	Yes	232	31	BC, B, NP, SUN, RKB, W, YP
Day	Chisholm	Yes	120	15	BLH, BC, B, NP, SUN, RKB, W, YP

KEY
BKT=Brook Trout
BLH=Bullhead
BC=Black Crappie
B=Bluegill
BRT=Brown Trout
CAT=Catfish (Channel and Flathead)

LAT=Lake Trout
LMB=Largemouth Bass
M=Muskie
NP=Northern Pike
PKS=Pink Salmon
RBT=Rainbow Trout

RKB=Rock Bass
SGR=Sauger
SMB=Smallmouth Bass
SPT=Splake
SUN=Sunfish
TM=Tiger Muskie

W=Walleye
WC=White Crappie
WHB=White Bass
YP=Yellow Perch

Fishing Waters

Tristan Publishing, Inc., believes that the following charts are accurate; however, we cannot guarantee or accept liability for their accuracy. The reader should contact the Minnesota DNR to verify the accuracy of the charts.

Name	Nearest Town	Public Access	Acres	Max. Depth	Fish Species
Deep	Gilbert	Yes	61	50	BC, B, LMB, NP, SUN, RKB, W, YP
Deepwater	Chisholm	Yes	22	37	BRT, RBT
Dewey	Chisholm	Yes	195	40	BC, B, NP, SUN, RKB, YP
Dinham	Melrude	Yes	206.8	25	BLH, BC, B, LMB, NP, SUN, W, YP
Dodo	Cotton	No	76	53	BC, B, LMB, NP, SUN, W, YP
Doherty	Buhl	Yes	71	16	BLH, BC, B, NP, SUN, YP
Dollar	Chisholm	Yes	12	32	BLH, B, NP, SUN, YP
Donna	Hoyt Lakes	Carry In	16	15	BC, B, NP
Dovre	Crane Lake	Yes	120	17	NP, YP
Dry	Ely	Carry In	82	44	BRT, SPT
Eagles Nest #1	Ely	Yes	322	76	BC, B, LMB, NP, SUN, RKB, SMB, W, YP
Eagles Nest #2	Ely	Yes	408	39	BC, B, LMB, NP, SUN, RKB, SMB, W, YP
Eagles Nest #3	Soudan	Yes	1001	49	BC, B, LMB, NP, SUN, RKB, SMB, W, YP
Eagles Nest #4	Ely	No	177	49	BC, B, LMB, NP, SUN, RKB, SMB, W, YP
East Twin	Ely	Carry In	191	22	BC, B, LMB, NP, SUN, RKB, SMB, W, YP
Echo	Orr	Yes	1054	10	BC, B, NP, SUN, RKB, SMB, W, YP
Ed Shave	Ely	Yes	82	17	B, NP, W, YP
Ek	Ray*	Carry In	89	19	BC, NP, YP
Elbow	Iron Junction	Yes	165	22	BLH, BC, B, LMB, NP, SUN, YP
Elbow	Orr	Yes	1659	60	BC, B, LMB, NP, SUN, RKB, SMB, W, YP
Elephant	Orr	Yes	742	30	BC, B, NP, SUN, SMB, W, YP
Elliot	Eveleth	Yes	398	13	BLH, BC, B, LMB, NP, SUN, W, YP
Ely	Eveleth	Yes	673	70	BC, B, LMB, NP, SUN, RKB, SMB, W, YP
Embarrass	Biwabik	Yes	442	19	BLH, BC, B, CAT, NP, RKB, W, YP
Emerald	Ely	Carry In	67	34	YP
Esquagama	Biwabik	Yes	366	90	BLH, BC, B, NP, SUN, RKB, W, YP
Eugene	Crane Lake	Yes	166	64	NP, YP
Everett	Ely	Carry In	109	15	BC, B, LMB, NP, RKB, SMB, W, YP
Fairy	Ely	Carry In	151	19	B, NP, RKB, W, YP
Fat	Crane Lake	Yes	102	50	LAT
Fenske	Ely	Yes	105	43	BC, B, LMB, NP, SMB, W, YP
Fig	Melrude	Yes	92	34	BLH, BC, NP, SUN, W, YP
Finberg	Hibbing	No	16	17	NP, SUN, YP
Finger	Ely	Carry In	287	60	NP, RKB, W
First	Ely	Carry In	42	30	BC, LMB, NP, RKB
Fish Lake	Duluth	Yes	3260	37	BLH, BC, B, NP, SUN, RKB, W, YP
Fishmouth	International Falls	No	32	28	NP, YP
Five Mile	Tower	Carry In	108	8	BC, B, LMB, NP, YP
Floodwood	Goodland	No	328	55	BLH, BC, B, LMB, NP, SUN, RKB, W, YP
Flowage	Duluth	No	106	15	BLH, BC, B, LMB, NP, SUN, RKB, W, YP
Forsyth Pit	Kinney	Yes	6	51	RBT
Foss	Ely	No	38	6	B, NP, SUN, YP
Four Mile	Tower	No	147	15	B, LMB, NP, YP
Fourteen	Buhl	No	375.5	14.5	BLH, BC, B, NP, SUN, W, YP
Franklin	Crane Lake	Yes	135	18	B, NP, W, YP
Frying Pan	Palo	No	69	39	BLH, BC, B, NP, SUN, RKB, W, YP
Gabrielson	Orr	Yes	15	18	B, NP, YP
Gannon	Crane Lake	No	89	18	NP, YP

Name	Nearest Town	Public Access	Acres	Max. Depth	Fish Species
Gate	Virginia	Yes	12	33	B
Ge-Be-On-Equat	Crane Lake	Carry In	607	55	NP, SMB, W, YP
George	Rollins	Yes	26.4	18	BC, LMB, NP, SUN, YP
Gilbert Pit	Gilbert	Yes	223	443	B, CAT, NP, SUN, RBT, RKB, SPT, W, YP
Godfrey-Glen Pit	Chisholm	No	2	10	BC
Gowan	Ely	Carry In	158	13	NP, W, YP
Grand	Twig	Yes	1592	24	BLH, BC, NP, SUN, W, YP
Grassy	Ely	Carry In	213	15	BC, B, LMB, NP, SUN, SMB, YP
Green	Ely	Carry In	141	20	B, NP, SUN, YP
Gull	Ely	Carry In	169	13	NP, SUN, YP
Gun	Crane Lake	Yes	158	135	LAT, SMB, YP
Gun	Ely	Carry In	337	57	B, NP, RKB, SMB, W
Half Moon	Eveleth	No	153	40	RBT
Hanson	Ely	Carry In	19	65	SPT
Harriet	Hibbing	Yes	55	49	BC, B, LMB, SUN, RKB, YP
Harris	Fairbanks	Yes	71	38	B, NP, SUN, W, YP
Hart	French River	Yes	10	10	BLH, BC, B, YP
Hart	Melrude	Carry In	44	20	BLH, BC, B, NP, SUN, RKB, W, YP
Headquarters	Gowan	No	60	24	BLH, NP, SUN, YP
Heikkila	Cromwell	No	93	10	BLH, NP, YP
Heritage	Crane Lake	Carry In	184	40	NP, RKB, W, YP
High	Ely	Carry In	277	66	BKT, B, RBT, SPT
Hobo	Ely	Carry In	74	15	BC, B, LMB, NP, W, YP
Hobson	Hibbing	No	64	42	BC, B, LMB, NP, SUN, SMB, YP
Holter	Ely	Carry In	23	16	NP, YP
Home	Ely	Carry In	85	24	NP, W, YP
Hook	Ely	Carry In	83	13	NP, YP
Horseshoe	Duluth	Carry In	90	7	BLH, BC, SUN, W, YP
Horseshoe	Eveleth	No	95	13	BLH, BC, B, NP, SUN, YP
Hustler	Crane Lake	Carry In	272	60	B, NP, RKB
Indian	Two Harbors	Yes	57.5	19	BC, B, NP, SUN, W, YP
Iron	Ely	Carry In	1851	60	BC, NP, RKB, SGR, SMB, W, YP
Island Lake	Duluth	Yes	7335.3	94	BLH, BC, B, M, NP, SUN, RKB, SGR, SMB, W, YP
Island	Goodland	Yes	227	65	BLH, BC, B, LMB, NP, SUN, W, YP
Island	Hibbing	No	128	12	BLH, NP, SUN, YP
Jacob	Ely	Carry In	24	50	BKT, RBT, SPT
Jacobs	Duluth	No	75	9	BLH, BC, B, NP, SUN, SMB, W, YP
James	Virginia	Yes	17	33	LMB, RBT
Janette	Goodland	Yes	137	23	BLH, BC, B, NP, SUN, W, YP
Jeanette	Buyck	Yes	580	15	NP, W, YP
Johnson	Crane Lake	Yes	1674	88	NP, SUN, RKB, SMB, W, YP
Johnson	Ely	Yes	465	18	BC, B, NP, SUN, RKB, W, YP
Jorgens	Ray	Carry In	64	21	NP, YP
Joseph	Babbitt	Yes	63.4	23	B, LMB, NP, SUN, W, YP
Judson Mine Pit	Buhl	Yes	18	64	SUN, RBT
Kabetogama	International Falls	Yes	25760	80	BC, B, NP, RKB, SGR, SMB, W, YP
Kabustasa	Orr	No	114	6.5	BC, B, NP, SUN, W, YP
Kangas	Babbitt	Carry In	22	15	NP, YP
Kaunonen	Embarrass	No	15	23	BLH, NP

KEY				
BKT=Brook Trout	**LAT**=Lake Trout	**RKB**=Rock Bass	**W**=Walleye
BLH=Bullhead	**LMB**=Largemouth Bass	**SGR**=Sauger	**WC**=White Crappie
BC=Black Crappie	**M**=Muskie	**SMB**=Smallmouth Bass	**WHB**=White Bass
B=Bluegill	**NP**=Northern Pike	**SPT**=Splake	**YP**=Yellow Perch
BRT=Brown Trout	**PKS**=Pink Salmon	**SUN**=Sunfish	
CAT=Catfish (Channel and Flathead)	**RBT**=Rainbow Trout	**TM**=Tiger Muskie	

Fishing Waters

Tristan Publishing, Inc., believes that the following charts are accurate; however, we cannot guarantee or accept liability for their accuracy. The reader should contact the Minnesota DNR to verify the accuracy of the charts.

Name	Nearest Town	Public Access	Acres	Max. Depth	Fish Species
Kelly	Kelly Lake	Yes	17	17	BLH, BC, B, NP, W, YP
Kendall	Eveleth	No	52	43	BC, LMB, SUN, YP
King	Rollins	Carry In	293	8	LMB, NP, SUN, RKB, W, YP
Kinney	Kinney	Yes	51	160	BKT, NP, YP
Kjostad	Orr	Yes	397	50	BC, B, NP, RKB, SMB, W, YP
Korb	Ely	Carry In	58	27	NP, YP
Kumpala	Aurora	No	74	39	BLH, BC, B, LMB, NP, SUN, W, YP
Lac La Croix	Ely	Carry In	34070	168	LAT, NP, RKB, SGR, SMB, W, YP
Lamb	Ely	Carry In	80	18	NP, YP
Leaf	Gilbert	No	49	25	BLH, BC, B, NP, SUN, W, YP
Leander	Buhl	Yes	247	45	BC, B, LMB, NP, SUN, W, YP
Leora	Cotton	Yes	269	35	BC, B, LMB, NP, SUN, W, YP
Linwood	Markham	No	251	34	BC, B, NP, SUN, RKB, W, YP
Little Alden	Duluth	Yes	81	29	BC, B, NP, SUN, RKB, SMB, W, YP
Little Armstrong	Ely	No	66	26	LMB, SMB, YP
Little Beartrack	Crane Lake	Carry In	53	35	SUN, RKB
Little Coyote	Rollins	No	40	15	LMB, NP, SUN, RKB, W, YP
Little Crab	Ely	Carry In	61	15	LMB, NP, RKB, SMB
Little Dry	Ely	Carry In	13	27	B, BRT, SPT
Little Elbow	Iron Junction	Yes	5	35	RBT
Little Finberg	Hibbing	No	130	18	NP, SUN, YP
Little Grand	Saginaw	Yes	71	8	BLH, BC, B, LMB, NP, SUN, W, YP
Little Hustler	Ely	Carry In	67	70	B, NP, SUN, RKB
Little Johnson	Crane Lake	Yes	481	28	NP, SMB, W, YP
Little Long	Ely	Yes	293	45	BC, B, LMB, NP, SUN, RKB, SMB, W, YP
Little Markham	Biwabik	No	42	25	BC, NP, W, YP
Little Sand	Virginia	No	94.3	14	BC, B, LMB, NP, SUN, W, YP
Little Sletten	Ely	Carry In	17	32	LMB
Little Stone	Two Harbors	Yes	181	17	BC, B, LMB, NP, SUN, W, YP
Little Sturgeon	Chisholm	Yes	266	22	BC, B, NP, SUN, RKB, W, YP
Little Trout	Crane Lake,	Carry In	239	95	LAT, NP, RKB, SMB, W, YP
Little Trout	Tower	Carry In	538	37	NP, RKB, SMB, W, YP
Little Vermillion	Crane Lake	No	1331	52	BLH, BC, B, NP, SUN, RKB, SGR, SMB, W, YP
Little	Ely	Carry In	61	24	NP, W, YP
Locator	International Falls	Yes	140	52	LMB, NP, SUN, RKB, YP
Loiten	International Falls	No	90.5	49	LMB, RKB
Long	Chisholm	Yes	267	36	BLH, BC, B, LMB, NP, SUN, W, YP
Long	Cotton	No	209.2	51	BLH, BC, B, NP, SUN, W, YP
Long	Crane Lake	Yes	409	18	NP, W, YP
Long	Eveleth	No	140	33	BLH, BC, B, LMB, NP, SUN, RKB, YP
Long	Makinen	Yes	395	14	BLH, BC, B, LMB, NP, SUN, W, YP
Longyear	Chisholm	Yes	158	18	BLH, BC, NP, SUN, W, YP
Loon	Aurora	Yes	290	85	BLH, BC, B, LMB, NP, SUN, RKB, W, YP
Loon	Crane Lake	Carry In	3101	70	BC, NP, RKB, SMB, W, YP
Lost	Biwabik	Yes	107	44	BLH, BC, B, LMB, NP, SUN, W, YP
Lost	Tower	Yes	768	20	BC, B, SUN, W, YP
Low	Ely	Yes	345	40	BC, B, LMB, NP, RKB, SMB, W, YP
Lower Comstock	Markham	No	161	30	BLH, BC, B, LMB, NP, SUN, RKB, W, YP
Lunetta	Ely	No	88	14	B, LMB, NP, RKB, SMB, YP
Lynx	Crane Lake	No	295	85	NP, RKB, W
Majestic	Eveleth	No	52	51	BLH, BC, B, NP, YP
Manganika	Virginia	No	158	24	BLH, BC, NP, YP
Maple Leaf	Alborn	No	89.6	51	BC, B, NP, SUN, W, YP

Name	Nearest Town	Public Access	Acres	Max. Depth	Fish Species
Marion	Crane Lake	Yes	163	13	B, NP, W, YP
Markham		No	264	29	BC, B, NP, SUN, YP
Martin	Brookston	No	71	77	BC, B, LMB, NP, SUN, YP
Mashkenode	Virginia	Yes	101	14	BLH, BC, B, NP, SUN, W, YP
Maude	Buyck	Yes	91	26	NP, W, YP
Maxine	Ely	No	37.3	21	B, LMB, NP, SUN, RKB, YP
McCormack	Chisholm	Yes	54	25	BLH, BC, B, NP, SUN, YP
McQuade	Hibbing	Yes	164	21	BLH, BC, B, NP, SUN, W, YP
Meander	Winton	Yes	139	25	B, SMB, YP
Merritt	Tower	Carry In	195	8	NP, YP
Miller Pit West	Aurora	Carry In	17	174	B
Miner's Pit West	Ely	Yes	138	140	BKT, B, LMB, SUN, RBT, RKB, SMB
Minister	Ely	Carry In	52	16	BC, B, LMB, NP, W, YP
Mirror	Duluth	Yes	18.2	27	BC, B, BRT, NP, SUN, YP
Mitchell	Ely	No	241	38	LMB, NP, SUN, RKB, SMB, W, YP
Moberg	Floodwood	Yes	35.5	27	BC, LMB, NP, SUN, YP
Moon	Eveleth	No	44	47	BC, B, LMB, NP, SUN, YP
Moose	Crane Lake	No	209	8	NP, W, YP
Moose	Orr	No	978	10	BLH, BC, B, LMB, NP, SUN, W, YP
Moose	Two Harbors	No	62.1	17	BLH, BC, B, NP, SUN, W, YP
Moran	Hibbing	Carry In	82	30	BLH, BC, B, LMB, NP, SUN, YP
Morcom	Melrude	Yes	178	6	BLH, BC, B, NP, SUN, YP
Morgan	Duluth	Yes	91	11	BLH, NP, SUN, YP
Mott Pit	Mt. Iron	Carry In	15	80	B, RBT, YP
Muckwa	Ely	Carry In	146	8.5	W, YP
Mud Hen	Makinen	Yes	166	9	BLH, BC, B, NP, SUN, W, YP
Mud	Ely	Yes	143	27	BLH, BC, B, LMB, NP, SUN, RKB, W, YP
Mudro	Ely	Carry In	95	76	NP, RKB, W, YP
Mukooda	Crane Lake	Yes	754	78	BC, B, LAT, LMB, NP, SUN, RKB, SMB, W, YP
Murphy	Central Lakes	Yes	395	24	BLH, BC, B, LMB, NP, SUN, W, YP
Myrtle	Orr	Yes	889	20	BLH, BC, B, LMB, NP, SUN, RKB, SMB, W, YP
Namakan	Ray	Yes	25130	150	BLH, BC, B, NP, SUN, RKB, SGR, SMB, W, YP
Neesh	Ely	Carry In	39	6	NP, YP
Neewin	Ely	Carry In	100	15	NP, YP
Nels	Ely	Yes	143	30	B, NP, SUN, RKB, W, YP
Net	Crane Lake	No	108	18	NP, SUN, YP
Nichols	Payne	Yes	413	31	BLH, BC, B, LMB, NP, SUN, W, YP
Nigh	Buyck	Yes	38	12	NP, W, YP
Nina Moose	Ely	No	430	6	NP, RKB, SMB, W, YP
Niswi	Ely	Carry In	119	8	NP, YP
Norberg	Ely	Yes	7	26	RBT
North Hegman	Ely	Carry In	101	30	NP, SMB
North Twin	Aurora	Yes	64	40	BLH, BC, B, LMB, NP, SUN, W, YP
North	Crane Lake	No	99	10	BC, NP, SUN, RKB, W, YP
Norway	Crane Lake	Carry In	58	37	NP, YP
O'Leary	Crane Lake	Yes	197	52	NP, SUN, SMB, W, YP
Ole	Ely	No	56	19	B, LMB, W, YP

KEY			
BKT=Brook Trout	LAT=Lake Trout	RKB=Rock Bass	W=Walleye
BLH=Bullhead	LMB=Largemouth Bass	SGR=Sauger	WC=White Crappie
BC=Black Crappie	M=Muskie	SMB=Smallmouth Bass	WHB=White Bass
B=Bluegill	NP=Northern Pike	SPT=Splake	YP=Yellow Perch
BRT=Brown Trout	PKS=Pink Salmon	SUN=Sunfish	
CAT=Catfish (Channel and Flathead)	RBT=Rainbow Trout	TM=Tiger Muskie	

Fishing Waters

Tristan Publishing, Inc., believes that the following charts are accurate; however, we cannot guarantee or accept liability for their accuracy. The reader should contact the Minnesota DNR to verify the accuracy of the charts.

Name	Nearest Town	Public Access	Acres	Max. Depth	Fish Species
One Pine	Ely	Yes	363	13	BC, B, LMB, NP, SUN, RKB, SMB, W, YP
Oriniack	Tower	Carry In	762	17	NP, RKB, W, YP
Otter	Ely	Carry In	78	17	B, NP, RKB, SMB
Otto	Brimson	Carry In	138	27	NP, SUN, SMB, YP
Oyster	Ely	Carry In	714	130	LAT, NP, SUN, RKB, YP
Paradise	Two Harbors	Yes	30	14	BC, NP, SUN, W, YP
Pauline	Buyck	Yes	62	25	NP, RKB, W, YP
Pekan	Ely	Carry In	36	23	SUN, YP
Pelican	Orr	Yes	10945	38	BLH, BC, B, LMB, NP, SUN, RKB, SMB, W, YP
Pequaywan	Rollins	Carry In	418.2	33	BLH, BC, NP, SUN, RKB, W, YP
Perch	Babbitt	Carry In	109	13	B, NP, SUN, W, YP
Perch	Chisholm	Yes	339	30	BC, NP, SUN, SMB, W, YP
Pfeiffer	Tower	Yes	55	26	BC, B, LMB, W, YP
Phantom	Ely	Carry In	52	10	NP, YP
Pickerel	Chisholm	Yes	28	47	BKT, RBT
Picket	Buyck	Yes	312	23	NP, W, YP
Picket	Ely	Carry In	66	9	B, NP, RKB, SMB, W, YP
Pike River	Tower	Yes	254	23	B, NP, RKB, W, YP
Pike	Hermantown	Yes	494	62	BC, B, LMB, NP, SUN, RKB, W, YP
Pine	Fairbanks	Carry In	430	14	B, NP, SUN, RKB, W, YP
Pine	Tower	Carry In	912	18	NP, SUN, RKB, W, YP
Pioneer	Cotton	Yes	81	42	BC, B, LMB, NP, SUN, RKB, YP
Pleasant	Eveleth	Yes	345	33	BLH, BC, B, LMB, NP, SUN, RKB, W, YP
Pocket	Ely	No	226	27	NP, RKB, W, YP
Prairie	Floodwood	Yes	848	47	BLH, BC, B, LMB, NP, SUN, RKB, W, YP
Profit	Crane Lake	Carry In	15	12	SUN, YP
Quarterline	Ray	Carry In	21	22	NP, YP
Rainy	International Falls	Yes	220800	161	BLH, BC, M, NP, RKB, SGR, SMB, W, YP
Ramshead	Ely	Carry In	480	10	NP, SUN, YP
Regenbogen	Ely	Carry In	10	34	BKT
Rice	Ely	Carry In	37	27	NP
Rocky	Ely	Carry In	116	40	NP, SUN, RKB, YP
Rose	Cotton	No	62	31	B, LMB, NP, SUN, W, YP
Round	Fairbanks	Carry In	311	6	BLH, NP, W, YP
Rush	Ely	Carry In	119	10	NP, RKB, SMB, W, YP
Ryan	International Falls	Carry In	37	12	NP, YP
Sabin	Aurora	Yes	146	600	B, LAT, NP, RBT, W
Sabin	Aurora	Yes	305	40	BLH, BC, B, NP, SUN, RKB, W, YP
Salo	Two Harbors	Yes	137	20	BLH, BC, B, NP, SUN, SMB, W, YP
Sand Point	Crane Lake	Yes	8869	184	BLH, BC, B, LMB, NP, RKB, SGR, SMB, W, YP
Sand	Hibbing	No	96	38	BLH, BC, B, LMB, NP, SUN, YP
Sand	Rollins	Yes	27	16	RBT
Sand	Virginia	No	701	15	BC, B, LMB, NP, SUN, W, YP
Schaeffer	Rollins	No	36	17	BC, NP, SUN, YP
Schelins	Independence	No	148	23	BC, B, LMB, NP, SUN, W, YP
Schisler		No	64	19	NP, W, YP
Schlamm	Ely	Carry In	65	6	B, NP, YP
Schubert	Cotton	No	205	24	BC, B, LMB, NP, SUN, RKB, SMB, W, YP
Schultz	Duluth	No	215	48	BLH, BC, NP, SUN, RKB, W, YP
Scott	Buhl	No	24	19	BLH, BC, B, NP, SUN

Name	Nearest Town	Public Access	Acres	Max. Depth	Fish Species
Section Fourteen	Makinen	Yes	140.1	27	BC, B, LMB, NP, SUN, RKB, W, YP
Serell	Ely	Carry In	37	34	NP, W, YP
Seven Beaver	Fairbanks	No	1410	5	NP, W, YP
Shagawa	Ely	Yes	2370	48	BC, B, NP, RKB, SMB, W, YP
Shannon	Chisholm	No	135	11	BC, B, NP, RKB, W, YP
Shell	Crane Lake	Carry In	484	15	B, LMB, NP, SUN, SMB, W, YP
Shipman Bass	Ely	Carry In	33	34	B, LMB, NP, YP
Shoe Pack	Chisholm	Carry In	41	22	BLH, BC, B, NP, SUN, YP
Shoepack	International Falls	Yes	306	24	B, M, YP
Side	Chisholm	Yes	372	32	BLH, BC, B, LMB, NP, SUN, RKB, W, YP
Silica	Ely	Carry In	49	16	B, NP, SUN, SMB
Silver	Biwabik	No	32	19	BLH, NP, W, YP
Silver	Biwabik	Yes	34	36	BC, B, LMB, NP, RKB
Silver	Virginia City	Yes	44	29	BLH, BC, B, LMB, NP, SUN, RKB, W, YP
Sinneeg	Ely	Carry In	157	32	NP, SUN, W, YP
Six Mile	Chisholm	Yes	84	14	BLH, BC, B, LMB, NP, SUN, W, YP
Six Mile	Tower	Carry In	104	22	B, LMB, NP, SUN
Skeleton	Tower	Yes	68	18	NP, YP
Sletten	Ely	Carry In	24	46	LMB, SUN, YP
Slim	Crane Lake	Carry In	121	42	NP, YP
Slim	Ely	Carry In	296	49	NP, W, YP
Smith	Brimson	Carry In	180	51	BC, NP, SUN, RKB, W, YP
South Hegman	Ely	Carry In	110	55	NP, SMB, YP
South Twin	Aurora	No	106	48	BC, B, NP, W, YP
South	Crane Lake	Carry In	35	10	NP, SUN, YP
Sparrow	Ely	Carry In	52	50	LMB, NP, SUN, W, YP
Spring Hole	Markham	No	1.2	16	BKT, NP
Spring	Crane Lake	Carry In	194	60	NP, SMB, YP
Spring	Two Harbors	Yes	97.3	25	BLH, BC, B, LMB, NP, SUN, YP
Spruce	Babbitt	No	N/A	7	W, YP
St. James Pit	Aurora	Yes	100	381	BKT, B, LAT, RBT, W
St. Louis River	Duluth	Yes	11500	27	BC, B, CAT, M, NP, SUN, RKB, SMB, W, YP
St. Mary's	Eveleth	Carry In	216	44	BLH, BC, B, LMB, NP, SUN, RKB, W, YP
Steep	Crane Lake	Carry In	86	40	NP, RKB
Stone	Rollins	Yes	206.2	17	BLH, BC, B, NP, SUN, W, YP
Stone	Zim	Yes	137	12	BLH, BC, B, NP, SUN, YP
Strand	Cotton	Yes	334	16	BC, B, NP, SUN, W, YP
Stuart	Ely	Carry In	752	40	NP, W, YP
Stubler Pit	Buhl	Yes	13	40	BC, B, YP
Sturgeon	Chisholm	Yes	1664	80	BLH, BC, B, NP, SUN, RKB, W, YP
Sullivan	Markham	Yes	31	7	BLH, B, SUN, YP
Sunday		No			BRT, SPT
Sunset	Cook	Yes	305	6	BC, NP, SUN, YP
Sunset	Twig	Carry In	67	54	BC, B, LMB, NP, SUN, W, YP
Sunshine	Duluth	No	78	37	BC, B, LMB, NP, SUN, RKB, W, YP
Susan	Cook	Yes	300	10	BC, NP, SUN, W, YP
Swan	Orr	Yes	80	11	BLH, BC, NP, SUN, YP

KEY				
BKT=Brook Trout	**LAT**=Lake Trout	**RKB**=Rock Bass	**W**=Walleye
BLH=Bullhead	**LMB**=Largemouth Bass	**SGR**=Sauger	**WC**=White Crappie
BC=Black Crappie	**M**=Muskie	**SMB**=Smallmouth Bass	**WHB**=White Bass
B=Bluegill	**NP**=Northern Pike	**SPT**=Splake	**YP**=Yellow Perch
BRT=Brown Trout	**PKS**=Pink Salmon	**SUN**=Sunfish	
CAT=Catfish (Channel and Flathead)	**RBT**=Rainbow Trout	**TM**=Tiger Muskie	

Fishing Waters

Tristan Publishing, Inc., believes that the following charts are accurate; however, we cannot guarantee or accept liability for their accuracy. The reader should contact the Minnesota DNR to verify the accuracy of the charts.

Name	Nearest Town	Public Access	Acres	Max. Depth	Fish Species
Takucmich	Crane Lake	Carry In	327	150	B, LAT, RKB, SMB
Tamarack	Ely	No	72	23	B, NP, W, YP
Tee	Ely	Carry In	36	25	YP
Tesoker	Crane Lake	Carry In	24	37	B, LMB, YP
Thirteen	Buhl	No	79	17	B, NP, SUN, SMB, YP
Thirty-Six	Cromwell	Yes	110	10	BLH
Thompson	Duluth	Yes	197	9	BLH, BC, B, LMB, NP, SUN, YP
Thumb	Ely	No	52	55	NP, RKB, W
Tooth	Crane Lake	Carry In	58	43	NP
Trout	Tower	Yes	7641	98	LAT, NP, SUN, RKB, SMB, W, YP
Trygg	Crane Lake	Carry In	25	35	BKT
Twin	Ely	Yes	239	51	LMB, NP, SUN, W, YP
Upper Comstock	Whiteface	Yes	271	28	BLH, BC, B, CAT, LMB, NP, SUN, RKB, W, YP
Upper Twin Pond	Duluth	Yes	1.7	5	BKT, BRT, LMB, RBT
Upstead	Silica	Yes	58	37	BC, B, LMB, NP, SUN, YP
Vermilion	Tower	Yes	40557	76	BLH, BC, B, LMB, M, NP, SUN, RKB, SMB, W, YP
Virginia	Virginia City	Yes	32	44	BLH, BC, B, LMB, NP, SUN, RKB, W, YP
War Club	International Falls	Yes	91	40	LMB, NP, SUN, RKB, YP
West Robinson	Ely	Yes	135	8	B, NP, SUN, YP
West Sturgeon	Chisholm	No	114	35	BLH, BC, B, NP, SUN, RKB, W, YP
West Twin	Brookston	Yes	107	18	BC, NP, SUN, W, YP
West Twin	Ely	Carry In	191	22	BC, B, NP, SUN, RKB, SMB, W, YP
West Two Rivers	Mt. Iron	Yes	1213	27	BLH, BC, NP, SUN, YP
Western	Ely	Carry In	41	12	NP, W, YP
Whisper	Ely	Carry In	43.6	25	B, LMB, W, YP
White Iron	Ely	Yes	3429	47	BC, B, LMB, NP, RKB, SMB, W, YP
White	McKinley	No	48	28	BLH, BC, B, LMB, NP, SUN, YP
White	Two Harbors	Yes	122.2	29	BC, LMB, NP, SUN, RKB, W, YP
Whiteface	Markham	Yes	5600	35	BC, B, NP, RKB, W, YP
Whitewater	Hoyt Lakes	Yes	1210	73	BLH, BC, B, NP, SUN, RKB, W, YP
Wild Rice	Duluth	Yes	2127	11	BC, NP, SUN, RKB, W, YP
Wilson	Cotton	Yes	54.6	14	BC, B, LMB, NP, RKB, W, YP
Winchester	Orr	Yes	360	50	BC, B, SUN, RKB, SMB, W, YP
Wolf	Ely	Yes	299	28	B, LMB, NP, SUN, RKB, SMB, W, YP
Wolf	Tower	Carry In	184	10	NP, SUN, SMB, W, YP
Wolf	Two Harbors	Yes	467	12	BC, B, NP, SUN, W, YP
Wynne	Aurora	Yes	279	52	BC, B, NP, RKB, W, YP
Yates	Kinney	No	16	50	BC, NP
Young	Melrude	Carry In	126	10	BLH, BC, NP
Scott					
Beason	Belle Plaine	Carry In	2.1	5.6	BLH, BC, B, NP, SUN
Cedar	New Prague	Yes	779.5	13	BLH, BC, B, LMB, NP, SUN, TM, W, YP
Cleary	Prior Lake	Yes	143	9	BLH, B, LMB, SUN, W
Crystal	Prior	No	32	26	BLH, BC, SUN
Cynthia	Prior	Yes	198	10	BLH, BC, B, SUN
Fish	Prior Lake	Yes	171	28	BLH, BC, B, LMB, NP, SUN, W, WC, YP
Gifford	Chaska	No	98	8	BLH, BC, B, NP, SUN, WC, YP
Hanrahan	Burnsville	Yes	67	7	BC, B, NP, SUN
McMahon	Prior Lake	Yes	110	14	BLH, BC, B, LMB, NP, SUN, W, YP
Mill Pond	Jordan	Yes	17	7	BC, B, NP, SUN, W, WC, YP
Murphy	Prior Lake	Carry In	70	17	BLH, BC, B, YP
O'Dowd	Shakopee	Yes	258	22	BLH, BC, B, LMB, M, NP, SUN, W, YP

Fishing Waters

Name	Nearest Town	Public Access	Acres	Max. Depth	Fish Species
Pike	Prior Lake	No	43	9	BLH, YP
Pleasant	Jordan	Yes	300	5	BLH, BC, B, LMB, SUN, YP
Prior	Prior Lake	Yes	810	60	BLH, BC, B, LMB, NP, SUN, W, WHB, YP
Schneider	Shakopee	Yes	36	9	BLH, BC, B, NP, SUN
Shakopee Pond	Shakopee	Yes	14	3	BLH, BC, B, NP, SUN, W
Spring	Prior Lake	Yes	580	37	BLH, BC, B, LMB, NP, SUN, W, WC, YP
Thole	Shakopee	Yes	105	12	BLH, BC, B, LMB, NP, SUN, W

Sherburne
Name	Nearest Town	Public Access	Acres	Max. Depth	Fish Species
Ann	Zimmerman	Yes	184	26	BC, B, LMB, NP, SUN, YP
Big	Big Lake	Yes	251	48	BLH, BC, B, LMB, NP, SUN, W, YP
Birch	Big Lake	Yes	151	18	BLH, BC, B, NP, SUN, W, YP
Briggs	Clear Lake	Yes	377	25	BLH, BC, B, LMB, NP, SUN, W, WC, YP
Camp	Clear Lake	No	79	34	BLH
Clear	Becker	No	109	25	BLH, BC, B, NP, SUN, W
Eagle	Big Lake	Yes	381	18	BLH, BC, B, LMB, NP, SUN, WC, YP
East Hunter	Zimmerman	No	54	7	BLH, BC, B, SUN, YP
Elk	Clear Lake	Yes	360	9	BLH, BC, B, LMB, NP, SUN, RKB, W, YP
Elk	Zimmerman	Yes	353	15	BLH, BC, B, LMB, NP, SUN, W, WC, YP
Fremont	Zimmerman	Yes	484	8	BLH, BC, B, YP
Julia	Clear Lake	Yes	142	15	BLH, BC, B, LMB, NP, SUN, W, YP
Long	Clearwater	No	182	26	BLH, BC, B, LMB, NP, SUN, W, YP
Mitchell	Big Lake	Yes	170	33	BLH, BC, B, LMB, NP, SUN, W, YP
Orono	Elk River	Yes	281	18	BLH, BC, B, NP, SUN, SMB, W, WC, YP
Pickerel	Clearwater	No	121	21	BLH, BC, B, NP, SUN, YP
Rush	Clear Lake	Yes	142	11	BLH, BC, B, LMB, NP, SUN, W, YP
Sandy	Zimmerman	Yes	62	41	BLH, BC, B, LMB, NP, SUN, YP
Thompson	Big Lake	Yes	95	22	BLH, BC, B, LMB, NP, SUN
Twin	Elk River	Yes	51	18	BLH, BC, B, LMB, NP, SUN
West Hunter	Zimmerman	Yes	58	6	BLH, BC, B, LMB, SUN, YP

Sibley
Name	Nearest Town	Public Access	Acres	Max. Depth	Fish Species
Clear	Gibbon	Yes	469	8	BLH, BC, B, NP, SUN, W, YP
Silver	Arlington	Yes	621	8	BLH, BC, B, SUN, W, WC, YP

Stearns
Name	Nearest Town	Public Access	Acres	Max. Depth	Fish Species
Achman	Avon	No	47	30	BLH, BC, B, LMB, NP, SUN, YP
Beaver	Luxemburg	Yes	152	27	BLH, BC, B, LMB, NP, SUN, RKB, W, YP
Becker	Richmond	Yes	176	20	BLH, BC, B, CAT, LMB, NP, SUN, W, YP
Big	Richmond	Yes	403	42	BLH, BC, B, LMB, NP, SUN, W, YP
Big Fish	Cold Spring	Yes	558	70	BLH, BC, B, LMB, NP, SUN, W, YP
Big Spunk	Avon	Yes	439.6	38	BLH, BC, B, LMB, NP, SUN, RKB, W, YP
Big Watab	Avon	Yes	227	123	BLH, BC, B, BRT, LMB, NP, SUN, RBT, RKB, W, YP

KEY			
BKT=Brook Trout	**LAT**=Lake Trout	**RKB**=Rock Bass	**W**=Walleye
BLH=Bullhead	**LMB**=Largemouth Bass	**SGR**=Sauger	**WC**=White Crappie
BC=Black Crappie	**M**=Muskie	**SMB**=Smallmouth Bass	**WHB**=White Bass
B=Bluegill	**NP**=Northern Pike	**SPT**=Splake	**YP**=Yellow Perch
BRT=Brown Trout	**PKS**=Pink Salmon	**SUN**=Sunfish	
CAT=Catfish (Channel and Flathead)	**RBT**=Rainbow Trout	**TM**=Tiger Muskie	

Fishing Waters

Tristan Publishing, Inc., believes that the following charts are accurate; however, we cannot guarantee or accept liability for their accuracy. The reader should contact the Minnesota DNR to verify the accuracy of the charts.

Name	Nearest Town	Public Access	Acres	Max. Depth	Fish Species
Black Oak	Melrose	Yes	119	19	BC, B, NP, SUN
Bolting	Cold Spring	No	104	36	BLH, BC, B, CAT, LMB, NP, W, YP
Brenzy Quarry	St. Cloud	No	0.5	N/A	RBT
Carnelian	Kimball	Yes	164	36	BLH, BC, B, LMB, NP, SUN, W, YP
Cedar Island	Richmond	Yes	998	75	BLH, BC, B, CAT, LMB, NP, SUN, W, YP
Cedar	Melrose	Yes	90	36	BLH, BC, B, LMB, NP, SUN, YP
Clear	Cold Spring	Yes	119	40	BLH, BC, B, LMB, NP, SUN, W, YP
Crooked	Clearwater	Yes	65	35	BC, B, LMB, NP, SUN, YP
Dallas	Clearwater	No	20	22	BLH, BC, B, LMB, NP, SUN, W, WC, YP
Deep	Richmond	No	48	54	B, LMB, NP, SUN
Eden	Eden Valley	Yes	263	77	BLH, BC, B, NP, SUN, W, YP
Feldgers	Clearwater	No	21	17	BLH, BC, B, LMB, NP, SUN, WC, YP
Fuller	Clearwater	No	35	28	BLH, B, NP, SUN
George	St. Cloud	Yes	9	32	BLH, BC, B, NP, SUN, W, YP
Goodners	Cold Spring	Yes	150	24	BLH, BC, B, LMB, NP, SUN, W, YP
Grand	Cold Spring	Yes	655	34	BLH, BC, B, LMB, NP, SUN, W, YP
Great Northern	Cold Spring	No	356	19	BLH, BC, B, CAT, NP, SUN, W, YP
Hinz	Clearwater	No	13	35	BLH, BC, B, LMB, NP, SUN, YP
Horseshoe	Richmond	Yes	550	57	BC, B, CAT, LMB, NP, SUN, SMB, W, YP
Hulbert	Clearwater	No	13	25	BLH, BC, B, LMB, NP, SUN, YP
Island	St. Joseph	No	120	41	BLH, BC, B, LMB, NP, SUN, YP
Kalla	Avon	No	103	48	BLH, BC, B, LMB, NP, SUN, W, YP
Kings	Freeport	Yes	194	44	BLH, BC, B, LMB, NP, SUN, W, YP
Knaus	Cold Spring	No	205	20	BLH, BC, B, CAT, LMB, NP, W, YP
Koop	Avon	No	57	54	BLH, BC, B, LMB, NP, SUN, YP
Koronis	Paynesville	Yes	3014	132	BLH, BC, B, NP, SUN, RKB, SMB, W, YP
Kraemer	St. Joseph	No	194	30	BLH, BC, B, LMB, NP, SUN, W, YP
Krays	Cold Spring	No	85	40	BLH, BC, B, CAT, NP, W, YP
Kreigle	Avon	No	126	66	BLH, BC, B, LMB, NP, SUN
Little Cedar Island	Richmond	Yes	33	20	BLH, BC, B, CAT, W
Little Rice	Richmond	No	54	24	BLH, BC, B, LMB, NP, SUN, YP
Long	Clearwater	Yes	49	38	BLH, BC, B, LMB, NP, SUN, W, YP
Long	Cold Spring	No	163	46	BLH, BC, B, LMB, NP, SUN, W, YP
Long	Richmond	Yes	460	35	BLH, BC, B, CAT, NP, SUN, W, YP
Long	St. Rosa	Yes	70	65	BLH, BC, B, LMB, NP, SUN, W, YP
Lower Spunk	Avon	No	280	27.5	BLH, BC, B, LMB, NP, SUN, RKB, W, YP
Maria	Clearwater	No	66	18	BLH, BC, B, LMB, NP, SUN, WC, YP
Maria	New Munich	Yes	100	45	BLH, BC, B, LMB, NP, SUN, YP
Marie	Fairhaven	Yes	141	36	BLH, BC, B, LMB, NP, SUN, W, YP
Melrose Red Quarry	St. Cloud	No	2	N/A	RBT
Middle Spunk	Avon	Yes	236.3	81	BLH, B, LMB, NP, SUN, RKB, W, YP
Minnie	Avon	No	20	59	BLH, BC, B, LMB, NP, SUN, YP
Mund	Clearwater	No	37	19	BLH, NP, SUN, YP
North Brown's	Eden Valley	Yes	324	41	BLH, BC, B, LMB, NP, SUN, W, YP
Oberg Quarry	St. Cloud	No	0.5	N/A	RBT
Ochotto	Avon	Yes	40	40	BC, B, LMB, NP, SUN, YP
Otter	Fairhaven	Yes	96	51	BC, B, LMB, NP, SUN, RKB, W
Pearl	Cold Spring	Yes	733	17	BLH, BC, B, LMB, NP, SUN, W, YP
Pelican	St. Anna	Yes	337	46	BLH, BC, B, LMB, NP, SUN, W, YP
Pine	Albany	Yes	107	79	BLH, BC, B, LMB, NP, SUN, W, YP
Pitts	Avon	No	93	18	BLH, BC, B, LMB, NP, SUN, YP
Pleasant	Pleasant Lake	Yes	222	33	BLH, BC, B, LMB, NP, SUN, W, YP

Name	Nearest Town	Public Access	Acres	Max. Depth	Fish Species
Quarry 11	St. Cloud	No	0.8	N/A	RBT
Quarry Pond	St. Cloud	No	2	N/A	RBT
Quinn	Clearwater	No	21	31	BLH, BC, B, LMB, NP, SUN, YP
Rice	Paynesville	Yes	1639	41	BLH, BC, B, LMB, NP, SUN, RKB, SMB, W, YP
Rossier	St. Joseph	No	33	31	BLH, BC, B, NP, SUN, RKB, W, WC
Sagatagan	St. Joseph	No	159	42	BLH, BC, B, LMB, NP, SUN, YP
Sand	Albany	Yes	202	12	BLH, BC, B, LMB, NP, SUN, W
Schmid	Avon	No	34	34	BLH, BC, B, LMB, NP, SUN, YP
Schneider	Richmond	Yes	54	52	BLH, BC, B, CAT, LMB, NP, SUN, YP
School Section	Kimball	Yes	188	12	BLH, BC, B, LMB, NP, SUN, YP
South Brown's	Eden Valley	No	97	5	BLH, NP
St. Anna	St. Rosa	Yes	119	107	BLH, BC, B, LMB, NP, SUN, W, YP
Stump	Avon	No	76	36	BLH, BC, B, NP, SUN, YP
Sylvia	Melrose	Yes	81	56	BC, B, LMB, NP, SUN, RKB, SMB, W, YP
Thielman Quarry	St. Cloud	No	0.5	N/A	RBT
Trabetusky Quarry	St. Cloud	No	1	N/A	RBT
Two Rivers	Holdingford	Yes	575	63	BLH, BC, B, LMB, NP, SUN, SMB, W, WC, YP
Uhlenkolts	New Munich	Yes	258	18	BLH, NP, SUN
Vails	Eden Valley	Yes	151	20	BLH, BC, B, NP, SUN, W, YP
Warner	Clearwater	Yes	27	38	BLH, BC, B, NP, SUN, W, WC
Watab	St. Joseph	No	88	54	BLH, BC, B, LMB, NP, SUN, W, WC
Willow	Kimball	No	186	4	BLH
Zumwalde	Richmond	No	106	23	BLH, BC, B, CAT, LMB, NP, SUN, W, YP
Steele					
Beaver	Ellendale	Yes	94	27	BC, B, LMB, NP, SUN, W, YP
Kohlmeier	Owatonna	Yes	32	14	BLH, BC, B, LMB, NP, SUN, W, YP
Stevens					
Charlotte	Cyrus	No	425	20	BLH, W, YP
Hattie	Alberta	Yes	477	9	BLH, NP, W, YP
Long	Cyrus	Yes	579	12	BLH, NP, SUN, W, YP
Page	Hancock	Yes	372	17	BLH, B, NP, SUN, W, YP
Perkins	Morris	Yes	512	13	BLH, BC, B, NP, W, WC, YP
Swift					
Camp	Swift Falls	Yes	203	26	BLH, BC, B, LMB, NP, SUN, W, YP
Monson	Sunburg	Yes	152	21	BLH, BC, B, LMB, NP, W, YP
Oliver	Appleton	Yes	416	35	BLH, BC, NP, SUN, W, YP
Todd					
Bass	Burtrum	Yes	113	82	BC, B, LMB, NP, SUN, W, YP
Bass	Grey Eagle	Yes	95	47	BLH, BC, B, LMB, NP, SUN, RKB, W, YP
Beauty	Long Prairie	Yes	237	27	BLH, BC, B, LMB, NP, SUN, W, YP
Big	Cushing	Yes	277	21	BLH, BC, B, LMB, NP, SUN, W, YP
Big Birch	Grey Eagle	Yes	2108	81	BLH, BC, B, LMB, NP, SUN, RKB, SMB, W, YP
Big Swan	Burtrum	Yes	918	45	BLH, BC, B, LMB, NP, SUN, RKB, W, YP

KEY	BKT=Brook Trout	LAT=Lake Trout	RKB=Rock Bass	W=Walleye
	BLH=Bullhead	LMB=Largemouth Bass	SGR=Sauger	WC=White Crappie
	BC=Black Crappie	M=Muskie	SMB=Smallmouth Bass	WHB=White Bass
	B=Bluegill	NP=Northern Pike	SPT=Splake	YP=Yellow Perch
	BRT=Brown Trout	PKS=Pink Salmon	SUN=Sunfish	
	CAT=Catfish (Channel and Flathead)	RBT=Rainbow Trout	TM=Tiger Muskie	

Fishing Waters

Tristan Publishing, Inc., believes that the following charts are accurate; however, we cannot guarantee or accept liability for their accuracy. The reader should contact the Minnesota DNR to verify the accuracy of the charts.

Name	Nearest Town	Public Access	Acres	Max. Depth	Fish Species
Buck	Burtrum	Yes	56	39	BLH, BC, B, LMB, NP, SUN, W, YP
Cedar	Little Sauk	Yes	158	28	BLH, BC, B, LMB, NP, SUN, W, YP
Charlotte	Long Prairie	Yes	148	84	BLH, BC, B, LMB, NP, SUN, RKB, W, YP
Coal	Browerville	Yes	167	25	BLH, BC, B, LMB, NP, SUN, W, YP
Dower	Staples	Yes	79	34	BLH, B, NP, SUN, W, YP
Fairy	Sauk Centre	Yes	297	37	BLH, BC, B, LMB, NP, SUN, SMB, W
Fawn	Lincoln	No	134	21	BLH, B, LMB, NP, SUN, RKB, W, YP
Fuller	Grey Eagle	Yes	54	47	BLH, BC, B, CAT, LMB, NP, SUN
Guernsey	West Union	Yes	125	19	BLH, BC, B, NP, SUN, RKB, W, YP
Hennessy	Grey Eagle	Yes	48	32	BLH, BC, B, LMB, NP, SUN, W
Horseshoe	Browerville	Yes	118	24	BLH, BC, B, LMB, NP, SUN, W, YP
Juergens	Little Sauk	No	118	22	BLH, BC, B, LMB, NP, SUN, W, YP
Lady	Grey Eagle	Yes	207	62	BLH, BC, B, LMB, NP, SUN, RKB, W, YP
Latimer	Round Prairie	No	193	30.5	BLH, BC, B, LMB, NP, SUN, W, YP
Lily	Sauk Center	Yes	56	38	BC, B, LMB, NP, SUN
Little Birch	Grey Eagle	Yes	838	89	BLH, BC, B, CAT, LMB, NP, SUN, RKB, SMB, W, YP
Little Osakis	Long Prairie	Yes	113	43	BLH, BC, B, NP, SUN, W, YP
Little Sauk	Sauk Center	Yes	268	29	BLH, BC, B, LMB, NP, SUN, W, YP
Little Swan	Pillsbury	Yes	149	67	BLH, BC, B, LMB, NP, SUN, W, YP
Long	Burtrum	Yes	372	63	BLH, BC, B, LMB, NP, SUN, RKB, W, YP
Long	Sauk Centre	Yes	98	35	BLH, BC, B, LMB, NP, SUN, YP
Long	Sauk Centre	Yes	215	36	BLH, BC, B, LMB, NP, SUN, W, YP
Maple	Little Sauk	Yes	367	23	BLH, BC, B, LMB, NP, SUN, W, YP
Mary	Upsala	Yes	104	58	BLH, BC, B, LMB, NP, SUN, W, YP
Mill	Long Prairie	Yes	160	18	BLH, BC, B, LMB, NP, SUN, YP
Mons	Swanville	Yes	86	80	BLH, BC, B, LMB, NP, SUN, W, YP
Moose	Burtrum	Yes	124	26	BLH, BC, B, LMB, NP, SUN, W, YP
Mound	Burtrum	Yes	273	57	BLH, BC, B, LMB, NP, SUN, RKB, W, YP
Mountain	Burtrum	No	51	44	BLH, BC, B, LMB, NP, SUN
Osakis	Osakis	Yes	6270	73	BLH, BC, B, LMB, NP, SUN, RKB, SMB, W, YP
Pepin	Swanville	Yes	41	34	BLH, BC, B, LMB, NP, SUN, RKB, W, YP
Pine Island	Cushing	Yes	234	26	BLH, BC, B, LMB, NP, SUN, W, YP
Rice	Browerville	Yes	785	8	BLH, BC, B, LMB, NP, SUN, YP
Sauk	Sauk Centre	Yes	2094	59	BLH, BC, B, LMB, NP, SUN, W, YP
Star	Lincoln	Yes	47	30	BC, B, LMB, NP, SUN
Thunder	Browerville	Yes	194	17	BLH, BC, B, LMB, NP, SUN, RKB, W, YP
Trace	Grey Eagle	Yes	252	6	BLH, SUN
Turtle	Staples	Yes	104	39	BLH, BC, B, LMB, NP, SUN, RKB, W, YP
Twin	Grey Eagle	Yes	314	43	BLH, BC, B, NP, SUN, YP
Traverse					
Mud	Wheaton	Yes	1640	6.5	BLH, BC, NP, SUN, RKB, W, WHB, WC, YP
Traverse	Browns Valley	Yes	11528	12	BLH, BC, B, CAT, NP, SUN, RKB, W, WHB, WC, YP
Wabasha					
Mississippi River	Cannon Falls	Carry In	N/A	N/A	BC, B, CAT, LMB, NP, SUN, PKS, RKB, SGR, SMB, W, WHB, WC, YP

Fishing Waters

Name	Nearest Town	Public Access	Acres	Max. Depth	Fish Species
Wadena					
Blueberry	Menahga	Yes	522	15	BLH, BC, B, NP, SUN, RKB, W, YP
Lower Twin	Menahga	Yes	391	26	BLH, BC, B, BRT, LMB, M, NP, SUN, RKB, W, YP
Spirit	Menahga	Yes	115	45	BLH, BC, B, LMB, NP, SUN, YP
Stocking	Menahga	Yes	343	22	BLH, BC, B, LMB, NP, SUN, RKB, W, YP
Waseca					
Clear	Waseca	Yes	652	34	BLH, BC, B, LMB, NP, W, YP
Elysian	Elysian	Yes	1902	13	BLH, BC, B, NP, SUN, W, YP
Lily	Elysian	Yes	59	23	BLH, B, NP, SUN, W, YP
Loon	Waseca	Yes	122	9	BLH, BC, B, CAT, LMB, SUN, YP
Reeds	Elysian	Yes	187	58	BLH, BC, B, LMB, NP, SUN, W, WC, YP
St. Olaf	New Richland	Yes	99	33	BC, B, NP, SUN, WC, YP
Toner's	Elysian	No	134	N/A	BLH, B, SUN
Washington					
Alice	Marine on St. Croix	Yes	25.1	9	BLH, BC, B, NP, SUN
Battle Creek	Woodbury	Yes	103	14	BLH, BC, LMB, NP, SUN, YP
Big Carnelian	Stillwater	Yes	463.6	66	BLH, BC, B, LMB, NP, SUN, W, YP
Big Marine	Forest Lake	Yes	1756	60	BLH, BC, B, LMB, NP, SUN, W, YP
Bone	Forest Lake	Yes	210	30	BLH, BC, B, NP, SUN, W, YP
Carver	Woodbury	Yes	51	36	BLH, BC, B, LMB, NP, SUN, YP
Clear	Forest Lake	Yes	424	28	BLH, BC, B, LMB, NP, SUN, TM, W, YP
Clear	St. Croix	No	31	27	BLH, B, LMB, NP, SUN, YP
Cloverdale	Stillwater	No	35	28	BLH, B, LMB, NP, W
DeMontreville	Lake Elmo	Yes	143	24	BLH, BC, B, LMB, NP, SUN, RKB, YP
East Boot	Marine on St. Croix	Yes	32.7	27	BLH, BC, LMB, NP, SUN
Edith	One Mile West	No	77	43	BC, B, LMB, NP
Elmo	Lake Elmo	Yes	206	140	BC, B, BRT, LMB, NP, SUN, RBT, TM, W, YP
Fish	White Bear Lake	No	21	34	BLH, BC, B, NP, SUN
Forest	Forest Lake	Yes	2251	37	BLH, BC, B, LMB, M, NP, SUN, RKB, W, WC, YP
Goose	Scandia	Yes	74.7	25	BLH, BC, B, LMB, NP, SUN, YP
Halfbreed	Forest Lake	Yes	74.5	34	BLH, BC, B, NP, SUN
Horseshoe	Lake Elmo	No	53	11.3	BLH, BC, B, LMB, NP, SUN, TM, YP
Jane	Lake Elmo	Yes	145	39	BLH, BC, B, LMB, NP, SUN, W, YP
Lily	Stillwater	Yes	35.9	51	BLH, BC, B, LMB, NP, SUN, W, YP
Little Carnelian	Stillwater	No	155	68	BLH, BC, B, LMB, NP, SUN, YP
Long	Maple Island	Yes	70.9	12	BLH, BC, B, NP, SUN, YP
Long	Pine Springs	Yes	48.5	34	BLH, BC, B, LMB, NP, SUN, YP
Long	Stillwater	No	110	22	BLH, B, SUN, W
Long	White Bear Lake	No	48	25	BLH, BC, B, NP, SUN
Loon	Stillwater	No	47	15	BLH, SUN, W
Lost	Mahtomedi	Yes	9.1	26	BLH, B, NP, SUN
Mays	St. Croix.	No	25	25	BLH, B, LMB, NP, SUN
Olson	North St. Paul	Yes	79	15	BLH, BC, B, LMB, NP, SUN, YP
Pine Tree	Dellwood	No	120	31	BLH, BC, B, LMB, SUN, W

KEY			
BKT=Brook Trout	**LAT**=Lake Trout	**RKB**=Rock Bass	**W**=Walleye
BLH=Bullhead	**LMB**=Largemouth Bass	**SGR**=Sauger	**WC**=White Crappie
BC=Black Crappie	**M**=Muskie	**SMB**=Smallmouth Bass	**WHB**=White Bass
B=Bluegill	**NP**=Northern Pike	**SPT**=Splake	**YP**=Yellow Perch
BRT=Brown Trout	**PKS**=Pink Salmon	**SUN**=Sunfish	
CAT=Catfish (Channel and Flathead)	**RBT**=Rainbow Trout	**TM**=Tiger Muskie	

Fishing Waters

Tristan Publishing, Inc., believes that the following charts are accurate; however, we cannot guarantee or accept liability for their accuracy. The reader should contact the Minnesota DNR to verify the accuracy of the charts.

Name	Nearest Town	Public Access	Acres	Max. Depth	Fish Species
Powers	Woodbury City	Yes	54	41	BLH, BC, B, LMB, NP, SUN, W, YP
Sand	Scandia	No	45	18	B, SUN
Shields	Forest Lake	Yes	26	27	BLH, BC, B, LMB, NP, SUN, W
South School	Withrow	Yes	124.4	26	BLH, BC, B, LMB, NP, SUN
Square	Stillwater	Yes	195	68	BLH, BC, B, LMB, NP, SUN, RBT, YP
St. Croix		Yes	8209	78	BLH, BC, B, CAT, LMB, M, NP, SUN, RKB, SGR, SMB, W, WHB, WC, YP
Sunset	White Bear Lake	Yes	124	17	BLH, BC, B, LMB, NP, SUN, W, YP
Tanners	Landfall	Yes	70	46	BLH, BC, B, CAT, LMB, NP, SUN, W, YP
West Boot	Marine on St. Croix	Yes	34.2	34	BLH, BC, LMB, NP, SUN, YP
White Bear	White Bear Lake	Yes	2416	83	BLH, BC, B, LMB, M, NP, SUN, RKB, SGR, SMB, W, YP
Watonwan					
Kansas	St. James	Yes	398	7	BLH, BC, LMB, SUN, W, YP
Long	St. James	Yes	264	13	BLH, BC, B, CAT, LMB, NP, SUN, W, YP
St. James	St. James	Yes	252	16	BLH, BC, B, CAT, LMB, NP, SUN, W, WC, YP
Wood	Comfrey	Yes	637	4.3	BLH, BC, NP, W, YP
Winona					
Goodview	Winona	Yes	66	26	BC, B, CAT, LMB, NP, SGR, W, WC, YP
Winona	Winona	Yes	319	38	BLH, BC, B, CAT, LMB, NP, SUN, SGR, W, WC, YP
Wright					
Albert	Buffalo	No	53	47	BLH, BC, B, LMB, NP
Ann	Howard Lake	Yes	386	18.5	BLH, BC, B, LMB, NP, SUN, W, YP
Augusta	Fairhaven	Yes	178	82	BLH, BC, B, LMB, NP, SUN, RKB, W, YP
Bass	Annandale	Yes	218	34	BLH, BC, B, LMB, NP, SUN, W, YP
Beebe	St. Michael	Yes	300	27	BLH, BC, B, LMB, NP, SUN, W, YP
Bertram	Monticello	Yes	100	44	BLH, BC, B, LMB, NP, SUN, YP
Birch	Buffalo	No	90	26	BLH, BC, B, NP, SUN, WC
Birch	Monticello	Yes	76	52	BLH, BC, B, LMB, NP, SUN, W
Black	Monticello	No	97	50	BLH, BC, B, LMB, NP, SUN
Brooks	Cokato	Yes	97	21	BLH, BC, B, NP, SUN
Buffalo	Buffalo	Yes	1552	33	BLH, BC, B, CAT, LMB, NP, SUN, SMB, W, YP
Camp	Maple Lake	Yes	108	52	BLH, BC, B, LMB, NP, SUN, W, YP
Caroline	Fairhaven	Yes	126	45	BLH, BC, B, LMB, NP, SUN, W, YP
Cassidy	Annandale	No	16	37	BLH, B, NP, SUN
Cedar	Annandale	Yes	837	108	BLH, BC, B, LMB, NP, SUN, RKB, W, YP
Cedar	Monticello	Yes	147	47	BLH, BC, B, LMB, NP, SUN, W
Charlotte	Hanover	Yes	235	46	BC, B, LMB, NP, SUN, W, YP
Chelgren	Dassel	No	57	24	BLH
Clearwater	Annandale	Yes	3196	73	BLH, BC, B, LMB, NP, RKB, SUN, W, YP
Cokato	Cokato	Yes	539	52	BLH, BC, B, CAT, LMB, NP, SMB, W, WC, YP
Collinwood	Dassel	Yes	584	28	BLH, BC, B, LMB, NP, SUN, W, YP
Constance	Buffalo	Yes	161	23	BLH, BC, B, LMB, NP, SUN, W, YP
Crawford	Montrose	Yes	109	19	BLH, B, LMB, SUN, W, YP
Dans	Annandale	No	73	27	BLH, BC, B, NP, SUN, WC, YP

Name	Nearest Town	Public Access	Acres	Max. Depth	Fish Species
Dean	Buffalo	Yes	173	20	BLH, BC, B, CAT, LMB, NP, SUN, SMB, W, YP
Deer	Buffalo	Yes	163	27	BLH, BC, B, CAT, LMB, NP, SUN, W, WC, YP
Dog	Winsted	No	94	25	BLH, BC, B, LMB, NP, SUN, WC, YP
Dutch	Howard Lake	Yes	153	21	BLH, BC, B, LMB, NP, SUN, WC, YP
Eagle	Maple Lake	Yes	244	38	BLH, BC, B, LMB, NP, SUN, W, YP
Emma	Howard Lake	Yes	177	17	BLH, BC, B, NP, SUN, W, YP
Fadden	Buffalo	No	19	48	BLH, BC, NP, SUN
First	Monticello	No	15	37	BLH, BC, B, LMB, NP, SUN, W, YP
Fish	Hasty	Yes	98	38	BLH, BC, B, LMB, NP, SUN, WC, YP
Foster	Dayton	No	121	10	BLH, BC, B, NP, W, WC
French	Annandale	Yes	332	50	BLH, BC, B, NP, SUN, W, WC, YP
Goose	Buffalo	Yes	42	14	BLH, BC, B, LMB, NP, SUN, WC, YP
Granite	Annandale	Yes	339	34	BLH, BC, B, LMB, NP, SUN, W, YP
Grass	Annandale	Yes	89	35	BLH, BC, B, NP, SUN, W, YP
Hidden	Annandale	No	7	32	BC, B, LMB, NP, SUN
Howard	Howard Lake	Yes	717	39	BLH, BC, B, LMB, NP, SUN, W, YP
Ida	Monticello	Yes	231	60	BLH, BC, B, LMB, NP, SUN, W, YP
Ida	Winsted	No	79	26	BLH, BC, B, LMB, NP, SUN, YP
Indian	Silver Creek	Yes	146	31	BLH, BC, B, LMB, NP, SUN, W, WC
John	Annandale	Yes	411	28	BLH, BC, B, LMB, NP, SUN, W
Limestone	Clearwater	Yes	188	34	BLH, BC, B, LMB, NP, SUN, W, YP
Little Eagle	Monticello	No	79	33	BLH, BC, B, LMB, NP, SUN
Little Rock	Maple Lake	No	36	51	BLH, BC, B, LMB, NP, SUN
Little Waverly	Waverly	Yes	330	12	BLH, BC, B, LMB, NP, SUN, W, YP
Locke	Clearwater	Yes	156	49	BLH, BC, B, LMB, NP, SUN, SMB, W, YP
Louisa	Kimball	Yes	179	44	BLH, BC, B, CAT, LMB, NP, SUN, W, YP
Maple	Maple Lake	Yes	777	76	BLH, BC, B, LMB, NP, SUN, W, YP
Maria	Maple Lake	No	108	20	BLH, B, NP, SUN, YP
Martha	Hanover	Yes	97	22	BLH, BC, B, LMB, NP, SUN
Mary	Maple Lake	Yes	209	102	BLH, BC, B, LMB, NP, SUN, W, YP
Mary	Winsted	Yes	196	47	BLH, BC, B, LMB, NP, SUN, W, WC, YP
Maxim	Annandale	No	47	18	BLH
Mink	Buffalo	Yes	91	36	BLH, BC, B, LMB, NP, SUN, WC
Mink	Maple Lake	Yes	301	39	BC, B, LMB, NP, SUN, W, YP
Mississippi River	Monticello	Yes	N/A	N/A	M, NP, SMB, W, YP
Moose	South Haven	Yes	88	43	BC, B, LMB, NP, SUN, YP
Mud	Cokato	Yes	55	65	BLH, BC, B, LMB, NP, SUN, W, YP
Mud	Monticello	No	24	37	BLH, BC, B, LMB, NP, YP
Nixon	Clearwater	Yes	56	67	BLH, BC, B, LMB, NP, SUN, YP
North Berthiaume	Buffalo	No	24	43	BLH, B, LMB, NP, SUN, YP
North Twin	Buffalo	No	42	58	BLH, BC, B, LMB, NP, SUN, YP
Pickeral	South Haven	No	19	37	BC, B, LMB, NP, SUN
Pleasant	Annandale	Yes	509	74	BC, B, LMB, NP, SUN, RKB, W, YP
Pulaski	Buffalo	Yes	702	87	BLH, BC, B, LMB, NP, SUN, RKB, W
Ramsey	Maple Lake	Yes	275	80	BLH, BC, B, LMB, NP, SUN, W, YP
Rice	Hasty	Yes	88	24	BLH, BC, B, LMB, NP, YP

KEY

BKT=Brook Trout	**LAT**=Lake Trout	**RKB**=Rock Bass	**W**=Walleye
BLH=Bullhead	**LMB**=Largemouth Bass	**SGR**=Sauger	**WC**=White Crappie
BC=Black Crappie	**M**=Muskie	**SMB**=Smallmouth Bass	**WHB**=White Bass
B=Bluegill	**NP**=Northern Pike	**SPT**=Splake	**YP**=Yellow Perch
BRT=Brown Trout	**PKS**=Pink Salmon	**SUN**=Sunfish	
CAT=Catfish (Channel and Flathead)	**RBT**=Rainbow Trout	**TM**=Tiger Muskie	

Fishing Waters

Tristan Publishing, Inc., believes that the following charts are accurate; however, we cannot guarantee or accept liability for their accuracy. The reader should contact the Minnesota DNR to verify the accuracy of the charts.

Name	Nearest Town	Public Access	Acres	Max. Depth	Fish Species
Rock	Maple Lake	Yes	175	37	BLH, BC, B, LMB, NP, SUN, W, WC, YP
Round	Howard Lake	Yes	48	28	BLH, BC, B, NP, SUN, WC
Scott	Haven	No	80	23	BLH, BC, B, CAT, LMB, NP, W, YP
Sheldon	Hasty	No	43	43	BLH, BC, B, LMB, NP, SUN, YP
Silver	Silver Creek	No	78	42	BLH, BC, B, LMB, NP, SUN, SMB, W, WC, YP
Smith	Howard Lake	Yes	226	5	BLH, SUN
Somers	Maple Lake	Yes	158	21	BC, B, LMB, NP, SUN, W, YP
South Berthiaume	Buffalo	No	24	73	BLH, BC, B, LMB, NP, SUN
South Twin	Buffalo	No	40	19	BLH, BC, B, LMB, NP, SUN, YP
Sugar	Annandale	Yes	1015	69	BLH, BC, B, LMB, M, NP, SUN, RKB, W, YP
Sullivan	Buffalo	Yes	73	58	BLH, BC, B, LMB, NP, SUN, W, YP
Sylvia	South Haven	Yes	652	78	BLH, BC, B, LMB, NP, SUN, RKB, W, YP
Tamarack	Buffalo	No	54	26	BLH, SUN
Twin	South Haven	Yes	872	97	BLH, BC, B, LMB, NP, SUN, RKB, W
Union	Haven	Yes	88.6	35	BLH, BC, B, CAT, LMB, NP, SUN, W, YP
Waverly	Waverly	Yes	485	70.5	BLH, BC, B, LMB, NP, SUN, W, YP
Wiegand	Clearwater	No	43	24	BLH, BC, B, LMB, NP, SUN, YP
Yaeger	Waverly	No	212	27	BLH, B, NP, SUN

Yellow Medicine

Name	Nearest Town	Public Access	Acres	Max. Depth	Fish Species
Curtis	Echo	Yes	440	8	BLH, SUN
Del Clark	Canby	Yes	154	30	BLH, BC, B, LMB, NP, SUN, W, YP
John	Porter	Yes	20	12	BLH, BC, B, LMB, NP, SUN, W, YP
Sylvan	Canby	No	15	5	BLH, BC, B, SUN, W, YP
Tyson	Wood Lake	Yes	147	8	BLH, B, NP, SUN, YP
Wood	Wood Lake	Yes	432	9	BLH, BC, CAT, SUN, W, YP

Index

Index

Index

Taxidermist: 32-33

Trolling: for muskies, 171-172; for northern, 165-166; for trout, 121

Trout: about, 103; bait for, 106-108; brookies, 110-111; downrigger, 112-113; drift, 118; fly-fishing, 104-105; ice fishing, 113-115; lake charts, 122-125; lures for, 106-108; splake; 111; spoons and spinners, 109-110; steelhead, 115-119; streams, 103-104; trolling, 121; when to fish, 38

Ultra-light outfit: 4

Walleye: about, 79-82; bait for, 88-93; casting, 95; hook, line and sinker, 93-94; ice fishing, 98-99; jigs, 96; lures for, 88-89; minnows as bait, 25; when to fish, 37, 84-88; where to catch, 82-83; wind effect on, 14

Wind: boating, 14-15; drift sock, 15; effect on fishing, 15

A special thanks to the North American Fishing Club
for having provided a number of fine photographs
placed throughout this book.

If you would like to become a member of the
North American Fishing Club, here's how to contact them:

North American Fishing Club
12301 Whitewater Drive
Minnetonka, MN 54343

1-800-843-6232
952-936-9333

www.fishingclub.com

Fish Stories

Date: _____   Weight: _____

Location: _____   Length: _____

Time: _____   Lure/Bait Used: _____

Fish Type: _____   Witness: _____

Notes: _____

_____

_____

_____

_____

More info or photo

Fish Stories

Date: _____ Weight: _____

Location: _____ Length: _____

Time: _____ Lure/Bait Used: _____

Fish Type: _____ Witness: _____

Notes: _____

_____

_____

_____

_____

More info or photo